INTRODUCTION TO

COBOL

A PRIMER AND PROGRAMMING GUIDE

INTRODUCTION TO

COBOL

A PRIMER AND PROGRAMMING GUIDE

ROSS A. OVERBEEK

W. E. SINGLETARY

REALWORLD SOFTWARE INC., SANFORD, FL

Addison-Wesley Publishing Company

Reading, Massachusetts • Menlo Park, California • Don Mills, Ontario • Wokingham, England
Amsterdam • Sydney • Singapore • Tokyo • Mexico City • Bogotá • Santiago • San Juan

This book is in the Addison-Wesley series in Data Processing

William B. Gruener
Sponsoring Editor

Cynthia Insolio Benn
Copy Editor

Hugh J. Crawford
Manufacturing Supervisor

Richard Hannus, Hannus Design Associates
Cover Designer

Marion E. Howe
Production Editor

Herbert Nolan
Production Manager

George Nichols
Illustrator

Martha H. Stearns
Managing Editor

Marcia Strykowski
Art Coordinator

Maria Szmauz
Text Designer

Library of Congress Cataloging-in-Publication Data

Overbeek, Ross A.
    Introduction to COBOL.

    Includes index.
    1. COBOL (Computer program language)   I. Singletary,
Wilson E.   II. Title.   III. Title: C.O.B.O.L.
QA76.73.C25O94   1986   001.64′24   84–14491
ISBN 0–201–16310–1

This text is designed to introduce students to the COBOL language. Our experience of teaching introductory COBOL courses for many years led us to realize that students have difficulty in learning from a text organized along the pattern of reference works, where topics are covered exhaustively in a single section. We also discovered that the most effective way to guide students' coding style was by using complete, properly structured example programs and asking students to write programs similar to these examples. We have therefore written this book to provide an effective tool for learning COBOL by using the following features.

Spiral Organization

Topics are introduced, used, and then revisited. Initially only the salient points of a topic are presented and they are immediately reinforced by a programming exercise. Later the topic is revisited allowing a gradual enrichment in terms of detail. By reinforcing the initial exposure with an exercise, the more advanced aspects of a topic are easier to understand.

Graduated Example Programs

The spiral organization is based on a carefully constructed set of example programs. As each example is presented, the student is introduced to just those aspects of COBOL required to understand the example. All the example programs are complete, properly structured, and well documented. To encourage the students to mimic the style of these programs, we have asked them to perform programming exercises that are intentionally similar to the examples.

Early Programming

Students are motivated by being able to write complete programs early in the course. We have therefore organized the initial sections of the text to allow programs to be written as quickly as possible. While Chapter 1 presents a short history of computing to give the student a perspective of the significance and rapid development of computing, we recommend that this be given as a reading assignment.

Structured Programming

Throughout the text we stress the importance of structured programming, accompanying the example programs with structured flowcharts. In a separate chapter, we look in depth at structured programming methodology, surveying the various types of design aids: pseudo-code, HIPO charts, Warnier diagrams.

Programming Techniques for the Commercial Environment

While covering all the essential features of ANS COBOL, we have emphasized those topics that will help students to write and maintain programs in the commercial environment.

Report logic To encourage the student to write programs that can be easily maintained, we have taken a slightly different approach to report logic. Following the Jackson design methodology, our presentation of report logic is based on the structure of the program reflecting the structure of the data processed by the program.

Editing data Our treatment of this everyday data processing task includes example editing code for the most common types of data that occur in real environments. These editing routines will be a valuable reference for the student.

Debugging Over 80 percent of all work on COBOL programs involves debugging and maintaining programs. We present a chapter that concentrates on the strategy to use for debugging programs.

Report Writer Although the use of Report Writer is limited in industry, we have included it in this book as a practical tool for producing simple reports.

Class Testing

Our presentation of COBOL in this book is the result of testing our ideas in classes at Northern Illinois University for several years. In addition, draft versions have been used at Elgin Community College and in an experimental high school class.

Acknowledgments

The book was criticized and proofread by numerous students and instructors. We wish to acknowledge our debt to all of those who made suggestions. In particular, we would like to thank Linda Mazer and Herman Prescott for detailed editing, the instructors at Northern Illinois University and Elgin Community College for constructive criticism, and the following reviewers for valuable suggestions:

Henry Austin, *Oakland Community College*
Norman D. Brammer, *Colorado State University*
Frank E. Cable, *Pennsylvania State University*
Ronald Cerruti, *City College of San Francisco*
David W. Chilson, *Bowling Green State University*

Richard F. Dempsey, *Pennsylvania State University*
Ray Fansleau, *American River College*
Joseph S. Kasprzyk, *Salem State College*
James T. Perry, *San Diego State University*
Oscar Poupart, *Schoolcraft College*
Eldon D. Werkheiser, *Pennsylvania State University*

Credits

Lisle, Illinois   R.A.O.
Deltona, Florida   W.E.S.

CONTENTS

Six Numeric Pictures and Basic Arithmetic

Seven Implementing the Decision Construct

Eight More Language Basics

Sixteen   Introduction to Report Logic

Seventeen   Report Logic Revisited

Eighteen   The Report Writer

L I S T   O F
E X A M P L E   P R O G R A M S

Just what COBOL mean

THE DEVELOPMENT AND ORGANIZATION OF COMPUTERS

INTRODUCTION   The first three sections of this chapter present a brief sketch of the history of the development of modern electronic computers. Perhaps the most exciting element of this history is the extremely rapid rate at which these machines have evolved since the completion of the first fully electronic computer in 1946. The remaining sections of the chapter are devoted to a consideration of the major components that make up a computer system and how these components relate to each other.

Not on exam.

1.1 In the Beginning

Human progress has depended to a large extent upon our species' ability to invent machines that extend our natural capabilities. Devices such as the lever, inclined plane, and wheel, which extend our physical capabilities, date to antiquity. Progress was fairly slow and steady so long as humans themselves or animals they harnessed served as the power source for machines. True, some intricate and remarkable machines were powered in this fashion: the spinning wheel, the loom, and the sewing machine are examples of literally man-powered machines that increased human speed and efficiency.

With the advent of independent power sources, however, progress along these lines began to increase exponentially. The invention of the steam engine was rapidly followed by the invention of the internal combustion engine. The machines invented to be powered by these engines gave human beings the ability to move mountains and reshape the earth. More recently the perfection of the jet engine has enabled us to fly faster than the speed of sound, and the rocket engine has given us the means to visit the moon and explore outer space. Even so, we have perhaps only begun to comprehend, dimly, the ultimate capabilities of machines. Engines powered by nuclear energy are still in the early experimental stage.

While the human species was busily engaged in extending its physical capabilities, a parallel, but perhaps less spectacular, development was taking place. Not content to extend only their physical capabilities, people were also striving to extend their mental capabilities. The abacus (Fig. 1.1) is an example of a computing device that is several thousands of years old. This device greatly enhanced the human ability to carry out arithmetic calculations. The first mechanical computing devices were invented by Pascal in 1642 and Leibniz

FIGURE 1.1 The abacus, an ancient manual computer. (Courtesy IBM Archives.)

in 1672 (Figs. 1.2 and 1.3). Pascal's calculator would perform addition and subtraction; Leibniz extended the power of the calculator by providing multiplication and division operations. These machines were the forerunners of the more recent manually operated desk calculators.

FIGURE 1.2 (a) Pascal (Historical Pictures Service-Chicago); and (b) his calculator, the Pascaline (courtesy IBM Archives).

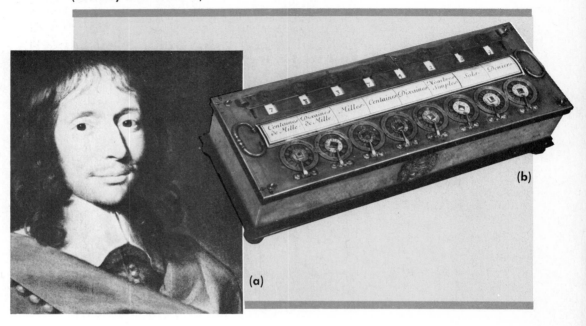

FIGURE 1.3 (a) Leibniz and (b) his calculator. (Courtesy IBM Archives.)

FIGURE 1.4   (a) Charles Babbage and (b) his "analytical machine." (Courtesy IBM Archives.)

(a)

(b)

The first automatic computing device was conceived by Charles Babbage (Fig. 1.4). Babbage spent more than 40 years perfecting plans and attempting to build a mechanical computer that would automatically carry out a prepared set of instructions. He died in 1871 without having completed a working model of his remarkable machine, but he had conceived many of the ideas that are incorporated into today's computers.

1.2 The Birth of the Electronic Computer

In 1944 Howard Aiken's IBM/Harvard Mark I Automatic Sequence Controlled Calculator (Fig. 1.5) was completed at Harvard University. This was the first general purpose digital computer, and it was, essentially, a realization of the general purpose computer first conceived by Charles Babbage almost 100 years earlier. The Mark I, although powered by electricity, could be classed as a mechanical machine. This computer employed a maze of electromechanical relays, mechanized wheels, and tabulating equipment.

The Mark I was used to generate mathematical tables, the purpose for which it was designed. It became obsolete, however, soon after it was completed because it simply was not fast enough. It operated at approximately 5 times the speed of a human being using a mechanical calculator.

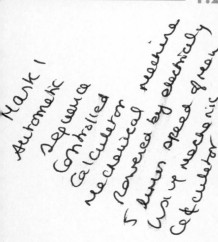

FIGURE 1.5 (a) Howard Aiken (courtesy Harvard University); and (b) the IBM/Harvard Mark I (courtesy IBM Archives).

(b)

(a)

ENIAC
1st electronic
Computer
faster then
MARK I by
factor 1000

Military

In 1946, 2 years after Mark I appeared, ENIAC (Electronic Numerical Integrator And Calculator) was completed at the Moore School of the University of Pennsylvania. The design and construction of ENIAC was supervised by the team of John W. Mauchly and J. Presper Eckert Jr. (Fig. 1.6). This was the first electronic computer to be built in the United States (Fig. 1.7).

In the design of ENIAC, the switching functions were performed by vacuum tubes rather than the electromagnetic relays used in Mark I. This computer was capable of performing 5000 additions or 1000 multiplications per second. Thus, ENIAC was faster than Mark I by a factor of about 1000. It is estimated that ENIAC could perform in 1 minute the number of calculations that a human being working with a mechanical calculator could perform in a full 40-hour week.

Because of its remarkable speed, ENIAC was a highly useful machine. It performed the task for which it was designed: computing ballistics tables for the military. It also worked on problems of weather forecasting, wind turnel design, and the study of cosmic rays.

Despite its usefulness, ENIAC had a number of severe drawbacks. It covered floor space 30 by 50 feet in area and weighed 30 tons. The more than 18,000 vacuum tubes and 500,000 soldered joints employed by ENIAC restricted its reliability. (It has been estimated that each time the power was shut off and then restored to ENIAC an average of 40 vacuum tube filaments would fail.) ENIAC also used 150 kilowatts of electricity, the equivalent of about 200 horsepower.

FIGURE 1.6   (a) John Mauchly and (b) J. Presper Eckert, inventors of the ENIAC. (Courtesy Sperry Corp.)

(a)

(b)

FIGURE 1.7 ENIAC, Electronic Numerical Integrator and Computer. (Courtesy Sperry Corp.)

[handwritten note in margin: had a patch cord type of arrangement connections had to be changed for each problem]

Though ENIAC employed the important concept of subroutines and contained some stored program features, it had still another serious fault. It was partially controlled by a patch cord type arrangement similar to a telephone switchboard. Because of this, several hours were required to manually change the patch cord connections each time a new problem was to be addressed by the machine. Mauchly and Eckert were acutely aware that this flaw would tend to offset ENIAC's speed.

Before ENIAC was completed, Mauchly and Eckert had begun the design of a machine that would not require the patch cord connections essential to ENIAC's operation. The computer they envisioned was dubbed EDVAC (Electronic Discrete Variable Automatic Computer). However, before EDVAC could be completed, Mauchly and Eckert had serious disagreements with the Moore School over the question of patent rights and left the University of Pennsylvania to form their own private company, the Eckert-Mauchly Computer Corporation. Their purpose was to design and build a Universal Automatic Computer (UNIVAC). UNIVAC was to be built for the U. S. Bureau of Standards on a Census Bureau contract, and to be used in tabulating the 1950 census.

Because of delays in the Bureau of Standards contract, Mauchly and Eckert were forced to take on another project in an attempt to gain more capital. This resulted in the production of BINAC (Binary Automatic Computer, Fig. 1.8), which was begun in 1947 for the Northrop Aircraft Company and completed

FIGURE 1.8 BINAC, Binary Automatic Computer. (Courtesy Sperry Corp.)

in 1949. BINAC is a landmark in the development of computers on several counts. BINAC was the first stored-program computer: it employed an all-binary system rather than the partially binary system used by EDVAC and could read magnetic tapes rather than punched cards. Moreover, BINAC was smaller, cheaper, and faster than ENIAC or EDVAC.

Two separate BINACs were built. These machines could work separately or in tandem to check on each other. This is another idea that has been used heavily in recent attempts to build "fail-safe" systems.

1.3 Three Generations of Commercial Computers

Because of a lack of finances Mauchly and Eckert sold their company to Remington Rand Corporation in February 1950. Thus, when UNIVAC 1 (Fig. 1.9) was completed under their direction in 1951, it became the world's first commercially produced electronic digital computer. UNIVAC's first assignment was to complete the 1950 census. A second UNIVAC 1 correctly projected Dwight D. Eisenhower to be the winner over Adlai Stevenson in the 1952 presidential election a mere 45 minutes after the polls had closed.

UNIVAC 1, formally dedicated in June 1951, ushered in what is now called the **first generation** of electronic computers. The computers of this generation were characterized by the fact that they utilized vacuum tubes for calculation, control, and, in some, for memory as well. Soon after the successful introduction of UNIVAC 1 a number of companies began the production of electronic computers. Notable among these were RCA, Philco, IBM, Burroughs, National Cash Register, General Electric, and Honeywell. If there was a dominant computer in this first generation it was the IBM 650 (Fig. 1.10), which was most popular in the years 1954–1959.

FIGURE 1.9 The UNIVAC 1, Universal Automatic Computer. (Courtesy Sperry Corp.)

FIGURE 1.10 The IBM 650 computer. (Courtesy IBM Archives.)

Perfection of the transistor gave rise to the **second generation** of computers. The transistor was much smaller than a vacuum tube, being no larger than a dime (Fig. 1.11). In addition, the transistor required much less power and, consequently, produced far less heat than a vacuum tube. This meant that, when computers were built which utilized transistors to perform the functions for which vacuum tubes were used in the first-generation machines, the size of an electronic computer could be greatly reduced. Transistors were also less expensive than vacuum tubes, and, because they contained no heated filaments that would burn out, they were much more reliable.

From about 1959 to 1965 second-generation computers were built. They were much smaller, less expensive, more reliable and faster than any of their first-generation predecessors. During this period IBM had taken the lead in the production of electronic computers, and this generation was dominated successively by the IBM 1620, the IBM 1401, and the IBM 7094 (Fig. 1.12).

The **third generation** of computers is characterized by the use of integrated circuits, which are miniaturized circuits, each of which is equivalent to hundreds of transistors. The use of integrated circuits allowed the packing density of switches to be increased by a factor of 100 or more. This increase in packing density resulted in a dramatic reduction in the size of computers. In addition, because the switches were so closely packed, the length of connections between switches was reduced correspondingly. This resulted in another significant increase in calculating speeds.

From 1965 to 1970 the third generation of computers was dominated by the IBM System/360 family of computers (Fig. 1.13). These machines ranged from models that were quite modest in capacity to some of the most sophisticated computers of the day. The interesting feature of this series of computers was that they were "upward compatible"; that is, it was assumed that any program that would run on any model in the series would run on any larger model.

Many advances in technology have been made since the third-generation computers came on the scene, but there is still no agreement as to what feature, or features, would characterize a fourth generation of computers.

FIGURE 1.11 The transistor, with transistor chips. (Courtesy IBM Archives.)

FIGURE 1.12   The IBM 7094 computer. (Courtesy IBM Archives.)

FIGURE 1.13   The IBM 370/158 computer. (Courtesy IBM Archives.)

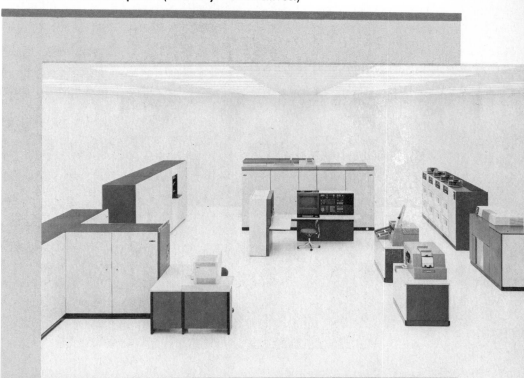

FIGURE 1.14 A large-scale integrated circuit (LSI). (Courtesy IBM Archives.)

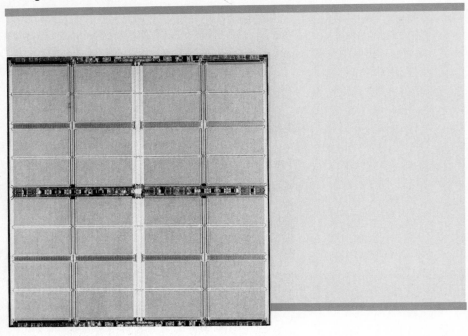

FIGURE 1.15 The CRAY X-MP Computer System. (Courtesy Cray Research, Inc.)

In the early 1970s the large-scale integrated circuit (LSI) was incorporated in the design of computers (Fig. 1.14). An LSI "chip," which is hardly larger than a fingernail, may contain the equivalent of thousands, or tens of thousands, of transistors. Semiconductor computer memories were developed based on the integrated circuit. Today, the CRAY 1 scientific computer developed by Cray Research, Inc., is based on technology that employs super-cooled circuits (Fig. 1.15).

LSDC

The increases in speed produced by computer technology in the past 30 years of development is truly mind-boggling. ENIAC 1 could perform 1000 multiplications per second. The CRAY 1, on the other hand, is capable of performing 240 million multiplications per second. Thus, if the ENIAC 1 could perform in one minute the amount of work that a human being working with a mechanical calculator could perform in a 40-hour week, the CRAY 1 can perform 80 man-years of work each second.

1.4 Computer Systems

A typical **computer system** consists of a configuration of **hardware devices** and a number of programs collectively referred to as **software.** The hardware configuration includes a **computer,** one or more **input devices,** one or more **output devices,** and one or more **auxiliary memory devices.** Figure 1.16 is a symbolic display of a computer system with the communication links indicated by directed line segments. The major components of the computer system are considered individually in the following sections.

FIGURE 1.16 Representation of a typical complete computer configuration.

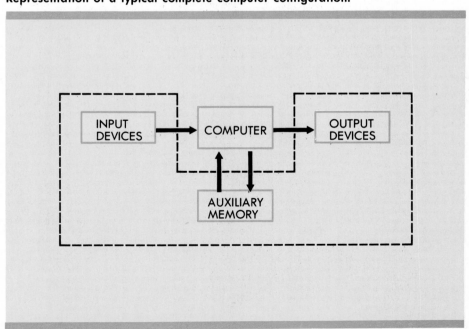

1.5 Computers

Generally speaking, a computer is a machine that is designed to accept a set of instructions (or program) and items of information (or data) from an input device, manipulate the data in various ways, and arrange the results in such a way as to produce useful output. Any computer that will perform these functions must contain an **input port,** an **output port,** a **memory,** and a **central processing unit (CPU).**

An input port is simply a device that will accept information from an external input device and transmit this information to the memory of the computer. An output port performs the inverse function of an input port. That is, it accepts information from the computer memory and transmits it to an external output device.

The memory is a device where information may be stored. The unit of memory required to store one character, such as a letter or digit, is called a **byte.** The capacity of memory is measured in terms of the number of bytes it contains. The common unit used to state memory capacities is the **K,** where a K consists of 1024 bytes. Since the capacities of computer memories have increased so dramatically in recent years another unit of memory has come into common usage. This is the **megabyte,** which consists of 1024K bytes. Information may be both transmitted to and retrieved from the computer memory. A memory that has this capacity to be both "written on" and "read from" is called a **random access memory (RAM).**

The central processing unit actually may be thought of as consisting of two separate units, the **control unit** and the **arithmetic-logic unit,** which perform quite distinct functions. The arithmetic-logic unit evaluates all arithmetic and logical expressions. This involves performing the arithmetic operations of addition, subtraction, multiplication, and division as well as evaluating expressions that contain the logical operators "and," "or," and "not." Closely related to the evaluation of logical expressions is the determination of the outcome of comparisons. The arithmetic-logic unit has the capacity to compare character strings as well as numerical items.

FIGURE 1.17 Representation of major components comprised by the standard microcomputer.

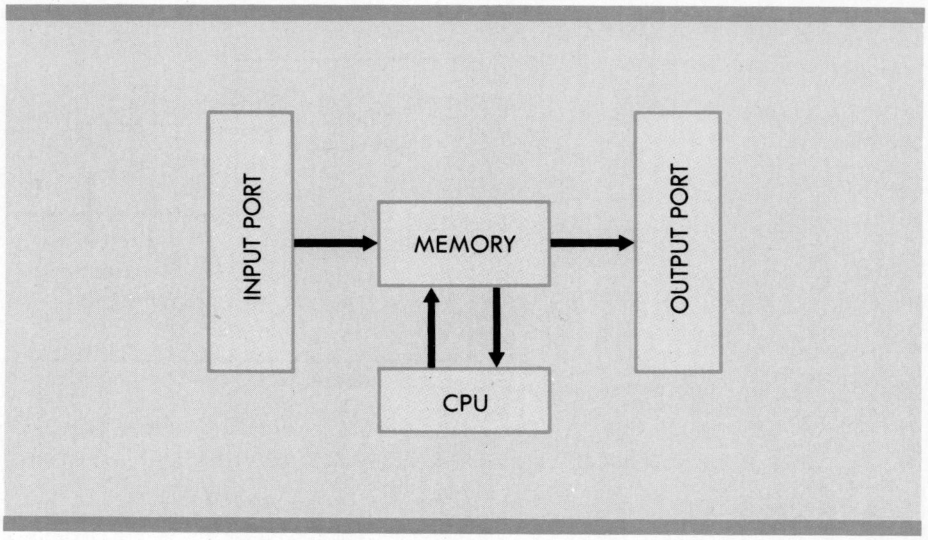

FIGURE 1.18 Standard **Z80** chip set, which includes all major components that make up the **Z80A** computer, arranged to conform with the diagram in Fig. 1.17.

The control unit generates the signals that determine what actions are to be taken by all of the other components of the computer. Instructions are fetched from memory by the control unit, which then deciphers these instructions and directs various components of the computer to take the appropriate actions. This, of course, includes directing the input and output ports to receive data or initiate output, directing the arithmetic-logic unit to perform required operations, and fetching and storing information in memory.

Figure 1.17 is a symbolic representation of the relationship of the components of a computer. Figure 1.18 is an actual photograph of the corresponding microcomputer components.

1.6 Input Devices

Input devices in common use may be divided into two groups. The first group requires that the data be prepared on a special medium before the input device transfers it to the computer. The second group, by contrast, allows information to be directly communicated to the computer.

The first group includes punched card readers, magnetic tape drives, magnetic disk drives, optical character readers, and magnetic ink character readers. For example, a keypunch machine is used to prepare punched cards, which can then be entered into a card reader. Key-to-tape devices are used to encode information on magnetic tapes before these tapes can be utilized by a tape drive. In each case the encoded information is transformed into a sequence of electrical impulses by the input device. These electrical impulses contain the information that is actually transmitted to the computer. Optical character readers are frequently utilized by universities to facilitate such functions as registration, recording of grades, and, yes, grading exams. Magnetic ink character readers are used by many of the larger banks to facilitate check processing.

The second group is referred to as **on-line terminals.** There are two types of on-line terminals, each of which has a typewriter-like keyboard for entering computer instructions and data. On-line terminals are capable of converting key strokes directly into electrical signals that are transmitted to the computer. This is possible because these terminals are directly connected to the computer by means of cables or telephone lines. The major difference between these two is that the visual display, or video, terminal has a video screen for the output of data whereas the typewriter terminal has a teleprinter for displaying output.

In Fig. 1.19 three types of common input devices are pictured.

FIGURE 1.19 Input devices: (a) card reader (courtesy IBM Archives); (b) video display terminal (courtesy of Hewlett-Packard Company); and (c) typewriter terminal (courtesy IBM Archives).

(a)

(b)

(c)

1.7 Output Devices

The most frequently used output devices include line printers, on-line terminals, magnetic tape drives, and magnetic disk drives. The line printers produce output in human-readable form. The speed at which these devices operate ranges over a rather wide spectrum, varying from 200 to 300 lines per minute for slower printers to 10,000 lines (approximately 200 pages) per minute for modern laser printers.

Output may be transmitted directly to on-line terminals via the cables or telephone lines that connect them to the computer. This output is then displayed on a video display screen or directed to a typewriter-like printer. Printed output is produced at a relatively slow speed in a typical range of from about 20 to 50 lines per minute.

Output directed to magnetic tape or disk drives is recorded in machine-readable form. This information may not be accessed by a human in any reasonable way without further processing. The major advantages of these devices are that the transfer rates are very high, even as compared to the fastest printers, and the fact that they have enormous storage capacities.

Two popular line printers are pictured in Fig. 1.20.

FIGURE 1.20 Two kinds of line printer: (a) IBM 3211 (courtesy IBM Archives); and (b) Model 9820 Laser Printer from DatagraphiX, an off-line page printer that operates at speeds up to 21,000 lines per minute (Courtesy DatagraphiX, ® Inc.)

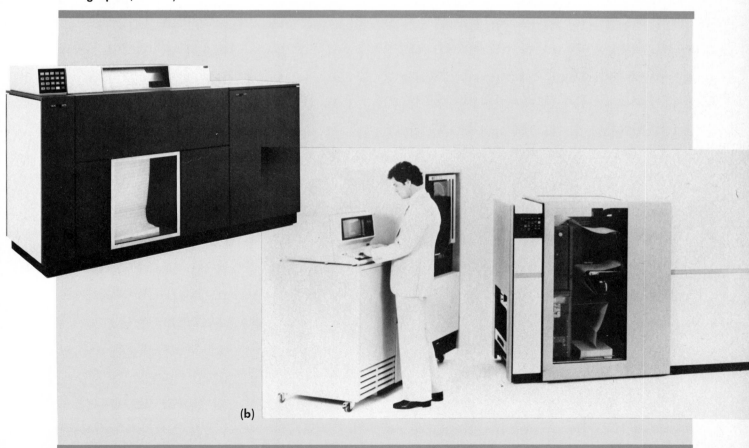

(b)

1.8 Auxiliary Storage Devices

Magnetic tape drives and magnetic disk drives are the most common auxiliary storage devices. Magnetic tapes and magnetic disks are capable of storing huge amounts of data. With either medium the information is recorded in patterns of magnetic particles. A magnetic tape is very similar in appearance to a common motion picture film, and, like the film, is stored on reels. A magnetic disk, on the other hand, looks like a phonograph record. These disks are normally clustered in a sealed container called a disk pack.

A fundamental difference between the magnetic tape and the magnetic disk is that the tape is a **sequential** storage medium, while the disk is a **random-access** storage medium. In the case of the sequential storage medium,

FIGURE 1.21 Auxiliary storage devices: (a) a hard disk drive (courtesy IBM Archives); (b) a tape drive; (c) a floppy disk (courtesy IBM Archives); and (d) a floppy disk drive (courtesy Radio Shack, a Division of Tandy).

it is necessary to read or write data items in a fixed sequence. Thus, in order to access any particular data item it is necessary to examine the data items in order until the desired one is encountered. In contrast, the data items on a magnetic disk may be accessed directly. This gives the use of magnetic disks a distinct advantage in many applications. The catch, of course, is that the tape drives are far less expensive. The nature of the application invariably dictates which of these two devices should be used.

Massive amounts of data can be stored on auxiliary storage devices. A tape or disk drive can have a storage capacity that is measured in billions of bytes. This is large indeed when compared to the 1- to 64-megabyte memory capacity of a typical large computer. Of course a price must be paid for this additional capacity. The transfer rate from a tape or disk drive is 1000 or more times slower than the transfer rate from computer memory.

A more recent innovation is the **floppy disk,** which is the standard auxiliary storage medium for the microcomputers that are becoming so commonplace. These disks also resemble a phonograph record, but they are quite flexible and are kept in individual paper covers rather than a sealed unit. Since these disks can be loaded into a disk drive individually, the computer user has a great deal of control over the management of the information contained on them. The capacity of a floppy disk is much less than the capacity of a *hard disk* (the term normally used to refer to disks that are not floppy). The usual capacity of a floppy disk is from about 140K to about 1.2 megabytes, while hard disks normally can be used to store from about 10 megabytes to several hundred megabytes per disk drive.

A hard disk drive, a tape drive, a floppy disk, and a floppy disk drive are pictured in Fig. 1.21.

1.9 Software

Systems software is a collection of programs that make the computer system accessible for normal usage. Most computer systems are supplied with a sizable library of software programs. Notable among these are the assemblers, compilers, input/output device control programs, and file management programs. These programs are of utmost importance if the computer system is expected to perform any useful functions whatever.

Any computer hardware configuration is virtually useless in the absence of systems software. The task of instructing a computer to perform even the most elementary tasks in the absence of systems software programs is simply too tedious and time consuming.

Perhaps the most important program in the software arsenal is the **operating system,** which is sometimes called the *master control program.* The requests of a user are made known to the operating system by means of systems commands. The operating system is then expected to handle all of the details that must be dealt with in order to comply with the user's commands. Such functions as supplying the appropriate compiler, allocating storage for the user's program and data, and controlling the operation of input and ouput devices are handled by the operating system.

A microcomputer hardware configuration and a large computer configuration are pictured in Fig. 1.22.

FIGURE 1.22 Computer hardware configurations: (a) for a microcomputer (courtesy IBM Archives); and (b) for a large computer.

(a)

(b)

S U M M A R Y

Efforts to construct devices that would relieve the tedium of making mathematical calculations date to antiquity. However, the first general purpose digital computer, Mark I, did not appear until 1944.

Two years later, in 1946, ENIAC, the first fully electronic computer was completed.

Three generations followed in relatively rapid succession. These computer generations were characterized respectively by the vacuum tube, the transistor, and integrated circuit. With each successive generation the size and energy requirements of these machines were greatly reduced while the reliability, speed, and memory capacities were dramatically increased.

Though improvements in computer technology have continued to accelerate, no single characteristic that would distinguish a fourth generation of computers has been identified. The CRAY 1 is currently capable of performing 80 man-years of work per second.

A computer system consists of a configuration of hardware devices and a number of programs collectively referred to as *software*.

The hardware includes a computer, one or more input devices, one or more output devices, and auxiliary memory devices.

The major components of the computer are a CPU, memory, and input and output ports. The CPU contains two principal components, the control unit and the arithmetic-logic unit.

The software is provided to make the computer system convenient to use. The central software program is the operating system, which automatically handles a multitude of routine chores that would otherwise be excessively tedious and time consuming.

REVIEW QUESTIONS

1.1 What ancient computing device is mentioned in this chapter?

1.2 Who were the two seventeenth-century scientists who perfected mechanical calculators?

1.3 The analytical engine employed many of the principles incorporated in modern computers. By whom was it conceived?

1.4 Who was responsible for completing the first general purpose computer?

1.5 What two men designed ENIAC, BINAC, and UNIVAC?

1.6 What components characterized the first, second, and third generation computers?

1.7 Name the types of devices incorporated in a typical hardware configuration.

1.8 What are the major components of a computer?

1.9 Name five input devices.

1.10 Name four output devices.

1.11 What devices are commonly used for auxiliary memory?

1.12 Name the two components of the CPU and briefly describe the function of each.

1.13 Describe two types of on-line terminals.

1.14 What device is commonly used for auxiliary storage in a microcomputer system?

1.15 What is the approximate range of capacities of floppy disks?

ELEMENTARY CONCEPTS

INTRODUCTION   In the first section of this chapter the need for and background of the COBOL language are briefly discussed. The notion of a computer program and the steps involved in developing a program are presented in Section 2.2. Section 2.3 introduces flowchart notation and the flowchart symbols used in this text. In Section 2.4 the need for structured programming is discussed and the basic structures of this discipline are considered. Primarily because of their historical significance, punched cards are the topic of Section 2.5.

2.1 The Origin of COBOL

Computers have been developed by a number of manufacturers, and each has produced a fairly large number of different models over the years. A common characteristic of the machines is that not one of them is capable of any action whatever unless it operates under the direction of a detailed set of instructions which is internally stored in the memory of the computer. These instructions are invariably encoded in binary bits (that is, they are represented as sequences of 0's and 1's) of information. Instructions are surely incomprehensible to the untrained eye and are indistinguishable from data items, which are stored in the same manner.

Such a detailed set of instructions is called an **object program.** The set of instructions of this type which a particular computer will accept is called the **machine language** or **object language** of that computer.

Each new make and model of computer had its own particular machine language. These languages were quite different and became more and more complex as computer technology continued to develop. The remarkably rapid advances in technology permitted the speed and internal storage size of the machines to be greatly increased with virtually every new model that appeared. This led to a situation in which any new computer model became obsolete in a short period of time. Each time that this occurred there was no choice but to discard the library of programs that had been developed for the outmoded computer. As you may imagine, the development of a new library of programs was an extremely expensive and time consuming task.

Assembler languages were developed to facilitate the writing of programs. These languages allowed **mnemonics** to be used for instruction **operation codes** and memory addresses. A program called an **assembler** was required to translate assembler language programs into machine language before they could be executed. For example, an encoded machine instruction might be

```
0101000000000101100000000001000
```

while the assembler instruction that the programmer specified was

```
ST 2,SUMVALS
```

Although assembler language programs were considerably easier to write and comprehend than the corresponding machine language programs, they were still machine specific. Each assembler language instruction is translated into exactly one machine language instruction. For this reason, an assembler language was compatible only with the computer for which it was designed.

It became obvious that two criteria had to be met if the use of electronic computers was ever to reach anything like its full potential. First, a method had to be developed that would allow users to write programs in a convenient and readily understandable language. The existing object languages were esoteric and highly diverse, and seemed to be diverging rather than becoming more similar. Second, some means had to be provided for transferring expensive libraries of programs from one model of computer to another.

A remarkable idea led to the simultaneous solution of both of these problems. The computer itself, operating under the direction of a sophisticated object language program, could accept as input a program written in another language and translate that program into object language. Such a translating program is called a **compiler,** and the language in which the input program is written is called a **source language.**

In 1957 the first really successful implementation of this idea was realized.

The source language used was FORTRAN (an acronym for FORmula TRANslator), and the machine was an IBM 704. As the name suggests, FORTRAN is a scientific or engineering oriented language. Although FORTRAN developed into a very satisfactory language for these applications, it was soon realized that it was not really satisfactory for business data processing applications.

In 1958 a committee of users and manufacturers was formed to study the problem of providing a language that would lend itself to the wide and unique class of business applications. In 1960 the first report of this committee, the **Conference on Data Systems Languages** (CODASYL), outlined the original specifications for the **COBOL** language. COBOL is a rather natural acronym for COmmon Business Oriented Language.

By the mid-1960s, satisfactory COBOL compilers had been developed by a number of computer manufacturers. The success of COBOL has been so great that for some years now it has been recognized as the predominant programming language in the world.

The standard for the COBOL language is specified by the **American National Standards Institute (ANSI).** It is our purpose here to introduce this version of the language, which we shall refer to as **American National Standard (ANS) COBOL.** While minor differences in the language do exist from one make of machine to another, the programs are easily adaptable from one to the other, and we shall not dwell on the differences.

2.2 Computer Programs

A **computer program,** or simply a **program,** is a detailed set of instructions written in strict accordance with the rules of some programming language. These instructions are intended to direct the computer to perform some specific task in an exact and unambiguous manner. If the program is in machine language, the instructions are carried out directly by the computer. If the program is in a higher level language such as FORTRAN or COBOL, the instructions must first be translated or compiled into machine language before being executed by the machine.

The rules governing the formation of correct statements in a language are collectively called the **syntax** of that language. In the case of higher level languages, the syntax specifies such things as the exact spelling of the **reserved words** that are a part of the language. The syntax also includes the way in which reserved words, symbols, and user-supplied names may be combined to form correct statements in the language. This sounds very much like the situation with respect to a natural language such as English, and indeed it is. The major difference that immediately impresses the novice programmer is that, unlike the human reader, the computer allows no deviation from the specified syntax. For example, the misspelling of a word in a COBOL program will cause that program to abort before reaching the execution phase. In this case, a listing of the program is output with appropriate error messages. Errors in spelling, punctuation, or spacing in program statements are called **syntactic errors.**

If the program is syntactically correct, the compilation is completed and the resulting object program is ready for execution. There is still no guarantee that the program does not contain an error in logic, because there is no way the computer can detect such errors before execution of the program has begun. Some errors in logic are detected by the computer during execution, and result in the printing of appropriate error messages. Most errors in logic, however, are beyond detection by the computer. After all, how could the machine anticipate that the programmer really meant something other than was written in the program? These errors result in output from the computer which is different from that intended by the programmer.

With these facts in mind, consider the steps involved in developing a usable program.

Step 1 The programmer must understand exactly what the program is intended to do.

Step 2 A precise plan or **algorithm** must be developed for accomplishing the purpose of the program.

Step 3 This algorithm must then be translated into the appropriate programming language.

Step 4 The program is then executed on the machine with trial data in an attempt to verify its correctness.

Step 1 is less innocuous than it may appear at first glance. The exact form in which input data is to be presented and the form in which output is to be generated are important considerations. All calculations to be made must be understood in complete detail. This normally requires a considerable amount of careful study and should not be rushed.

Step 2 is where the ingenuity of the programmer comes into full play. Not only must an exact plan for solving the problem be developed, but efficiency of the plan must be considered. The mark of a good programmer is the ability to conceive and create effective algorithms. Once an algorithm has been developed, it is usual practice to represent it diagrammatically with a flowchart. This will be discussed in the next sections.

Step 3 requires a thorough understanding of the syntax of the programming language. Considerations of efficiency also come into play here, but this is usually a less demanding task than Step 2.

Step 4 can be the most tedious and time consuming of all if the first three steps have not been carefully carried out. Several runs may be necessary in order to remove all syntactic errors if sufficient care is not exercised in step 3. When the program is actually executed it is important that it be tested against all feasible contingencies (insofar as this is possible). If logical errors are present, the programmer must return to step 2 and repeat steps 2, 3, and 4.

A programmer, like a musician, learns by doing. One may learn a great deal by reading books on programming or music, but a true virtuoso can never develop in the absence of hours of controlled practice.

2.3 Flowcharts

Among the many notations available for designing the logic of programs, flowcharts have been chosen for this book because this is the notation most readily comprehensible to beginners. Flowcharts are graphs that are used to pictorially display the logic of programs schematically. When the logic of a program is moderately complicated, a flowchart can serve two very important purposes. First, it is an essential aid in the construction of the algorithm, providing a useful tool for checking the logic of the algorithm. Second, it can serve as a valuable part of the documentation of the finished program. In fact, many commercial operations require flowcharts as a part of program documentation.

Pictorial representation of logic
① algorithm
② documentation

Table 2.1 Summary of flowchart symbols

Flowchart symbol	Name	Symbol use
parallelogram	**Input/output**	Used for all input and output operations such as reading cards and printing lines.
rectangle	**Process**	Used for operations or groups of operations such as data transfer and arithmetic.
diamond	**Decision**	Used to represent a decision that can be made by the computer.
rounded rectangle	**Terminal**	Used to represent the beginning and end of a program or subroutine.
rectangle with top bar	**Subroutine**	Represents a sequence of instructions called a *subroutine,* which is defined separately.

The reason for this is that someone who is unfamiliar with the logic of the program can understand it more easily from the flowchart than from the program itself.

A summary of the flowchart symbols to be used in this text is presented in Table 2.1. The symbols in a flowchart are connected through the use of directed line segments (arrows) to indicate the order in which the statements are to be executed. The reader with prior programming experience will notice that no connectors (on-page or off-page) have been included in the set of flowchart symbols shown in Table 2.1. This is because there is no use of these symbols in the examples presented in this text, and we strongly discourage their use.

2.4 Structured Programming

As programming problems become larger and more complex, correct solutions are increasingly difficult to design. More care is required at the flowcharting stage to ensure that the resulting program will produce satisfactory results. The flowcharting task is a design problem. All routines and subroutines must be designed in such a way as to ensure that they will work together correctly and simply.

Each programming task poses a unique set of problems, but there are some design criteria that apply to every program:

Clarity   The logic of the program should be easy to understand not only by the designer but to others as well.

Modularity   A program should be broken down functionally into procedures and subprograms that interact with each other. It is possible to understand very large programs (20–500 modules) only if they are analyzed in this way.

functionally independent structure

Ease of modification   Very few programs survive for long without some changes being made. Programs should be designed so that modifications can be made easily.

Correctness   An algorithm that has been designed with simplicity will be easier to verify. In such cases, coding the program becomes a routine chore.

Structured programming techniques have been designed and adopted as an aid in satisfying these criteria.

The germ of the idea of structured programming came from a paper presented to the International Colloquium on Algebraic Linguistics and Automata Theory in Israel in 1964. In this paper Corrado Bohm and Guiseppe Jacopini proved that any programming logic can be expressed using sequential processes and only two control structures.

The first large-scale application of structured programming in a commercial setting took place during the years 1969 to 1972. The highly publicized "New York Times Project" was carried out by the IBM Corporation during these years. The remarkable success of this project, and the publicity that it received, led to general acceptance of structured programming by the mid-1970s.

Although other improved programming technologies were also employed in the New York Times Project, the use of structured programming is credited with a large measure of its success. Programmer productivity, as measured in the number of debugged lines of code produced per day, was markedly increased. In addition, remarkably few errors were detected in the code. In fact, only 21 errors were found in a total of more than 83,000 lines of code—fewer than 3 errors per 10,000 lines. This is a clear indication that most errors can be avoided through the use of proper programming techniques.

The COBOL language has some minor drawbacks as a vehicle for supporting structured programming. These can be overcome, however, at the expense of some minor inconveniences. The remainder of this section is focused on the implementation of structured programs in COBOL, and the examples throughout the text are all presented via structured flowcharts and structured COBOL programs.

The three basic constructs allowed in implementing structured COBOL programs are sequence, decision, and loop structures:

1. **Sequence structures**   consist of a sequence of COBOL statements that are to be executed in the precise order in which they occur.

2. **Decision structures**   select which of two other structures is to be executed next. Either, but not both, of the structures to be selected may be empty. The decision structures are implemented by use of the IF statement in COBOL.

3. **Loop structures**   allow the statements constituting a subroutine to be executed repetitively. The PERFORM statement is used to implement loop structures in COBOL.

Figure 2.1 presents flowcharts that illustrate the logic of these three basic constructs.

An important feature of each of these constructs is that each has but a single entry and a single exit point. For this reason program segments that implement these constructs are relatively easy to check for correctness. In order to isolate errors, it is frequently necessary to apply various inputs only at the single entry point and check the corresponding results at the single exit point.

FIGURE 2.1 The allowable constructs in a structured program.

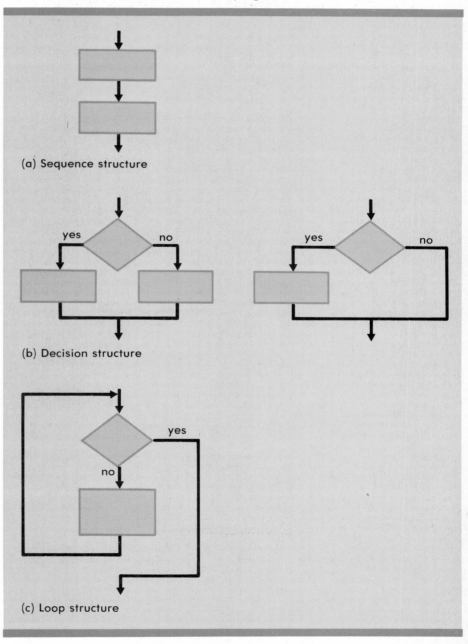

A **structured flowchart** is one that can be derived from a flowchart containing only a simple process block by the repeated replacement of simple process blocks by any of the three basic structures shown in Fig. 2.1.

A **structured program** is a program that faithfully represents the logic of a structured flowchart.

Several examples of simple structured flowcharts are presented in Fig. 2.2.

Figure 2.2 (a) depicts a decision structure in which a process block has been replaced by a sequence construct. Figure 2.2 (b) is a loop structure in which a process block has again been replaced by a sequence structure. Figure 2.2 (c) is a decision structure in which each of the process blocks has been replaced by a decision structure. Figure 2.2 (d) is a decision structure that could be formed by replacing the right process block by a sequence of two

FIGURE 2.2 Examples of structured logic.

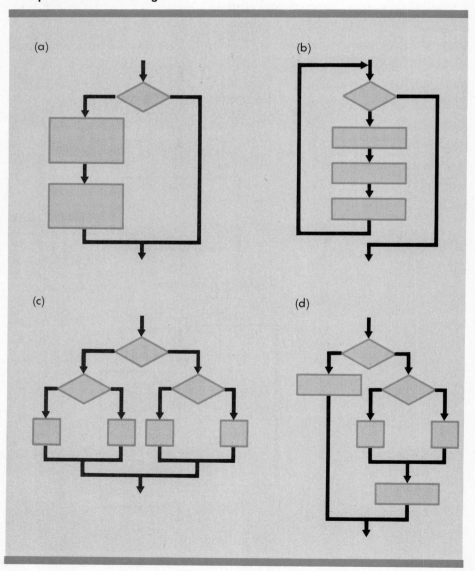

process blocks and then replacing the first of these process blocks with a decision structure.

Several examples of unstructured flowcharts are presented in Fig. 2.3. Try to determine why each of these examples is not structured before continuing.

You may have observed that both Fig. 2.3 (a) and 2.3 (b) depict structures that contain a backward branch (that is, a branch to a symbol in the flowchart which precedes the symbol from which the branch emanates), and that the branch is to a process block. None of the basic structures has this form. Figures 2.3 (c) and 2.3 (d) contain backward branches that emanate from decision

FIGURE 2.3 Examples of improperly structured logic.

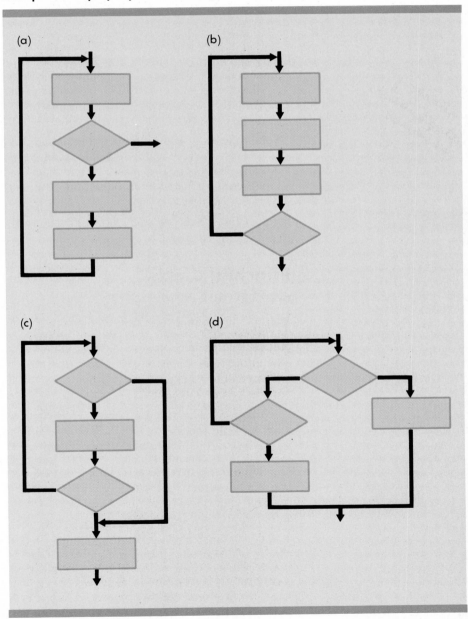

symbols. The loop structure, which is the only basic structure with a backward branch, does not allow a branch to emanate from a decision symbol.

2.5 **Advantages of Structured Programming**

The discipline of structured programming imposes constraints on the production of programs which tend to force them to satisfy the four criteria described in the preceding section: clarity, modularity, ease of modification, and correctness. How these criteria are satisfied is outlined below.

1. Structured programs may be read sequentially line by line with comprehension. This is because each logical segment of the program must have a single entry and a single exit point. Satisfying this constraint means avoiding the random branching permitted by ad hoc programming practices. It adds greatly to the clarity of programs, rendering them far more understandable to individuals other than the programmer.

2. The nature of the structures allowed in structured programs tends to force these programs to be broken down into functionally independent modules. Thus the overall logic of the program can be readily understood, and the details can be filled in by studying the individual modules.

3. Modification of structured programs is a relatively easy task. This is true because each of the modules is functionally independent and has a single entry and a single exit point. Hence any module may be modified without affecting the functional operation of any other module in the program.

4. The correctness of a structured program may be established by confirming the correctness of each individual module.

2.6 **Punched Cards**

Until quite recently the punched card was the medium used almost exclusively for entering information into the computer. Today, most information is keyed directly to disk. It is worthwhile, however, to have a basic understanding of punched cards because of the vast influence their use has had on the art of computing. For example, the standard coding forms for COBOL, FORTRAN, and assembler language are all designed for 80-column input lines because punched cards have 80 columns.

The standard punched card is rectangular in shape and measures $7\frac{3}{4}$ by $3\frac{1}{4}$ inches. These cards are divided into 80 vertical columns, which are numbered near the top and again at the bottom of the card. Twelve punch positions are associated with each vertical column. The lower 10 of these positions are numbered 0 through 9, while the upper two, called the 12 and 11 punches, are not numbered on the card.

The idea behind the encoding of information on punched cards is really quite simple. With each character that can be represented on the card, there is associated a unique punch position or combination of punch positions. Thus any of the numerals 0 to 9, the letters A to Z, or the special characters ?, /, %, etc. can be represented in any one of the 80 columns of the card by the appropriate combination of punches.

It is not important to know which punches are associated with the various characters because the appropriate code is punched into a column of the card

FIGURE 2.4 A punched card.

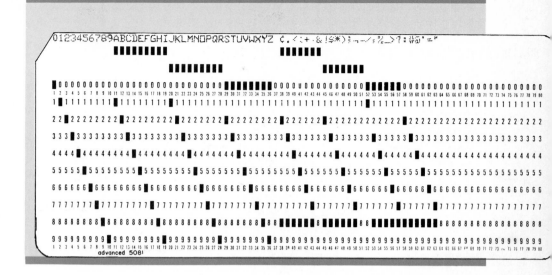

when a key of the keypunch is depressed. In addition, the corresponding character is printed at the top of the card above that column. Figure 2.4 illustrates a punched card into which all the legal characters have been punched. You can easily decipher the character code by studying this illustration.

SUMMARY

Any action performed by a computer is carried out under the direction of a computer program. A computer can execute only object language instructions, which are encoded as sequences of 0's and 1's. Each object language is specific to a particular model of computer.

An assembler language allows instructions to be written in terms of mnemonics and such instructions are translated into object language by an assembler.

The development of compilers allowed programs to be written in higher level languages. Such programs are transferable from one machine to another.

The original specifications for COBOL were outlined by the Conference on Data Systems Languages (CODASYL) in 1958. The U. S. standard for the COBOL language is specified by the American National Standards Institute (ANSI).

A computer program is a detailed set of instructions written in accordance with the syntactic rules of some programming language. The two types of errors that occur in computer programs are syntactic and logical.

The flowchart notation is one among many notations that are used to design and represent the logic of programs. A flowchart is a graph that schematically displays the logic of a program.

Structured programming is a discipline for writing programs which produces demonstrable dividends. The three constructs allowed in structured programs are sequence, decision, and loop constructs.

Structured programs are, for the most part, clearer to read, more logically separated into modules, easier to modify, and more easily tested for correctness than programs written by ad hoc techniques.

REVIEW QUESTIONS

2.1   How are machine language instructions encoded?

sequence of binary bit

2.2   What is an assembler language?

allows use of mnemonics for operation codes of memory addresses.

2.3   What is the major disadvantage of writing programs in machine or assembler language? *Can be run on only one type of machine. Machine specific. not easily readable*

2.4   When and by what conference were the original specifications for the COBOL language outlined? *Conference on Data System Languages*

2.5   COBOL is an acronym for what phrase?

2.6   What is a computer program? *detailed instructions in accordance with rules of a programming language*

2.7   What are the rules called that specify how statements in a language must be formed? *Syntax*

2.8   What two types of errors occur in programs? *syntactic logical*

2.9   What types of errors are likely to be detected by a compiler? *syntactic*

2.10   What are the four major steps in developing a program?

2.11   What is a flowchart? *graphic/schematic/pictorial representation of logic*

2.12   Sketch and name the five flowchart symbols used in this text.

*Input/output
Terminal
decision
Process
subroutine*

2.13   When and on what project was the first commercial application of structured programming made? *New York Times project*

2.14   Name and sketch the three basic constructs allowed in structured flowcharts. *Decision/or structure Loop structure Sequence structures*

2.15   What are the four major advantages to be realized from the use of structured programming? *1. clarity 2. Modular 3. ease of modification 4. correctness*

2.10   a) understanding problem to be solved

b) formulate algorithm

c) translate " to programming language

d) execute the program using trial data.

CHAPTER THREE

BASIC ELEMENTS OF COBOL

INTRODUCTION   In this chapter just enough of the basics of COBOL are introduced to allow a simple program to be written. In Section 3.1 the COBOL coding form and the format of COBOL input lines are discussed and an extremely simple COBOL program is displayed both as it would appear written on coding forms and as programs will be displayed in the remainder of the text. Sections 3.2–3.5 contain brief descriptions of the four divisions that each COBOL program must contain. The simplest formats of some of the COBOL statements used in each of these divisions are presented. Section 3.6 introduces several basic definitions and indicates two of the formatting conventions used throughout the text.

3.1 **The COBOL Coding Form**

COBOL programs are normally prepared on special coding forms identical or similar to those illustrated in Fig. 3.1. The coding form is divided into 80 vertical columns. The reason for this is that the length of source input lines was standardized when all source programs were input via punched cards, which had 80 columns. Thus each line of a source program, whether input from cards or from a terminal, is assumed to be of length 80, corresponding to one line of the coding form.

The first six columns of the form provide a field for associating an identifying page and line number with each line of the program. The sole purpose of these numbers was to facilitate the reordering of the source deck if by some chance the cards should become disordered. Unfortunately, it was not an uncommon occurrence for a large deck of cards to be dropped. In the event of such an accident, it was an extremely tedious and time consuming task to reorder the cards without sequence numbers. The common practice was to use the first three columns to number the pages 001, 002, etc. The columns 4–6 were used to number the lines on a page. These line numbers were usually in multiples of 10. Thus, the number 011090 might refer to the ninth line of the eleventh page of the coding forms. The reason for numbering the lines by tens rather than numbering them consecutively was to allow for the addition of lines that might have been omitted. Thus line 045 could have been inserted between lines 040 and 050.

The COBOL statements of the program are written in columns 8 through 72. Of these, columns 8 and 12 are distinguished by broken lines and are worthy of special note. Column 8 is referred to as the A margin and column 12 is referred to as the B margin. Each COBOL statement, depending upon its function, is required to start in the A margin or in or beyond the B margin. Note that each of the statements of the program depicted in Fig. 3.1 begins in one of these two margins.

The last eight columns are reserved for an identifying name that would be common to each line of the source program. The sole purpose of this name is to identify a particular source line with the program of which it is a part.

If an asterisk appears in column 7, it serves as an indication that the entire line is to be treated as a comment. In this case, the line is simply reproduced in the program listing without further examination. Such comments are used extensively throughout this text for the purpose of adding documentation to programs.

The blank lines appearing on the coding form are intended to be represented by blank lines in the source program. Such lines create additional spacing in the program listing produced by the compiler. This spacing is used to enhance the readability of the program listing.

Since virtually all source programs are currently entered via terminals, it is common practice to leave columns 1 through 6 and 73 through 80 of the source input lines blank. After all, disk files are far less likely to become scrambled than card decks. Therefore, all programs and program segments in the remainder of this text will be displayed in the format illustrated in Fig. 3.2. The COBOL statements in this figure constitute a complete program.

This program reads a single record that contains the name of an author, the title of a book, and the price of the book and prints a single line that contains this information in a somewhat altered sequence. As you will see, however, the rules of the COBOL language require that the program contain considerably more than a simple statement of the facts that a record is to be read and a line is to be printed.

The COBOL language was designed in such a way as to force the programmer to organize the lines of the source program into readily identifiable segments. There are four different types of segments, called **divisions, sections, paragraphs,** and **file descriptions.** Each segment of the program begins with a segment header, which serves to identify it. The segment headers are required to begin in the A margin.

The most inclusive segments of code are the **divisions,** and each COBOL program is required to contain the following four division headers in the order given:

```
IDENTIFICATION DIVISION.
ENVIRONMENT DIVISION.
DATA DIVISION.
PROCEDURE DIVISION.
```

In our example the ENVIRONMENT DIVISION contains the two section headers

```
CONFIGURATION SECTION.
INPUT-OUTPUT SECTION.
```

The DATA DIVISION contains the single section header

```
FILE SECTION.
```

These are the only section headers that are required to appear in each COBOL program.

Examples of paragraph headers in the sample program are

```
PROGRAM-ID.
SOURCE-COMPUTER.
OBJECT-COMPUTER.
FILE-CONTROL.
```

These paragraph headers are also required as a part of each COBOL program.

A period is required as the last symbol of all division, section, and paragraph headers.

Each file description header begins with the letters FD in columns 8 and 9, and these are followed by a programmer-supplied name, which begins in the B margin. The following file description header appears in our example:

```
FD PRINT-FILE
```

The words IDENTIFICATION, DIVISION, and PROGRAM-ID are examples of words that are reserved for narrowly defined purposes in the COBOL language. Such words are called **reserved words.** There are over 200 COBOL reserved words. A complete list of these reserved words appears in Appendix A. When a reserved word is used in a program, it must be correctly spelled and cannot be used for any other than its intended purpose. This will, most assuredly, cause the novice programmer some anguish, but you will quickly learn to avoid illegal use of these words and to exercise caution when spelling them.

Some names in each COBOL program are composed by the programmer. These are called **user-supplied names.** Examples from the program in Fig. 3.2 are

```
EXAMPLE1
PRINT-FILE
PRICE-OUT
```

The programmer is allowed a wide degree of freedom in composing such names. However, all user-supplied names must conform to the following rules:

FIGURE 3.1 A program on coding forms.

COBOL Coding Form

SEQUENCE	COBOL STATEMENT
001010	IDENTIFICATION DIVISION.
020	PROGRAM-ID. EXAMPLE1.
030	AUTHOR. W E SINGLETARY.
040	
050	***
060	*
070	* THIS PROGRAM READS ONE INPUT RECORD CONTAINING INFORMATION
080	* ABOUT A BOOK. THE FIELDS IN THE INPUT RECORD ARE
090	*
100	* THE AUTHOR OF THE BOOK
110	* THE TITLE OF THE BOOK
120	* AND THE PRICE OF THE BOOK.
130	*
140	* THE PROGRAM THEN PRINTS THE FIELDS ON A SINGLE PRINT LINE.
150	*
160	***** → ************
170	
180	
190	ENVIRONMENT DIVISION.
200	CONFIGURATION SECTION.
210	

PROGRAM EXAMPLE 1   PROGRAMMER WES   PAGE 1 OF 4

COBOL Coding Form

IBM

GX28-1464-5 U/M 050*
Printed in U.S.A.

PAGE **2** OF **4**

SYSTEM

PROGRAM **EXAMPLE 1**

PROGRAMMER **WES**

CARD FORM =

PUNCHING INSTRUCTIONS

SEQUENCE		A	B	COBOL STATEMENT
002	010		SOURCE-COMPUTER. IBM-370.
	020		OBJECT-COMPUTER. IBM-370.
	030		
	040		INPUT-OUTPUT SECTION.
	050		FILE-CONTROL.
	060		
	070		SELECT INPUT-FILE ASSIGN TO UR-S-SYSIN.
	080		SELECT PRINT-FILE ASSIGN TO UR-S-SYSPRINT.
	090		
	100		DATA DIVISION.
	110		FILE SECTION.
	120		
	130	*	THIS FILE IS USED TO READ THE INPUT RECORD.
	140		
	150	FD	INPUT-FILE
	160		LABEL RECORDS ARE OMITTED
	170		DATA RECORD IS INPUT-RECORD.
	180		
	190	01	INPUT-RECORD
	200		05 AUTHOR-IN PIC X(20).
	210		05 TITLE-IN PIC X(40).
	220		05 PRICE-IN PIC X(6).
	230		05 FILLER PIC X(14).
	240		

Continued

*A standard card form, IBM Electro C61897, is available for punching source statements from this form. Instructions for using this form are given in any IBM COBOL reference manual. Address comments concerning this form to IBM Corporation, LDS Publishing, Dept. J04, 1501 California Ave., Palo Alto, Ca. 94304

* Number of forms per pad may vary slightly

FIGURE 3.1 Continued

IBM COBOL Coding Form

GX28-1464-5 U/M 050*
Printed in U.S.A.

SYSTEM
PROGRAM EXAMPLE 1
PROGRAMMER WES
DATE
PUNCHING INSTRUCTIONS: GRAPHIC / PUNCH
PAGE 3 OF 4
CARD FORM #

```
SEQUENCE  A   B                                  COBOL STATEMENT
003010 * THIS FILE IS USED TO WRITE OUT THE SINGLE PRINT LINE.
   020
   030  FD  PRINT-FILE
   040      LABEL RECORDS ARE OMITTED
   050      DATA RECORD IS PRINT-LINE.
   060
   070  01  PRINT-LINE.
   080      05  FILLER              PIC X(22).
   090      05  PRICE-OUT           PIC X(6).
   100      05  FILLER              PIC X(5).
   110      05  AUTHOR-OUT          PIC X(20).
   120      05  FILLER              PIC X(5).
   130      05  TITLE-OUT           PIC X(40).
   140      05  FILLER              PIC X(35).
   150
   160  PROCEDURE DIVISION
   170
   180      OPEN INPUT INPUT-FILE.
   190      OPEN OUTPUT PRINT-FILE.
   200
   210      READ INPUT-FILE AT END STOP RUN.
   220
```

*A standard card form, IBM Electro C61897, is available for punching source statements from this form. Instructions for using this form are given in any IBM COBOL reference manual. Address comments concerning this form to IBM Corporation, LDS Publishing, Dept. J04, 1501 California Ave., Palo Alto, Ca. 94304

* Number of forms per pad may vary slightly

COBOL Coding Form

GX28-1464-5 U/M 050*
Printed in U.S.A.

IBM

SYSTEM		
PROGRAM	EXAMPLE 1	
PROGRAMMER	WES	

PUNCHING INSTRUCTIONS

GRAPHIC		
PUNCH		

CARD FORM #

PAGE 4 OF 4

SEQUENCE			COBOL STATEMENT
(PAGE)	(SERIAL)	A / B	
0 0 4	0 1 0		MOVE SPACES TO PRINT-LINE.
	0 2 0		MOVE PRICE-IN TO PRICE-OUT.
	0 3 0		MOVE AUTHOR-IN TO AUTHOR-OUT.
	0 4 0		MOVE TITLE-IN TO TITLE-OUT.
	0 5 0		
	0 6 0		WRITE PRINT-LINE.
	0 7 0		
	0 8 0		CLOSE INPUT-FILE.
	0 9 0		CLOSE PRINT-FILE.
	1 0 0		
	1 1 0		STOP RUN.

IDENTIFICATION

* A standard card form, IBM Electro C61897, is available for punching source statements from this form. Instructions for using this form are given in any IBM COBOL reference manual. Address comments concerning this form to IBM Corporation, LDS Publishing, Dept. J04, 1501 California Ave., Palo Alto, Ca. 94304

* Number of forms per pad may vary slightly

Rule 1 A name can contain any of the alphabetic characters A to Z, the numeric characters 0 to 9, and the hyphen (-).

Rule 2 A name cannot exceed 30 characters in length.

Rule 3 A name cannot begin or end with a hyphen, although hyphens may occur anywhere else in the name.

Rule 4 A name cannot contain a blank.

Rule 5 Except in the case of a program name or a paragraph name in the procedure division, a name is required to contain at least one alphabetic character.

Rule 6 A name cannot be a COBOL reserved word.

In addition to satisfying these rules, the name of the program itself (the PROGRAM-ID) should not exceed eight characters in length and cannot contain any hyphens. In addition, the first character of the program name should be alphabetic.

We shall now discuss each of the four divisions in just enough detail to enable the reader without previous experience with COBOL to write very simple programs similar to that given in Fig. 3.2.

FIGURE 3.2 EXAMPLE1: a program to list one record.

```
      IDENTIFICATION DIVISION.
      PROGRAM-ID. EXAMPLE1.
      AUTHOR. W E SINGLETARY.

 ********************************************************************
 *
 * THIS PROGRAM READS ONE INPUT RECORD CONTAINING INFORMATION
 * ABOUT A BOOK. THE FIELDS IN THE INPUT RECORD ARE
 *
 *        THE AUTHOR OF THE BOOK
 *        THE TITLE OF THE BOOK
 *    AND THE PRICE OF THE BOOK.
 *
 * THE PROGRAM THEN PRINTS THE FIELDS ON A SINGLE PRINT LINE.
 *
 ********************************************************************


      ENVIRONMENT DIVISION.
      CONFIGURATION SECTION.

      SOURCE-COMPUTER. IBM-370.
      OBJECT-COMPUTER. IBM-370.

      INPUT-OUTPUT SECTION.
      FILE-CONTROL.

          SELECT INPUT-FILE ASSIGN TO UR-S-SYSIN.
          SELECT PRINT-FILE ASSIGN TO UR-S-SYSPRINT.
```

```
      DATA DIVISION.
      FILE SECTION.

   *  THIS FILE IS USED TO READ THE INPUT RECORD.

      FD   INPUT-FILE
           LABEL RECORDS ARE OMITTED
           DATA RECORD IS INPUT-RECORD.

      01   INPUT-RECORD.
           05   AUTHOR-IN         PIC X(20).
           05   TITLE-IN          PIC X(40).
           05   PRICE-IN          PIC X(6).
           05   FILLER            PIC X(14).

   *  THIS FILE IS USED TO WRITE OUT THE SINGLE PRINT LINE.

      FD   PRINT-FILE
           LABEL RECORDS ARE OMITTED
           DATA RECORD IS PRINT-LINE.

      01   PRINT-LINE.
           05   FILLER            PIC X(22).
           05   PRICE-OUT         PIC X(6).
           05   FILLER            PIC X(5).
           05   AUTHOR-OUT        PIC X(20).
           05   FILLER            PIC X(5).
           05   TITLE-OUT         PIC X(40).
           05   FILLER            PIC X(35).

      PROCEDURE DIVISION.

           OPEN INPUT INPUT-FILE.
           OPEN OUTPUT PRINT-FILE.

           READ INPUT-FILE AT END STOP RUN.

           MOVE SPACES TO PRINT-LINE.
           MOVE PRICE-IN TO PRICE-OUT.
           MOVE AUTHOR-IN TO AUTHOR-OUT.
           MOVE TITLE-IN TO TITLE-OUT.

           WRITE PRINT-LINE.

           CLOSE INPUT-FILE.
           CLOSE PRINT-FILE.

           STOP RUN.
```

3.2 The IDENTIFICATION DIVISION

The IDENTIFICATION DIVISION in our first example consists of just three lines:

```
IDENTIFICATION DIVISION.
PROGRAM-ID. EXAMPLE1.
AUTHOR. W E SINGLETARY.
```

The first of these is, of course, the division header. The second line consists of the paragraph header PROGRAM-ID., which must be followed by a blank, and the user-supplied program name. Every COBOL program is required to contain these two lines with variation in the program name only. The third line is not required, but is usually included to identify the author of the program.

3.3 The ENVIRONMENT DIVISION

The ENVIRONMENT DIVISION of the program EXAMPLE1 consists of the following lines:

```
ENVIRONMENT DIVISION.
CONFIGURATION SECTION.

SOURCE-COMPUTER. IBM-370.
OBJECT-COMPUTER. IBM-370.

INPUT-OUTPUT SECTION.
FILE-CONTROL.

    SELECT INPUT-FILE ASSIGN TO UR-S-SYSIN.
    SELECT PRINT-FILE ASSIGN TO UR-S-SYSPRINT.
```

[handwritten margin note: Name each file & assign to input / output device]

Each of the lines in this example is required to be included in the program. Very little information must be supplied by the programmer in an ENVIRONMENT DIVISION. In the CONFIGURATION SECTION, the names of the computer on which the program is to be compiled (the source computer) and the computer that is to execute the program (the object computer) must be supplied. The program is usually, as in this case, compiled and executed by the same computer. Furthermore, the names are fixed in most cases by the given installation and are, therefore, the same for all programs written in that particular shop.

In the FILE-CONTROL paragraph of the INPUT-OUTPUT SECTION, the programmer must name each file to be utilized by the program and assign it to an input or output device. These device names vary from vendor to vendor and are also usually fixed for a given installation, so we shall not dwell on the various possibilities here. The format for the SELECT statement is

SELECT file-name ASSIGN TO system-name.

The capitalized words that are underlined are required; the file-name is a user-supplied name; and the system-name is the name of an input or output device. The system-names given in the example refer to the card reader and the line printer for our particular purposes. The capitalized words that are not underlined may be omitted.

Although the IDENTIFICATION and ENVIRONMENT divisions may seem to represent an imposing block of code when viewed by the novice, they are actually completely routine and should cause no worry. The bulk of the programming effort goes into the DATA and PROCEDURE divisions, which constitute the real meat of the program.

3.4 The DATA DIVISION

The DATA DIVISION of a COBOL program may contain a WORKING-STORAGE SECTION as well as a FILE SECTION. We shall defer a discussion of the WORKING-STORAGE SECTION until later. The FILE SECTION must furnish complete specifications of all input and output files and records to be utilized by the program. When the card reader is being used for input and the line printer for output, an input record is a single card and an output record is a single printed line. A file is a collection of related data records. Note that a file may contain only a single record, as in the following example, but generally it will contain many records.

We will now consider in some detail the file and record descriptions in our sample program. The FILE SECTION of the DATA DIVISION of the program is listed below.

```
* THIS FILE IS USED TO READ THE INPUT RECORD.

  FD    INPUT-FILE
        LABEL RECORDS ARE OMITTED
        DATA RECORD IS INPUT-RECORD.

  01    INPUT-RECORD.
        05  AUTHOR-IN            PIC X(20).
        05  TITLE-IN             PIC X(40).
        05  PRICE-IN             PIC X(6).
        05  FILLER               PIC X(14).

* THIS FILE IS USED TO WRITE OUT THE SINGLE PRINT LINE.

  FD    PRINT-FILE
        LABEL RECORDS ARE OMITTED
        DATA RECORD IS PRINT-LINE.

  01    PRINT-LINE.
        05  FILLER               PIC X(22).
        05  PRICE-OUT            PIC X(6).
        05  FILLER               PIC X(5).
        05  AUTHOR-OUT           PIC X(20).
        05  FILLER               PIC X(5).
        05  TITLE-OUT            PIC X(40).
        05  FILLER               PIC X(35).
```

The file-name given in the file description must be the same as that given in the SELECT statement of the INPUT-OUTPUT SECTION. If these names are not identical, the program will not be executed.

The line LABEL RECORDS ARE OMITTED must be used for every card and printer file. This has the effect of informing the compiler that there are no beginning and ending labels for these files. Labels are associated with tape and disk files, however, and the LABEL RECORDS clause plays an important role in such cases. A discussion of these matters is deferred to Chapter 16.

The DATA RECORD clause serves to assign a user-supplied name to the input and output records.

File Section: Complete specification of all input and output data records and files.

File collection of releaddale records.

Margin

[handwritten margin notes: 01 — name following it refers to an entire record]

[handwritten margin notes: Filler data cause that can't be referenced by name]

The 01 beginning in the A margin serves to indicate that the name following it refers to an entire record. This statement is somewhat redundant since the name must be the same as that given in the DATA RECORD IS clause preceding it. The statement is required, however, by the rules of the COBOL language. The 01 is referred to as a level number.

Records are made up of fields. A field is simply a string of adjacent columns. The statements with the level number 05 are used to describe these fields. The name FILLER is used to denote any field that is not to be referred to by name in this particular program. The PICTURE clause describes the length of the field and the type of data (alphabetic, alphanumeric, or numeric) that the field is to contain. The letter X is used to denote a field that is alphanumeric (that is, it may contain letters, numbers, and special characters) and the number following it in parentheses indicates the length of the field.

Thus, the first and third of the 05 level field descriptions in the specification of PRINT-LINE indicate that the first 22 positions and positions 29–34 of the output record contain alphanumeric data and will not be referenced by name in the program. The second 05 level field description assigns the user-supplied name PRICE-OUT to the alphanumeric data field represented by the printer positions 23–28. Note that the total number of positions described is 133, which provides one column for specifying line spacing and 132 print characters per line. The maximum number of print characters per line varies with the type of printer being used. Most printers allow lines of 132 characters. The examples in this text use 132-character print lines, but note that some printers allow fewer characters.

Group items may be further subdivided in a record description by the use of higher level numbers, but this subject will not be discussed here.

3.5 The PROCEDURE DIVISION

The PROCEDURE DIVISION of the program EXAMPLE1 is listed below.

```
PROCEDURE DIVISION.

        OPEN INPUT INPUT-FILE.
        OPEN OUTPUT PRINT-FILE.

        READ INPUT-FILE AT END STOP RUN.

        MOVE SPACES TO PRINT-LINE.
        MOVE PRICE-IN TO PRICE-OUT.
        MOVE AUTHOR-IN TO AUTHOR-OUT.
        MOVE TITLE-IN TO TITLE-OUT.

        WRITE PRINT-LINE.

        CLOSE INPUT-FILE.
        CLOSE PRINT-FILE.

        STOP RUN.
```

Clearly, the PROCEDURE DIVISION consists of a sequence of statements for manipulating the files and records specified and assigned symbolic names in preceding divisions of the COBOL program.

An OPEN statement is required for each input and output file to be utilized by the program. These statements specify whether the file is an input or output

file and must occur in the PROCEDURE DIVISION before any attempt is made
to access data on these files. The formats of these statements are

```
OPEN INPUT file-name
OPEN OUTPUT file-name
```

Before the run is completed, all files must be closed. This is accomplished
with a statement in the format:

```
CLOSE file-name
```

The READ statement simply causes the input file to be read. For the
moment, we will tacitly assume that an input record will be present. Thus, the
AT END clause will never be executed. This clause will be dealt with in detail
in the next chapter.

The MOVE verb is a powerful COBOL tool and is used to move data from
an input area or from storage to an output record or another storage area.
The first MOVE statement,

```
MOVE SPACES TO PRINT-LINE.
```

causes the space reserved for the PRINT-LINE to be filled with blanks. This
has the effect of erasing any "garbage" characters that may remain from a
previous use of this space. The second MOVE statement,

```
MOVE PRICE TO PRICE-OUT.
```

causes the field PRICE in the input record to be moved to the field called
PRICE-OUT in the output record. The general format of this statement is

```
MOVE data-name-1 TO data-name-2
```

The WRITE statement has the format

```
WRITE record-name
```

This simply causes the output record named to be printed.

Finally, the statement

```
STOP RUN
```

terminates execution of the program.

We will include sample input and output for most of our programs. This
should make it easier for you to determine precisely what results are produced
by the statements in the program. The program of EXAMPLE1 produced the
line

```
                          2.95   AYN RAND   ATLAS SHRUGGED
```

as output, when the following record was used as input:

```
AYN RAND        ATLAS SHRUGGED        2.95
```

3.6 Some Remarks on Syntax

In the statement formats presented throughout this text the uppercase (capitalized) underlined words are called **key words** and must be present where
indicated. The other uppercase words are optional and may be omitted if
desired. The lowercase words are generic terms that must be replaced by user-
supplied names.

An **imperative statement** is a statement that specifies a specific uncon-ditional action to be taken by the object program. All of the statements in the PROCEDURE DIVISION of EXAMPLE1, other than the READ statement, are imperative statements. The READ statement is not considered imperative, because it includes an action that will be taken conditionally (we will cover this in more detail later). The following definitions, which do not appear in the ANSI COBOL manual, are convenient for this exposition.

A **simple imperative statement** is an imperative statement formed in accordance with one of the imperative statement formats.

A **composite imperative statement** is a sequence of simple imperative statements each separated from the next by one or more blanks. When the term "imperative statement" is used, it is intended to refer to a composite imperative statement unless otherwise qualified.

An **imperative sentence** is an imperative statement terminated by a period followed by a space.

The necessity for allowing composite imperative statements will become clear when conditional statements are introduced.

With these definitions in mind, consider two alternative ways of writing the PROCEDURE DIVISION of EXAMPLE1. The first is as follows:

```
OPEN INPUT INPUT-FILE
OPEN OUTPUT PRINT-FILE

READ INPUT-FILE AT END STOP RUN.

MOVE SPACES TO PRINT-LINE
MOVE PRICE-IN TO PRICE-OUT
MOVE AUTHOR-IN TO AUTHOR-OUT
MOVE TITLE-IN TO TITLE-OUT

WRITE PRINT-LINE

CLOSE INPUT-FILE
CLOSE PRINT-FILE

STOP RUN.
```

In this first alternative the entire PROCEDURE DIVISION is written as two imperative sentences.

```
OPEN INPUT INPUT-FILE OPEN OUTPUT PRINT-FILE
READ INPUT-FILE AT END STOP RUN.
MOVE SPACES TO PRINT-LINE
MOVE PRICE-IN TO PRICE-OUT MOVE AUTHOR-IN TO
AUTHOR-OUT.
MOVE TITLE-IN TO TITLE-OUT WRITE PRINT-LINE
CLOSE INPUT-FILE CLOSE OUTPUT-FILE STOP RUN.
```

In this alternative the same PROCEDURE DIVISION is shown with more than one simple imperative statement written on some lines.

One of the prime objectives in writing code is to produce programs that are easily comprehended by others and can be easily modified. In order to achieve this goal, a number of formatting conventions that are not required by the syntax of the COBOL language are followed in all of the programs presented in this text. The two conventions that should be apparent in the example are

Rule 1 Each simple imperative statement is written on a separate line.

Rule 2 Unless there is a reason for doing otherwise, each line contains a separate sentence.

S U M M A R Y

COBOL source input lines are limited to a maximum of 80 characters. Of these columns 1–6 are used to assign page and line numbers to the individual lines. An asterisk in column 7 indicates that the entire line is to be treated as a comment. Column 8 is referred to as the *A margin.* All headers for DIVISIONS, SECTIONS, PARAGRAPHS, and FILE DESCRIPTIONS must begin in column 8. All COBOL statements must begin in or beyond column 12, which is referred to as the *B margin* and may not extend beyond column 72. Columns 73–80 are reserved for program identification.

The most inclusive segments of code in a COBOL program are the divisions, and each COBOL program must contain the following four divisions in the order shown:

```
IDENTIFICATION DIVISION
ENVIRONMENT DIVISION
DATA DIVISION
PROCEDURE DIVISION
```

The IDENTIFICATION DIVISION contains information about the program such as the name of the program and the name of the author.

The ENVIRONMENT DIVISION specifies the hardware to be used to process the program and ties the internal COBOL file names to the actual physical files.

The DATA DIVISION contains complete descriptions of all input and output records and specifies all work areas to be utilized by the program. A data item, often referred to as a **field,** is a contiguous set of characters. A data item that is not further subdivided—and, hence, may be referenced only in its entirety—is called an **elementary data item.**

Often data items are divided into several subdata items. Such data items are called **group data items.** For example, the data item "date" may be divided into month, day, and year, and represented in the form

mmddyy

Such a division has the advantage of allowing reference to the subdata items.

A **record** is a collection of data items that refer to a single logical entity. For example, an employee record might contain the fields *employee number, name, address, hourly rate,* etc.

A **file** is a collection of related records. Although a file may contain only a single record, most files will contain many records. For example, an employee file would contain an individual record for each employee.

The PROCEDURE DIVISION contains the sequence of statements that are to be carried out to achieve the purpose of the program.

The COBOL verbs introduced with accompanying simple statement formats are

OPEN   must be used to initialize processing of a file

CLOSE   must be used to terminate processing of a file

MOVE   used to move data from one field to another

READ   used to access a record from a file
WRITE   used to write a record to a file
STOP   used to terminate execution of the program

R E V I E W   Q U E S T I O N S

[handwritten margin notes: Page and line numbers / Division section Paragraph FD / hypha A-2 09]

3.1   For what purpose are columns 1–6 of a source statement reserved?

3.2   Name the COBOL program segments that must have a header.

3.3   In what column must a header begin?   *8*   *A nothing – #*

3.4   What does an asterisk in column 7 signify?   *Comment*

3.5   What characters may be included in COBOL user-supplied names?

3.6   What is the maximum length of a user-supplied name?   *30*

3.7   Name the four divisions of a COBOL program and briefly describe the function of each.   *Identification, environment,*

3.8   How are hardware devices assigned to files?   *Select statement. File control.*

3.9   What statement signifies whether a file is to be used for input or for output?   *open statement*

3.10   What COBOL verbs are used in the PROCEDURE DIVISION of the second program presented in this chapter?   *open close move stop read write*

P R O G R A M M I N G   E X E R C I S E S

For each of the following exercises you are to write a program that reads a single input record and prints one or more lines from data in the input record. These programs should be patterned after EXAMPLE1.

3.1   Read a single record containing the following information:

Columns	Contents
1–9	Social security number
10–12	Unused
13–32	Person's name
33–80	Unused

Print out a single line containing the information from the record. The following format should be used:

Columns	Contents
1–10	Spaces
11–19	Social security number
20–26	Spaces
27–46	Name
Rest	Spaces

of processing any number of input records. The flowcharts for EXAMPLE2 are the subject of Fig. 4.1, and the complete program listing is given in Fig. 4.2. The program in Fig. 4.2 was run with the following input records:

```
AYN RAND         ATLAS SHRUGGED       2.95
JACK LONDON      MARTIN EDEN          3.25
ALDOUS HUXLEY    APE AND ESSENCE      1.85
```

The program produced the following output:

```
         2.95    AYN RAND         ATLAS SHRUGGED
         3.25    JACK LONDON      MARTIN EDEN
         1.85    ALDOUS HUXLEY    APE AND ESSENCE
```

As you study the example, note the slightly different format of the OPEN statement that was used. The following statement was used rather than two separate OPEN statements:

```
OPEN INPUT INPUT-FILE
     OUTPUT PRINT-FILE.
```

It is quite acceptable to OPEN both input and output files in a single statement. In fact it is possible to OPEN several input and several output files in a single

FIGURE 4.1   The logic of EXAMPLE2.

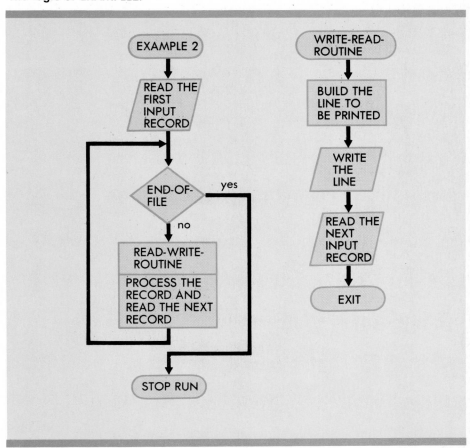

FIGURE 4.2 EXAMPLE2: a program to list multiple records.

```
      IDENTIFICATION DIVISION.
      PROGRAM-ID. EXAMPLE2.
      AUTHOR. W E SINGLETARY.

      ***********************************************************
      *
      * THIS PROGRAM IS SIMILAR TO EXAMPLE1, EXCEPT
      * THAT THIS PROGRAM WILL LIST ANY NUMBER OF INPUT RECORDS.
      * THE PROGRAM WILL PROCESS INPUT UNTIL END-OF-FILE OCCURS.
      *
      * THE FIELDS ON EACH INPUT RECORD ARE
      *
      *         THE AUTHOR OF THE BOOK
      *         THE TITLE OF THE BOOK
      *     AND THE PRICE OF THE BOOK.
      *
      ***********************************************************


      ENVIRONMENT DIVISION.
      CONFIGURATION SECTION.

      SOURCE-COMPUTER. IBM-370.
      OBJECT-COMPUTER. IBM-370.

      INPUT-OUTPUT SECTION.
      FILE-CONTROL.

          SELECT INPUT-FILE ASSIGN TO UR-S-SYSIN.
          SELECT PRINT-FILE ASSIGN TO UR-S-SYSPRINT.

      DATA DIVISION.
      FILE SECTION.

      ***********************************************************
      *
      * THIS FILE IS USED TO READ THE INPUT RECORDS.  EACH RECORD
      * CONTAINS DATA ON A SINGLE BOOK.
      *
      ***********************************************************

      FD  INPUT-FILE
          LABEL RECORDS ARE OMITTED
          DATA RECORD IS INPUT-RECORD.

      01  INPUT-RECORD.
          05  AUTHOR-IN        PIC X(20).
          05  TITLE-IN         PIC X(40).
          05  PRICE-IN         PIC X(6).
          05  FILLER           PIC X(14).
```

```
**************************************************************
*
* THE INFORMATION FROM THE INPUT RECORDS IS PRINTED
* OUT USING THIS FILE.  THERE WILL BE ONE LINE
* PRINTED FOR EACH BOOK DESCRIBED IN THE INPUT FILE.
*
**************************************************************

  FD  PRINT-FILE
      LABEL RECORDS ARE OMITTED
      DATA RECORD IS PRINT-LINE.

  01  PRINT-LINE.
      05  FILLER             PIC X(22).
      05  PRICE-OUT          PIC X(6).
      05  FILLER             PIC X(5).
      05  AUTHOR-OUT         PIC X(20).
      05  FILLER             PIC X(5).
      05  TITLE-OUT          PIC X(40).
      05  FILLER             PIC X(35).

  WORKING-STORAGE SECTION.

**************************************************************
*
* THE EOF-FLAG IS SET TO 'Y' WHEN END-OF-FILE IS REACHED.
*
**************************************************************

  01  EOF-FLAG              PIC X VALUE IS 'N'.

  PROCEDURE DIVISION.

      OPEN INPUT INPUT-FILE
           OUTPUT PRINT-FILE.

      READ INPUT-FILE AT END MOVE 'Y' TO EOF-FLAG.

      PERFORM WRITE-READ-ROUTINE UNTIL EOF-FLAG = 'Y'.

      CLOSE INPUT-FILE
            PRINT-FILE.

      STOP RUN.
```

Continued

FIGURE 4.2 Continued

```
***************************************************************
*
* THIS SUBROUTINE PRINTS THE CONTENTS A RECORD WHICH HAS
* ALREADY BEEN READ AND ATTEMPTS TO READ THE NEXT RECORD.
*
***************************************************************

  WRITE-READ-ROUTINE.

      MOVE SPACES TO PRINT-LINE.
      MOVE PRICE-IN TO PRICE-OUT.
      MOVE AUTHOR-IN TO AUTHOR-OUT.
      MOVE TITLE-IN TO TITLE-OUT.

      WRITE PRINT-LINE.

      READ INPUT-FILE AT END MOVE 'Y' TO EOF-FLAG.
```

statement. For example, the following statement would OPEN two input and three output files:

```
OPEN INPUT   NORMAL-TRANSACTIONS
             EXCEPTIONAL-TRANSACTIONS
     OUTPUT  DAILY-REPORT
             QUARTERLY-SUMMARY
             ERROR-REPORT.
```

A more general format for the CLOSE statement is also used in the example. The statement

```
CLOSE INPUT-FILE
      PRINT-FILE.
```

causes both of the files to be closed.

Particular attention should be focused on the use of the data item EOF-FLAG in this example. When the program is compiled, an initial value of 'N' is assigned to this item. The first time that an attempt is made to execute the READ statement with no input record available to be read, an end-of-file condition is detected. This initiates execution of the AT END phrase in the READ statement, which causes the value of EOF-FLAG to be changed to 'Y'. At this time, the condition in the PERFORM statement, EOF-FLAG = 'Y' assumes a logical value of 'TRUE'.

The discussion of the execution of the PERFORM statement indicates that this will, in turn, cause execution of the program to be transferred to the statement following the PERFORM. This will simply result in the closing of the input and output files and termination of the execution of the program.

The use of loop constructs is the key to the use of computers in performing data processing tasks. Be certain that you understand this example before going on.

S U M M A R Y

The WORKING-STORAGE SECTION of the DATA DIVISION provides an area for defining all records and noncontiguous data items that are not a part of external data files. The VALUE clause may be used to assign initial values to data items in the WORKING-STORAGE SECTION during compilation of the program.

The AT END phrase in the READ statement is used to deal with end-of-file conditions. The READ statement is a conditional statement when this phrase is included.

The relational operators LESS THAN, EQUAL TO, and GREATER THAN may be used to form simple logical relations. Each of these operators may be preceded by the unary logical operator NOT, and the symbols <, =, and > may be substituted for the corresponding operators.

In this text, the term "subroutine" will be used to refer to paragraphs in the PROCEDURE DIVISION of a COBOL program which are accessed through use of the PERFORM statement.

The PERFORM statement with an UNTIL phrase is used in conjunction with subroutines to implement the loop construct in COBOL programs.

R E V I E W   Q U E S T I O N S

4.1   What is the purpose of the WORKING-STORAGE SECTION?

4.2   Which clause may be used to assign initial values to data items in WORKING-STORAGE?

4.3   What is the purpose of the AT END phrase in the READ statement?

4.4   What is the scope of the AT END phrase?

4.5   List all allowable forms of the relational operators.

4.6   Describe the structure of a subroutine.

4.7   Where do the subroutines occur in relation to the main routine?

4.8   Give the two formats for the PERFORM statement introduced in this chapter.

4.9   How is the loop construct implemented in COBOL?

4.10   What determines the end of a paragraph in the PROCEDURE DIVISION?

P R O G R A M M I N G   E X E R C I S E S

Exercises 4.1–4.11 of this set require that you look at the exercises at the end of Chapter 3. Those exercises required that you write a program that read only a single input card. These exercises are identical to those, except that the program that you write must accept any number of input records, printing the appropriate line or lines for each input record.

4.12   Write a program that reads a set of input records that conform to the following format:

Columns	Contents
1–20	Name
21–29	Social security number
30–32	Golf score
33–80	Spaces

For every two input records, a single line should be printed using the following format:

Columns	Contents
1–10	Spaces
11–30	Name from the first record of a pair
31–35	Spaces
36–44	Social security number from the first record of a pair
45–48	Spaces
49–51	Score from first record
52–75	Spaces
76–95	Name from second record
96–100	Spaces
101–109	Social security number from the second record
110–113	Spaces
114–116	Score from second record
Rest	Spaces

You may assume that there will be an even number of input records.

CHAPTER FIVE

PAGE AND COLUMN HEADINGS

INTRODUCTION In Sections 5.1–5.4 the specifics required for building and printing page and column headings and properly controlling the vertical spacing of the printer are discussed. The mechanics of specifying page and column headings and the directions necessary to have them printed at the top of a page are presented in Section 5.5.

The example provided in Section 5.6 is included to illustrate the use of the new material introduced in the first five sections of the chapter.

5.1 Constants

The COBOL language provides for the use of three types of constants in the DATA and PROCEDURE divisions of a COBOL program. These are the numeric constants, the nonnumeric constants or literals, and the figurative constants. Of these, the numeric and nonnumeric constants are defined by the programmer, while the figurative constants are COBOL reserved words that have been assigned special meanings or values. A **constant** is a form of data that is not changed during the execution of a program. Constants play an important role in the construction of COBOL programs, and each of these three types is discussed in some detail below.

A **numeric constant** is a constant that represents a numeric quantity and can be used in arithmetic operations. The use of numeric constants will be illustrated when the COBOL statements for performing the arithmetic operations are introduced. For the moment, the following rules for the formation of numeric constants are stated and several examples are given:

Rule 1   A numeric constant can contain from 1 to 18 digits, a plus or minus sign, and a decimal point (note that blanks are not allowed).

Rule 2   If a sign is present, it must be the leftmost character of the constant.

Rule 3   If there is no sign, the quantity represented by the constant is assumed to be positive.

Rule 4   A decimal point can occur anywhere in the constant except as the rightmost character. Whole numbers are represented by constants without a decimal point.

Examples of numeric constants are as follows:

```
.005

13.786

-874.3

96

-.047

-1
```

A **nonnumeric constant** is a constant that can be used to represent arbitrary character strings. These constants are very convenient for use in composing page and column headings and messages of various types. The rules for forming nonnumeric constants are

Rule 1   The beginning and end of a nonnumeric constant must be delimited by a single quotation mark.

Rule 2   A nonnumeric constant can contain from 1 to 120 characters other than the quotation marks.

Rule 3   Any valid COBOL character (alphabetic, numeric, or special) other than a single quotation mark can appear between the single quotation marks, which delimit the constant.

Rule 4 To embed a quotation mark in a literal, use two consecutive quotation marks.

Following are several examples of nonnumeric literals.

```
'CLASS LISTING'
'PAYROLL REPORT'
'EMPLOYEE''S NAME'
'10,000'
'$-0+*'
'12.03'
```

Our next example program illustrates the use of nonnumeric constants in the data division of a program.

A **figurative constant,** as stated earlier, is a COBOL reserved word. Reserved words have been assigned a special meaning or value by the developers of COBOL. The two most commonly used figurative constants are SPACES and ZEROS (or ZEROES; either spelling is acceptable).

We have previously used the constant SPACES in statements of the form

```
MOVE SPACES TO field-1.
```

This, as we have seen, has the effect of assigning a blank to each position of field-1.

In the same way, a zero can be assigned to each position of field-1 by a statement of the form

```
MOVE ZEROS TO field-1.
```

There are several other figurative constants, and two of these will be discussed in a later section.

5.2 The VALUE Clause

VALUE clauses may be used to assign initial values to elementary data items (that is, data items that are not further subdivided) in the WORKING-STORAGE SECTION of the DATA DIVISION. This use of the VALUE clause is not permitted in the FILE SECTION. The general format for the VALUE clause is

```
VALUE IS literal
```

where the literal may be any type of literal consistent with the PICTURE clause used in specifying the corresponding data item.

Several valid data descriptions employing the VALUE clause are listed below.

```
05  FILLER          PIC X(48)  VALUE IS SPACES.
05  FILLER          PIC X(13)  VALUE IS 'EMPLOYEE LIST'.
05  FILLER          PIC X(8)   VALUE IS 'BIRTHDAY'.
```

Note that when a literal is assigned as a value, its length should match the length specification in the PICTURE clause.

The value specified in a VALUE clause is assigned to the corresponding data item during compilation of the program. That is, the data item has been initialized to the value before execution of the statements in the program begins.

5.3 SPECIAL NAMES

A SPECIAL-NAMES paragraph may be included in the CONFIGURATION SEC-
TION of the ENVIRONMENT DIVISION of a COBOL program. The use of this
paragraph in this book will be to define a mnemonic that can be used in the
WRITE statement to advance the printer to the top of the next page. Printer
channel 1, which normally means top of page, is referenced by C01. It is
standard practice on many COBOL compilers to use this paragraph to facilitate
advancing the printer to the top of a page, but the reader is warned that the
practice used at a particular facility should be checked to determine whether
this is valid for the compiler in use there.

The paragraph that is used for this purpose in the next example program
is

```
SPECIAL-NAMES.
    C01 IS TOP-OF-PAGE.
```

The details of how this mnemonic may be used in the WRITE statement are
covered in the next section.

5.4 The ADVANCING Phrase in the WRITE Statement

The ADVANCING phrase gives the programmer the flexibility of controlling
the positioning of the printed lines in the output file. One form of this clause
is

$$\underline{\text{AFTER}} \text{ ADVANCING constant-1} \begin{bmatrix} \text{LINE} \\ \text{LINES} \end{bmatrix}$$

The value of constant-1 must be a positive integer less than 100. In this case,
the printed page is advanced the number of lines specified by constant-1. The
AFTER ADVANCING phrase establishes the value in the first position of the
printed record. As mentioned earlier, this character is the carriage control that
determines the line spacing for the printer. The word LINES is optional, thus

```
AFTER ADVANCING 1
```

can be used.

The other form of the AFTER ADVANCING phrase used is

```
AFTER ADVANCING mnemonic-name
```

where mnemonic-name is a function-name given in the special-names paragraph of the environment division.

The following examples illustrate the use of the ADVANCING phrase. The
statement

```
WRITE OUTPUT-LINE AFTER ADVANCING 1
```

causes single spacing to occur before the line is printed. The statement

```
WRITE OUTPUT-LINE AFTER ADVANCING TOP-OF-PAGE
```

causes the line to be printed at the top of the next page.

5.5 Page and Column Headings

Page and column headings are required as part of most meaningful printed output. A typical report, for example, would require a minimum of four distinct record descriptions for printed records—the page header, a column header, a detail line corresponding to the data items being processed, and a summary line. When multiple output record formats are required, it is common (and preferred) practice to define the record formats in the WORKING-STORAGE SECTION and include the description of a single print line, or buffer, in the FILE SECTION. This permits initial values to be assigned to the fields in the record descriptions and can dramatically reduce the number of MOVE statements required in the PROCEDURE DIVISION.

An example should help to clarify this concept. Suppose that the following record descriptions were included in the WORKING-STORAGE SECTION.

```
01   PAGE-HEADER.
     05   FILLER      PIC X(1).
     05   FILLER      PIC X(48) VALUE IS SPACES.
     05   FILLER      PIC X(13) VALUE IS 'EMPLOYEE LIST'.
     05   FILLER      PIC X(71) VALUE IS SPACES.

01   COLUMN-HEADER.
     05   FILLER      PIC X(1).
     05   FILLER      PIC X(28) VALUE IS SPACES.
     05   FILLER      PIC X(13) VALUE IS 'EMPLOYEE NAME'.
     05   FILLER      PIC X(27) VALUE IS SPACES.
     05   FILLER      PIC X(8)  VALUE IS 'BIRTHDAY'.
     05   FILLER      PIC X(56) VALUE IS SPACES.
```

Also suppose that the following record description had been included in the FILE SECTION.

```
01   OUTPUT-LINE      PIC X(133).
```

Then the following statements could have been used in the PROCEDURE DIVISION to print the page and column headings at the top of a new page.

```
MOVE PAGE-HEADER TO OUTPUT-LINE.
WRITE OUTPUT-LINE AFTER ADVANCING TOP-OF-PAGE.

MOVE COLUMN-HEADER TO OUTPUT-LINE.
WRITE OUTPUT-LINE AFTER ADVANCING 2 LINES.
```

Actually, there is a format for the WRITE statement that includes a FROM phrase. This would allow each of the pairs of lines listed above to be replaced by a single line. The format for the FROM phrase is

```
FROM identifier-1
```

Using this option, the two pairs of lines to print the headings could be replaced by

```
WRITE OUTPUT-LINE FROM PAGE-HEADER
     AFTER ADVANCING TOP-OF-PAGE.

WRITE OUTPUT-LINE FROM COLUMN-HEADER
     AFTER ADVANCING 2 LINES.
```

Each of these statements has precisely the same effect as the corresponding pair of statements which it replaces.

The reader should note that the lines defined in the page and column headers just shown have been padded to a full 133 characters. This is not strictly necessary, because of the fact that when a shorter nonnumeric data item is moved to a longer one, the longer field is filled to the right with blanks. A more complete discussion of the MOVE statement is given in Chapter 8.

5.6 EXAMPLE3—A Simple Report with Headers

The purpose of this section is to present a program that illustrates the printing of page and column headings. Specifically, the program positions the printer to the top of a page and prints a page heading. Then, after proper spacing, it prints column headings. After this is done, a file of input records, each of which contains an employee name and a birth date, is read and this information is printed in the appropriate columns. The flowchart for this program is presented in Fig. 5.1. The complete program listing follows in Fig. 5.2.

FIGURE 5.1   The logic of EXAMPLE3.

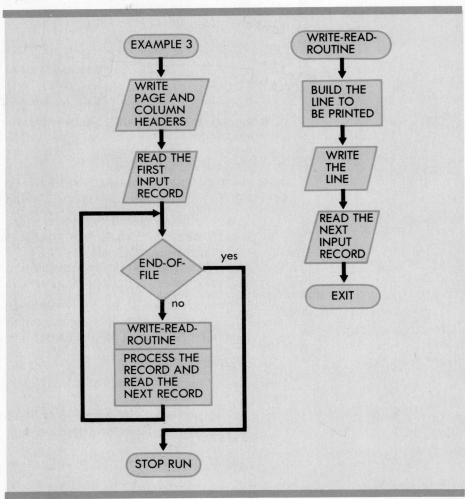

FIGURE 5.2 EXAMPLE3: a report with page and column headers.

```
IDENTIFICATION DIVISION.
PROGRAM-ID. EXAMPLE3.
AUTHOR. W E SINGLETARY.

************************************************************
*
* THIS PROGRAM READS A SET OF RECORDS CONTAINING EMPLOYEE
* NAMES AND BIRTHDAYS.  THE INFORMATION FROM THE RECORDS IS
* LISTED UNDER APPROPRIATE PAGE AND COLUMN HEADERS.  NOTE
* THE USE OF THE "AFTER ADVANCING" OPTION ON THE WRITE
* STATEMENT.
*
************************************************************

ENVIRONMENT DIVISION.

CONFIGURATION SECTION.
SOURCE-COMPUTER. IBM-370.
OBJECT-COMPUTER. IBM-370.

SPECIAL-NAMES.
    C01 IS TOP-OF-PAGE.

INPUT-OUTPUT SECTION.
FILE-CONTROL.

    SELECT EMPLOYEE-FILE ASSIGN TO UR-S-SYSIN.
    SELECT REPORT-FILE ASSIGN TO UR-S-SYSPRINT.

DATA DIVISION.
FILE SECTION.

************************************************************
*
* THIS FILE IS USED TO READ THE RECORDS CONTAINING NAMES
* AND BIRTHDAYS.
*
************************************************************

FD  EMPLOYEE-FILE
    LABEL RECORDS ARE OMITTED
    DATA RECORD IS INPUT-RECORD.

01  INPUT-RECORD.
    05   NAME-IN       PIC X(20).
    05   FILLER        PIC X.
    05   BIRTHDAY-IN   PIC X(8).
    05   FILLER        PIC X(51).
```

Continued

FIGURE 5.2 Continued

```
****************************************************************
*
* THIS FILE IS USED TO LIST THE CONTENTS OF THE RECORDS.  NOTE
* THE AFTER ADVANCING OPTION CAUSES THE FIRST BYTE OF THE
* PRINT LINE TO BE USED AS A CARRIAGE CONTROL CHARACTER.
*
****************************************************************

  FD  REPORT-FILE
      LABEL RECORDS ARE OMITTED
      DATA RECORD IS OUTPUT-LINE.

  01  OUTPUT-LINE.
      05  FILLER        PIC X(29).
      05  NAME-OUT       PIC X(20).
      05  FILLER        PIC X(20).
      05  BIRTHDAY-OUT   PIC X(8).
      05  FILLER        PIC X(56).

  WORKING-STORAGE SECTION.

****************************************************************
*
* EOF-FLAG IS SET TO 'Y' WHEN END-OF-FILE OCCURS.
*
* PAGE-HEADER AND COLUMN-HEADER ARE USED TO PRINT HEADERS AT
*          THE TOP OF THE FIRST PAGE OF OUTPUT.
*
****************************************************************

  01  EOF-FLAG        PIC X       VALUE IS 'N'.

  01  PAGE-HEADER.
      05  FILLER        PIC X(1).
      05  FILLER        PIC X(48) VALUE IS SPACES.
      05  FILLER        PIC X(13) VALUE IS 'EMPLOYEE LIST'.
      05  FILLER        PIC X(71) VALUE IS SPACES.

  01  COLUMN-HEADER.
      05  FILLER        PIC X(1).
      05  FILLER        PIC X(28) VALUE IS SPACES.
      05  FILLER        PIC X(13) VALUE IS 'EMPLOYEE NAME'.
      05  FILLER        PIC X(27) VALUE IS SPACES.
      05  FILLER        PIC X(8)  VALUE IS 'BIRTHDAY'.
      05  FILLER        PIC X(56) VALUE IS SPACES.
```

```
    PROCEDURE DIVISION.
        OPEN INPUT EMPLOYEE-FILE
             OUTPUT REPORT-FILE.

        MOVE PAGE-HEADER TO OUTPUT-LINE.
        WRITE OUTPUT-LINE AFTER ADVANCING TOP-OF-PAGE.

        MOVE COLUMN-HEADER TO OUTPUT-LINE.
        WRITE OUTPUT-LINE AFTER ADVANCING 3 LINES.

        MOVE SPACES TO OUTPUT-LINE.
        WRITE OUTPUT-LINE AFTER ADVANCING 1.

        READ EMPLOYEE-FILE AT END MOVE 'Y' TO EOF-FLAG.

        PERFORM WRITE-READ-ROUTINE UNTIL EOF-FLAG = 'Y'.

        CLOSE EMPLOYEE-FILE
              REPORT-FILE.

        STOP RUN.

    ****************************************************************
    *
    * THE FOLLOWING SUBROUTINE PRINTS THE FIELDS FROM THE LAST
    * INPUT RECORD AND ATTEMPTS TO READ THE NEXT RECORD.
    *
    ****************************************************************

    WRITE-READ-ROUTINE.

        MOVE SPACES TO OUTPUT-LINE.
        MOVE NAME-IN TO NAME-OUT.
        MOVE BIRTHDAY-IN TO BIRTHDAY-OUT.

        WRITE OUTPUT-LINE AFTER ADVANCING 1.

        READ EMPLOYEE-FILE AT END MOVE 'Y' TO EOF-FLAG.
```

first character is a carriage control character—these control the positioning of the line printed.

In this example the group data items PAGE-HEADER and COLUMN-HEADER specify a complete output record. Because, in this case, an output record is a printed line, each of these items describes the format of a complete line. It may be assumed that the first character of the printed record is reserved for a carriage control character that controls the positioning of the printed line. This character is never printed and the appropriate character is inserted by the COBOL compiler if the program is correctly coded. For this reason the first field of PAGE-HEADER is specified to be of length 1 and is designated as an alphanumeric character. This field should always be given this characterization and no value need be assigned to it. However, we could have accomplished the same effect by omitting the first field and making the length of the second field 49 rather than 48.

In EXAMPLE3 the first WRITE statement causes the printer to be advanced to the top of a page before PAGE-HEADER is printed. The second WRITE statement effects triple spacing between PAGE-HEADER and COLUMN-HEADER. The third WRITE statement, of course, causes single spacing before each output record is printed.

There is a requirement that, if the AFTER ADVANCING phrase is used in one WRITE statement for a given file, then it must be used in all WRITE statements for that output file.

We ran EXAMPLE3 with the following input:

```
ROSS OVERBEEK          5/16/49
BILL JACOBS            2/11/45
MAY LOO                10/28/53
```

The program produced the following output:

```
                              EMPLOYEE LIST


        EMPLOYEE NAME                    BIRTHDAY

        ROSS OVERBEEK                    5/16/49
        BILL JACOBS                      2/11/45
        MAY LOO                          10/28/53
```

SUMMARY

The COBOL language provides numeric, nonnumeric, and figurative constants. The numeric and nonnumeric constants are defined by the user, and rather detailed rules govern their formation. The figurative constants are COBOL reserved words whose values are determined by the system.

VALUE clauses may be used to assign initial values to elementary data items in the WORKING-STORAGE SECTION.

A SPECIAL-NAMES paragraph may be added to the CONFIGURATION SECTION of the ENVIRONMENT DIVISION. This paragraph is used here to assign C01 the name TOP-OF-PAGE, which may then be used in advancing the printer to the top of the next page.

Vertical positioning of print lines is controlled by use of the ADVANCING phrase in WRITE statements.

It is often convenient to describe records in the WORKING-STORAGE SECTION, where the VALUE clause may be used to advantage. These records can then be printed by first moving them to a record in an output file. This is most easily accomplished by using the FROM phrase in a WRITE statement.

REVIEW QUESTIONS

5.1   Name the three types of COBOL constants and give an example of each.

5.2   When are the values specified in VALUE clauses assigned to data items?

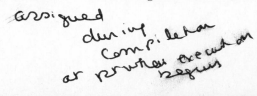

5.3   Where may VALUE clauses be used?

5.4   What use is made of the SPECIAL-NAMES paragraph in EXAMPLE3?

5.5   Where must this paragraph be placed?

5.6   How is vertical positioning of print lines controlled?

5.7   What specific phrase could be used to advance the printer 10 lines?

5.8   Where should the record descriptions for page and column headings be specified?

5.9   What advantage can be gained through not giving detailed record descriptions of the headers in output records?

5.10   What phrase may be used to conveniently print headers that are not defined as records in output files?

PROGRAMMING EXERCISES

5.1–5.7 Take the first seven exercises from the set at the end of Chapter 3 and add the following features.

a) Any number of input records may be used as input.

b) Appropriate page and column headings should be printed at the top of the page.

c) Double-spacing should occur before the first line corresponding to a given input record is printed. Successive lines corresponding to the same input record should be single-spaced.

CHAPTER SIX

NUMERIC PICTURES AND BASIC ARITHMETIC

INTRODUCTION In the preceding chapters all of the PICTURE clauses have specified only alphanumeric data. Alphanumeric data items cannot be used as operands in arithmetic operations. In Section 6.1 the PICTUREs for numeric and numeric edited data items are introduced in enough detail to allow the manipulation and output of numeric data.

Section 6.2 introduces basic forms of the arithmetic statements. While the formats displayed there are far from complete, they provide enough details to permit the usual arithmetic operations to be performed.

In Section 6.3 an example that illustrates the use of arithmetic statements is displayed.

6.1 The PICTURE Clause

In the examples considered thus far, all of the PICTURE clauses have specified fields that were to be occupied by alphanumeric data items. The values assigned to these fields were character strings that could contain any valid COBOL character (numeric, alphabetic, or special). An alphanumeric field cannot, however, be used in arithmetic operations. In the ensuing discussion field specifications for numeric data items and the means provided for editing such fields to formats that are appropriate for output will be discussed.

Four distinct groups of PICTURE clauses provided for specifying data fields are considered below. They are

Alphabetic items	PICTURE consists of A's only.
Alphanumeric items	PICTURE consists of X's only.
Numeric items	PICTURE consists of 9's and a V or 9's only. A leading S can be used to indicate a sign (the use of signed values will be covered in Chapter 8).
Numeric edited items	PICTURE consists of 9's, Z's, and a decimal point.

With these PICTUREs a sequence of A's, X's, 9's or Z's can be represented by a single occurrence of the appropriate symbol followed by a repeat factor enclosed in parentheses. For example,

```
PIC XXXXX
```

and

```
PIC X(5)
```

are interpreted identically.

The use of PICTURE clauses specifying alphabetic fields is not common, because the only allowable characters in such fields are the letters A to Z and the blank. This is hardly adequate even for names, which may contain periods and possibly hyphens. For this reason name fields are usually specified by alphanumeric rather than alphabetic PICTURE clauses.

Numeric items that are to be read from input records, such as cards, do not usually contain a decimal point. Field specifications for such items are illustrated below. For example, the clause

```
PIC 9999.
```

reserves storage for four numeric digits (0 to 9). This indicates a whole number. In specifying fields for decimal numbers a V must be used in the PICTURE to indicate the desired location of the decimal point. For example, the clause

```
PIC 9(4)V9(2).
```

could be used to represent a field that is to allow for six decimal digits, two of which are to follow the decimal point. Of course, this same specification could have been given alternatively as

```
PIC 9999V99.
```

In the last two PICTURE clauses presented, the V represents an implied decimal point. This does not occupy a position in the input record and should not be included in the length of the input field. That is to say, the numerals

     `123456`

read from an input record into a field specified by one of these PICTURE clauses would be treated by the computer as the decimal number

     `1234.56`

The picture associated with this data item is seven characters in length, but, obviously, the representation in the input record occupies only six positions. This is the standard technique used for the input of numeric items.

Numeric edited fields are used to specify the form in which numeric data is to be output. A numeric edited field normally contains editing symbols (such as decimal points, etc.). For this reason such fields cannot be used in any arithmetic operation. With a few minor exceptions, all numeric data should be moved to numeric edited fields before being moved to an output record. Moving numeric data items to numeric edited fields provides a facility for inserting characters such as dollar signs, commas, and decimal points into these fields to make the output more meaningful.

In its crudest form the PICTURE for a numeric edited data item contains only 9's and a decimal point. In computing the length of the edited field, the decimal must be counted as a character position. This does not apply to fields specified for whole numbers, because no decimal point is involved. As an example, the PICTURE for a numeric edited field to receive the number 123.45 could be specified by 999.99. Here the specified field is of length 6. It is also permissible to use a repeat factor or factors in a PICTURE for a numeric edited field. Thus the field for this item could have been specified by the equivalent PICTURES 9(3).99 or 9(3).9(2).

If leading zeroes are present in the data item to be received in a numeric edited field, the printing of these can be suppressed by using Z's. The Z's appear in the initial positions of the PICTURE specification. This causes any leading zeroes occurring in the sending field which correspond to a Z in the receiving field to be replaced by a blank. As an example, if the clause:

     `PIC ZZZZ.99`

is specified for a field that is to receive the value 0034.56, the edited result will have a value of 34.56.

A common mistake of beginning programmers is to attempt to use numeric edited data items in arithmetic operations. It is important to remember that such items are in printable format, but are not in numeric format. Any attempt to use such an item in an arithmetic operation will be detected as an error.

Table 6.1 should help you understand the effect of moving a numeric item to a numeric edited field. Note the effects of truncation when the receiving field contains fewer digits than the sending field.

Caution: Be certain that the receiving field is at least as long as the sending field. Data is moved from a numeric sending field to a numeric edited field as the result of the execution of a MOVE statement.

The use of the PICTURE clauses presented above is illustrated in the next example program, which also introduces the arithmetic verbs.

Table 6.1 The effects of moving a numeric item to a numeric edited field

Sending field		Receiving field	
Picture	Data	Picture	Edited result
9999V99	123456	9999.99	1234.56
9999V99	003456	9999.99	0034.56
9999V99	123456	ZZZZ.99	1234.56
9999V99	000123	ZZZZ.99	1.23
9(4)V99	000123	ZZ99.99	01.23
9(4)V99	000012	Z(4).99	.12
9(3)V999	123456	Z(4).99	123.45
9(5)V9	123456	9(4).99	2345.60
9(5)V9(3)	12345678	Z(4).99	2345.67

6.2 The Arithmetic Verbs

There are two distinct formats for statements beginning with each of the four arithmetic verbs (ADD, SUBTRACT, MULTIPLY, and DIVIDE). For example, the two formats associated with the ADD verb are

```
ADD field-1 TO field-2

ADD field-1 field-2 GIVING field-3
```

The effect of the first of these is simply to add the contents of field-1 to the contents of field-2 and to store the result in field-2. Of course, the original contents of field-2 are lost when execution of the statement occurs. With the second form, the contents of field-1 and field-2 are again added, but in this case the result is stored in field-3. With the first form, field-1 is unaltered, and with the second, both field-1 and field-2 remain unchanged.

The use of numeric literals is also allowed in these statements. In the first format, field-1 may be a numeric literal, and in the second, either field-1 or field-2 may be a numeric literal. The receiving field—that is, field-2 in the first format and field-3 in the second—however, must be the name of a data field. *Note:* field-3 may be a numeric edited field.

The formats for arithmetic statements using the SUBTRACT, MULTIPLY, and DIVIDE verbs are similar to those given for the ADD verb. The statement formats for these verbs are

```
SUBTRACT field-1 FROM field-2
SUBTRACT field-1 FROM field-2 GIVING field-3

MULTIPLY field-1 BY field-2
MULTIPLY field-1 BY field-2 GIVING field-3

DIVIDE field-1 INTO field-2
DIVIDE field-1 INTO field-2 GIVING field-3
```

In each case the use of the first format causes the result to replace the contents of field-2. It should be noted that, when a DIVIDE statement is executed using integer fields, the remainder, if any, is dropped. The following two examples illustrate this, if it is assumed that TOTAL, TOTAL-NUMBERS, and AVERAGE all have integer values (that is, if the picture clauses for these fields contain no implied decimal point).

```
DIVIDE TOTAL-NUMBERS INTO TOTAL.
```

Execution of this statement has the following result:

FIELD NAME:	TOTAL	TOTAL-NUMBERS
VALUE BEFORE:	43	10
VALUE AFTER:	Ø4	10

```
DIVIDE TOTAL-NUMBERS INTO TOTAL GIVING AVERAGE.
```

The results of the execution of this statement are

FIELD NAME:	TOTAL	TOTAL-NUMBERS	AVERAGE
VALUE BEFORE:	43	10	?
VALUE AFTER:	43	10	4

6.3 EXAMPLE4—A Program to Summarize Gasoline Expenditures

An algorithm for processing an unspecified number of gasoline purchases, EXAMPLE4, is presented in the flowcharts shown in Fig. 6.1. The input file is to consist of a set of records, each of which is to contain the number of gallons and the price per gallon for a single purchase. This information together with the total price paid is to be printed for each individual purchase. Finally, after the entire file has been processed, the grand total number of gallons, the total cost of all the purchases, and the average cost per gallon are to be printed.

The complete program listing for EXAMPLE4 is presented in Fig. 6.2. This program was run with the following input data:

```
10201150
12001149
09501139
15001129
04001180
```

The program produced the following output:

```
        GASOLINE EXPENDITURES

        GALLONS  PRICE   COST

          10.20  1.150  11.73
          12.00  1.149  13.78
           9.50  1.139  10.82
          15.00  1.129  16.93
           4.00  1.180   4.72

TOTALS:   50.70         57.98   AVERAGE PRICE = 1.14   # PURCHASES =   5
```

FIGURE 6.1 The logic of EXAMPLE4.

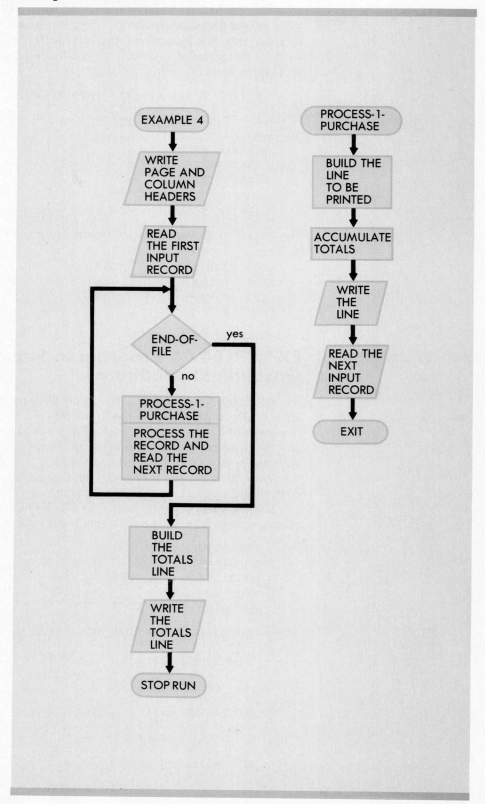

FIGURE 6.2 EXAMPLE4: a program illustrating arithmetic verbs.

```
      IDENTIFICATION DIVISION.
      PROGRAM-ID. EXAMPLE4.
      AUTHOR. W E SINGLETARY.

  *****************************************************************
  *
  * THIS PROGRAM ILLUSTRATES THE USE OF ARITHMETIC VERBS,
  * NUMERIC LITERALS, AND NUMERIC PICTURES.
  *
  * IT READS IN A SET OF RECORDS, EACH OF WHICH REPRESENTS
  * A SINGLE PURCHASE OF GASOLINE.  EACH RECORD CONTAINS THE
  * NUMBER OF GALLONS THAT WERE PURCHASED AND THE PRICE
  * PAID PER GALLON.  THE PROGRAM PRINTS THIS INFORMATION,
  * AS WELL AS THE PRICE PAID (FOR EACH PURCHASE).  FINALLY,
  * AFTER ALL OF THE INPUT RECORDS HAVE BEEN PROCESSED, THE
  * PROGRAM PRINTS
  *
  *        THE TOTAL NUMBER OF GALLONS PURCHASED,
  *        THE TOTAL COST,
  *    AND THE AVERAGE COST PER GALLON.
  *
  *****************************************************************

      ENVIRONMENT DIVISION.

      CONFIGURATION SECTION.
      SOURCE-COMPUTER. IBM-370.
      OBJECT-COMPUTER. IBM-370.

      SPECIAL-NAMES.
          C01 IS TOP-OF-PAGE.

      INPUT-OUTPUT SECTION.
      FILE-CONTROL.

          SELECT INPUT-FILE ASSIGN TO UR-S-SYSIN.
          SELECT OUTPUT-FILE ASSIGN TO UR-S-SYSPRINT.
```

continued

FIGURE 6.2 Continued

```
     DATA DIVISION.
     FILE SECTION.

*****************************************************************
*
* THIS FILE IS USED TO READ THE INPUT RECORDS.  EACH RECORD
* CONTAINS THE NUMBER OF GALLONS IN COLUMNS 1-4.  THERE IS AN
* ASSUMED DECIMAL POINT AFTER THE LEFT TWO DIGITS (THUS, 1234
* WOULD REPRESENT 12.34 GALLONS).  COLUMNS 5-7 GIVE THE PRICE
* PER GALLON (WITH TWO DIGITS TO THE RIGHT OF THE ASSUMED
* DECIMAL POINT).
*
*****************************************************************

     FD   INPUT-FILE
          LABEL RECORDS ARE OMITTED
          DATA RECORD IS INPUT-RECORD.

     01   INPUT-RECORD.
          05   GALLONS-IN              PIC 99V99.
          05   PRICE-IN                PIC 9V999.
          05   FILLER                  PIC X(72).

*****************************************************************
*
* THIS FILE IS USED TO PRODUCE THE REPORT ON GASOLINE
* EXPENDITURES.  ONE LINE WILL BE PRINTED PER PURCHASE, AS
* WELL AS TOTALS AT THE END OF THE REPORT.
*
*****************************************************************

     FD   OUTPUT-FILE
          LABEL RECORDS ARE OMITTED
          DATA RECORD IS PRINT-LINE.

     01   PRINT-LINE.
          05   FILLER                  PIC X(30).
          05   GALLONS-OUT             PIC ZZ.99.
          05   FILLER                  PIC X(10).
          05   PRICE-OUT               PIC Z.999.
          05   FILLER                  PIC X(7).
          05   PURCHASE-AMOUNT         PIC ZZZ.99.
          05   FILLER                  PIC X(70).
```

```
   WORKING-STORAGE SECTION.

   *********************************************************
   *
   * EOF-FLAG IS SET TO 'Y' WHEN END-OF-FILE OCCURS.
   *
   * COST IS SET TO THE COST OF ONE PURCHASE.
   *
   * TOTAL-GALLONS IS USED TO ACCUMULATE THE TOTAL NUMBER OF
   *    GALLONS THAT WERE PURCHASED
   *
   * TOTAL-COST IS USED TO ACCUMULATE THE TOTAL AMOUNT PAID
   *
   * NUMBER PURCHASES IS USED TO COUNT THE NUMBER OF PURCHASES
   *
   * PAGE-HEADER AND COLUMN-HEADER ARE USED TO PRINT HEADERS AT
   *          THE TOP OF THE FIRST PAGE OF OUTPUT.
   *
   * TOTALS-LINE IS USED TO PRINT THE FINAL TOTALS
   *
   *********************************************************

      01  MISC-FIELDS.
          05   EOF-FLAG              PIC X            VALUE IS 'N'.
          05   COST                  PIC 9999V99.

      01  ACCUMULATORS.
          05   TOTAL-GALLONS         PIC 99999V99     VALUE IS 0.
          05   TOTAL-COST            PIC 999999V99    VALUE IS 0.
          05   NUMBER-PURCHASES      PIC 9(3)         VALUE IS 0.

      01  PAGE-HEADER.
          05   FILLER                PIC X(1).
          05   FILLER                PIC X(35)        VALUE IS SPACES.
          05   FILLER                PIC X(21)        VALUE IS
                                                      'GASOLINE EXPENDITURES'.
          05   FILLER                PIC X(76)        VALUE IS SPACES.

      01  COLUMN-HEADER.
          05   FILLER                PIC X(1).
          05   FILLER                PIC X(28)        VALUE IS SPACES.
          05   FILLER                PIC X(7)         VALUE IS 'GALLONS'.
          05   FILLER                PIC X(9)         VALUE IS SPACES.
          05   FILLER                PIC X(5)         VALUE IS 'PRICE'.
          05   FILLER                PIC X(9)         VALUE IS SPACES.
          05   FILLER                PIC X(4)         VALUE IS 'COST'.
          05   FILLER                PIC X(70)        VALUE IS SPACES.
```

continued

FIGURE 6.2 Continued

```
01    TOTALS-LINE.
      05    FILLER                PIC X(20)        VALUE IS SPACES.
      05    FILLER                PIC X(8)         VALUE IS 'TOTALS: '.
      05    TOT-GALLONS           PIC ZZZZ.99.
      05    FILLER                PIC X(20)        VALUE IS SPACES.
      05    TOT-COST              PIC ZZZZZ.99.
      05    FILLER                PIC X(5)         VALUE IS SPACES.
      05    FILLER                PIC X(16)        VALUE IS
                                                   'AVERAGE PRICE = '.
      05    AVG-PRICE             PIC Z.99.
      05    FILLER                PIC X(4)         VALUE IS SPACES.
      05    FILLER                PIC X(14)        VALUE IS
                                                   '# PURCHASES = '.
      05    NUM-PURCHASES         PIC ZZ9.
      05    FILLER                PIC X(24)        VALUE IS SPACES.

PROCEDURE DIVISION.
    OPEN INPUT INPUT-FILE
         OUTPUT OUTPUT-FILE.

    MOVE PAGE-HEADER TO PRINT-LINE.
    WRITE PRINT-LINE AFTER ADVANCING TOP-OF-PAGE.

    MOVE COLUMN-HEADER TO PRINT-LINE.
    WRITE PRINT-LINE AFTER ADVANCING 2 LINES.

    MOVE SPACES TO PRINT-LINE.
    WRITE PRINT-LINE AFTER ADVANCING 1.

    READ INPUT-FILE AT END MOVE 'Y' TO EOF-FLAG.

    PERFORM PROCESS-1-PURCHASE UNTIL EOF-FLAG = 'Y'.

    PERFORM PRINT-TOTALS-LINE.

    CLOSE INPUT-FILE
          OUTPUT-FILE.

    STOP RUN.
```

```
***********************************************************************
*
* THE FOLLOWING SUBROUTINE PROCESSES THE PRECEEDING RECORD   AND
* THEN ATTEMPTS READ ANOTHER RECORD.
*
***********************************************************************

   PROCESS-1-PURCHASE.
       MOVE SPACES TO PRINT-LINE.
       MOVE GALLONS-IN TO GALLONS-OUT.
       MOVE PRICE-IN TO PRICE-OUT.
       MULTIPLY GALLONS-IN BY PRICE-IN GIVING COST.
       MOVE COST TO PURCHASE-AMOUNT.

       ADD GALLONS-IN TO TOTAL-GALLONS.
       ADD COST TO TOTAL-COST.
       ADD 1 TO NUMBER-PURCHASES.

       WRITE PRINT-LINE AFTER ADVANCING 1.

       READ INPUT-FILE AT END MOVE 'Y' TO EOF-FLAG.

***********************************************************************
*
* THE FOLLOWING SUBROUTINE PRINTS THE FINAL LINE CONTAINING
* THE SUMMARY VALUES.
*
***********************************************************************

   PRINT-TOTALS-LINE.
       MOVE TOTAL-GALLONS TO TOT-GALLONS.
       MOVE TOTAL-COST TO TOT-COST.
       DIVIDE TOTAL-GALLONS INTO TOTAL-COST GIVING AVG-PRICE.
       MOVE NUMBER-PURCHASES TO NUM-PURCHASES.
       MOVE TOTALS-LINE TO PRINT-LINE.
       WRITE PRINT-LINE AFTER ADVANCING 3 LINES.
```

SUMMARY

A PICTURE for alphanumeric data items is specified using X's only or an X followed by a repeat factor enclosed in parentheses. A PICTURE for numeric data items contains 9's and possibly an occurrence of V. The V is used to indicate an implied decimal point and is not counted in the length of the input field. Repeat factors are allowed both preceding and following the V. Numeric edited PICTUREs may contain 9's, Z's, and a decimal point. The decimal point is counted in the length of the output field. Both the 9's and Z's represent integer positions; however, the Z's are used to suppress leading zeroes.

Two formats are presented for each of the ADD, SUBTRACT, MULTIPLY, and DIVIDE arithmetic verbs. In the first format, the operation causes the contents of the second operand to be replaced by the result. The second format of the statement causes both of the operands to remain unchanged, and the result replaces the contents of a third operand.

R E V I E W   Q U E S T I O N S

6.1   What characters may be used in the PICTURE for an alphanumeric data item?   *X's*

6.2   What characters may be used in the PICTURE for a numeric data item?   *9A's*

6.3   What characters may be used in the PICTURE for a numeric edited data item?   *9's Z's*

6.4   What does the character V represent?

6.5   Is the V counted in the length of the field?

6.6   What use is made of the character Z?   *suppress leading zero, replace by blank*

6.7   Are the occurrences of Z's counted in the length of the field?

6.8   Does a decimal point count in the length of a numeric edited field?

6.9   Which of the arithmetic statements in the first format cause the second operand to be altered?

6.10 Which of the operands is altered in arithmetic statements in the second format?

P R O G R A M M I N G   E X E R C I S E S

6.1   Suppose that a firm has savings accounts with several banks. A distinct rate of interest is earned on each account. Write a program to read in any number of input records using the following format:

Columns	Contents
1–20	Name of the bank
21–27	Amount (99999V99)
28–31	Rate of interest (99V99)
32–80	Spaces

a) Write a program that will produce a report with appropriate headers such that a single line is printed for each account.

b) Calculate a summary at the end of the report containing

Total amount

Number of accounts

Average amount per account

Average interest rate

To calculate the average interest rate, sum the individual amounts times their corresponding interest rates, and then divide by the total amount.

6.2 Suppose that a store attached to each item or group of items an input record in the following format:

Columns	Contents
1–5	A unique number identifying the item
6–8	The number of units of the given item
9–13	Total value of merchandise represented by the item or set of items (999V99)

a) Print a report with appropriate headers such that for each input record, the information on the record, along with the amount per unit, is displayed.

b) Print a totals line containing:

Total number of input records

Total amount

Average amount per input record

6.3 Suppose that an individual wished to utilize a computer to balance his checking account. As input to the program there would be three types of input records.

FIRST RECORD

Columns	Contents
1–7	Last month's ending balance (99999V99)
8–80	Spaces

SECOND RECORD

Columns	Contents
1–7	Sum of deposits made this month (99999V99)
8–80	Spaces

THE REST OF THE RECORDS

Columns	Contents
1–7	Amount of a check
8–80	Spaces

Print a report with appropriate headings and labels such that

a) One line is printed for each input record, and

b) The balance (assume that this will be positive) is printed at the end of the report. Include in this totals line the number of checks (you may assume that there will be some checks) and the average amount per check.

6.4 Read in a sequence of test scores (ranging from 0 to 100). The format of the input records will be:

Columns	Contents
1–3	Score
4–80	Spaces

Print a report with appropriate headings and spacing. For each input record a single line should be printed, and at the end of the report there should be a totals line that contains the following information:

a) The sum of the scores

b) The number of scores

c) The average score

IMPLEMENTING THE DECISION CONSTRUCT

INTRODUCTION Section 7.1 introduces the COMPUTE statement. This statement can be used to express complex arithmetic expressions much more economically than they can be expressed with the basic arithmetic statements alone. As an added advantage, complex arithmetic expressions may be more readily comprehended when written in the form allowed by the COMPUTE statement.

The IF statement, which permits implementation of the decision construct in the COBOL language, is the subject of Section 7.2.

Comparisons are discussed in Section 7.3. The existence of alphanumeric as well as numeric data items makes the evaluation of the outcome of comparisons a nontrivial matter.

Use of DISPLAY statements as a debugging tool and a convenient means of displaying error messages is briefly touched upon in Section 7.4.

A simple payroll program is listed in Section 7.5 to illustrate the concepts introduced in the previous sections of the chapter.

7.1 The COMPUTE Statement

For many data processing applications little computation is required. In these cases the arithmetic verbs ADD, SUBTRACT, MULTIPLY, and DIVIDE are sufficient. There are, however, situations in which fairly complicated arithmetic expressions must be evaluated. If this is the case, the use of the COBOL arithmetic verbs introduced earlier may become quite cumbersome. The COMPUTE statement provides the flexibility necessary to express complicated arithmetic computations in a compact, easily readable form. When COMPUTE statements are used, symbols are employed, rather than arithmetic verbs, to indicate the arithmetic functions. These symbols are displayed in the following table:

Symbol	Meaning
+	Addition
−	Subtraction
/	Division
*	Multiplication
**	Exponentiation

The format of the COMPUTE statement is

    COMPUTE field-1 = expression

where expression is any arithmetic expression represented in terms of the arithmetic symbols, numeric fields, and literals. For example,

```
COMPUTE WAGES = RATE * HOURS
COMPUTE AVERAGE = TOTAL / NUMBER
COMPUTE DISC = (A ** 2 + B ** 2) ** .5
```

are all valid COBOL COMPUTE statements.

The allowable use of parentheses for COBOL expressions conforms to the usual conventions learned in high school algebra courses. There are rules governing the evaluation of arithmetic expressions from which parentheses are omitted. The novice is advised, however, to use a sufficient number of parentheses to ensure that a given expression will be evaluated correctly, and to make certain that the number of left parentheses is the same as the number of right parentheses.

Note: Each arithmetic operator used in an arithmetic expression must be preceded and followed by a space. This rule applies to the equality symbol as well as the symbols +, −, *, /, and **.

As an example of the economy achieved by the use of COMPUTE statements, consider the following sequence of statements for computing overtime pay:

```
SUBTRACT 40 FROM HRS GIVING OVERTIME-HRS.
MULTIPLY HOURLY-RATE BY 1.5 GIVING OVERTIME-RATE.
MULTIPLY OVERTIME-HRS BY OVERTIME-RATE GIVING OVERTIME-PAY.
```

An equivalent calculation using a COMPUTE statement can be written as follows:

```
COMPUTE OVERTIME-PAY = (HRS - 40) * (HOURLY-RATE * 1.5).
```

In the first calculation the intermediate results, OVERTIME-HRS and OVERTIME-

RATE, are introduced. A line of code is required to define fields for each of these results in the WORKING-STORAGE SECTION of the DATA DIVISION. Assuming that this must be done, the COMPUTE statement presented here replaces five lines of code.

7.2 The IF Statement

The use of PERFORM statements with an UNTIL clause has been presented in previous examples. There a condition was used to determine how often to PERFORM the subroutine. The use of IF statements to test conditions will be discussed here. The logical decision implemented by a single IF statement is relatively simple. However, with several IF statements seemingly very complex patterns of logic can be implemented. Structured COBOL programs derive their capacity to implement complex data processing algorithms largely through the use of PERFORM and IF statements.

The format for the IF statement is

```
IF condition statement-1 ELSE statement-2
```

where

Condition is a conditional statement of the form discussed in Section 4.3.

Statement-1 is one or more COBOL statements.

Statement-2 is one or more COBOL statements.

It should be obvious from the format of the IF statement that such a statement may require several lines on the coding form. The recommended method of writing these statements is illustrated in the following example:

```
IF HOURS IS GREATER THAN 40
    COMPUTE OV-PAY = ((HRS - 40) * (RATE * 1.5))
    MULTIPLY RATE BY 40 GIVING REG-PAY
ELSE
    MOVE ZEROES TO OV-PAY
    MULTIPLY RATE BY HRS GIVING REG-PAY.
```

This format for presenting the IF statement aids greatly in the documentation of the program. The scope of the IF statement is clearly delineated, as are the scopes of statement-1 and statement-2. This presentation has the following characteristics:

1. The word IF and the condition appear on the first line or lines.
2. The statements of statement-1 occur next and are indented and vertically aligned, one to a line.
3. The word ELSE appears on a line by itself and is vertically aligned with the word IF.
4. The statements of statement-2 occur next and are indented and vertically aligned, one to a line.

When the IF statement is executed, the validity of the condition is checked. If the condition is valid, the statements of statement-1 are executed, and control passes to the statement following the period that concludes the IF sentence. Otherwise, the statements of statement-2 are executed and control passes to the statement following the IF sentence.

The ELSE clause may be omitted entirely if it is unnecessary. That is, the IF statement can be written in the following format:

```
IF condition statement-1
```

When an IF statement in this format is executed, the statements in statement-1 are executed only if the condition is valid. Otherwise control is passed directly to the statement following the IF statement. An example of an IF statement in this format is

```
IF LINE-COUNT IS GREATER THAN 45
    PERFORM HEADER-ROUTINE.
```

Caution should be exercised in the writing of IF statements. The scope of the IF statement extends to, and only to, the first occurrence of a period following the word IF. The misplacement or omission of a period in such statements usually cannot be detected as a syntax error by the compiler. Such an error can lead to erroneous and often perplexing results when the program is executed.

The preceding examples illustrate a point that has not been made earlier. They demonstrate the fact that a COBOL statement can be broken after any word and continued on the following line. Actually, a statement can be continued for any number of lines. The only exception arises when the break must occur in the body of an alphanumeric constant. In this exceptional case the line that is broken must be continued through column 72. In the continuation line a hyphen must appear in column 7, and the continuation of the literal (including single quotes at the beginning and end) must begin in column 12 or beyond. As an example,

```
01  PG-HEADER    PICTURE IS X(50) VALUE IS 'SEMI-MONTHLY PAYROL
-           'L REPORT OF SIMPSON ENTERPRISES'.
```

indicates a correct continuation of an alphanumeric constant. The continuation of literals is generally considered poor practice and is discouraged.

The use of IF statements is illustrated in EXAMPLE5.

7.3 Comparisons in COBOL

When numeric operands are compared using the relational operators $<$, $>$, or $=$, the result of the comparison is decided with respect to the algebraic values of the operands. Zero is considered a unique value, regardless of sign. Unsigned numeric operands are considered to be positive for purposes of comparison.

When nonnumeric operands or two operands, one of which is numeric and one of which is nonnumeric, are compared, the comparison is made with respect to the binary collating sequence of the character set. The collating sequence for the EBCDIC character encoding used on most IBM machines, in ascending order, is as follows:

1.   (space)
2. . (period or decimal point)
3. < (less than symbol)
4. ((left parenthesis)
5. + (plus sign)
6. $ (dollar sign)

7.   *   (asterisk)

8.   )   (right parenthesis)

9.   ;   (semicolon)

10.   -   (hyphen)

11.   /   (slash)

12.   ,   (comma)

13.   >   (greater than symbol)

14.   '   (single quotation mark)

15.   =   (equal sign)

16.   "   (double quotation mark)

17.   A   thru   Z

18.   0   thru   9

Another character encoding that is commonly used, the American Standard Code for Information Interchange (ASCII), uses the following sequence:

1.   (space)

2.   "   (double quotation mark)

3. $ (dollar sign)

4.   '   (single quotation mark)

5.   ((left parenthesis)

6.   )   (right parenthesis)

7.   *   (asterisk)

8.   +   (plus sign)

9.   ,   (comma)

10.   -   (hyphen)

11.   .   (period)

12.   /   (slash)

13.   0   thru   9

14.   ;   (semicolon)

15.   <   (less than symbol)

16.   =   (equal sign)

17.   >   (greater than symbol)

18.   A   thru   Z

We have listed only a portion of each collating sequence, but you should be able to detect that there are some significant differences. The major difference that you should be familiar with is the difference in order between numeric and alphabetic characters.

If only one of the operands specified is numeric, it must be an integer. In that case, it is treated as if it were an alphanumeric data item of the same size. The contents of the alphanumeric operand are then compared to this operand as if both of the operands were alphanumeric.

The length of an operand is the total number of characters that it contains. All group items are treated as nonnumeric operands.

Two cases arise in the comparison of nonnumeric operands.

[handwritten margin note: if all pairs of ch. are = thru last pair = if not = comparison stops at the 1st pair of unequal]

Case 1   Comparison of operands of equal size.

If all pairs of characters compare equally through the last pair, the operands are considered to be equal.

If the two operands are not equal, the comparison stops at the first (leftmost) pair of unequal characters. The operand whose character in that position is higher in the collating sequence is determined to be greater.

Case 2   Comparison of operands of unequal size.

If the operands are of unequal size, comparison proceeds as though the shorter operand were extended on the right by a sufficient number of spaces to make the operands of equal size.

7.4 The DISPLAY Verb

Occasionally a program will fail to perform as expected. In such cases it is necessary to locate and correct the errors that have caused the malfunction. This process of locating and correcting errors is called **debugging.** In many instances the errors may be obvious. However, in some cases the errors can be extremely difficult to detect. One very useful tool that can be used in locating errors (or "bugs") is the DISPLAY verb. The format of a DISPLAY statement is

$$\underline{\text{DISPLAY}} \quad \left\{ \begin{matrix} \text{literal-1} \\ \text{identifier-1} \end{matrix} \right\} \quad \left[\begin{matrix} \text{literal-2} \\ \text{identifier-2} \end{matrix} \right] \; \ldots$$

When the DISPLAY statement is executed, the specified items are displayed contiguously in the printed listing. For example,

```
DISPLAY 'EOF-FLAG = ' EOF-FLAG
```

would cause

```
EOF-FLAG = N
```

to be printed if the variable EOF-FLAG contained the value N.

The DISPLAY statement should not be used to print items that require formatting. However, in addition to being an invaluable debugging tool, it is often useful for printing error messages.

7.5 EXAMPLE5—A Simple Payroll Program

Our next sample program, EXAMPLE5, is designed to print a simple payroll report. A page header including the page number is printed at the top of each page. After triple-spacing, column headers are printed. Double-spacing is effected before the first report line is printed; after this, single-spacing occurs after each report line until the number of print lines reaches 40. After 40 lines have been printed, the entire process is repeated with the appropriate page number printed at the top of each new page.

The actual report is quite simple. An input file, with each record containing a name, a pay rate, and the number of hours worked, serves as input. Each report line is to contain a name, pay rate, hours worked, regular pay, overtime pay, and gross pay.

The program has been designed using the principles of structured programming presented earlier. The flowchart for the main routine is given in Fig. 7.1. There are four subroutines in addition to the main routine. The flowcharts for these subroutines are presented in Figs. 7.2 and 7.3.

A cursory glance should be sufficient to verify that each of these flowcharts is structured. One point of particular interest is that the HEADER-ROUTINE is called by both the main routine and the PRINT-ROUTINE. This causes no problems because the main routine can call any of the subroutines, and a subroutine can call any other subroutine of which it is not a part.

The PRINT-ROUTINE in this program is of special interest. It utilizes a new form of the AFTER ADVANCING phrase. In the statement

```
WRITE PRINT-BUFF FROM PRINT-LINE
       AFTER ADVANCING N-LINES
```

N-LINES is an identifier specifying a numeric field that contains an integer giving the number of lines to advance before printing. As you will see when

FIGURE 7.1 The logic of EXAMPLE5.

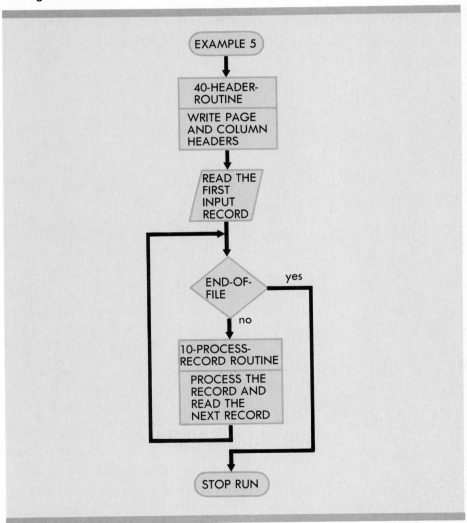

FIGURE 7.2 The logic of EXAMPLE5.

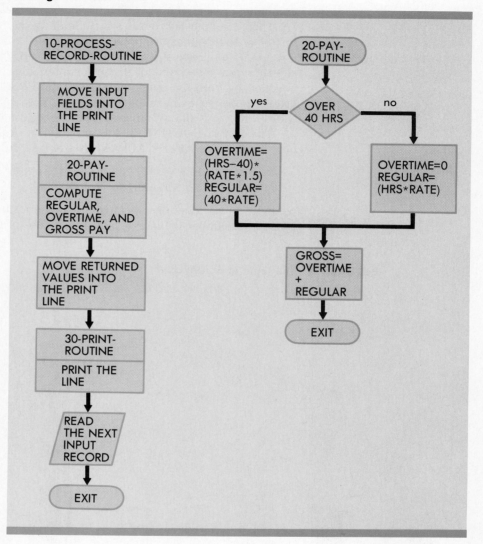

you study the program, this ability to assign a value to N-LINES to control the number of lines to advance can be very useful. Notice that page and column headers are printed when necessary. The routine that calls PRINT-ROUTINE must set N-LINES to 2 for double-spacing. Otherwise, single-spacing will automatically occur. Study the logic of PRINT-ROUTINE carefully because it is used in almost all of the remaining programs in this text.

The coding of any program should be a straightforward, routine task once the program has been properly designed and structured flowcharts have been produced. The complete listing of EXAMPLE5 is shown in Fig. 7.4.

We ran EXAMPLE5 with the following input:

```
JOHN ADAMS        0780 4200
HANK BAKER        0940 4140
MARY CAXTON       0960 4000
```

FIGURE 7.3   The logic of EXAMPLE5.

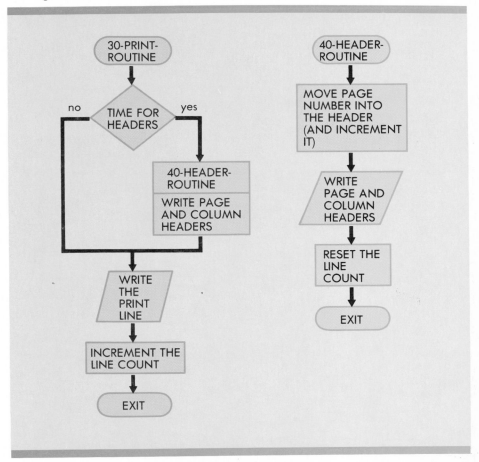

```
RANDY DANISH        0600 3500
ROSS OVERBEEK       1000 3000
JOHN SMITH          0860 4250
PETER ZARROW        1540 4100
```

The program produced the following output:

	PAYROLL				PAGE 1
EMPLOYEE NAME	RATE	HRS	REGULAR	OVERTIME	GROSS
JOHN ADAMS	7.80	42.00	312.00	23.40	335.40
HANK BAKER	9.40	41.40	376.00	19.74	395.74
MARY CAXTON	9.60	40.00	384.00	.00	384.00
RANDY DANISH	6.00	35.00	210.00	.00	210.00
ROSS OVERBEEK	10.00	30.00	300.00	.00	300.00
JOHN SMITH	8.60	42.50	344.00	32.25	376.25
PETER ZARROW	15.40	41.00	616.00	23.10	639.10

FIGURE 7.4 Continued

```
01  PRINT-LINE.
    05   FILLER          PIC X(25).
    05   NAME-OUT        PIC X(20).
    05   FILLER          PIC X(5).
    05   RATE-OUT        PIC ZZZ.99.
    05   FILLER          PIC X(3).
    05   HRS-OUT         PIC ZZ.99.
    05   FILLER          PIC X(4).
    05   REGULAR-PAY     PIC ZZZ.99.
    05   FILLER          PIC X(5).
    05   OVER-TIME       PIC ZZZ.99.
    05   FILLER          PIC X(5).
    05   GROSS-PAY       PIC ZZZ.99.
    05   FILLER          PIC X(25).

01  PAGE-HEADER.
    05   FILLER          PIC X(1).
    05   FILLER          PIC X(51)    VALUE IS SPACES.
    05   FILLER          PIC X(7)     VALUE IS 'PAYROLL'.
    05   FILLER          PIC X(54)    VALUE IS SPACES.
    05   FILLER          PIC X(5)     VALUE IS 'PAGE '.
    05   PG-NUM          PIC ZZ9.

01  COLUMN-HEADER.
    05   FILLER          PIC X(1).
    05   FILLER          PIC X(24)    VALUE IS SPACES.
    05   FILLER          PIC X(13)    VALUE IS 'EMPLOYEE NAME'.
    05   FILLER          PIC X(14)    VALUE IS SPACES.
    05   FILLER          PIC X(4)     VALUE IS 'RATE'.
    05   FILLER          PIC X(4)     VALUE IS SPACES.
    05   FILLER          PIC X(3)     VALUE IS 'HRS'.
    05   FILLER          PIC X(4)     VALUE IS SPACES.
    05   FILLER          PIC X(7)     VALUE IS 'REGULAR'.
    05   FILLER          PIC X(4)     VALUE IS SPACES.
    05   FILLER          PIC X(8)     VALUE IS 'OVERTIME'.
    05   FILLER          PIC X(5)     VALUE IS SPACES.
    05   FILLER          PIC X(5)     VALUE IS 'GROSS'.
    05   FILLER          PIC X(25)    VALUE IS SPACES.

PROCEDURE DIVISION.
    OPEN INPUT INPUT-FILE
        OUTPUT OUTPUT-FILE.

    PERFORM 40-HEADER-ROUTINE.
    READ INPUT-FILE AT END MOVE 'Y' TO EOF-FLAG.

    PERFORM 10-PROCESS-RECORD-ROUTINE UNTIL EOF-FLAG = 'Y'.

    CLOSE INPUT-FILE
        OUTPUT-FILE.

    STOP RUN.
```

```
**********************************************************************
*
* THIS ROUTINE PROCESSES THE INPUT RECORD THAT HAS ALREADY BEEN
* READ AND THEN ATTEMPTS TO READ THE NEXT RECORD.
*
**********************************************************************

 10-PROCESS-RECORD-ROUTINE.
     MOVE SPACES TO PRINT-LINE.
     MOVE NAME-IN TO NAME-OUT.
     MOVE RATE TO RATE-OUT.
     MOVE HRS TO HRS-OUT.
     PERFORM 20-PAY-ROUTINE.
     MOVE REG-PAY TO REGULAR-PAY.
     MOVE OV-PAY TO OVER-TIME.
     PERFORM 30-PRINT-ROUTINE.
     READ INPUT-FILE AT END MOVE 'Y' TO EOF-FLAG.

**********************************************************************
*
* THIS ROUTINE COMPUTES THE GROSS-PAY FOR THE EMPLOYEE.
*
**********************************************************************

 20-PAY-ROUTINE.
     IF HRS > 40 THEN
         COMPUTE OV-PAY = ((HRS - 40) * (RATE * 1.5))
         COMPUTE REG-PAY = 40 * RATE
     ELSE
         MOVE 0 TO OV-PAY
         COMPUTE REG-PAY = HRS * RATE.

     ADD OV-PAY REG-PAY GIVING GROSS-PAY.

**********************************************************************
*
* THIS ROUTINE PRINTS A LINE (STARTING ON A NEW PAGE IF
* NECESSARY).
*
**********************************************************************

 30-PRINT-ROUTINE.
     IF LINE-COUNT > 50 THEN
         PERFORM 40-HEADER-ROUTINE.
     WRITE PRINT-BUFF FROM PRINT-LINE
         AFTER ADVANCING N-LINES.
     ADD N-LINES TO LINE-COUNT.
     MOVE 1 TO N-LINES.
```

continued

FIGURE 7.4 Continued

```
****************************************************************
*
* THIS ROUTINE IS INVOKED TO PRINT PAGE AND COLUMN HEADERS..
* IT RESETS THE LINE-COUNT TO 6 (THE NUMBER OF THE NEXT LINE
* ON THE PAGE).
*
****************************************************************

  40-HEADER-ROUTINE.
      MOVE PAGE-NO TO PG-NUM.
      ADD 1 TO PAGE-NO.
      WRITE PRINT-BUFF FROM PAGE-HEADER
          AFTER ADVANCING TOP-OF-PAGE.
      WRITE PRINT-BUFF FROM COLUMN-HEADER
          AFTER ADVANCING 3 LINES.
      MOVE 2 TO N-LINES.
      MOVE 6 TO LINE-COUNT.
```

SUMMARY

A COMPUTE statement can be used in lieu of a sequence of basic arithmetic statements to perform a complex arithmetic calculation. The expressions allowed in COMPUTE statements permit arithmetic expressions to be written in a format that is as near to that of ordinary algebra as is possible. The operational symbols $+$, $-$, $/$, $*$, and $**$ are used to represent addition, subtraction, division, multiplication, and exponentiation, respectively. Parentheses may be used in accordance with the familiar algebraic rules.

The COBOL IF statement is represented by the format

IF condition statement-1 ELSE statement-2

where both statement-1 and statement-2 are permitted to represent more than one COBOL statement. The ELSE clause may be omitted if the situation warrants.

In order to improve readability of the program, it is very important to consistently follow indenting conventions that clearly portray the scope of each alternative.

Comparisons of numeric operands are evaluated with respect to the algebraic values of the operands. Comparisons of nonnumeric operands are evaluated lexicographically with respect to the binary collating sequence. Mixing of numeric and nonnumeric operands is not recommended, but mixed operands are compared as if both were nonnumeric.

The DISPLAY statements provide a convenient means of displaying the contents of key fields at various points during the execution of a program. When used in this manner, they are a powerful debugging tool. These statements are also useful for displaying error messages.

Handwritten margin note (top left): Express computation / Compact readable / form

R E V I E W   Q U E S T I O N S

7.1   What is the main advantage of using COMPUTE statements?

7.2   Name the operational symbols allowed in COMPUTE statements and indicate the meaning of each. *+ − * ** /* *rules of algebra*

7.3   How is the use of parentheses governed in COMPUTE statements?

7.4   What do statement-1 and statement-2 represent in the format of the IF statement? *COBOL statements*

7.5   State the rules suggested for displaying IF statements.

7.6   What terminates the scope of an IF statement? *Period next*

7.7   When may the ELSE clause be omitted in an IF statement? *wherever unnecessary*

7.8   How is the comparison of numeric operands evaluated?

7.9   How is the comparison of mixed operands evaluated?

7.10 How is the length of an operand determined? *No: of characters.*

Handwritten margin notes (left): IF condition / statement COBOL / ELSE / statement

Handwritten notes (bottom): 7.8 according to algebraic value of operands. Zero is considered unique (i.e. −0 = +0) and unsigned values concerned +ve. 7.9 numeric field which must be an integer is considered converted to an alphanumeric field of the same size

Large handwritten circled note: IMP

P R O G R A M M I N G   E X E R C I S E S

7.1   Compute a weekly payroll using the following input format:

Columns	Contents
1–20	Name
21	Space
22–25	Rate (99V99)
26	Space
27–30	Hours worked (99V99)
31	'M' or 'S' indicating married or single
32–33	Number of dependents
34–80	Spaces

Calculate the gross pay just as in the example program. Also calculate the following:

FICA deduction = 5.2% of the gross pay

State tax deduction = 2.5% of (gross pay − (number of dependents * 20))

Federal tax deduction = 9.7% of (gross pay − (number of dependents * 12)) if a person is married

= 12.5% of (gross pay − (number of dependents * 12)) if a person is single

Net pay = gross pay − deductions.

For each input record, an appropriately formatted print line should be written. Besides the page and column headers, there should be 40 lines printed per page.

7.2   Write a program to balance a checkbook. The input records will have the following formats:

FIRST RECORD

Columns	Contents
1	0
2–8	Beginning balance
9–80	Spaces

REMAINING RECORDS

Columns	Contents
1	1 indicates a check 2 indicates a deposit
2–8	Amount
9–80	Spaces

On the printed output, appropriate headers should be used. Forty detail lines (nonheaders) should be printed per page. The output line should have the following format:

Position	Contents
1–10	Spaces
11–18	Amount if the corresponding record was a check
19–20	Spaces
21–28	Amount if the corresponding record was a deposit
29–30	Spaces
31–33	Service charge
34–35	Spaces
36–43	Remaining balance
44–133	Spaces

The service charge for an item is as follows:

$.10	For a deposit
$.10	For a check less than $100
$.15	For a check greater than or equal to $100

Note that the report contains a running balance, with checks appearing in one column and the deposits in another column. At the end of the report print the sum of the checks, the sum of the deposits, and the sum of the service charges.

7.3   Suppose that your company owns a computer and that another company rents time on the computer. For each block of time that the machine is rented out, a single input record is produced using the following format:

Columns	Contents
1–7	Starting time (for example, 11:10AM)
8	Space
8–15	Ending time
16–80	Spaces

No block of time will be greater than 24 hours, and the rental on the computer is $350 per hour. Print a report with appropriate headers and 40 detail lines per page. Each detail line should contain the information from one input record and the computer charge. At the end of the report print the total charge.

7.4   Rewrite the report described in Exercise 7.3, but use the following rental rates:

$350/hr for the hours 8:00 A.M. to 5:00 P.M.

$200/hr for the hours 5:00 P.M. to 8:00 A.M.

7.5   Read in a set of scores for students. The following input record format should be used:

Columns	Contents
1–20	Student's name
21	Space
22–30	Social security number
31	Space
32–34	Test score
35–80	Spaces

Write a report with one printed line for each input record. There should be appropriate page and column headers, and there should be a total of 50 lines printed per page, including blank lines. A double-spaced line counts as two lines. There may be more than one input record for a student; in that case, double-space before printing the first line, and single-space for each consecutive score. Thus, the rules for spacing are

a) If an input record has the same social security number as the previous record, single-space before printing the corresponding line of the report.

b) Otherwise, double-space before printing.

At the end of the report, print the average test score.

CHAPTER EIGHT

MORE LANGUAGE BASICS

INTRODUCTION In this chapter a number of COBOL elements that are essential for the production of quality programs are discussed. In particular, the facility for handling signed numbers is presented, in Section 8.1. Obviously, some provision for dealing with negative numbers must be provided.

More particulars concerning the formatting of printed output are detailed in Section 8.2. In Section 8.3 the particulars governing the execution of the MOVE statement are explained in some detail.

Section 8.4 deals with options available for use in arithmetic statements, and complete formats for these statements are displayed there. The facility that allows names to be assigned to conditions that may be encoded in input records as single characters is the subject of Section 8.5. Finally, an example that illustrates the use of the tools presented in Sections 8.1–8.5 is displayed in Section 8.6.

8.1 Signed Numbers

Up to this point, no provision for handling negative numbers has been discussed. The examples presented thus far have been written with the tacit assumption that all numeric items input to the program would be positive, and that no negative numbers would arise in the course of arithmetic operations performed on these numeric items. Of course, these assumptions are not realistic in all data processing environments. The facilities provided by the COBOL language for dealing with signed numbers are discussed below.

When a signed number is to be entered into an input field, the picture for the input field must include an S as its first character. If the S is not included, the sign associated with the number is simply dropped. For example, a receiving field specified by

        PIC S9(4)V99

could be used as a field to receive a six-digit number that is assumed to be signed. The S serves as indication to the compiler that the sign of the number should be preserved. If no S is included in the picture for a receiving field, any indicated operational sign for a number entered into this field is dropped and the number is considered to be positive.

To input a signed numeric field, you may place the sign in any of four locations: it can precede the actual digits; it can follow the digits; it can be "overpunched" on the first digit; or it can be "overpunched" on the last digit. In the first two cases (in which the sign is not overpunched), the sign occupies an extra position in the input field. Hence, a picture of S9(4)V99 would occupy seven positions, not six. On the other hand, if the sign is overpunched, it does not count in the length of the field. "Overpunch" in this context refers to altering a digit to some other value to encode both the sign and the digit as a single character. This practice occurred quite often when punched cards were used, but it is seldom employed anymore.

To specify exactly how the sign will be represented in a signed numeric field, you should use a SIGN clause.

$$\text{[SIGN IS]}\begin{Bmatrix}\underline{\text{LEADING}}\\\underline{\text{TRAILING}}\end{Bmatrix}\quad\text{[\underline{SEPARATE} CHARACTER]}$$

The option SEPARATE CHARACTER is used to indicate that the sign is not overpunched. You must specify LEADING or TRAILING. Thus,

        PIC S9(4)V99 SIGN IS LEADING SEPARATE CHARACTER

specifies a seven-character field in which the first character will be occupied with the sign (+ or −). On the other hand,

        PIC S9(4)V99 SIGN IS TRAILING

specifies a six-character field in which the sign is encoded in the rightmost position of the field. If the SIGN clause is omitted, the sign is normally overpunched into the rightmost position. However, this default condition can vary with different types of computers and different compilers. Therefore, if you do need to specify that an input field may contain a sign, it is a good practice to include the SIGN clause to make the location of the sign completely clear.

8.2 Editing Printed Output

The use of the decimal point and the letter Z for editing numeric data for printed output was discussed briefly in Section 6.1. The COBOL language provides a rather extensive set of symbols for editing purposes. The most frequently used of these symbols are discussed in this section. The sole purpose of these editing features is to edit numeric data into more readable form.

Simple insertion editing is accomplished by use of the symbols: , (comma), B (space), / (slash), and 0 (zero). When one of these insertion characters is used in a picture, it is counted in the length of the output item, and it represents the position in that item where insertion will occur. The examples in Table 8.1 should serve to illustrate this type of editing.

Floating insertion editing is accomplished using two or more occurrences of one of the symbols: $, −, or + as the leftmost symbols in the picture of the numeric edited item. When floating insertion is employed in a picture, the insertion character should appear in the position immediately to the left of the leftmost position that a digit (from the sending field) is expected to occupy. In addition, the insertion character should occur in all digit positions in the case of a whole number, or in all digit positions to the left of the decimal point in the case of a decimal number. There is also a requirement that at least two occurrences of the insertion character appear to the left of any occurrence of a comma or decimal point in the picture. All floating insertion character occurrences are counted in the length of the receiving field. Table 8.2 illustrates this type of editing.

Make special note of the following points. The use of the floating currency symbol always causes the printing of a single occurrence of this symbol. Use of the floating + symbol causes the printing of one occurrence of a + or − symbol, depending upon the sign of the numeric field. Use of the − symbol causes the printing of one occurrence of this symbol only when the numeric field being edited has a negative sign.

Table 8.1 Simple insertion editing

Sending field		Receiving field		
Picture	Data	Picture	Length	Edited result
S9(4)V99	123456	Z,ZZZ.99	8	1,234.56
S9(4)V99	123	Z,ZZZ.99	8	1.23
S9(4)	0012	ZZZ,Z00	7	1,200
S9(4)	1234	ZZZ,Z00	7	123,400
S9(9)	267121454	999B99B9999	11	267 12 1454
S9(6)	110226	99/99/99	8	11/02/26

Table 8.2 Floating insertion editing

Sending field		Receiving field		
Picture	**Data**	**Picture**	**Length**	**Edited result**
S9(4)V99	123456	$$,$$$.99	9	$1,234.56
S9(4)V99	123	$$,$$$.99	9	$1.23
S9(4)V99	123456	++,+++.99	9	+1,234.56
S9(4)V99	−123456	++,+++.99	9	−1,234.56
S9(4)V99	123456	−−,−−−.99	9	1,234.56
S9(4)V99	−123456	−−,−−−.99	9	−1,234.56
S9(4)V99	1234	−−,−−−.99	9	12.34

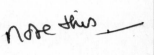

note this

Zero suppression and character insertion editing may be accomplished by use of the asterisk symbol (*). The principal use of this type of editing is to prevent the easy alteration of amounts printed on checks. Examples of its use are shown in Table 8.3.

Fixed insertion editing may be effected using the debit symbol (DB) or the credit symbol (CR). These symbols are used most frequently when a field representing an amount of money is to be designated as positive or negative. Table 8.4 illustrates the use of these symbols. The debit and credit symbols each add two to the length of the receiving field. Also note that these symbols are printed only when the sending field has a negative sign.

This discussion of the COBOL editing symbols should suffice for the purposes of this text, but it is by no means complete. For further details, you will need to read the COBOL manual published by the vendor of the particular (source) computer you intend to employ.

① add 2 to the length of field
② are only printed when sending field has a −ve sign,
③ disregarded otherwise

Table 8.3 Zero suppression and character insertion editing

Sending field		Receiving field		
Picture	**Data**	**Picture**	**Length**	**Edited result**
S9(4)V99	123456	$*,***.99	9	$1,234.56
S9(4)V99	001234	$*,***.99	9	$***12.34
S9(4)V99	000012	$*,***.99	9	$*****.12

Table 8.4 Fixed insertion editing

Sending field		Receiving field		
Picture	Data	Picture	Length	Edited result
S9(4)V99	123456	$$,$$$.99CR	11	$1,234.56
S9(4)V99	−123456	$$,$$$.99CR	11	$1,234.56CR
S9(4)V99	1234	$$,$$$.99DB	11	$12.34
S9(4)V99	−1234	$$,$$$.99DB	11	$12.34DB

001234

8.3 The COBOL MOVE Statement

Several examples introduced earlier have employed the MOVE statement. How-ever, no general rules governing the action produced by these statements have been considered. These general rules are discussed in what follows.

As a start, it should be observed that every group data item in either a sending or receiving field is considered to be an alphanumeric item. The MOVE statement permits the following types of moves:

An alphanumeric data item can be moved to an alphanumeric, a numeric, or a numeric edited receiving field. If the receiving field is numeric or numeric edited, the sending field should contain only numeric digits.

A numeric data item, or a numeric constant, can be moved to an alphanu-meric, numeric, or numeric edited receiving field.

A numeric edited item can be moved only to an alphanumeric field.

When an alphanumeric data item is the receiving field, characters are moved from the sending to the receiving field starting with the leftmost characters of each field. If the receiving field is shorter than the sending field, the excess characters in the sending field are ignored. If the receiving field is longer, excess character positions are filled with blanks.

Some examples should help to clarify these remarks. Here, it is assumed that the fields are described as follows:

```
01  AREA1.                    01  AREA2.
    02  X    PIC X(4).            02  Z1    PIC X.
    02  Y    PIC X(3).            02  Z2    PIC X.
```

Some typical MOVE statements, with the conditions of the sending and receiving fields before and after execution of the MOVE statements, are presented in Table 8.5. In these examples the underline (__) is used to indicate a space.

When a numeric field is moved to another numeric field, or to a numeric edited item, the following rules apply. First the numbers are aligned by the decimal point. If the receiving field is shorter, digits are truncated from one or both ends of the number in the sending field. If the receiving field is longer, empty positions are filled with zeroes at one or both ends.

Table 8.5 Typical MOVE statements between nonnumeric fields

MOVE statements	(before MOVE)		(after MOVE)
MOVE X TO Y.	X	ABCD	same
	Y	CAT	ABC
MOVE 'JONES' TO Y.	Y	CAT	JON
MOVE X TO AREA2.	X	ABCD	same
	AREA2	ME	AB
MOVE Y TO X.	Y	CAT	same
	X	ABCD	CAT_
MOVE '3' TO X.	X	ABCD	3___
MOVE AREA2 TO X.	AREA2	ME	same
	X	ABCD	ME__
MOVE AREA1 TO AREA2.	AREA1	ABCDCAT	same
	AREA2	ME	AB
MOVE AREA2 TO AREA1.	AREA2	ME	same
	AREA1	ABCDCAT	ME_____

Several numeric fields are listed below. Table 8.6 gives examples illustrating moves between these fields. In these examples, V represents the implied decimal point.

```
01   NUM1   PIC 9(4).        01   NUM3   PIC 9(5).
01   NUM2   PIC 99V99.       01   NUM4   PIC 999V999.
```

Table 8.6 Moves between numeric fields

MOVE statements	(before MOVE)		(after MOVE)
MOVE NUM1 TO NUM2.	NUM1	1234	same
	NUM2	25V20	34V00
MOVE NUM2 TO NUM1.	NUM2	25V20	same
	NUM1	1234	0025
MOVE NUM1 TO NUM3.	NUM1	1234	same
	NUM3	65432	01234
MOVE NUM3 TO NUM1.	NUM3	65432	same
	NUM1	1234	5432
MOVE NUM2 TO NUM4.	NUM2	25V20	same
	NUM4	123V456	025V200
MOVE NUM4 TO NUM1.	NUM4	123V456	same
	NUM1	1234	0123
MOVE NUM4 TO NUM2.	NUM4	123V456	same
	NUM2	25V20	23V45
MOVE 100 TO NUM2.	NUM2	25V20	00V00
MOVE 1.5 TO NUM1.	NUM1	1234	0001

8.4 The Arithmetic Statement: Options and General Formats

The formats given previously for the ADD and SUBTRACT statements allowed for the addition of two operands or the subtraction of one operand from another. There are more general formats for these statements which allow for the utilization of any number of operands. These more general formats for the ADD statement are

```
ADD field-1 [field-2] ... TO field-m
ADD field-1  field-2 ... GIVING field-m
```

The data name in the square brackets is optional; the three dots following it imply that as many more data names as you wish could follow. The words ADD, TO, and GIVING are underlined to indicate that they are COBOL reserved words required in these statements. The words field-1 and field-m are required user-supplied data names. Of course the fields or data names, except the receiving field, could also be numeric literals. The general formats for the ADD statement, which reflect this fact, are

$$\text{ADD} \begin{Bmatrix} \text{literal-1} \\ \text{field-1} \end{Bmatrix} \begin{bmatrix} \text{literal-2} \\ \text{field-2} \end{bmatrix} \dots \underline{\text{TO}} \text{ field-m}$$

$$\text{ADD} \begin{Bmatrix} \text{literal-1} \\ \text{field-1} \end{Bmatrix} \begin{Bmatrix} \text{literal-2} \\ \text{field-2} \end{Bmatrix} \begin{bmatrix} \text{literal-3} \\ \text{field-3} \end{bmatrix} \dots \underline{\text{GIVING}} \text{ field-m}$$

The braces indicate that one of the enclosed choices must be included. The square brackets indicate that one of the enclosed choices may optionally be included. The other conventions are the same as those given previously.

From this discussion it should be obvious that the following two statements are correct COBOL statements.

```
ADD 16.97 STATE-TAX FED-TAX FICA TO DEDUCTIONS.
ADD 16.97 STATE-TAX FED-TAX FICA GIVING DEDUCTIONS.
```

Applying these format conventions to the SUBTRACT statement formats yields the following:

$$\underline{\text{SUBTRACT}} \begin{Bmatrix} \text{literal-1} \\ \text{field-1} \end{Bmatrix} \begin{bmatrix} \text{literal-2} \\ \text{field-2} \end{bmatrix} \dots \underline{\text{FROM}} \text{ field-m}$$

$$\underline{\text{SUBTRACT}} \begin{Bmatrix} \text{literal-1} \\ \text{field-1} \end{Bmatrix} \begin{bmatrix} \text{literal-2} \\ \text{field-2} \end{bmatrix} \dots \underline{\text{FROM}} \begin{Bmatrix} \text{literal-m} \\ \text{field-m} \end{Bmatrix}$$

$$\underline{\text{GIVING}} \text{ field-n}$$

With either of these two formats, all the fields and literals preceding the word FROM are added together. In the first case this sum is subtracted from field-m, and this result replaces the value of field-m. In the second, the result of the addition is subtracted from field-m or literal-m and the result is stored in field-n.

The preceding formats illustrate most of the conventions used in the presentation of statement formats in technical COBOL manuals. These conventions will be employed in this text from this point on. As an aid to the reader, they are briefly summarized in the following list.

1. All words printed entirely in capital letters are COBOL reserved words.

2. All words printed in lowercase letters represent information to be supplied by the user.

3. All underlined COBOL reserved words are required unless the portion of the format in which they are contained is optional.

4. Braces ({ }) enclosing a stack of items indicate that one of the items in the stack is required.

5. Square brackets ([ ]) enclosing a stack of items indicate that one of the items in the stack can be used or that all can be omitted as the program requires.

6. The ellipses (...) following an item indicate that the item can be repeated as many times as desired.

An option useful with any of the arithmetic statements is the ROUNDED option. When this option is used, the word ROUNDED is included in the arithmetic statement immediately following the name of the data field that is to receive the result of the arithmetic operation. Thus the following statements are valid:

```
ADD A TO B ROUNDED

SUBTRACT B FROM C GIVING D ROUNDED

COMPUTE Z ROUNDED = X + Y * W
```

When the PICTURE for the receiving field indicates fewer decimal positions than the result to be stored in that field, the excess digits are dropped if the ROUNDED option is not used. However, if the ROUNDED option is used, the result is rounded before being stored. As an example, suppose that the following conditions exist.

X		Y		Z
PICTURE	contents	PICTURE	contents	PICTURE
99V999	70.708	99V999	20.291	99V99

Then, if the statement

```
ADD X Y GIVING Z
```

is executed, the resulting value of Z is 90.99. However, if the statement

```
ADD X Y GIVING Z ROUNDED
```

is executed, the resulting value of Z is 91.00. The ROUNDED option is particularly convenient when values in dollars and cents are used in arithmetic computations.

The final option to be discussed in conjunction with the arithmetic statements is the ON SIZE ERROR option. When this option is used, the phrase

```
ON SIZE ERROR statement
```

(where the statement is any unconditional, i.e., imperative, statement) is included at the end of the arithmetic statement. The effect of this option is to cause the imperative statement in the option clause to be executed in the event that the receiving field for the result of the arithmetic operation has fewer decimal positions before the decimal point than are required to accommodate the result. If such a condition occurs and the option is not used, the results are unpredictable.

As an example, suppose the following conditions exist.

	X		Y		Z
PICTURE	contents	PICTURE	contents	PICTURE	
99V99	89.72	99V99	12.04	99V99	

Then, if the statement

```
ADD X Y GIVING Z ON SIZE ERROR PERFORM ERROR-RTN
```

were executed, the result of the addition would be 101.76. In this case a size error would occur and a branch would be made to ERROR-RTN. The use of ON SIZE ERROR is not recommended. Rather, care should be exercised to assure that all fields are sized to accommodate the largest possible value that could be assigned to them.

If you do use an ON SIZE ERROR, you should be aware that the imperative statement (which is invoked when the condition occurs) is terminated by the next period. Thus,

```
IF HOURS-WORKED > 40
    ADD OVERTIME-PAY TO TOTAL-PAY
        ON SIZE ERROR MOVE 'Y' TO SIZE-ERROR-FLAG
    ADD OVERTIME-HOURS TO TOTAL-OVERTIME-HOURS.
```

contains an error. The field TOTAL-OVERTIME-HOURS is incremented only when the SIZE ERROR occurs. The proper way to code the logic would be

```
IF HOURS-WORKED > 40
    PERFORM ADD-OVERTIME.
        .
        .
        .
ADD-OVERTIME.
    ADD OVERTIME-PAY TO TOTAL-PAY
        ON SIZE ERROR MOVE 'Y' TO SIZE-ERROR-FLAG.
    ADD OVERTIME-HOURS TO TOTAL-OVERTIME-HOURS.
```

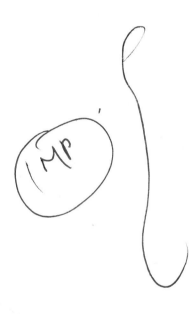

More complete formats for the arithmetic statements using the conventions summarized previously are shown in Fig. 8.1.

The REMAINDER option with the second form of the DIVIDE statement is rarely used; however, it can be useful occasionally. If this option is used, the remainder of the division operation is stored in the data area specified by field-4.

8.5 Condition-Names

The use of coded values in a particular data field to indicate which of a variety of conditions prevails is common practice in data processing applications. In most instances a coded value contains no inherent clue as to which condition it represents. As a particular example, the initial section of the record description for the INPUT-RECORD in our next program is

```
01  INPUT-RECORD.
    02  TYPE-CODE        PIC X.
```

FIGURE 8.1 The syntax of arithmetic statements.

```
      ⎧literal-1⎫⎡literal-2⎤
ADD   ⎨         ⎬⎢         ⎥ ... TO field-m [ROUNDED]
      ⎩field-1  ⎭⎣field-2  ⎦
      [ON SIZE ERROR statement]


      ⎧literal-1⎫⎡literal-2⎤⎡literal-3⎤
ADD   ⎨         ⎬⎢         ⎥⎢         ⎥ ... GIVING field-m
      ⎩field-1  ⎭⎣field-2  ⎦⎣field-3  ⎦
      [ROUNDED] [ON SIZE ERROR statement]


            ⎧literal-1⎫⎡literal-2⎤
SUBTRACT    ⎨         ⎬⎢         ⎥ ... FROM field-m
            ⎩field-1  ⎭⎣field-2  ⎦
      [ROUNDED] [ON SIZE ERROR statement]


            ⎧literal-1⎫⎡literal-2⎤            ⎧literal-m⎫
SUBTRACT    ⎨         ⎬⎢         ⎥ ... FROM   ⎨         ⎬
            ⎩field-1  ⎭⎣field-2  ⎦            ⎩field-m  ⎭
      GIVING field-n [ROUNDED] [ON SIZE ERROR statement]


            ⎧literal-1⎫
MULTIPLY    ⎨         ⎬ BY field-2 [ROUNDED]
            ⎩field-1  ⎭
      [ON SIZE ERROR statement]


            ⎧literal-1⎫      ⎧literal-2⎫
MULTIPLY    ⎨         ⎬ BY   ⎨         ⎬ GIVING field-3
            ⎩field-1  ⎭      ⎩field-2  ⎭
      [ROUNDED] [ON SIZE ERROR statement]


          ⎧literal-1⎫
DIVIDE    ⎨         ⎬ INTO field-2 [ROUNDED]
          ⎩field-1  ⎭
      [ON SIZE ERROR statement]


          ⎧literal-1⎫        ⎧literal-2⎫
DIVIDE    ⎨         ⎬ INTO   ⎨         ⎬ GIVING field-3
          ⎩field-1  ⎭        ⎩field-2  ⎭
      [ROUNDED] [REMAINDER field-4]
      [ON SIZE ERROR imperative-statement]


COMPUTE field-1 [ROUNDED] = arithmetic expression
      [ON SIZE ERROR statement]
```

Here a value of "C" in the TYPE-CODE field represents a check, while a value of "D" represents a deposit. These single-letter codes do provide a clue as to the type of transaction the input record represents, but the codes 1 and 2 could have been used as easily.

The COBOL language provides a feature that allows the programmer to associate a name with the condition indicated by a particular code value that may appear in a given field. This is accomplished through the use of 88-level items in the data division of the program. The following section of code from EXAMPLE6 illustrates this technique.

```
01  INPUT-RECORD.
    02  TYPE-CODE          PIC X.
        88  IT-IS-A-CHECK VALUE IS 'C'.
        88  IT-IS-A-DEPOSIT VALUE IS 'D'.
```

In this program segment the two 88-level items define **condition-names.** These statements do not define new fields, nor do they assign a value to any field. The sole purpose of each of these statements is to associate a name with a code value that is indicative of the condition reflected by that particular value. These condition-names can then be used in statements where the corresponding code values would otherwise occur. This can greatly enhance the readability of program listings. For example,

```
IF IT-IS-A-CHECK
    MOVE AMOUNT-IN TO CHECK-OUT
```

may be used in place of

```
IF TYPE-CODE = 'C'
    MOVE AMOUNT-IN TO CHECK-OUT
```

The format describing the proper method of defining a condition-name is

$$
88 \text{ condition-name} \begin{cases} \underline{VALUE} \text{ IS literal-1} \\ \underline{VALUES} \text{ ARE literal-1 } \underline{THRU} \text{ literal-2} \end{cases}
$$

The condition-name is associated with the contents of the most recent previously defined elementary data item. The condition named prevails if the value of that data item with which it is associated is literal-1 or a value in the range literal-1 through literal-2, depending upon which option is specified.

As an example illustrating the use of a condition-name that represents a range of values, consider the following statements, which define the field MONTH-OF-REPORT.

```
02  MONTH-OF-REPORT          PIC 99.
    88  FIRST-QUARTER         VALUES ARE 1 THRU 3.
    88  SECOND-QUARTER        VALUES ARE 4 THRU 6.
    88  THIRD-QUARTER         VALUES ARE 7 THRU 9.
    88  FOURTH-QUARTER        VALUES ARE 10 THRU 12.
```

In this case, the statement

```
IF THIRD-QUARTER PERFORM CALC-DIVIDEND-3.
```

would cause a branch to CALC-DIVIDEND-3 if MONTH-OF-REPORT had a value of 7, 8, or 9.

The use of condition-names is recommended for two reasons:

1. Their use can considerably enhance the readability of a program listing.

2. If at some point a decision is made to change the codes used with respect to a given program, these changes can be effected by simply making the appropriate changes in the 88-level items provided condition-names have been used. Careful consideration of the alternative will indicate how much of an advantage this can be.

8.6 EXAMPLE6—A Program to Balance a Checkbook

The program presented in this section demonstrates a number of the features introduced in the five preceding sections. The program is to process an input file and utilize the input data to balance a checkbook. The first record in the file contains the beginning balance. The remaining records represent transactions, which may be checks or deposits. The beginning balance is printed, and for each transaction the type and amount of the transaction and the resulting balance are printed. After all of the transactions have been processed the following information is printed: final balance, number of checks, total amount of all checks, the average amount per check, the number of deposits, the total of all deposits, and the average amount per deposit.

The flowcharts for the main program and two of the subroutines are given in Figs. 8.2 and 8.3. The complete program listing follows the flowcharts, in Fig. 8.4. The PRINT-ROUTINE and HEADER-ROUTINE are not included in Fig. 8.3 since the logic of these two routines is identical to that of the corresponding routines in EXAMPLE5.

Particular attention should be given to the print routine in this example. Observe that this print routine is almost a duplicate of the print routine used in EXAMPLE6. Carefully note the techniques used in these routines, as they provide a generic prototype of the print routine that is required in each report program.

As in previous programs, we use 01-level items in WORKING-STORAGE to group data items into logically related categories. For example, the lines:

```
01   FLAGS.
     02   EOF-FLAG          PIC X VALUE IS 'N'.
          88   EOF-HAS-OCCURRED VALUE IS 'Y'.


01   PRINT-VARIABLES.
     02   N-LINES           PIC 9 VALUE IS 1.
     02   LINE-COUNT        PIC 99.
     02   PAGE-NO           PIC 999 VALUE IS 1.


01   ACCUMULATORS.
     02   BALANCE           PIC S9(6)V99 VALUE IS 0.
     02   NUM-CHECKS        PIC 9(4) VALUE IS 0.
     02   CHECKS-TOTAL      PIC 9(6)V99 VALUE IS 0.
     02   NUM-DEPOSITS      PIC 9(4) VALUE IS 0.
     02   DEPOSITS-TOTAL    PIC 9(6)V99 VALUE IS 0.
```

group the flags, print variables, and accumulators into readily identifiable categories. The use of this technique is highly recommended. In large programs, requiring many noncontiguous items, the grouping of items in this way can add significantly to the documentation of the program.

We ran EXAMPLE6 using the following input records:

```
B  00010670
C  00005200
C  00003980
D  00004630
C  00005000
```

FIGURE 8.2 The logic of EXAMPLE6.

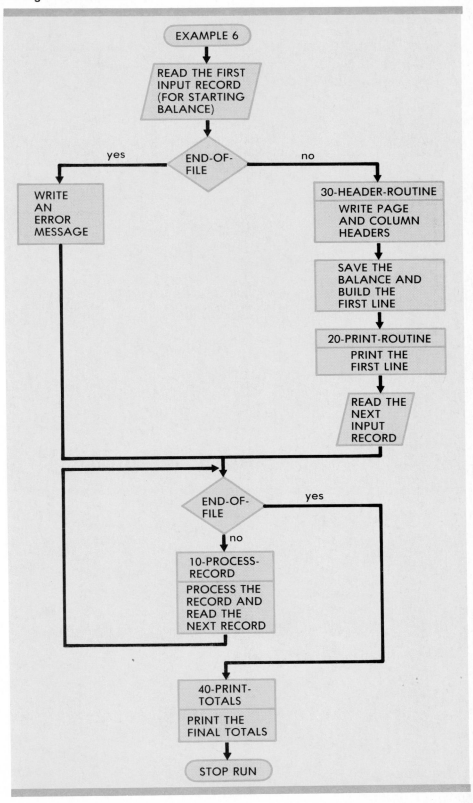

FIGURE 8.3 The logic of EXAMPLE6.

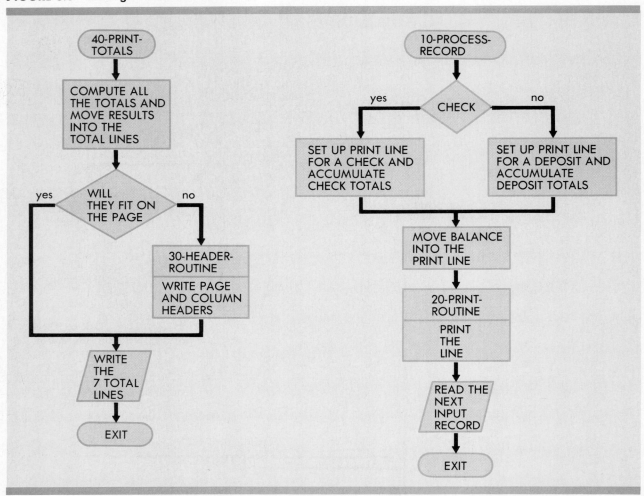

The program produced the following output:

```
C H E C K I N G   A C C O U N T   R E P O R T                    PAGE  1


                        CHECKS          DEPOSITS        BALANCE

                                                        106.70
                        52.00                            54.70
                         9.80                            44.90
                                         46.30           91.20
                        50.00                            41.20


        FINAL BALANCE:            41.20
        NUMBER CHECKS:                3
        AMOUNT OF CHECKS:       $111.80
        AVERAGE CHECK:          $37.27
        NUMBER DEPOSITS:              1
        AMOUNT OF DEPOSITS:     $46.30
        AVERAGE DEPOSIT:        $46.30
```

FIGURE 8.4 EXAMPLE6—a program to balance a checkbook.

```
      IDENTIFICATION DIVISION.
      PROGRAM-ID. EXAMPLE6.
      AUTHOR. W E SINGLETARY.

      ****************************************************************
      *
      * THIS PROGRAM CAN BE USED TO BALANCE A CHECKBOOK.  THE FIRST
      * INPUT RECORD CONTAINS THE BEGINNING BALANCE.  THE REMAINING
      * RECORDS REPRESENT CHECKS OR DEPOSITS.  FOR EACH SUCH RECORD
      * THE AMOUNT AND REMAINING BALANCE IS PRINTED.   AT THE END THE
      * FINAL BALANCE, NUMBER OF CHECKS, TOTAL AMOUNT OF THE CHECKS,
      * THE AVERAGE AMOUNT PER CHECK, THE NUMBER OF DEPOSITS, TOTAL
      * AMOUNT DEPOSITED, AND THE AVERAGE DEPOSIT ARE PRINTED.
      *
      ****************************************************************

      ENVIRONMENT DIVISION.

      CONFIGURATION SECTION.
      SOURCE-COMPUTER. IBM-370.
      OBJECT-COMPUTER. IBM-370.

      SPECIAL-NAMES.
          C01 IS TOP-OF-PAGE.

      INPUT-OUTPUT SECTION.
      FILE-CONTROL.

          SELECT INPUT-FILE ASSIGN TO UR-S-SYSIN.
          SELECT OUTPUT-FILE ASSIGN TO UR-S-SYSPRINT.
```

continued

FIGURE 8.4 Continued

```
   DATA DIVISION.
   FILE SECTION.

************************************************************************
*
* THIS FILE CONTAINS A RECORD WITH THE STARTING BALANCE,
* FOLLOWED BY RECORDS REPRESENTING CHECKS AND DEPOSITS.
* THE FIRST CHARACTER OF EACH RECORD GIVES THE TYPE OF THE
* RECORD.   THE VALUES ARE
*
*         B - BEGINNING BALANCE (FIRST RECORD ONLY)
*         C - CHECK
*         D - DEPOSIT
*
* THE AMOUNT-IN FIELD IS SHOWN AS SIGNED, SINCE THE BEGINNING
* BALANCE COULD BE NEGATIVE.  ALL CHECKS AND DEPOSITS SHOULD
* HAVE POSITIVE AMOUNTS (THAT IS, FOR A CHECK THE AMOUNT WILL
* BE SUBTRACTED FROM THE CURRENT BALANCE).
*
************************************************************************

   FD   INPUT-FILE
        LABEL RECORDS ARE OMITTED
        DATA RECORD IS INPUT-RECORD.

   01   INPUT-RECORD.
        05   TYPE-CODE        PIC X.
             88   IT-IS-A-CHECK          VALUE IS 'C'.
             88   IT-IS-A-DEPOSIT        VALUE IS 'D'.
        05   FILLER           PIC X.
        05   AMOUNT-IN        PIC S9(6)V99.
        05   FILLER           PIC X(70).
```

```
****************************************************************
*
* THIS FILE IS USED TO PRINT THE REPORT.  CHECKS AND DEPOSITS
* ARE PRINTED IN SEPARATE COLUMNS, ALONG WITH THE RUNNING
* TOTAL.
*
****************************************************************

  FD  OUTPUT-FILE
      LABEL RECORDS ARE OMITTED
      DATA RECORD IS PRINT-BUFF.

  01  PRINT-BUFF          PIC X(133).

  WORKING-STORAGE SECTION.

****************************************************************
*
* EOF-FLAG IS SET TO 'Y' WHEN END-OF-FILE OCCURS.
*
* N-LINES IS SET TO THE NUMBER OF LINES TO ADVANCE BEFORE
*          PRINTING A LINE
*
* LINE-COUNT CONTAINS THE NUMBER OF THE NEXT LINE ON A PAGE.
*
* PAGE-NO CONTAINS THE PAGE NUMBER OF THE NEXT PAGE OF THE
*          REPORT.
*
* BALANCE CONTAINS THE RUNNING BALANCE.
*
* NUM-CHECKS CONTAINS THE TOTAL NUMBER OF CHECKS
*
* CHECKS-TOTAL CONTAINS THE TOTAL AMOUNT OF THE CHECKS
*
* NUM-DEPOSITS CONTAINS THE TOTAL NUMBER OF DEPOSITS
*
* DEPOSITS-TOTAL CONTAINS THE TOTAL AMOUNT DEPOSITED
*
* PRINT-LINE IS USED TO BUILD THE LINES TO BE PRINTED.
*
* PAGE-HEADER AND COLUMN-HEADER ARE USED TO PRINT HEADERS AT
*          THE TOP OF THE FIRST PAGE OF OUTPUT.
*
```

continued

FIGURE 8.4 Continued

```
*  TOTS-LINE-1 IS THE TOTALS LINE WITH THE FINAL BALANCE
*
*  TOTS-LINE-2 IS THE TOTALS LINE WITH THE NUMBER OF CHECKS
*
*  TOTS-LINE-3 IS THE TOTALS LINE WITH THE TOTAL OF THE CHECKS
*
*  TOTS-LINE-4 IS THE TOTALS LINE WITH THE AVERAGE CHECK AMOUNT
*
*  TOTS-LINE-5 IS THE TOTALS LINE WITH THE NUMBER OF DEPOSITS
*
*  TOTS-LINE-6 IS THE TOTALS LINE WITH THE TOTAL OF DEPOSITS
*
*  TOTS-LINE-7 IS THE TOTALS LINE WITH THE AVERAGE DEPOSIT AMOUNT
*
************************************************************************

   01  FLAGS.
       05   EOF-FLAG           PIC X          VALUE IS 'N'.
            88   EOF-HAS-OCCURRED             VALUE IS 'Y'.


   01  PRINT-VARIABLES.
       05   N-LINES            PIC 9.
       05   LINE-COUNT         PIC 99.
       05   PAGE-NO            PIC 999        VALUE IS 1.


   01  ACCUMULATORS.
       05   BALANCE            PIC S9(6)V99 VALUE IS 0.
       05   NUM-CHECKS         PIC 9(4)       VALUE IS 0.
       05   CHECKS-TOTAL       PIC 9(6)V99   VALUE IS 0.
       05   NUM-DEPOSITS       PIC 9(4)       VALUE IS 0.
       05   DEPOSITS-TOTAL     PIC 9(6)V99   VALUE IS 0.


   01  PRINT-LINE.
       05   FILLER             PIC X(25).
       05   CHECK-OUT          PIC ZZZ,ZZZ.99.
       05   FILLER             PIC X(5).
       05   DEPOSIT-OUT        PIC ZZZ,ZZZ.99.
       05   FILLER             PIC X(5).
       05   BALANCE-OUT        PIC ---,---.99.


   01  PAGE-HEADER.
       05   FILLER             PIC X(1).
       05   FILLER             PIC X(10)      VALUE IS SPACES.
       05   FILLER             PIC X(45)      VALUE IS
            'C H E C K I N G   A C C O U N T   R E P O R T'.
       05   FILLER             PIC X(10)      VALUE IS SPACES.
       05   FILLER             PIC X(5)       VALUE IS 'PAGE '.
       05   PG-NUM             PIC ZZ9.
```

```
01  COLUMN-HEADER.
    05  FILLER          PIC X(1).
    05  FILLER          PIC X(28)     VALUE IS SPACES.
    05  FILLER          PIC X(6)      VALUE IS 'CHECKS'.
    05  FILLER          PIC X(7)      VALUE IS SPACES.
    05  FILLER          PIC X(8)      VALUE IS 'DEPOSITS'.
    05  FILLER          PIC X(8)      VALUE IS SPACES.
    05  FILLER          PIC X(7)      VALUE IS 'BALANCE'.

01  TOTS-LINE-1.
    05  FILLER          PIC X(10)     VALUE IS SPACES.
    05  FILLER          PIC X(20)     VALUE IS 'FINAL BALANCE:'.
    05  FINAL-BALANCE   PIC ---,---.99.

01  TOTS-LINE-2.
    05  FILLER          PIC X(10)     VALUE IS SPACES.
    05  FILLER          PIC X(26)     VALUE IS 'NUMBER CHECKS:'.
    05  TOT-NUM-CHECKS  PIC ZZZ9.

01  TOTS-LINE-3.
    05  FILLER          PIC X(10)     VALUE IS SPACES.
    05  FILLER          PIC X(20)     VALUE IS
                                      'AMOUNT OF CHECKS:'.
    05  TOT-AMT-CHECKS  PIC $$$,$$$.99.

01  TOTS-LINE-4.
    05  FILLER          PIC X(10)     VALUE IS SPACES.
    05  FILLER          PIC X(20)     VALUE IS
                                      'AVERAGE CHECK:'.
    05  AVERAGE-CHECK   PIC $$$,$$$.99.

01  TOTS-LINE-5.
    05  FILLER          PIC X(10)     VALUE IS SPACES.
    05  FILLER          PIC X(26)     VALUE IS
                                      'NUMBER DEPOSITS:'.
    05  TOT-NUM-DEPOSITS
                        PIC ZZZ9.

01  TOTS-LINE-6.
    05  FILLER          PIC X(10)     VALUE IS SPACES.
    05  FILLER          PIC X(20)     VALUE IS
                                      'AMOUNT OF DEPOSITS:'.
    05  TOT-AMT-DEPOSITS
                        PIC $$$,$$$.99.

01  TOTS-LINE-7.
    05  FILLER          PIC X(10)     VALUE IS SPACES.
    05  FILLER          PIC X(20)     VALUE IS
                                      'AVERAGE DEPOSIT:'.
    05  AVERAGE-DEPOSIT PIC $$$,$$$.99.
```

continued

FIGURE 8.4 Continued

```
    PROCEDURE DIVISION.
        OPEN INPUT INPUT-FILE
            OUTPUT OUTPUT-FILE.

        READ INPUT-FILE AT END MOVE 'Y' TO EOF-FLAG.
        IF EOF-HAS-OCCURRED
            MOVE ' *** EMPTY INPUT FILE ***' TO PRINT-BUFF
            WRITE PRINT-BUFF AFTER ADVANCING TOP-OF-PAGE
        ELSE
            PERFORM 30-HEADER-ROUTINE
            MOVE AMOUNT-IN TO BALANCE
            MOVE SPACES TO PRINT-LINE
            MOVE BALANCE TO BALANCE-OUT
            PERFORM 20-PRINT-ROUTINE
            READ INPUT-FILE AT END MOVE 'Y' TO EOF-FLAG.

        PERFORM 10-PROCESS-RECORD-ROUTINE UNTIL EOF-HAS-OCCURRED.

        PERFORM 40-PRINT-TOTALS.

        CLOSE INPUT-FILE
            OUTPUT-FILE.

        STOP RUN.


    ****************************************************************
    *
    * THIS ROUTINE PROCESSES THE INPUT RECORD THAT HAS ALREADY BEEN
    * READ AND THEN ATTEMPTS TO READ THE NEXT RECORD.
    *
    ****************************************************************

    10-PROCESS-RECORD-ROUTINE.
        MOVE SPACES TO PRINT-LINE.

        IF IT-IS-A-CHECK
            MOVE AMOUNT-IN TO CHECK-OUT
            SUBTRACT AMOUNT-IN FROM BALANCE
            ADD 1 TO NUM-CHECKS
            ADD AMOUNT-IN TO CHECKS-TOTAL
        ELSE
            MOVE AMOUNT-IN TO DEPOSIT-OUT
            ADD AMOUNT-IN TO BALANCE
            ADD 1 TO NUM-DEPOSITS
            ADD AMOUNT-IN TO DEPOSITS-TOTAL.

        MOVE BALANCE TO BALANCE-OUT.

        PERFORM 20-PRINT-ROUTINE.
        READ INPUT-FILE AT END MOVE 'Y' TO EOF-FLAG.
```

```
*********************************************************************
*
* THIS ROUTINE PRINTS A LINE (STARTING ON A NEW PAGE IF
* NECESSARY).
*
*********************************************************************

 20-PRINT-ROUTINE.
     IF LINE-COUNT > 50
         PERFORM 30-HEADER-ROUTINE.
     WRITE PRINT-BUFF FROM PRINT-LINE
         AFTER ADVANCING N-LINES.
     ADD N-LINES TO LINE-COUNT.
     MOVE 1 TO N-LINES.


*********************************************************************
*
* THIS ROUTINE IS INVOKED TO PRINT PAGE AND COLUMN HEADERS..
* IT RESETS THE LINE-COUNT TO 6 (THE NUMBER OF THE NEXT LINE
* ON THE PAGE).
*
*********************************************************************

 30-HEADER-ROUTINE.
     MOVE PAGE-NO TO PG-NUM.
     ADD 1 TO PAGE-NO.
     WRITE PRINT-BUFF FROM PAGE-HEADER
         AFTER ADVANCING TOP-OF-PAGE.
     WRITE PRINT-BUFF FROM COLUMN-HEADER
         AFTER ADVANCING 3 LINES.
     MOVE 2 TO N-LINES.
     MOVE 6 TO LINE-COUNT.
```

continued

FIGURE 8.4 Continued

```
***********************************************************************
*
* THIS ROUTINE PRINTS THE LAST 7 TOTALS LINES.  IF THE
* COUNT SHOWS THAT THE SEVEN LINES WOULD NOT FIT ON THE
* CURRENT PAGE, THE TOTALS WILL BE PRINTED ON A NEW PAGE.
*
***********************************************************************

 40-PRINT-TOTALS.
     MOVE BALANCE TO FINAL-BALANCE.
     MOVE NUM-CHECKS TO TOT-NUM-CHECKS.
     MOVE CHECKS-TOTAL TO TOT-AMT-CHECKS.
     IF NUM-CHECKS = 0
         MOVE 0 TO AVERAGE-CHECK
     ELSE
         DIVIDE NUM-CHECKS INTO CHECKS-TOTAL
             GIVING AVERAGE-CHECK ROUNDED.
     MOVE NUM-DEPOSITS TO TOT-NUM-DEPOSITS.
     MOVE DEPOSITS-TOTAL TO TOT-AMT-DEPOSITS.
     IF NUM-DEPOSITS = 0
         MOVE 0 TO AVERAGE-DEPOSIT
     ELSE
         DIVIDE NUM-DEPOSITS INTO DEPOSITS-TOTAL
             GIVING AVERAGE-DEPOSIT ROUNDED.

     IF LINE-COUNT > 45
         PERFORM 30-HEADER-ROUTINE.
     WRITE PRINT-BUFF FROM TOTS-LINE-1
         AFTER ADVANCING 3 LINES.
     WRITE PRINT-BUFF FROM TOTS-LINE-2
         AFTER ADVANCING 1.
     WRITE PRINT-BUFF FROM TOTS-LINE-3
         AFTER ADVANCING 1.
     WRITE PRINT-BUFF FROM TOTS-LINE-4
         AFTER ADVANCING 1.
     WRITE PRINT-BUFF FROM TOTS-LINE-5
         AFTER ADVANCING 1.
     WRITE PRINT-BUFF FROM TOTS-LINE-6
         AFTER ADVANCING 1.
     WRITE PRINT-BUFF FROM TOTS-LINE-7
         AFTER ADVANCING 1.
```

S U M M A R Y

When signed numeric data items are to be processed, the character S must be the first character of the PICTUREs for such items. In addition, the SIGN clause should specify exactly how the sign will be represented in the input field.

Simple insertion editing allows the use of the symbols: , (comma), B (space), / (slash), and 0 (zero). These symbols, used in a PICTURE, are counted in the length of the output item, and represent the positions where the insertion will occur.

Floating insertion editing is indicated by use of sequences of the symbols: $, −, and +. One occurrence of the insertion symbol must appear in the PICTURE in the position preceding the position which the first significant digit may occupy. At least two occurrences of a floating insertion symbol must appear in the PICTURE to the left of any comma or decimal point.

The * may be used for zero suppression and character editing.

The MOVE statement may be used to

1. move an alphanumeric field to another alphanumeric field;
2. move a numeric data item or a numeric constant to an alphanumeric, numeric, or numeric edited field;
3. move a numeric edited item to an alphanumeric field.

The ROUNDED and SIZE ERROR phrases may, optionally, be used in arithmetic statements.

Condition-names are used to equate names to condition codes in order that the conditions can be referred to by name rather than a cryptic code.

R E V I E W   Q U E S T I O N S

8.1   In what way is the PICTURE for a signed numeric data item unique?

8.2   What information does the SIGN clause contain?

8.3   What symbols may be used for simple insertion editing?

8.4   What symbols are used for floating insertion?

8.5   What rules apply to the use of floating insertion characters?

8.6   How may the * be used for zero suppression?

8.7   What symbols may be used in fixed insertion editing to indicate the sign of the numeric output item?

8.8   What types of fields can act as receiving fields when moving a numeric data item?

8.9   To which fields may a numeric edited item be moved?

8.10   Is use of the SIZE ERROR phrase recommended?

8.11   Of what importance is the ROUNDED phrase?

8.12   What purpose do condition names serve?

PROGRAMMING EXERCISES

8.1   Suppose that a mail order firm keeps track of its sales by entering an input record in the following format for each transaction.

Columns	Contents
1–6	Item identification number
7–11	Value of the item
12–14	Number of items sold. If a set of items is returned, this field will contain a negative number
15	This field will contain a 'C', if the item was purchased with a charge card. Otherwise, it will contain spaces.
16–80	Spaces

Print a report containing one line per input record. The information on the input record should all appear on the printed line, as well as the amount represented by the input record (number of items times amount per item). The amount fields should include dollar signs. If the calculated amount ever exceeds $99,999.99, an error message should be printed; use an ON SIZE ERROR clause to check for the error. At the end of the report the total amount should be printed. Use condition-names for the end-of-file flag and the "charge card" flag. The format of the report should be as follows:

```
                        SALES REPORT

     ITEM        VALUE        # SOLD       AMOUNT       CHARGED

    264355        3.35          18          60.30          NO
    287499       10.95           2          21.90          YES
       .            .            .            .             .
       .            .            .            .             .

        TOTAL AMOUNT SOLD    = 1802.90
        TOTAL AMOUNT CHARGED =  632.00
```

8.2   Suppose that a bank wished to determine the average amount of money in its customers' checking accounts. The first step might be to prepare input records in the following format:

Columns	Contents
1–9	Social security number
10	Spaces
11–19	Amount (possibly negative)
20	This field will contain a 'B' for a business account. Otherwise, it will contain a 'P' for personal account.
22–80	Spaces

Write a program to print a report containing

a) One line (properly edited) for each input record.

b) A summation line at the end containing

Total number of accounts

Total amount

Average balance (rounded)

Total number of business accounts

Total amount of business accounts

Average amount per business account

Total number of personal accounts

Total amount in personal accounts

Average balance in personal accounts

If any average balance exceeds $9,999.99, an error should be detected by using ON SIZE ERROR. Use condition-names for the end-of-file flag and the field giving the type of the account.

8.3 Write a program that, when given the dimensions of a plot of land and the price of the land, computes the cost of the land per square foot. Specifically, the program should accept input records in the following format:

Columns	Contents
1–4	Width of the land in feet
5	Space
6–9	Length of the plot of land in feet
10	Space
11–17	Price of the plot of land
18–80	Spaces

The program should produce one printed line for each input record. The line should contain

a) All the information on the input record (with the price properly edited).

b) The price per square foot (rounded).

If a dimension is accidentally given the value 0, an error will occur when an attempt is made to calculate the price per square foot. In this case, use the ON SIZE ERROR clause to detect the error and cause an error message to be printed.

8.4 Assume that a stockbroker has had input records prepared using the following format:

Columns	Contents
1–9	Client's social security number
10–17	Profit or loss made last year
18	This field will contain 'T' if the amount is taxable
19–80	Spaces

Write a program to create a report containing

a) One properly edited print line for each input record

b) Summation lines giving the total number of accounts, the total amount of profit or loss, the average profit or loss (rounded), the total amount of taxable income, the average taxable income (rounded), the total amount of nontaxable income, and the average amount of nontaxable income (rounded)

Edit all dollar amounts, using character insertion editing to put asterisks between the $ and first printed digit of the amount. Use condition names for the end-of-file flag and the code indicating whether or not an amount is taxable.

SINGLE-LEVEL TABLES

INTRODUCTION Tables are sets of contiguous, or logically consecutive, data items that have the same format. Many data processing applications require the manipulation of tables. The COBOL language contains several features that are intended to facilitate the processing of data in tabular form.

The OCCURS clause, which is the subject of Section 9.1, eliminates the need for separate DATA DIVISION entries to define the repeated data items that occur in tables. This clause also generates the mechanism that is required to allow the entries in a table to be referenced through the use of subscripts.

In Section 9.2 a format for the PERFORM statement containing a VARYING phrase is discussed. The resulting statement, which we shall simply refer to as the PERFORM. . .VARYING statement, provides the means for conveniently processing each data item in a table individually through the use of a single PERFORM statement.

An example program, which illustrates the features introduced in the previous sections of the chapter, is discussed and displayed in Section 9.3.

- Tables are set of contiguous or logically contiguous data items that have same format
-
    occurs clause

9.1 The OCCURS Clause

The OCCURS clause provides a convenient way of describing data items that contain a number of fields with identical descriptions. The format of the OCCURS clause is

<u>OCCURS</u> integer TIMES

The OCCURS clause can be used to describe the repeated occurrence of any data format that is not at the 01- or 77-level.

Suppose, for example, that we wish to reserve storage for eight numbers to be read from an input record, each with the format 9(10). The record description,

```
01   NUMBERS-REC.
     05   NUM1          PIC 9(10).
     05   NUM2          PIC 9(10).
                .
                .
                .
     05   NUM8          PIC 9(10).
```

could be used for this purpose. However, a more compact way of describing this record would be

```
01   NUMBERS-REC.
     05 NUM PIC 9(10) OCCURS 8 TIMES.
```

In order to refer to any one of these eight items, a subscript must be used. The subscript is an integer enclosed in parentheses. For example, the first item with the data name NUM is referenced as NUM (1), the second as NUM (2), etc. Note that a space must separate the data name from the opening parenthesis when subscripts are used.

The OCCURS clause can be used to describe repeated occurrences of a group item, as well as an elementary item. For example, the statements

```
01   DATE-TABLE.
     05   DATE-ENTRY OCCURS 10 TIMES.
          10   MONTH        PIC 99.
          10   DAY          PIC 99.
          10   YEAR         PIC 9999.
```

set aside storage for 10 dates, each of which contains a month, day, and year. The year associated with the eighth date entry is referenced by YEAR (8).

A data name can also be used as a subscript, but the data name used must have a PICTURE clause that defines an integer field. For example,

```
DATE-ENTRY (NUM)
```

refers to DATE-ENTRY (6) if NUM has the value 6 at the time the statement containing this reference is executed.

The OCCURS clause is primarily used in programs that require the manipulation of data in tabular form. An important point to remember is that VALUE clauses cannot be used in conjunction with fields defined by an OCCURS clause.

9.2 The PERFORM. . .VARYING Statement

The next example, EXAMPLE7, illustrates the use of another format of the PERFORM statement, which has rather extensive applications. This form of the PERFORM statement is included in ANS COBOL because of the frequent occurrence of loops in data processing applications.

The format of the PERFORM statement under discussion is

```
PERFORM procedure-name-1

    VARYING field-1 FROM {literal-1} BY {literal-2}
                         {field-2  }    {field-3  }

        UNTIL condition-1
```

In this format field-1, field-2, and field-3 must have integer values, and literal-1 and literal-2 must be numeric constants that represent integers. It is a requirement of ANS COBOL that the value of literal-1 or field-2 be positive. It is occasionally useful to assign a negative value to literal-2.

When this statement is executed, field-1 is initially assigned the value represented by literal-1 or field-2. The condition is checked, and, if it is not satisfied, procedure-name-1 is executed. Then field-2 is incremented by the value of literal-2 or field-3. The condition is again checked and if it is not satisfied, the subroutine is executed again. This continues until condition-1 is found to be satisfied and control is then passed to the next statement in the program. Of course, if condition-1 is satisfied initially, the range of the PERFORM statement is not executed and control passes to the next statement at once. The flowchart of Fig. 9.1 illustrates the logic of this form of the PERFORM statement.

FIGURE 9.1 The logic of the PERFORM statement.

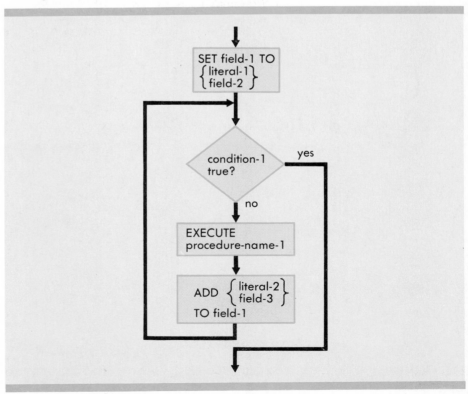

9.3 EXAMPLE7—A Program to Summarize Student Aptitude Scores

The program EXAMPLE7 was designed to illustrate the use of the OCCURS clause and the PERFORM...VARYING statement. This program reads input records that contain the name of a student and five aptitude test scores. The format for each of these records is as shown in Fig. 9.2. The output produced is to contain a record corresponding to each input record. The program produces a report similar to the following:

```
          STUDENT  APTITUDE  SCORES                          PAGE    1



  NAME         ENGLISH    MATH    SOC STUD    NAT SCI    WORD USE    TOTAL    AVERAGE

JOHN ARTIN        26       29        24         29         26        134        27
JUDY BLISS        31       27        30         29         29        146        29
MAY CARTWRIGHT    21       26        25         22         26        120        24
ROBERT MOSS       29       33        29         30         28        149        30

AVERAGES:         27       29        27         28         27        137        28
```

The flowcharts for EXAMPLE7 are displayed in Figs. 9.3–9.5 and the complete program listing (Fig. 9.6) follows the flowcharts. For Fig. 9.5, flowcharts for 40-PRINT-ROUTINE and 50-HEADER-ROUTINE are identical to those of previous programs; 70-MOVE-AVG-SCORE is a single statement that computes the average for the Ith column. Uses of the OCCURS clause in both the FILE SECTION and WORKING-STORAGE SECTION of the DATA DIVISION should be studied. Note also the use of the PERFORM...VARYING as well as the independent uses of subscripts in the PROCEDURE DIVISION.

FIGURE 9.2 Input record format for EXAMPLE7.

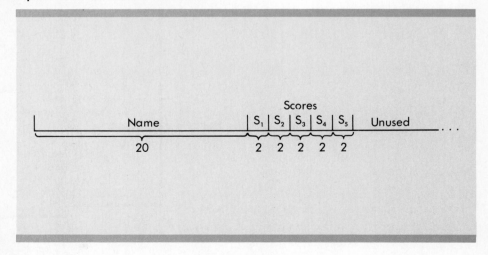

FIGURE 9.3 The logic of EXAMPLE7.

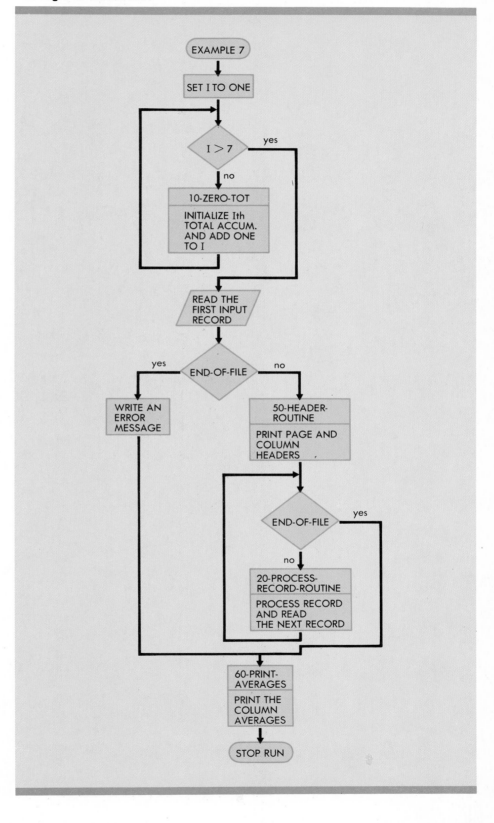

FIGURE 9.4   The logic of EXAMPLE7.

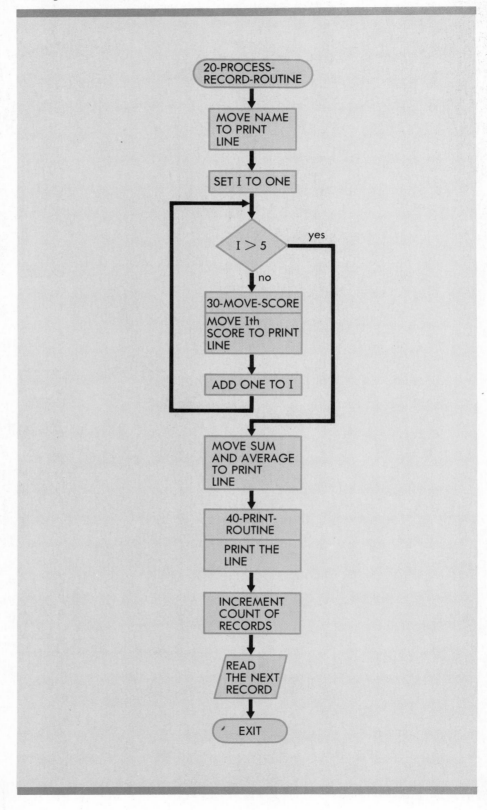

FIGURE 9.5 The logic of EXAMPLE7.

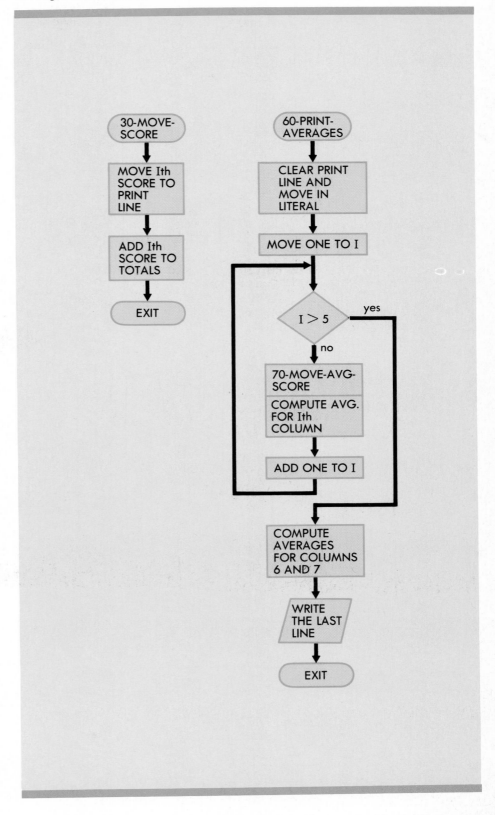

FIGURE 9.6 EXAMPLE7—a program to summarize student aptitude scores.

```
       IDENTIFICATION DIVISION.
       PROGRAM-ID. EXAMPLE7.
       AUTHOR. W E SINGLETARY.


       ***********************************************************
       *
       * THIS PROGRAM CAN BE USED TO PRINT STUDENT APTITUDE SCORES.
       * EACH INPUT RECORD GIVES FIVE TEST SCORES FOR A SINGLE
       * STUDENT.  THE TEST SCORES REPRESENT
       *
       *     1) ENGLISH USAGE
       *     2) MATH USAGE
       *     3) SOC. STUDIES READING
       *     4) NATURAL SCIENCE READING
       *     5) WORD USAGE
       *
       * FOR EACH STUDENT THE FIVE SCORES, ALONG WITH THEIR SUM
       * AND AVERAGE, ARE DISPLAYED.
       *
       * AFTER ALL INPUT RECORDS ARE DISPLAYED AVERAGES FOR
       * EACH OF THE COLUMNS WILL BE PRINTED.
       *
       ***********************************************************

       ENVIRONMENT DIVISION.

       CONFIGURATION SECTION.
       SOURCE-COMPUTER. IBM-370.
       OBJECT-COMPUTER. IBM-370.

       SPECIAL-NAMES.
           C01 IS TOP-OF-PAGE.

       INPUT-OUTPUT SECTION.
       FILE-CONTROL.

           SELECT INPUT-FILE ASSIGN TO UR-S-SYSIN.
           SELECT OUTPUT-FILE ASSIGN TO UR-S-SYSPRINT.
```

```
DATA DIVISION.
FILE SECTION.

*********************************************************************
*
* THIS FILE CONTAINS ONE RECORD PER STUDENT.  EACH RECORD
* CONTAINS A NAME AND FIVE TEST SCORES.
*
*********************************************************************


FD  INPUT-FILE
    LABEL RECORDS ARE OMITTED
    DATA RECORD IS INPUT-RECORD.

01  INPUT-RECORD.
    05  NAME-IN           PIC X(20).
    05  SCORE-IN          PIC 99 OCCURS 5 TIMES.
    05  FILLER            PIC X(50).

*********************************************************************
*
* THIS FILE IS USED TO PRINT THE REPORT.  ONE LINE IS PRINTED
* FOR EACH STUDENT.  AT THE END AVERAGES ARE PRINTED FOR EACH
* COLUMN.
*
*********************************************************************

FD  OUTPUT-FILE
    LABEL RECORDS ARE OMITTED
    DATA RECORD IS PRINT-BUFF.

01  PRINT-BUFF          PIC X(133).
```

continued

FIGURE 9.6 Continued

```
 WORKING-STORAGE SECTION.

*****************************************************************
*
* EOF-FLAG IS SET TO 'Y' WHEN END-OF-FILE OCCURS.
*
* N-LINES IS SET TO THE NUMBER OF LINES TO ADVANCE BEFORE
*         PRINTING A LINE
*
* LINE-COUNT CONTAINS THE NUMBER OF THE NEXT LINE ON A PAGE.
*
* PAGE-NO CONTAINS THE PAGE NUMBER OF THE NEXT PAGE OF THE
*         REPORT.
*
* I IS USED AS A SUBCRIPT.
*
* SUM-SCORE ACCUMULATES THE SUM OF ONE STUDENT'S SCORES
*
* AVG-SCORE GETS SET TO THE AVERAGE SCORE FOR ONE STUDENT
*
* COLUMN-TOTALS CONTAINS TOTALS FOR EACH OF THE COLUMNS, AS
*    WELL AS A COUNT OF THE NUMBER OF RECORDS INCLUDED IN THE
*    TOTALS.
*
* PRINT-LINE IS USED TO BUILD THE LINES TO BE PRINTED.
*
* PAGE-HEADER AND COLUMN-HEADER ARE USED TO PRINT HEADERS AT
*         THE TOP OF THE FIRST PAGE OF OUTPUT.
*
*****************************************************************


 01   FLAGS.
      05  EOF-FLAG          PIC X          VALUE IS 'N'.
          88  EOF-HAS-OCCURRED             VALUE IS 'Y'.
```

```
01   PRINT-VARIABLES.
     05   N-LINES         PIC 9.
     05   LINE-COUNT      PIC 99.
     05   PAGE-NO         PIC 999      VALUE IS 1.


01   MISC.
     05   I               PIC 99.
     05   SUM-SCORES      PIC 999.
     05   AVG-SCORE       PIC 99.


01   COLUMN-TOTALS.
     05   COL-TOTAL       PIC 9(7) OCCURS 7 TIMES.
     05   NUMBER-OF-RECS  PIC 9(6)      VALUE IS 0.


01   PRINT-LINE.
     05   FILLER          PIC X(21).
     05   NAME-OUT        PIC X(20).
     05   FILLER          PIC X(10).
     05   SCORES-OUT OCCURS 5 TIMES.
          10   SCORE-OUT  PIC Z9.
          10   FILLER     PIC X(7).
     05   FILLER          PIC X(3).
     05   SUM-SCORES-OUT  PIC ZZ9.
     05   FILLER          PIC X(6).
     05   AVG-SCORE-OUT   PIC Z9.


01   PAGE-HEADER.
     05   FILLER          PIC X(1).
     05   FILLER          PIC X(38)     VALUE IS SPACES.
     05   FILLER          PIC X(45)     VALUE IS
          'S T U D E N T    A P T I T U D E    S C O R E S'.
     05   FILLER          PIC X(20)     VALUE IS SPACES.
     05   FILLER          PIC X(5)      VALUE IS 'PAGE '.
     05   PG-NUM          PIC ZZ9.
```

FIGURE 9.6   Continued

```
01   COLUMN-HEADER.
     05   FILLER           PIC X(1).
     05   FILLER           PIC X(22)      VALUE IS SPACES.
     05   FILLER           PIC X(4)       VALUE IS 'NAME'.
     05   FILLER           PIC X(21)      VALUE IS SPACES.
     05   FILLER           PIC X(9)       VALUE IS 'ENGLISH'.
     05   FILLER           PIC X(9)       VALUE IS '   MATH'.
     05   FILLER           PIC X(9)       VALUE IS 'SOC STUD'.
     05   FILLER           PIC X(9)       VALUE IS 'NAT SCI'.
     05   FILLER           PIC X(9)       VALUE IS 'WORD USE'.
     05   FILLER           PIC X(3)       VALUE IS SPACES.
     05   FILLER           PIC X(9)       VALUE IS ' TOTAL '.
     05   FILLER           PIC X(9)       VALUE IS 'AVERAGE'.


PROCEDURE DIVISION.
    OPEN INPUT INPUT-FILE
         OUTPUT OUTPUT-FILE.

    PERFORM 10-ZERO-TOT VARYING I FROM 1 BY 1
         UNTIL I > 7.

    READ INPUT-FILE AT END MOVE 'Y' TO EOF-FLAG.
    IF EOF-HAS-OCCURRED
         MOVE ' *** EMPTY INPUT FILE ***' TO PRINT-BUFF
         WRITE PRINT-BUFF AFTER ADVANCING TOP-OF-PAGE
    ELSE
         PERFORM 50-HEADER-ROUTINE
         PERFORM 20-PROCESS-RECORD-ROUTINE
             UNTIL EOF-HAS-OCCURRED.

    PERFORM 60-PRINT-AVERAGES.

    CLOSE INPUT-FILE
          OUTPUT-FILE.

    STOP RUN.

*********************************************************************
*
* THIS ROUTINE JUST ZEROES TOTALS ACCUMULATORS.
*
*********************************************************************

 10-ZERO-TOT.
     MOVE 0 TO COL-TOTAL (I).
```

```
*****************************************************************
*
* THIS ROUTINE PROCESSES THE INPUT RECORD THAT HAS ALREADY BEEN
* READ AND THEN ATTEMPTS TO READ THE NEXT RECORD.
*
*****************************************************************

 20-PROCESS-RECORD-ROUTINE.
     MOVE SPACES TO PRINT-LINE.
     MOVE NAME-IN TO NAME-OUT.

     MOVE 0 TO SUM-SCORES.
     PERFORM 30-MOVE-SCORE VARYING I FROM 1 BY 1
         UNTIL I > 5.

     MOVE SUM-SCORES TO SUM-SCORES-OUT.
     ADD SUM-SCORES TO COL-TOTAL (6).
     COMPUTE AVG-SCORE ROUNDED = SUM-SCORES / 5.
     MOVE AVG-SCORE TO AVG-SCORE-OUT.
     ADD AVG-SCORE TO COL-TOTAL (7).
     PERFORM 40-PRINT-ROUTINE.
     ADD 1 TO NUMBER-OF-RECS.
     READ INPUT-FILE AT END MOVE 'Y' TO EOF-FLAG.

*****************************************************************
*
* THIS ROUTINE MOVES A SCORE TO THE PRINT LINE AND ADDS IT
* TO THE TOTAL OF THE SCORES.
*
*****************************************************************

 30-MOVE-SCORE.
     MOVE SCORE-IN (I) TO SCORE-OUT (I).
     ADD SCORE-IN (I) TO SUM-SCORES.
     ADD SCORE-IN (I) TO COL-TOTAL (I).


*****************************************************************
*
* THIS ROUTINE PRINTS A LINE (STARTING ON A NEW PAGE IF
* NECESSARY).
*
*****************************************************************

 40-PRINT-ROUTINE.
     IF LINE-COUNT > 50
         PERFORM 50-HEADER-ROUTINE.
     WRITE PRINT-BUFF FROM PRINT-LINE
         AFTER ADVANCING N-LINES.
     ADD N-LINES TO LINE-COUNT.
     MOVE 1 TO N-LINES.
```

continued

FIGURE 9.6 Continued

```
    ********************************************************************
    *
    * THIS ROUTINE IS INVOKED TO PRINT PAGE AND COLUMN HEADERS..
    * IT RESETS THE LINE-COUNT TO 6 (THE NUMBER OF THE NEXT LINE
    * ON THE PAGE).
    *
    ********************************************************************

     50-HEADER-ROUTINE.
         MOVE PAGE-NO TO PG-NUM.
         ADD 1 TO PAGE-NO.
         WRITE PRINT-BUFF FROM PAGE-HEADER
             AFTER ADVANCING TOP-OF-PAGE.
         WRITE PRINT-BUFF FROM COLUMN-HEADER
             AFTER ADVANCING 3 LINES.
         MOVE 2 TO N-LINES.
         MOVE 6 TO LINE-COUNT.


    ********************************************************************
    *
    * THIS ROUTINE PRINTS THE LAST LINE, WHICH GIVES THE AVERAGES
    * FOR EACH OF THE COLUMNS.
    *
    ********************************************************************

     60-PRINT-AVERAGES.
         MOVE SPACES TO PRINT-LINE.
         MOVE 'AVERAGES:' TO NAME-OUT.
         PERFORM 70-MOVE-AVG-SCORE VARYING I FROM 1 BY 1
             UNTIL I > 5.
         COMPUTE SUM-SCORES-OUT ROUNDED =
             COL-TOTAL (6) / NUMBER-OF-RECS.
         COMPUTE AVG-SCORE-OUT ROUNDED =
             COL-TOTAL (7) / NUMBER-OF-RECS.

         WRITE PRINT-BUFF FROM PRINT-LINE
             AFTER ADVANCING 3 LINES.

    ********************************************************************
    *
    * THIS ROUTINE MOVES THE AVERAGE OF ONE COLUMN TO THE PRINT
    * LINE.
    *
    ********************************************************************

     70-MOVE-AVG-SCORE.
         COMPUTE SCORE-OUT (I) ROUNDED =
             COL-TOTAL (I) / NUMBER-OF-RECS.
```

SUMMARY

A table is a set of contiguous data items with identical formats. A subscript is an integer whose value identifies a particular element in a table. In ANS COBOL a subscript is expressed by enclosing an integer, or a variable that evaluates to an integer value, in parentheses.

The OCCURS clause allows repeated data items to be defined without the necessity of using separate entities in the DATA DIVISION. When a table is specified through the use of an OCCURS clause, the facilities for referencing particular elements in the table through the use of subscripts are established.

The PERFORM...VARYING statement provides the facility to perform a function on each element, or a selected set of elements, in a table sequentially. Two integer parameters in this statement allow initial and increment values to be specified for a subscript. The valuation of a condition determines when execution of the statement is complete. Execution of the statement proceeds as follows:

Step 1 The value of the subscript is set to the initial value.

Step 2 The condition is evaluated, and, if it is not satisfied, the function is performed on the table element specified by the value of the subscript. Otherwise, control is passed to the next statement in the program.

Step 3 The value of the subscript is incremented by the increment value and control is passed to step 2.

REVIEW QUESTIONS

9.1 What is a table?

9.2 What is a subscript?

9.3 Can a VALUE clause be specified for an item subordinate to an OCCURS clause?

9.4 What do the three integer values in the VARYING phrase specify?

9.5 How does the use of the OCCURS clause reduce the number of lines required in a program?

9.6 In what ways can use of the PERFORM...VARYING statement reduce the number of lines required in a program?

PROGRAMMING EXERCISES

9.1 A company employs six salespersons. Whenever any of the six salespersons makes a sale, an input record is created using the following format:

Columns	Contents
1	Salesperson's number (1–6)
2	Space
3–9	Amount of sale (99999V99)
10–80	Spaces

At the end of the month these input records are to be used to print a report that appears as follows:

```
                              SALES REPORT                        PAGE 1

             SALESPERSON 1      SALESPERSON 2      SALESPERSON 3 ...

               987.10
                                                     10.00
                                                     36.50
                                    24.50
                 .                    .                .
                 .                    .                .
                 .                    .                .
   TOTALS      1257.80              544.60            84.20 ...
```

Note that for every input record read, the amount should be printed under the correct salesperson's column. Thus, only one amount should be printed per line, and where it appears depends upon the number of the salesman who executed the transaction. At the end of the report a single totals line should be printed. Write the program to produce the month-end report.

9.2   a) Read in a set of up to 50 test scores (the scores range from 0 to 100). Each test score will be punched into the first three columns of an input record.

b) Calculate the average test score.

c) Print out each test score (one per line) and the difference between the given score and the average of the scores.

d) At the end of the report, print the number of test scores above the average score and the number of test scores below or equal to the average test score.

9.3   Suppose that a loan company had input records for its accounts using the following format:

Columns	Contents
1–20	Name of person who opened the account
21–29	Social security number of that person
30–78	Seven account fields, which contain

  1. Amount overdue since the first day of the current month

  2. Amount overdue at least one month, but not two months

  .
  .
  .

7. Amount overdue six
months or more

79–80   Spaces

Write a program that simply reads the input records, prints the information from each input record on a single line, and prints a totals line at the end of the report. Appropriate page and column headers should be used.

9.4   A company that sells office equipment has had a single input record created for each type of product it sells. The format of these records is

Columns	Contents
1–20	Description of product
21–26	Number of items sold this month
27–80	Nine fields containing the number of items sold in each of the last nine months

Write a report that prints one line for each input record. The line should display all the information on the input record, the average number of items sold per month for the last nine months, and the difference between the number of items sold this month and the average for the last nine months.

9.5   Suppose that a set of up to 100 name and address records has been created using the following format:

Columns	Contents
1–20	Name
21–40	1st line of address
41–60	2nd line of address
61–80	3rd line of address

Write a program that performs the following tasks:

a) The program should first read the input records, storing the information from the records in a table.

b) The program should then print out each entry in the table. Up to four lines should be produced for each entry (do not print blank lines).

c) The program should then compress the table by removing duplicate entries. To simplify the task, you may assume that the input records will be sorted into ascending order before they are submitted to the program. Thus, duplicates will reside in adjacent entries in the table.

d) Print the remaining entries in the compressed table.

9.6   Write a program to compute the average scores per game for each of 10 basketball players on a team. The program should take as input any number of records, each of which will contain a player number in columns 1–2 (the value should range from 01 to 10) and a score in columns 4–6. After all of the input records have been read the program should produce the following output for each player:

```
PLAYER  2 PLAYED IN  9 GAMES WITH AN AVERAGE OF 17 POINTS
```

9.7   Write a program that can be used to compute average scores for bowlers. Each input record should conform to the following format:

Columns	Contents
1–20	Name of bowler
21–50	1 to 10 bowling scores (Each score is three digits, and spaces are used for "empty" scores.)
51–80	Unused

For each input record, the program should print a single line giving the bowler's name, scores, and average score. The program should include proper page and column headers, and should print 55 lines per page.

9.8   This exercise involves encoding and decoding short messages. You are to write a program that reads messages, encodes the messages, and decodes the messages back to the original text (to make sure that the encoding works as expected). The program first reads a record that contains the alphabetic characters in the first 26 columns. The characters can occur in any order. When messages are encoded, every 'A' in a message will be replaced by the first character in this first record, every 'B' by the second character, and so forth. Thus, the first record establishes the encoding scheme (which is, granted, a fairly straightforward approach). For example, if the first record contained

```
ZYXWVUTSRQPONMLKJIHGFEDCBA
```

then the message "The Eagle has landed" would be encoded as GSV VZTOV TZH OZMWVW. After reading the first record the program should read records (of up to 80 characters) that each contain a message. Your program should print the original message, encode it, print the encoded version, decode the message, and print the decoded message (which should be identical with the original). Thus, each input message should cause three lines of output to be printed. For this assignment, you will find it convenient to have two tables in working storage. Each will contain 26 one-character entries. The first table should be initialized to the letters A, B, ... Z. The second should contain the records read from the first record. The input record should be defined as a table of 80 one-character entries. The program should print page headers, and print up to 50 lines per page.

MULTI-DIMENSIONAL TABLES

INTRODUCTION   Occasionally a situation arises in a data processing application which could be dealt with more succinctly through the use of two- or three-dimensional tables. The central aim of this chapter is to introduce the tools provided by COBOL for dealing with such situations.

The REDEFINES clause is discussed in Section 10.3 because it provides a convenient means for initializing the values of table elements. The use of the OCCURS clause in defining multidimensional tables is examined in Section 10.4, and the method of referencing the individual entries in such tables is discussed. The use of the AFTER clause in the PERFORM ... VARYING statement as a means of implementing the orderly augmentation of multidimensional table subscripts during the execution of a single PERFORM statement is explained in Section 10.5.

10.1 Level-Numbers

The level-numbers 01 through 49 are used to indicate the hierarchical relationship of data items within a logical record. When an item at any of these levels is followed immediately by an item or items with a higher level-number, the items with the higher level-number are considered to be subordinate to the item with the lower level-number.

In the examples considered thus far, we have used the level-number 01 to indicate a logical record, and the level-number 05 for all of the elementary data items subordinate to the record. The first entry in a record description must have an 01 level-number, but a great deal of freedom is allowed with the level-numbers for subordinate items. A well-established custom (probably a holdover from the days when the use of punched cards was prevalent) is to assign multiples of 5 as level-numbers to successive subordinate levels (e.g., 05, 10, 15, etc.). Most practical applications require hierarchies of data which are at least three levels deep.

The following example should help to clarify these concepts.

```
01   STUDENT-RECORD.
     05   NAME                        PIC X(20).
     05   SOC-SEC-NO.
          10   SOC-SEC1               PIC 999.
          10   SOC-SEC2               PIC 99.
          10   SOC-SEC3               PIC 9999.
     05   HOME-ADDRESS.
          10   STREET-ADDRESS.
               15   NUM               PIC 99999.
               15   STREET            PIC X(14).
          10   CITY-ADDRESS.
               15   CITY              PIC X(15).
               15   STATE             PIC X(12).
               15   ZIP               PIC 99999.
```

All data items subordinate to a particular data item can be referenced independently. For example, NAME, SOC-SEC-NO, and HOME-ADDRESS are all data items subordinate to STUDENT-RECORD. Any one of these data items can be referenced by name. All of these, with the exception of NAME, are group data items. That is, they are further subdivided. NAME is an elementary data item. As such, it must have a PICTURE clause. HOME-ADDRESS has two subordinate group items, STREET-ADDRESS and CITY-ADDRESS. Either of these items could be referenced independently, as could any one of the elementary items subordinate to them.

Several facts are worthy of note with respect to level-numbers in record descriptions. The level-numbers from 02 through 49 may begin in column 12 or beyond. Here the indenting of each of the successive subordinate levels by four spaces graphically depicts the interdependence of the fields. Only elementary items can have PICTURE clauses. And indeed, they must have PICTURE clauses.

10.2 The DATA RECORDS Clause

Most data processing applications require that several formats be provided for the records in both the input file, or files, and the output files. This requirement has been addressed in previous examples in the case of the output file. Records in several different formats have been constructed in WORKING-STORAGE and written to the output file using the WRITE ... FROM sentence. A tacit assumption has been made, however, that the input file will contain records that are all in the same format. This restriction is unrealistic. For example, practically all input files will contain an initial record that provides a date and perhaps other information about the other records in the file. In fact, an input file that may be used to update an existing file will probably contain records that may be used to delete or add records to the existing file as well as records that indicate alterations to be made to records in that file. If allowance is made for the initial record as well as each of these three types of records, the input file would contain records in each of four distinct formats.

The DATA RECORDS clause provides the facility for defining multiple record formats for a given file. The format for this clause is

$$\underline{DATA} \left\{ \begin{array}{l} \underline{RECORD} \ IS \\ \underline{RECORDS} \ ARE \end{array} \right\} data\text{-}name\text{-}1 \ [data\text{-}name\text{-}2] \ ...$$

Each record entered from the file by the execution of a READ statement occupies the same storage area. The different formats specified simply redefine the fields in this storage area. These fields can be referenced through the use of the data names that occur in any of the several record formats. There should be some particular field which occurs in the same position in each of the record descriptions and which contains a code that can be used to identify the correct record format to be used to process a particular record. When this determination has been made, a routine can be selected to process the given record.

10.3 The REDEFINES Clause

The REDEFINES clause provides the means for assigning alternative formats to an area of storage. The following example should help to clarify the use of this clause.

```
01   REC-IN.
     05   TRAN-CODE              PIC 9.

     05   FIRST-ALTERNATIVE.
          10   M-CODE            PIC X.
          10   AGE               PIC 999.

     05   SECOND-ALTERNATIVE REDEFINES FIRST-ALTERNATIVE.
          10   SEX-CODE          PIC X.
          10   WEIGHT-1          PIC 999.
```

In this example, FIRST-ALTERNATIVE and SECOND-ALTERNATIVE both describe the same area in REC-IN.

The idea of redefining the format of a storage area should be familiar to you by now, for this is precisely what is accomplished by specifying multiple record formats in the DATA RECORDS ARE clause. The REDEFINES clause, however, provides more flexibility in that

1. it provides a facility for redefining portions of records, and

2. it can be used to redefine areas in working storage.

The general format of the REDEFINES clause is

```
level-number data-name-1 REDEFINES data-name-2
```

For example,

```
05  LABEL-2 REDEFINES LABEL-1 PIC 99.
```

causes LABEL-2 to redefine the area previously described by LABEL-1.

Several important restrictions govern the use of the REDEFINES clause. These are as follows:

Rule 1   The level-numbers of data-name-1 and data-name-2 must be identical. Thus,

```
05  SOC-SEC.
    10  SOC-1                PIC X(9).
    10  ALT-SOC REDEFINES SOC-SEC.
        15  A-SOC            PIC 9(9).
```

is invalid because ALT-SOC has a level-number of 10 while SOC-SEC has a level-number of 05.

Rule 2   The REDEFINES clause which contains the format of data-name-1 must immediately follow the last statement in the description of data-name-2, or must follow another REDEFINES clause which also gives an alternative format for data-name-2. For example,

```
01  REC-IN.
    05  SOC-SEC.
        10  S-1              PIC X(3).
        10  S-2              PIC X(2).
        10  S-3              PIC X(4).
    05  M-CODE               PIC X.
    05  S-NUM REDEFINES SOC-SEC   PIC 9(9).
```

is invalid because M-CODE falls between S-NUM and the description of the field that S-NUM redefines.

Rule 3   Data-name-2 must not contain an OCCURS clause in its definition (but data-name-1 can).

Rule 4   The lengths of the storage areas described by data-name-1 and data-name-2 must agree exactly unless they are 01-level items. In the case of fixed-length records, the lengths should agree for 01-level items as well.

Rule 5   An 01-level entry in the FILE SECTION must not be redefined with a REDEFINES clause. The DATA RECORDS ARE option is used for this purpose.

Rule 6   Since the REDEFINES clause is used only for the purpose of creating an alternative format for a previously described area, a VALUE IS clause cannot be used in the statements describing data-name-1. If a value is to be assigned initially to the given area, this must be done in the description of data-name-2.

Two common uses of the REDEFINES clause are illustrated in the following two program segments. The first segment is a redefinition of just a section of a record, UPDATE-REC. That redefinition is as follows:

```
01   UPDATE-REC.
     05   TRAN-KEY.
          10   PRODUCER        PIC X(4).
          10   VOLUME-ID       PIC X(15).
     05   TRAN-CODE            PIC X.
          88   ADD-TRANSACTION     VALUE IS 'A'.
          88   CHANGE-TRANSACTION VALUE IS 'C'.
          88   DELETE-TRANSACTION VALUE IS 'D'.

     05   ADD-TRAN.
          10   ARTIST          PIC X(10).
          10   TITLE           PIC X(20).
          10   IN-STOCK        PIC 9(4).
          10   ON-ORDER        PIC 9(4).
          10   PRICE           PIC 99V99.
          10   FILLER          PIC X(18).

     05   CHANGE-TRAN REDEFINES ADD-TRAN.
          10   FIELD-CODE      PIC 9.

          10   NEW-ARTIST.
               15   ARTIST     PIC X(10).
               15   FILLER     PIC X(49).

          10   NEW-TITLE REDEFINES NEW-ARTIST.
               15   TITLE      PIC X(20).
               15   FILLER     PIC X(39).

          10   NEW-IN-STOCK REDEFINES NEW-ARTIST.
               10   ADJUST-SIGN PIC X.
               10   ADJUST-BY   PIC 9(4).
               10   FILLER      PIC X(54).

          10   NEW-ON-ORDER REDEFINES NEW-ARTIST.
               15   ADJUST-SIGN PIC X.
               15   ADJUST-BY   PIC 9(4).
               15   FILLER      PIC X(54).

          10   NEW-PRICE REDEFINES NEW-ARTIST.
               15   PRICE      PIC 99V99.
               15   FILLER     PIC X(55).

          10   NEW-HISTORY REDEFINES NEW-ARTIST.
               15   HISTORY-SUB PIC 99.
               15   HIST-VALUE  PIC 9(4).
               15   FILLER      PIC X(53).

          10   A-SALE-THIS-WEEK REDEFINES NEW-ARTIST.
               15   SALES-SIGN PIC X.
               15   NUMBER-SOLD PIC 9(4).
               15   FILLER      PIC X(54).
```

No alternative format is specified for the first 20 positions of the record. However, ADD-TRAN and CHANGE-TRAN give alternative formats for the remaining 60 positions. Within CHANGE-TRAN seven alternative descriptions for positions 22 through 80 of the record are specified.

The second common use of the REDEFINES clause is the initialization of values in a table. The following statements assign initial values to M-TABLE.

```
01  M-VALS.
    05  FILLER          PIC X(4) VALUE 'ANTH'.
    05  FILLER          PIC X(4) VALUE 'ART'.
    05  FILLER          PIC X(4) VALUE 'BIOL'.
    05  FILLER          PIC X(4) VALUE 'CHEM'.
    05  FILLER          PIC X(4) VALUE 'ECON'.
    05  FILLER          PIC X(4) VALUE 'ENGL'.
    05  FILLER          PIC X(4) VALUE 'FORL'.
    05  FILLER          PIC X(4) VALUE 'HIST'.
    05  FILLER          PIC X(4) VALUE 'MATH'.
    05  FILLER          PIC X(4) VALUE 'PHIL'.
    05  FILLER          PIC X(4) VALUE 'PHYS'.
    05  FILLER          PIC X(4) VALUE 'POLI'.
    05  FILLER          PIC X(4) VALUE 'PSYC'.
    05  FILLER          PIC X(4) VALUE 'SOCI'.
    05  FILLER          PIC X(4) VALUE 'UNSP'.

01  M-TAB REDEFINES M-VALS.
    05  M-TABLE OCCURS 15 TIMES PIC X(4).
```

Thus, M-TABLE (1), M-TABLE (2), ..., M-TABLE (15) take as values the abbreviations for departments in a university. The importance of this technique to initialize the values in a table should become apparent from subsequent examples.

10.4 Multidimensional Tables

All of the tables that we have discussed in previous sections were one-dimensional tables. That is, any data item in those tables could be referenced using a single subscript. Very rarely you will find it necessary to use tables of two or three dimensions. To illustrate this concept, consider a master file for saving information on all products sold by some company. Each item record in the file will contain the data associated with a single product. Suppose that it is necessary to keep detailed sales history totals for each product. Further, suppose that the products are each sold at four separate stores. The following record description includes the statements required to define the appropriate history fields.

```
01  PRODUCT-RECORD.
    05  PRODUCT-NUMBER          PIC 9(5).
    05  PRODUCT-DESCRIPTION     PIC X(20).
    05  PRICE                   PIC 9(4)V99.
    05  IN-STOCK                PIC 9(5).
    05  HISTORY-DATA.
        10  ONE-DAYS-HISTORY OCCURS 366 TIMES.
            15  ONE-STORES-SALES OCCURS 4 TIMES
                                    PIC 9(4).
```

Note that each record contains history for 366 days. Each day's history contains four numeric fields. Thus, each record contains 1464 distinct numeric history fields. To reference a specific value of ONE-STORES-SALES requires two subscripts; the first specifies the day, and the second specifies which store. For example,

```
ONE-STORES-SALES (32, 3)
```

would reference the number of sales at store 3 on February 1 (since February 1 is the thirty-second day of the year).

The preceding example involves a two-dimensional table, because two separate subscripts are required to reference the lowest level data items. Just as with one-dimensional tables, the subscripts can be specified as data items. Thus,

```
ONE-STORES-SALES (DAY-SUB, STORE-SUB)
```

is valid. To see exactly how to manipulate a two-dimensional table, consider the problem of displaying the total sales so far this year for a given product. The following short section of code accomplishes this simple task (assuming that PRODUCT-RECORD contains a valid record):

```
01   SUBSCRIPTS.
        05   DAY-SUB            PIC 999.
        05   STORE-SUB          PIC 9.
        05   SUM-OF-SALES       PIC 9(6).
        .
        .
        .

     MOVE 0 TO SUM-OF-SALES.
     PERFORM SUM-UP-A-DAY
         VARYING DAY-SUB FROM 1 BY 1 UNTIL
         DAY-SUB > 366.
     DISPLAY 'TOTAL SALES =' SUM-OF-SALES.
        .
        .
        .

 SUM-UP-A-DAY.
        PERFORM SUM-UP-A-STORE
            VARYING STORE-SUB FROM 1 BY 1 UNTIL
            STORE-SUB > 4.

 SUM-UP-A-STORE.
        ADD ONE-STORES-SALES (DAY-SUB, STORE-SUB) TO
            SUM-OF-SALES.
        .
        .
        .
```

The previous example illustrated two-dimensional tables. Three-dimensional tables are quite similar—they just require one more subscript. For example, if each of the four stores had up to five separate salespersons, and if we needed to record exactly how many sales each person made, we could define the record as

```
01   PRODUCT-RECORD.
     05   PRODUCT-NUMBER           PIC 9(5).
     05   PRODUCT-DESCRIPTION      PIC X(20).
     05   PRICE                    PIC 9(4)V99.
     05   IN-STOCK                 PIC 9(5).
     05   HISTORY-DATA.
          10   ONE-DAYS-HISTORY OCCURS 366 TIMES.
               15   ONE-STORES-SALES OCCURS 4 TIMES.
                    20   ONE-PERSONS-SALES OCCURS 5 TIMES
                                   PIC 9(4).
```

In this case, three subscripts are required. Thus,

```
ONE-PERSONS-SALES (DAY-SUB, STORE-SUB, PERSON-SUB)
```

could be used to reference a single value, assuming that the three subscripts all contain valid values.

10.5 The PERFORM . . . VARYING Revisited

The PERFORM ... VARYING statement was introduced in the preceding chapter, and a discussion of how it could be used to augment the values referenced by an identifier in an orderly fashion during the execution of a PERFORM statement was discussed. However, if the elements in a multidimensional table are to be traversed in an orderly fashion, the values of two or more identifiers must be augmented. The same format of the PERFORM statement could be used to accomplish this, but this requires the use of a PERFORM statement in a subroutine referenced by a PERFORM statement. The following example should help to clarify this.

Suppose that ARRAY is a three-dimensional table and that the three identifiers SUB-1, SUB-2, and SUB-3 are used to represent the first, second, and third subscripts, respectively. Then, the following section of symbolic code could be used to transverse the elements of ARRAY in an orderly fashion.

```
PERFORM SUBRTN-1 VARYING SUB-1
     FROM literal-1 BY literal-2
     UNTIL condition-1.


               .
               .
               .


SUBRTN-1.
     PERFORM SUBRTN-2 VARYING SUB-2
          FROM literal-3 BY literal-4
          UNTIL condition-2.


               .
               .
               .
```

```
SUBRTN-2.
     PERFORM SUBRTN-3 VARYING SUB-3
          FROM literal-5 BY literal-6
          UNTIL condition-3.

                         .
                         .
                         .

SUBRTN-3.

                    .
                    .
                    .
```

As a more concrete example, suppose that ARRAY is a three-dimensional table with dimensions 10, 10, and 10. Then, the following segment of code could be used to sum all of the elements of ARRAY.

```
PERFORM SUBRTN-1 VARYING SUB-1 FROM 1 BY 1
     UNTIL SUB-1 > 10.

                    .
                    .
                    .

SUBRTN-1.
     PERFORM SUBRTN-2 VARYING SUB-2 FROM 1 BY 1
          UNTIL SUB-2 > 10.

                    .
                    .
                    .

SUBRTN-2.
     PERFORM SUBRTN-3 VARYING SUB-3 FROM 1 BY 1
          UNTIL SUB-3 > 10.

                    .
                    .
                    .

SUBRTN-3.
     ADD ARRAY (SUB-1, SUB-2, SUB-3) TO SUM-OF-ENTRIES.

                    .
                    .
                    .
```

The designers of the COBOL language, realizing the convenience it could provide, implemented a single statement that could be used to replace the three PERFORM statements used in these two examples. This is the PERFORM ... VARYING statement with AFTER clauses.

```
PERFORM procedure-name-1
        VARYING identifier-1 FROM {literal-1    }
                                  {identifier-2 }

           BY {literal-2    } UNTIL condition-1
              {identifier-3 }

        AFTER identifier-4 FROM {literal-3    }
                                {identifier-5 }

           BY {literal-4    } UNTIL condition-2
              {identifier-6 }

        AFTER identifier-7 FROM {literal-5    }
                                {identifier-8 }

           BY {literal-6    } UNTIL condition-3
              {identifier-9 }
```

The statement to replace the three PERFORM statements in the last example is

```
PERFORM SUBRTN-3 VARYING SUB-1 FROM 1 BY 1
    UNTIL SUB-1 > 10
    AFTER SUB-2 FROM 1 BY 1 UNTIL SUB-2 > 10.
    AFTER SUB-3 FROM 1 BY 1 UNTIL SUB-3 > 10.
```

Flowcharts depicting the logic of the PERFORM ... VARYING statement with one and two AFTER phrases are presented in Figs. 10.1 and 10.2, respectively.

Particular attention should be given to the fact, as illustrated in the flowcharts, that a PERFORM ... VARYING statement with one or more AFTER phrases performs in exactly the same way as the nested PERFORM ... statements introduced in the first example. Several advantages are gained through the use of the AFTER phrase:

The statement encountered initially makes it clear that a multidimensional table is being processed.

There is no need to search for three subroutines, since this form of the PERFORM ... VARYING statement requires only one.

The code that is produced is much clearer to read. Such code is the mark of a good programmer.

10.6 EXAMPLE8—A Program to Print an Appointment Calendar

In order to illustrate the use of multidimensional tables, we have written an example that will print a calendar of appointments for the coming week. It might be used by anyone that has regularly scheduled appointments, such as a doctor or administrator. The program accepts as input an initial **date record,**

FIGURE 10.1 The logic of the PERFORM . . . VARYING statement (one AFTER phrase).

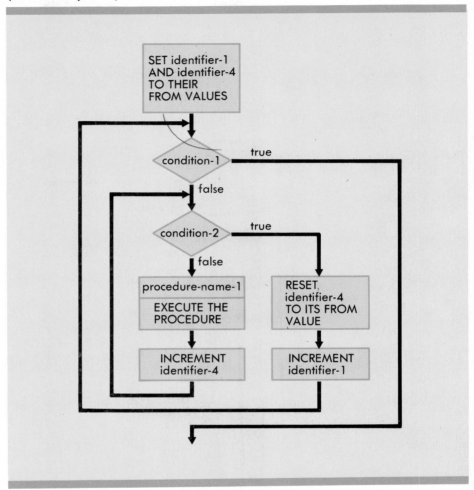

followed by input records that represent scheduled appointments. The use of two distinct types of input records forces (or at least strongly motivates) the use of the DATA RECORDS ARE clause in the file definition for the input file.

The date record will contain the date of the first day in the week. The date will occur in the first eight columns of the record. The remaining input records contain the fields defining a scheduled appointment: the name, day, time slot, and reason for the appointment. The day is specified as a two-character code, which causes a table lookup to be required to change the code into a subscript for the specified day (thus, TH would be used to determine that the appointment was scheduled for the 4th day of the week). Each day is broken up into 16 half-hour time slots, which are numbered from 1 to 16. These correspond to appointments from 8:30 A.M. through 4:00 P.M. Figure 10.3 presents an example of the output of the program.

The logic for the program is depicted in Figs. 10.4–10.8. The actual program follows the flowcharts. The output in Fig. 10.3 was produced by submitting the following records as input to the program.

FIGURE 10.2   The logic of the PERFORM . . . VARYING statement (two AFTER phrases).

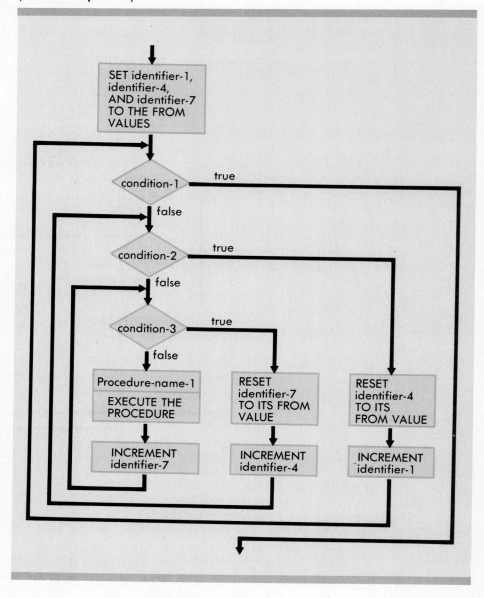

```
11/14/83
MARY BAKER            M 02SCHEDULING CONFLICT
JOHN LOOMIS           M 04MIDTERM
GARY ADAMS            T 12DISCUSS EXCHANGES
CAROL MATSON          M 11EVALUATE TESTS
RICHARD MATSUMOTO     M 06DISC. COMPUTER USAGE
CASPER MARTIN         TH03EVALUATE TESTS
MARY LINDHOLM         T 14CREATE FINAL EXAM
JOHN LOOMIS           T 16RESCHEDULED MIDTERM
JOAN SORENSEN         F 01REVIEW PRES. VISIT
CATHERINE WILLIAMS    F 03RETAKE FINAL EXAM
```

FIGURE 10.3   Sample output from EXAMPLE8.

```
                                    APPOINTMENTS

                          FOR THE WEEK OF NOVEMBER 14, 1983


                    MONDAY          TUESDAY      WEDNESDAY      THURSDAY          FRIDAY

                                                                             JOAN SORENSEN
    8:30                                                                      REVIEW PRES. VISIT


    9:00     MARY BAKER
             SCHEDULING CONFLICT

                                                             CASPER MARTIN    CATHERINE WILLIAMS
    9:30                                                     EVALUATE TESTS   RETAKE FINAL EXAM


   10:00     JOHN LOOMIS
             MIDTERM

   10:30


   11:00     RICHARD MATSUMOTO
             DISC. COMPUTER USAGE

   11:30

   12:00

   12:30

    1:00

    1:30     CAROL MATSON
             EVALUATE TESTS


    2:00                     GARY ADAMS
                             DISCUSS EXCHANGES


    2:30

    3:00                     MARY LINDHOLM
                             CREATE FINAL EXAM


    3:30

    4:00                     JOHN LOOMIS
                             RESCHEDULED MIDTERM
```

We have omitted flowcharts for the subroutines 10-EMPTY-A-SLOT, 20-READ-INPUT, 30-PROCESS-A-RECORD, 50-GET-DAY, 80-MOVE-NAMES, and 90-MOVE-REASONS, because they are essentially trivial. In addition, we have not explicitly shown all of the loops controlled by a PERFORM ... VARYING; that is, we occasionally have used a single block showing a call to a subroutine to represent a loop in which the subroutine is called a fixed number of times.

FIGURE 10.4 The logic of EXAMPLE8.

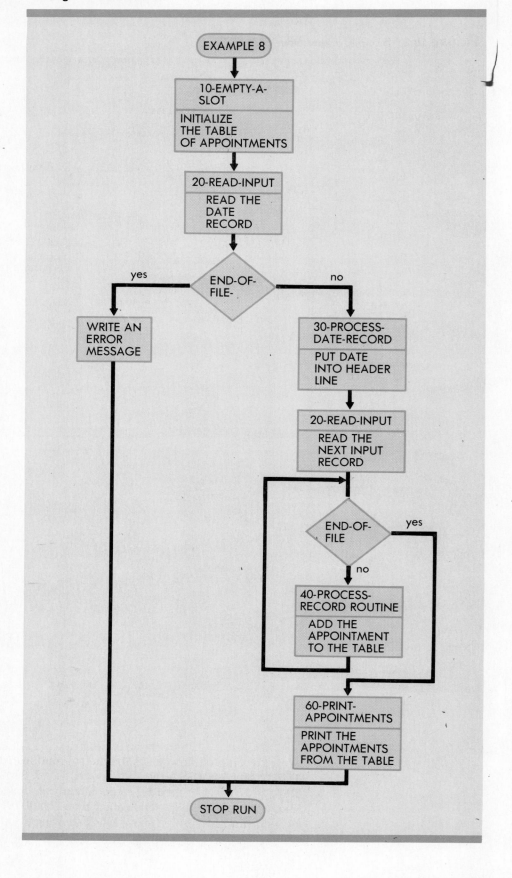

FIGURE 10.5   The logic of EXAMPLE8.

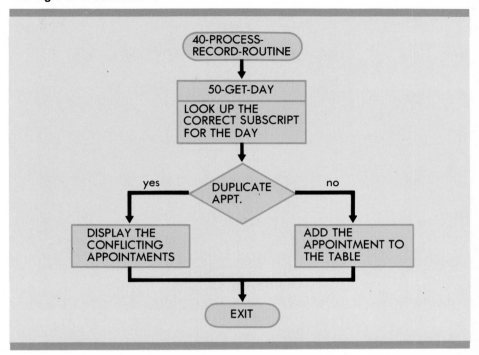

FIGURE 10.6   The logic of EXAMPLE8.

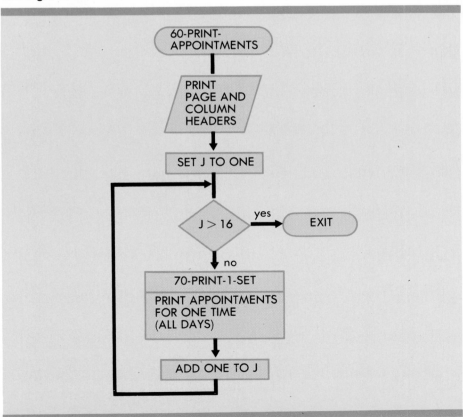

FIGURE 10.7   The logic of EXAMPLE8.

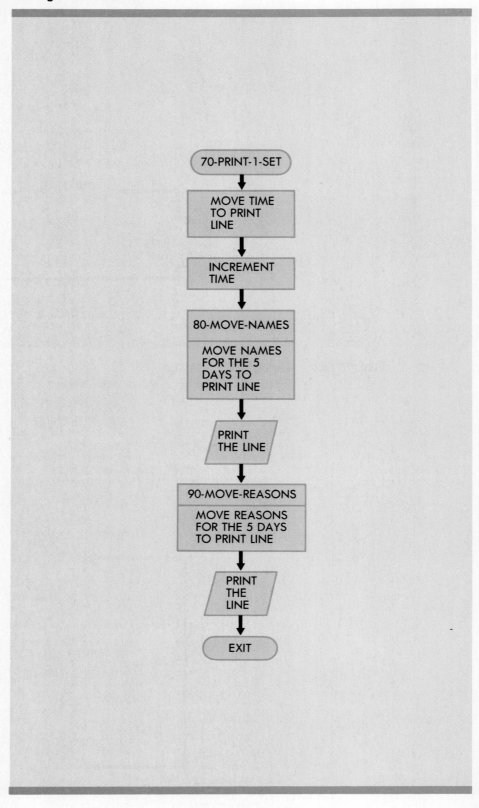

FIGURE 10.8   EXAMPLE8—a program to generate an appointment calendar.

```
IDENTIFICATION DIVISION.
PROGRAM-ID. EXAMPLE8.
AUTHOR. W E SINGLETARY.

*******************************************************************
*
* THIS PROGRAM IS USED TO DISPLAY APPOINTMENTS FOR 1 WEEK.  IT
* READS IN A "DATE RECORD" AS THE FIRST INPUT RECORD.  THIS
* RECORD CONTAINS JUST THE DATE OF MONDAY (SO A HEADER OF
* THE FORM
*
*               WEEK OF NOVEMBER  12, 1983
*
* CAN BE PRINTED).  AFTER THE DATE RECORD, THERE CAN BE ANY
* NUMBER OF RECORDS, EACH OF WHICH REPRESENTS A SINGLE
* APPOINTMENT.  ONCE ALL OF THE APPOINTMENT RECORDS HAVE
* BEEN READ, THEN ALL OF THE APPOINTMENTS FOR THE WEEK ARE
* DISPLAYED.
*
*******************************************************************

ENVIRONMENT DIVISION.

CONFIGURATION SECTION.
SOURCE-COMPUTER. IBM-370.
OBJECT-COMPUTER. IBM-370.

SPECIAL-NAMES.
    C01 IS TOP-OF-PAGE.

INPUT-OUTPUT SECTION.
FILE-CONTROL.

    SELECT INPUT-FILE ASSIGN TO UR-S-SYSIN.
    SELECT OUTPUT-FILE ASSIGN TO UR-S-SYSPRINT.
```

continued

FIGURE 10.8 Continued

```
 DATA DIVISION.
 FILE SECTION.

****************************************************************
*
* THIS FILE IS USED TO READ THE INPUT RECORDS.  THE FIRST
* RECORD IS THE DATE RECORD.  IT SHOULD CONTAIN A DATE OF
* THE FORM MM/DD/YY IN THE FIRST 8 COLUMNS.  ALL OF THE
* REMAINING RECORDS REPRESENT SINGLE APPOINTMENTS.  EACH
* APPOINTMENT SPECIFIES
*
*    A) A NAME
*    B) A DAY OF THE WEEK (M, T, W, TH, F).  HERE SINGLE
*       LETTER CODES SHOULD BE FOLLOWED BY A BLANK.
*    C) AN APPOINTMENT SLOT.  THE DAY FROM 8:30AM TO 4:30PM
*       IS DIVIDED INTO 16 HALF-HOUR SLOTS.
*    D) A NOTE INDICATING THE REASON FOR THE APPOINTMENT
*
****************************************************************

 FD   INPUT-FILE
      LABEL RECORDS ARE OMITTED
      DATA RECORDS ARE DATE-RECORD, APPT-RECORD.

 01   DATE-RECORD.
      05   DATE-OF-MONDAY.
           10   MM          PIC 99.
           10   FILLER      PIC X.
           10   DD          PIC 99.
           10   FILLER      PIC X.
           10   YY          PIC 99.
      05   FILLER           PIC X(72).

 01   APPT-RECORD.
      05   NAME-IN          PIC X(20).
      05   DAY-CODE         PIC XX.
      05   SLOT             PIC 99.
      05   REASON-IN        PIC X(20).
      05   FILLER           PIC X(36).
```

```
****************************************************************
*
* THIS FILE IS USED TO PRINT THE APPOINTMENTS.  ONLY A SINGLE
* PAGE IS PRINTED, WITH A SEPARATE COLUMN FOR EACH OF THE
* DAYS (MONDAY - FRIDAY).
*
****************************************************************

  FD  OUTPUT-FILE
      LABEL RECORDS ARE OMITTED
      DATA RECORD IS PRINT-BUFF.

  01  PRINT-BUFF                 PIC X(133).

  WORKING-STORAGE SECTION.

****************************************************************
*
* EOF-FLAG IS SET TO 'Y' WHEN END-OF-FILE OCCURS.
*
* MONTH-TABLE IS USED TO CONVERT THE MONTH NUMBER INTO A
*     MORE READABLE VERSION IN THE PAGE HEADERS
*
* DAY-CODE-TABLE IS USED TO CONVERT THE 2-CHARACTER DAY
*     CODES INTO NUMBERS FROM 1-5 (SUBSCRIPTS INTO THE
*     APPOINTMENT TABLE).
*
* APPOINTMENT-TABLE CONTAINS THE APPOINTMENTS FOR THE WEEK.
*
* I AND J ARE USED AS SUBSCRIPTS.
*
* APPT-TIME GIVES THE TIME OF THE NEXT APPOINTMENT
*
* PRINT-LINE IS USED TO BUILD THE LINES TO BE PRINTED.
*
* PAGE-HEADER-1, PAGE-HEADER-2, AND COLUMN-HEADER ARE USED
*     TO PRINT HEADERS ON THE PAGE.
*
*
****************************************************************

  01  FLAGS.
      05  EOF-FLAG               PIC X      VALUE IS 'N'.
          88  EOF-HAS-OCCURRED              VALUE IS 'Y'.
```

continued

FIGURE 10.8 Continued

```
01  MONTH-TABLE.
    05  FILLER                  PIC X(9)   VALUE IS 'JANUARY'.
    05  FILLER                  PIC X(9)   VALUE IS 'FEBRUARY'.
    05  FILLER                  PIC X(9)   VALUE IS 'MARCH'.
    05  FILLER                  PIC X(9)   VALUE IS 'APRIL'.
    05  FILLER                  PIC X(9)   VALUE IS 'MAY'.
    05  FILLER                  PIC X(9)   VALUE IS 'JUNE'.
    05  FILLER                  PIC X(9)   VALUE IS 'JULY'.
    05  FILLER                  PIC X(9)   VALUE IS 'AUGUST'.
    05  FILLER                  PIC X(9)   VALUE IS 'SEPTEMBER'.
    05  FILLER                  PIC X(9)   VALUE IS 'OCTOBER'.
    05  FILLER                  PIC X(9)   VALUE IS 'NOVEMBER'.
    05  FILLER                  PIC X(9)   VALUE IS 'DECEMBER'.
01  MONTH-ACCESS                REDEFINES MONTH-TABLE.
    05  MONTH                   PIC X(9) OCCURS 12 TIMES.

01  DAY-CODE-TABLE.
    05  FILLER                  PIC X(2)   VALUE IS 'M'.
    05  FILLER                  PIC X(2)   VALUE IS 'T'.
    05  FILLER                  PIC X(2)   VALUE IS 'W'.
    05  FILLER                  PIC X(2)   VALUE IS 'TH'.
    05  FILLER                  PIC X(2)   VALUE IS 'F'.
01  DAY-ACCESS                  REDEFINES DAY-CODE-TABLE.
    05  DAY-CD                  PIC X(2) OCCURS 5 TIMES.

01  APPOINTMENT-TABLE.
    05  APPT-FOR-1-DAY          OCCURS 5 TIMES.
        10  ONE-APPT            OCCURS 16 TIMES.
            15  NAME            PIC X(20).
            15  REASON          PIC X(20).

01  SUBSCRIPTS.
    05  I                       PIC 99.
    05  J                       PIC 99.

01  APPT-TIME.
    05  NEXT-HOUR               PIC 99     VALUE IS 8.
    05  NEXT-MINUTES            PIC 99     VALUE IS 30.

01  PRINT-LINE.
    05  FILLER                  PIC X(1).
    05  APPT-TIME-OUT.
        10  APPT-HOUR           PIC Z9.
        10  APPT-COLON          PIC X.
        10  APPT-MINUTES        PIC 99.
    05  FILLER                  PIC X(3).
    05  ONE-COLUMN              OCCURS 5 TIMES.
        10  NAME-OR-REASON-OUT PIC X(20).
        10  FILLER              PIC X(2).
```

```
01  PAGE-HEADER-1.
    05  FILLER              PIC X(1).
    05  FILLER              PIC X(48) VALUE IS SPACES.
    05  FILLER              PIC X(23) VALUE IS
    'A P P O I N T M E N T S'.

01  PAGE-HEADER-2.
    05  FILLER              PIC X(43) VALUE IS SPACES.
    05  FILLER              PIC X(16) VALUE IS
                            'FOR THE WEEK OF'.
    05  MONTH-OUT           PIC X(9).
    05  FILLER              PIC X      VALUE IS SPACES.
    05  DD-OUT              PIC Z9.
    05  FILLER              PIC X(2)  VALUE IS ', '.
    05  YYYY-OUT.
        10  YY-FIRST-2      PIC X(2)  VALUE IS '19'.
        10  YY-OUT          PIC 99.

01  COLUMN-HEADER.
    05  FILLER              PIC X(12) VALUE IS SPACES.
    05  FILLER              PIC X(22) VALUE IS 'MONDAY'.
    05  FILLER              PIC X(22) VALUE IS 'TUESDAY'.
    05  FILLER              PIC X(22) VALUE IS 'WEDNESDAY'.
    05  FILLER              PIC X(22) VALUE IS 'THURSDAY'.
    05  FILLER              PIC X(22) VALUE IS 'FRIDAY'.


PROCEDURE DIVISION.
    OPEN INPUT INPUT-FILE
        OUTPUT OUTPUT-FILE.

    PERFORM 10-EMPTY-A-SLOT VARYING I FROM 1 BY 1 UNTIL I > 5
            AFTER J FROM 1 BY 1 UNTIL J > 16.

    PERFORM 20-READ-INPUT.
    IF EOF-HAS-OCCURRED
        MOVE ' *** EMPTY INPUT FILE ***' TO PRINT-BUFF
        WRITE PRINT-BUFF AFTER ADVANCING TOP-OF-PAGE
    ELSE
        PERFORM 30-PROCESS-DATE-RECORD
        PERFORM 20-READ-INPUT
        PERFORM 40-PROCESS-RECORD-ROUTINE
            UNTIL EOF-HAS-OCCURRED
        PERFORM 60-PRINT-APPOINTMENTS.

    CLOSE INPUT-FILE
        OUTPUT-FILE.

    STOP RUN.
```

continued

FIGURE 10.8 Continued

```
     ***********************************************************
     *
     * THIS ROUTINE INITIALIZES AN ENTRY IN THE APPOINTMENT-TABLE
     * TO ALL SPACES.
     *
     ***********************************************************

      10-EMPTY-A-SLOT.
          MOVE SPACES TO NAME (I, J).
          MOVE SPACES TO REASON (I, J).

     ***********************************************************
     *
     * THIS ROUTINE READS INPUT RECORDS, SETTING EOF-FLAG TO 'Y'
     * WHEN END-OF-FILE OCCURS.
     *
     ***********************************************************

      20-READ-INPUT.
          READ INPUT-FILE AT END MOVE 'Y' TO EOF-FLAG.

     ***********************************************************
     *
     * THIS ROUTINE PROCESSES THE DATE RECORD.  THIS SIMPLY AMOUNTS
     * TO CONVERTING THE MONTH AND YEAR INTO THE FORMS REQUIRED
     * FOR THE PAGE HEADER AND MOVING THE VALUES INTO THE HEADER.
     *
     ***********************************************************

      30-PROCESS-DATE-RECORD.
          MOVE MONTH (MM) TO MONTH-OUT.
          MOVE DD TO DD-OUT.
          MOVE YY TO YY-OUT.
```

```
****************************************************************
*
* THIS ROUTINE PROCESSES THE INPUT RECORD THAT HAS ALREADY BEEN
* READ AND THEN ATTEMPTS TO READ THE NEXT RECORD.
*
****************************************************************

 40-PROCESS-RECORD-ROUTINE.
     PERFORM 50-GET-DAY VARYING I FROM 1 BY 1
         UNTIL DAY-CODE = DAY-CD (I).

     IF NAME (I, SLOT) = SPACES
         MOVE NAME-IN TO NAME (I, SLOT)
         MOVE REASON-IN TO REASON (I, SLOT)
     ELSE
         DISPLAY 'BOTH ' NAME-IN ' AND ' NAME (I, SLOT)
                 ' ARE SCHEDULED FOR ' DAY-CODE
                 ' SLOT ' SLOT.

     PERFORM 20-READ-INPUT.

****************************************************************
*
* THIS ROUTINE IS A NULL ROUTINE.  ALL OF THE SEARCHING
* LOGIC IS EXPRESSED IN THE PERFORM THAT INVOKES IT.
*
****************************************************************

 50-GET-DAY.
     EXIT.

****************************************************************
*
* THIS ROUTINE PRINTS THE PAGE OF APPOINTMENTS.
*
****************************************************************

 60-PRINT-APPOINTMENTS.
     WRITE PRINT-BUFF FROM PAGE-HEADER-1
         AFTER ADVANCING TOP-OF-PAGE.
     WRITE PRINT-BUFF FROM PAGE-HEADER-2
         AFTER ADVANCING 2 LINES.
     WRITE PRINT-BUFF FROM COLUMN-HEADER
         AFTER ADVANCING 3 LINES.

     MOVE SPACES TO PRINT-LINE.
     PERFORM 70-PRINT-1-SET VARYING J FROM 1 BY 1
         UNTIL J > 16.
```

continued

FIGURE 10.8   Continued

```
********************************************************************
*
* THIS ROUTINE PRINTS THE APPOINTMENTS FOR A GIVEN TIME OF THE
* DAY.
*
********************************************************************

  70-PRINT-1-SET.
      MOVE NEXT-HOUR TO APPT-HOUR.
      MOVE ':' TO APPT-COLON.
      MOVE NEXT-MINUTES TO APPT-MINUTES.
      IF NEXT-MINUTES = 30
          ADD 1 TO NEXT-HOUR
          MOVE 0 TO NEXT-MINUTES
      ELSE
          MOVE 30 TO NEXT-MINUTES.

      IF NEXT-HOUR > 12
          SUBTRACT 12 FROM NEXT-HOUR.

      PERFORM 80-MOVE-NAMES VARYING I FROM 1 BY 1
          UNTIL I > 5.
      WRITE PRINT-BUFF FROM PRINT-LINE
          AFTER ADVANCING 2.

      MOVE SPACES TO APPT-TIME-OUT.
      PERFORM 90-MOVE-REASONS VARYING I FROM 1 BY 1
          UNTIL I > 5.
      WRITE PRINT-BUFF FROM PRINT-LINE
          AFTER ADVANCING 1.

********************************************************************
*
* THIS ROUTINE MOVES THE NAMES FOR APPTS AT A GIVEN TIME TO
* THE PRINT LINE.
*
********************************************************************

  80-MOVE-NAMES.
      MOVE NAME (I, J) TO NAME-OR-REASON-OUT (I).

********************************************************************
*
* THIS ROUTINE MOVES THE REASONS FOR APPTS AT A GIVEN TIME TO
* THE PRINT LINE.
*
********************************************************************

  90-MOVE-REASONS.
      MOVE REASON (I, J) TO NAME-OR-REASON-OUT (I).
```

S U M M A R Y

Level-numbers are used to indicate the hierarchical relationship of data items. They may take on values from 01 to 49. Normally, the values 01, 05, 10, 15, ... are used, with each higher level indented by four spaces.

When a file will be used to process records that can occur in several formats (i.e., there may be more than one type of record in the file), you should use DATA RECORDS ARE in the file description (followed by the multiple formats).

To assign alternate formats to the same area of storage you can use the REDEFINES clause. There are two common uses:

1. To specify alternate formats for portions of a single record, you can use a REDEFINES clause within a record description.

2. A REDEFINES clause can be used to create an initialized table.

A multidimensional table can be used to represent data in which a single table entry must itself include a table. When processing a multidimensional table, it is frequently convenient to use AFTER phrases in a PERFORM ... VARYING statement.

R E V I E W   Q U E S T I O N S

10.1 Why are level-numbers of 01, 05, 10, ... used, rather than 01, 02, 03, ...?

10.2 When you write a program that accesses a file containing records in several formats, you normally use DATA RECORDS ARE to specify the multiple formats. When an actual record has been read, how can the program determine the type of the record (i.e., which of the formats should be used to process the contents of the record)?

10.3 If you are using a REDEFINES clause to create an initialized table in working storage, should the definition with the OCCURS precede or follow the definition with the actual values? Does it matter?

10.4 You have seen that it is possible to use an AFTER phrase in a PERFORM ... VARYING to process the entries in a multidimensional table. Why might this practice be discouraged? (Some programmers do actually feel that the AFTER phrase should not be used in a PERFORM ... VARYING statement.)

P R O G R A M M I N G   E X E R C I S E S

10.1 Suppose that a company has five salespersons. The company keeps track of the sales made by each of these people for each of the 13 weeks in a quarter (i.e., a fiscal quarter of a year). Each week a single record is created for each of the salespersons, giving that person's sales for the previous week. Write a program that reads in these records as input (up to 5 × 13 = 65 records) and writes a sales report. The report should contain one line for each salesperson. This line should list the sales for each of the 13 weeks, as well as average sales per week (divide the total

COMPLEX CONDITIONS AND NESTED IF STATEMENTS

INTRODUCTION The tools that the COBOL language provides for making complex logical decisions are discussed in this chapter. Class tests are introduced in Section 11.1 as a means of performing basic editing of input data fields. The logical connectives and their use in expressing complex logical conditions are introduced and illustrated in Section 11.2.

Section 11.3 deals with the formation and evaluation of nested IF statements, which can, in many instances, be used as an alternative to complex conditions. The implementation of two patterns of logic that require the use of special techniques is also considered.

Several rather subtle errors that frequently occur in the implementation of the logic to express complex logical conditions are exposed in Section 11.4. Finally, EXAMPLE9 illustrates the use of most of the language elements and techniques covered in the earlier sections.

11.1 Class Tests for Numeric and Alphabetic Fields

The sample programs presented thus far have allowed the input of records that may have contained erroneous fields that could lead to the abnormal termination of program execution. For instance, a field described with a numeric PICTURE clause may actually have contained a nonnumeric character. As an example, suppose a field, AMOUNT, is described as follows:

```
05   AMOUNT              PIC 999V99.
```

This field can be read from an input record that contains alphabetic characters in some of the field positions. If this occurs, execution of the program will be abnormally terminated with an error message the first time an arithmetic operation involving AMOUNT is attempted.

Occasional data entry errors occur inevitably in an environment where thousands of records are entered daily. It is important that programs be written in such a way as to avoid the abnormal termination of execution when erroneous data is encountered. The following two statements should indicate just how important this can be.

1. The machine operator present when the program is executed may not be able to detect which field is invalid. Hence, a correction of the invalid input record and a rerun of the program may not be attempted. To an operator who has probably never written a COBOL program, an error message may seem cryptic at best.

2. In any event, the program must be run once in order to detect each such invalid input record. Thus, if a program is to process 10,000 input records, 20 of which contain invalid data, the correct output can be obtained only after the twenty-first run.

The COBOL language does provide a facility for detecting invalid characters in alphabetic as well as numeric fields. In practice, most programs are written in such a way that all numeric fields are verified on input. In the event an invalid character is detected, a detailed error message is printed and execution of the program is continued. This verification is accomplished by using an IF statement in the following format.

$$\underline{IF}\ field\text{-}1\ IS\ [\underline{NOT}] \left\{ \begin{array}{l} \underline{NUMERIC} \\ \underline{ALPHABETIC} \end{array} \right\} statement\text{-}1$$

A field is numeric if it contains only numeric digits and an operational sign, and a field is alphabetic if it contains only alphabetic characters and blanks. Thus, the statement

```
IF AMOUNT IS NOT NUMERIC
    PERFORM ERROR-ROUTINE.
```

has the effect of testing the contents of AMOUNT for the presence of characters other than digits. If such a character is detected, a branch is made to ERROR-ROUTINE and the processing is continued. In subsequent examples, a verification check will be present for each numeric field that is input.

The verification of alphabetic fields is not as useful as the verification of numeric fields. However, the statement

```
IF NAME IS NOT ALPHABETIC
    PERFORM BAD-NAME.
```

effects a branch to BAD-NAME in case a character other than an alphabetic character or a blank occurs in NAME.

For two reasons the verification of alphabetic fields is not as important as the verification of numeric fields.

1. An alphabetic field is not likely to be processed in such a way as to cause abnormal termination of the execution of a program in the case in which it contains an invalid character.

2. Name fields are often meant to contain periods and possibly other punctuation, such as hyphens. Obviously, such fields should not be verified to be alphabetic.

We shall present a more detailed discussion of editing input data in Chapter 15. For now, it is quite enough to understand how the class tests can be used to catch many common input errors.

11.2 Complex Conditions

Conditions are used in both PERFORM and IF statements. As we noted earlier, a condition can be either true or false. The conditions that we discussed before were all **simple conditions.** Actually, we have introduced three distinct types of simple conditions so far.

1. A **relation condition** causes two data items to be compared. For example,

    ```
    HOURS-WORKED > 40
    ```

    is a relation condition.

2. A **condition-name** causes a given data item to be tested to determine whether or not it has a specified value or a value in a specified range. The name and the specified value or value range are given in an 88-level item. For example, in EXAMPLE8 EOF-HAS-OCCURRED was a condition-name.

3. A **class** condition causes the test for alphabetic or numeric contents, as described in the last section. Thus,

    ```
    IF HOURS-WORKED IS NOT NUMERIC
        DISPLAY '*** INVALID HOURS WORKED ***'.
    ```

    uses a class test.

These simple conditions are adequate for most tests. However, you will find it necessary occasionally to be able to specify more complex conditions. For example, suppose that you wish to PERFORM the subroutine PROCESS-DATA only when both ERROR-FLAG and EOF-FLAG contain the character 'N'. To do this you would use

```
IF ERROR-FLAG = 'N' AND EOF-FLAG = 'N'
    PERFORM PROCESS-DATA.
```

Here we have an example of a complex condition formed with the AND operator. In general

```
condition-1 AND condition-2
```

is true only if both condition-1 and condition-2 are true. You can form complex conditions using several AND operators. Thus,

```
IF HOURS-WORKED IS NUMERIC AND
   WAGE-RATE IS NUMERIC AND
   SOC-SEC-NUM IS NUMERIC

   DISPLAY 'INPUT VALUES ARE OK'.
```

is an example of a complex condition constructed with two AND operators. If you wish, you can use parentheses to show grouping. For example, the previous condition might be given as

```
(HOURS-WORKED IS NUMERIC AND
 WAGE-RATE IS NUMERIC) AND
 SOC-SEC-NUM IS NUMERIC
```

If you are using several AND operators, it does not matter which way the conditions are grouped, so parentheses would not normally be used. You will see examples a little further on, however, in which the groupings do matter (involving both AND and OR operators).

The OR operator is used when you wish the condition to be true if either (or both) of two given conditions are true. For example, suppose that you wished to DISPLAY an error message if either the HOURS-WORKED or the WAGE-RATE field were not numeric. To do this you might use

```
IF HOURS-WORKED IS NOT NUMERIC OR
   WAGE-RATE IS NOT NUMERIC

   DISPLAY '*** INVALID INPUT VALUES ***'.
```

In general

```
condition-1 OR condition-2
```

is false only when both condition-1 and condition-2 are false. You can use several OR operators to build a complex condition that will be true unless all of the connected conditions are false. For example,

```
WAGE-RATE > 20.00 OR
HOURS-WORKED > 60 OR
HOURS-WORKED = 0
```

is a complex condition that is false only when each of the three connected conditions are false.

Before continuing, let's consider a number of complex conditions and how they would be evaluated. Throughout the rest of this section, we will need to refer to specific fields to illustrate the evaluation of conditions. Table 11.1 gives the field names and contents that we shall use.

Now consider the conditions in Table 11.2 and make sure you understand why each one evaluates to the value (true or false) that we show for it.

Sometimes it is necessary to construct a complex condition using both AND and OR operators. For example, suppose that you wished to print a warning message if the CASH-ON-HAND is below $600 and the DAY-IN is less than 26, or if CASH-ON-HAND is below $800 and DAY-IN is less than 16. To do this you might code

```
IF (CASH-ON-HAND < 600 AND DAY-IN < 26) OR
   (CASH-ON-HAND < 800 AND DAY-IN < 16)

   DISPLAY '*** WARNING CASH ON HAND IS TOO LOW ***'.
```

(handwritten margin note: "and both have to be true — or either or both")

Table 11.1

Field	Picture	Contents
ERROR-FLAG	X	N
EOF-FLAG	X	Y
CASH-ON-HAND	9(4)V99	0150V00
MONTH-IN	99	10
DAY-IN	99	28

Note that the parentheses make it clear exactly how to group the conditions. In this case the grouping really does matter, since

```
IF CASH-ON-HAND < 600 AND (DAY-IN < 26 OR
       CASH-ON-HAND < 800) AND DAY-IN < 16

       DISPLAY '*** WARNING CASH ON HAND IS TOO LOW ***'.
```

will cause the warning message to be printed only if CASH-ON-HAND is below $600. In general, you should always use parentheses if a complex condition contains both AND and OR operators. People frequently find it difficult to evaluate complex conditions, so we recommend that you study the examples in Table 11.3 carefully. To evaluate a complex expression, first evaluate the simple conditions. Then work "from the inside out."

There is one more logical operator that you can use to construct complex conditions—the NOT operator. In general

```
NOT condition-1
```

evaluates to true if condition-1 is false (and to false if condition-1 is true).

Table 11.2

Condition	Value
EOF-FLAG = 'N' AND MONTH-IN > 5	False
EOF-FLAG = 'N' OR MONTH-IN > 5	True
CASH-ON-HAND > 100.00 AND MONTH-IN > 6 AND MONTH-IN IS NOT = 12	True
DAY-IN > 0 AND DAY-IN < 32	True
MONTH-IN = 0 OR MONTH-IN > 12	False

Table 11.3

Condition	Value
(EOF-FLAG = 'N' AND MONTH-IN > 5) OR (EOF-FLAG = 'Y' AND MONTH-IN < 11)	True
(EOF-FLAG = 'N' OR MONTH-IN > 5) AND (EOF-FLAG = 'Y' OR MONTH-IN < 11)	True
(CASH-ON-HAND > 100.00 AND MONTH-IN > 10) OR (CASH-ON-HAND < 200.00 AND MONTH-IN > 11)	False
(DAY-IN > 0 AND DAY-IN < 32) OR ERROR-FLAG = 'Y'	True
(MONTH-IN = 0 OR MONTH-IN > 12) AND ERROR-FLAG = 'Y'	False

Thus,

```
IF NOT (ERROR-FLAG = 'N' AND EOF-FLAG = 'N')
    DISPLAY '*** WARNING - ERROR OR EOF OCCURRED ***'.
```

is equivalent to

```
IF ERROR-FLAG IS NOT = 'N' OR EOF-FLAG IS NOT = 'N'
    DISPLAY '*** WARNING - ERROR OR EOF OCCURRED ***'.
```

In either case the message will be printed if either flag is set to 'Y'. Now consider a few more examples, as shown in Table 11.4.

Let us summarize the rules that we have presented.

Rule 1 Simple conditions can be evaluated by examining, and perhaps comparing, the contents of particular data items.

Rule 2 Complex conditions can be constructed from simple conditions and the logical operators AND, OR, and NOT. The rules for evaluating a condition built from these operators are as follows:

Table 11.4

Condition	Value
NOT (EOF-FLAG = 'N' AND MONTH-IN < 5)	True
(EOF-FLAG = 'N' OR MONTH-IN > 5) AND (NOT (EOF-FLAG = 'Y' OR MONTH-IN < 11))	False
NOT (CASH-ON-HAND < 50 OR CASH-ON-HAND > 500)	True

    a) (condition-1 AND condition-2) is true exactly when condition-1 and condition-2 are both true.

    b) (condition-1 OR condition-2) is true if either or both of the connected conditions is true.

    c) (NOT condition) is true if condition is false. If condition is true, then (NOT condition) is false.

Rule 3   Use parentheses to clarify exactly how a complex condition is to be evaluated if more than one type of logical operator occurs in the condition.

11.3 Nested IF Statements

Recall that in Chapter 7 the following format for the IF statement was discussed.

```
IF condition statement-1 ELSE statement-2
```

where

1. **Condition** is a conditional statement.
2. **Statement-1** is one or more COBOL statements.
3. **Statement-2** is one or more COBOL statements.

Attention is directed to the fact that no restrictions are placed on the statements that make up statement-1 and statement-2. This allows the possibility that statement-1, or statement-2, or both may contain conditional statements. These possibilities will be explored in this section. In that discussion statement-1 will sometimes be referred to as the IF block and condition-2 as the ELSE block. When an IF statement contains embedded IF statements, it is referred to as a **nested IF statement.**

Perhaps the simplest example of a nested IF statement is provided by an IF statement without an ELSE phrase, which contains an IF statement that also contains no ELSE phrase. Such a statement may be abstractly represented by

```
IF C1
    IF C2
        S1.
```

In this example C1 and C2 represent conditions and S1 represents a statement or IF block. In the following discussion it will be convenient, for purposes of exposition, to use the symbols S1, S2, ... to represent statements and the symbols C1, C2, ... to represent conditions.

A **flowchart** representing the logic of this statement is presented in Fig. 11.1. It should be noted that the condition C1 is evaluated and if this yields a value of true condition C2 is evaluated. Finally, the statement S1 is executed only if both S1 and S2 are true.

You may have noticed that this statement could be replaced with the single IF statement represented by

```
IF C1 AND C2
    S1.
```

In the vast majority of cases, this type of replacement of a nested IF statement by one or more simple IF statements containing complex logical conditions

FIGURE 11.1   A nested IF structure (first example).

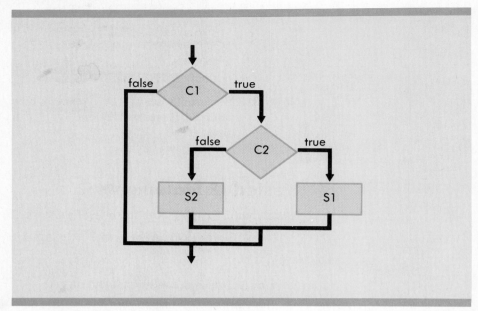

will yield equivalent logic. Beware, however, there are unusual situations in which the logic will not be the same. Some of these cases are covered in Section 11.4.

The matter of whether nested IF statements or IF statements with compound logical conditions should be used is largely a matter of taste. However, for most programmers, the decision of which to use is influenced by a set of programming standards provided by the development environment. Some of the standards manuals that we have seen over the years have contained restrictions such as

1. No more than three logical connectives may be used in a complex logical condition.
2. IF statements may not be nested to a depth greater than two.

As a programmer you must comply with the constraints that are imposed by the standards manual to which you are subject. But, if no such restrictions are imposed, avoid writing nested IF statements or complex logical conditions that are so complex as to render them inordinately difficult to comprehend. Such statements lead to programs that are difficult to check for programming errors and difficult to maintain because others may find it a tough job to follow the logic.

Two rules are of particular importance when writing or determining the effect of nested IF statements.

Rule 1   The scope of an IF block extends to its paired ELSE phrase or until the end of the sentence if no ELSE is encountered. The scope of an ELSE block extends to the end of the sentence. (Recall that a sentence is terminated with a period followed by a space.)

Rule 2   Each ELSE phrase is paired with the immediately preceding IF which has not already been paired with an ELSE phrase.

In documenting nested IF statements we will follow the convention of indenting each nested IF statement four spaces with respect to the immediately preceding IF statement to which it applies. ELSE phrases will be aligned with the IF statements to which they apply.

A slightly more complicated example will serve to illustrate the importance of the first of the two rules just given. Consider the following statement:

```
IF C1
    IF C2
        S1
    ELSE
        S2.
```

The logic of this statement is depicted in Fig. 11.2.

This same logic could be realized without the use of a nested IF statement as follows:

```
IF C1 AND C2
    S1.
IF C1 AND NOT C2
    S2.
```

Suppose, however, that the period were omitted at the end of the first of the two IF statements. Then, the indentation just employed would not reflect the logic of the resulting statement, which would be properly indented as follows:

```
IF C1 AND C2
    S1
    IF C1 AND NOT C2
        S2.
```

The logic for this statement is represented by the flowchart in Fig. 11.3. This flowchart should be studied in enough detail so that you understand that, in

FIGURE 11.2 Nested IF structure (second example).

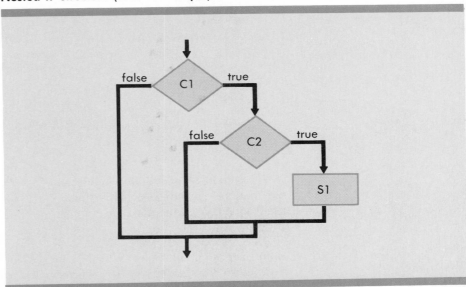

FIGURE 11.3   Nested IF structure (third example).

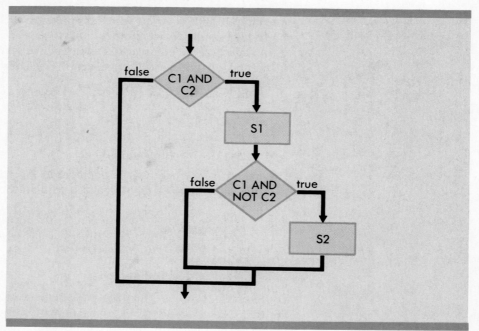

this case, the statements in S2 could never be executed. The moral is that the omission of periods can lead to logical errors that may be difficult to trace. This should also serve to emphasize the point that the function of the compiler is in no way influenced by indentation. In fact, as we will illustrate later, the compiler treats these statements exactly as it would if they were written on a single line.

A somewhat more complicated pattern of logic which frequently arises is presented in Fig. 11.4. This logic can be expressed in COBOL with a statement of the following form:

```
IF C1
        IF C2
                S1
        ELSE
                S2
ELSE
        IF C3
                S3
        ELSE
                S4.
```

If you have any doubt about whether the use of indentation and the convention of writing each individual statement on a different line improves the readability of program listings, consider the following form of this statement.

```
IF C1 IF C2 S1 ELSE S2 ELSE IF C3 S3 ELSE S4.
```

Both of these versions are syntactically correct; the compiler simply does not distinguish the difference. However, the first version is by far the simpler of the two for a human to comprehend at a glance.

FIGURE 11.4 Nested IF structure (fourth example).

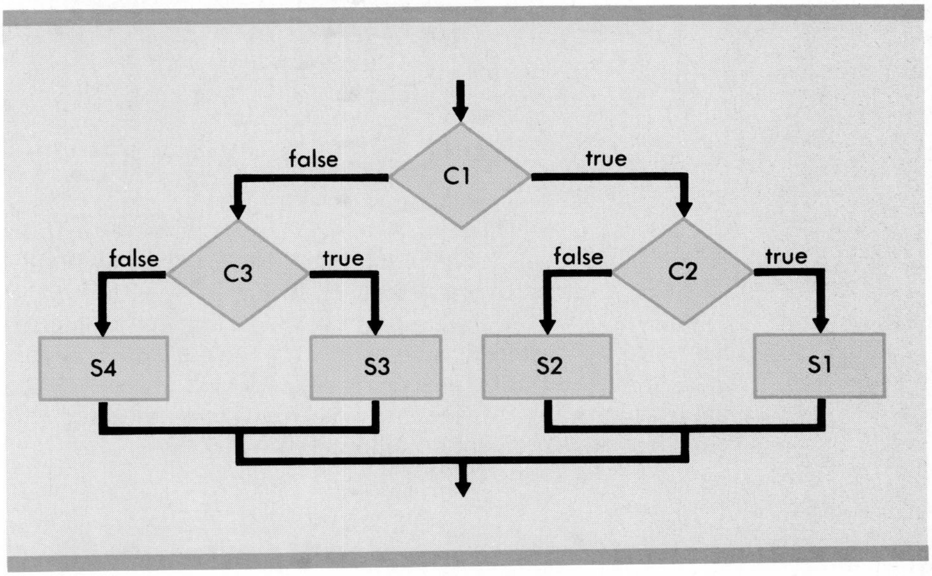

Another pattern of logic which is not uncommon is one that requires an imperative statement preceding an IF statement in either the IF or the ELSE block of an outer IF statement. An example of this form of logic is given in Fig. 11.5. This pattern of logic may be easily implemented in COBOL by a statement such as the following:

FIGURE 11.5 Nested IF structure (fifth example).

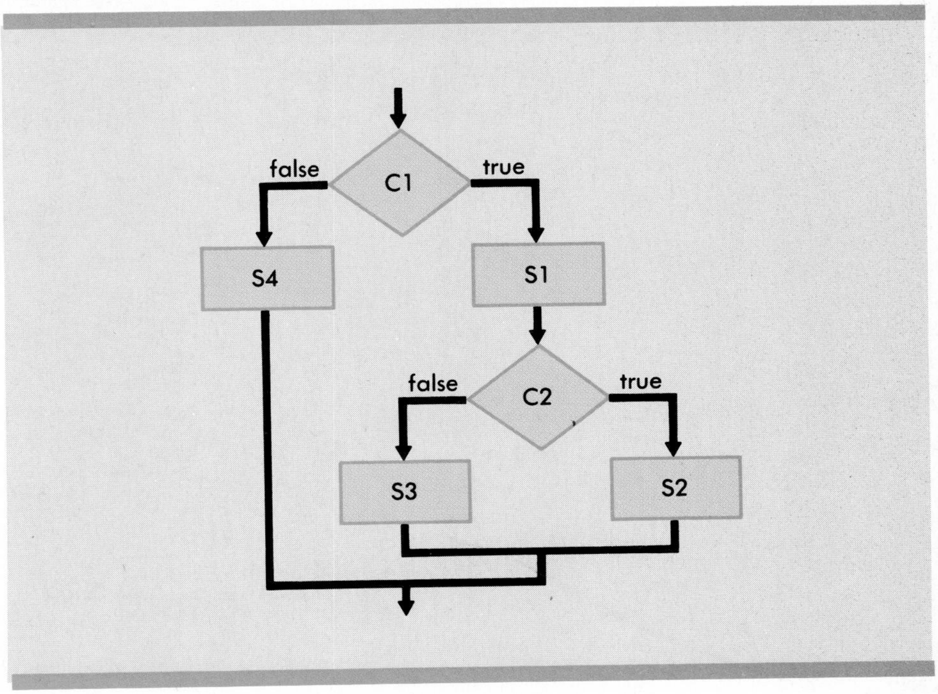

```
IF C1
     S1
     IF C2
          S2
     ELSE
          S3
ELSE
     S4.
```

There are a couple of patterns of logic which, because of the rule that deals with the pairing of ELSE phrases with IF's, require special attention. The first of these is given in Fig. 11.6.

It is a useful exercise to attempt to implement this logic directly by using nested IF statements. A problem arises, however, in the fact that this forces S3 to be executed only in the IF or the ELSE block of the inner IF statement. This problem can be easily circumvented through the use of a PERFORM statement as follows:

```
IF C1
          PERFORM INNER-DECISION-CONSTRUCT
          S3
     ELSE
          S4.
              .
              .
              .

INNER-DECISION-CONSTRUCT.
     IF C2
          S1
     ELSE
          S2.
```

FIGURE 11.6   **Nested IF structure (sixth example).**

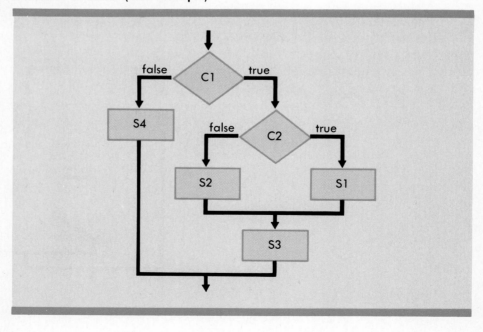

FIGURE 11.7   Nested IF structure (seventh example).

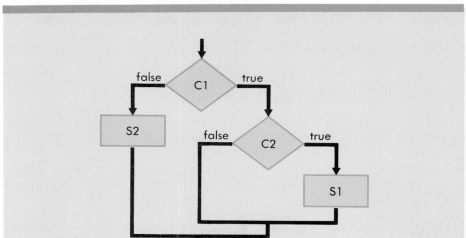

The other pattern of logic that we wished to consider has the form shown in Fig. 11.7. The problem here is that the ELSE phrase that must be paired with the outer IF statement will be paired with the inner IF statement, which contains no ELSE phrase. Try it!

The designers of COBOL foresaw this difficulty and allowed the words NEXT SENTENCE to be substituted for either the IF or the ELSE block of an IF statement. If the NEXT SENTENCE branch is taken, control is passed to the statement immediately following the IF statement. Thus the following statement would implement the logic of Fig. 11.7.

```
IF C1
      IF C2
            S1
      ELSE

            NEXT SENTENCE
ELSE
      S2.
```

Several subtle errors that can occur when complex conditions are used in IF statements are discussed in the next section.

11.4 Subtle Errors That Arise in the Use of Complex Conditions

There are a few subtle errors that are commonly made in the use of conditional expressions. The first class of such errors are violations of the following rule:

> When a complex condition is evaluated, every simple condition contained in the complex condition must be capable of evaluation.

For example, in Chapter 8 we presented a simple program to balance a checkbook.

The first input record processed by the program is supposed to contain a 'B' in column 1 (to indicate that the record is the "balance record" that gives the starting balance in the checking account). In that program we did not check for all possible input errors. We did check for an empty input file, but we did not check for a missing balance record. Now that we have explained the importance of editing input data, you should understand why such checks are required. The following code might be considered as a way to check for a missing balance record.

```
IF EOF-HAS-OCCURRED OR (TYPE-CODE NOT = 'B')
    MOVE ' *** MISSING BALANCE RECORD ***'
        TO PRINT-BUFF
    WRITE PRINT-BUFF AFTER ADVANCING TOP-OF-PAGE
ELSE
    normal processing
```

[handwritten note: Mutually exclusive situations so split up and make simple.]

There is a serious error in this code. In the case in which end-of-file has occurred, only one of the two simple conditions can be evaluated. That is, if end-of-file has occurred, then the condition (TYPE-CODE NOT = 'B') is neither true nor false. It cannot be evaluated, since the field TYPE-CODE refers to a field in the current input record. The proper way to check for a missing balance record would be

```
IF EOF-HAS-OCCURRED
    MOVE ' *** EMPTY INPUT FILE ***'
        TO PRINT-BUFF
    WRITE PRINT-BUFF AFTER ADVANCING TOP-OF-PAGE
ELSE
    IF TYPE-CODE NOT = 'B'
        MOVE ' *** MISSING BALANCE RECORD'
            TO PRINT-BUFF
        WRITE PRINT-BUFF AFTER ADVANCING TOP-OF-PAGE
    ELSE
        normal processing
```

Here the condition (TYPE-CODE NOT = 'B') will be evaluated only when end-of-file has not yet occurred.

A similar problem can occur when you are searching a table for a specified value. For example, consider the example in Chapter 10, EXAMPLE8. There we gave a program that printed out a person's appointments for one week. The following section of code was given to convert the abbreviation for a day into a subscript in the range 1 to 5.

```
PERFORM 40-GET-DAY VARYING I FROM 1 BY 1
    UNTIL DAY-CODE = DAY-CD (I).
            .
            .
            .
40-GET-DAY.
    EXIT.
```

This code works quite well, as long as the value in DAY-CODE actually occurs in the table. If it does not, however, the program will fail. To correct this, one might be tempted to use the following code:

```
        PERFORM 40-GET-DAY VARYING I FROM 1 BY 1
            UNTIL (I > 5) OR (DAY-CODE = DAY-CD (I)).
        IF I > 5
            error processing
        ELSE
            normal processing
            .
            .
            .
    40-GET-DAY.
        EXIT.
```

This code fails, because (DAY-CODE = DAY-CD (I)) cannot be evaluated when
I > 5. The proper way to make the check is as follows:

```
        PERFORM 40-GET-DAY VARYING I FROM 1 BY 1
            UNTIL (I = 5) OR (DAY-CODE = DAY-CD (I)).
        IF DAY-CODE NOT = DAY-CD (I)
            error processing
        ELSE
            normal processing
            .
            .
            .
    40-GET-DAY.
        EXIT.
```

Before leaving this class of error, it is worth pointing out that many COBOL
compilers will actually generate code that "works" for each of the two errors
we have pointed out. This has caused many programmers to become sloppy
about checking for such errors. A program may thus run for several years and
then fail when a new version of the COBOL compiler is used to compile it.
You should be very careful to write only conditional expressions that you are
certain will always evaluate properly.

Another common error involves the use of an AT END phrase on a READ
statement. Consider the following code:

```
    IF NOT EOF-HAS-OCCURRED
        READ INPUT-FILE AT END MOVE 'Y' TO EOF-FLAG
        PERFORM 10-PROCESS-RECORD UNTIL EOF-HAS-OCCURRED.

    PERFORM 20-PROCESS-TOTALS.
```

[handwritten annotation left:] Read in the Middle of an if. Read is considered part of an imperative, Perform will be done only after no further records are read.

[handwritten annotation right:] Perform statement will be considered part of at end phrase.

Suppose that the programmer intended this code to check for end-of-file, and
then to read and process records until end-of-file occurs. Will this code work?
The answer is no. In the case in which end-of-file has not yet occurred, no
further records will be read. This happens because the statement

```
    PERFORM 10-PROCESS-RECORD UNTIL EOF-HAS-OCCURRED
```

is considered to be part of the AT END phrase. The AT END phrase is terminated
by the next period. In cases where this problem can arise, we recommend
creating a separate, small routine to read records. For example, the following
code works.

```
IF NOT EOF-HAS-OCCURRED
   PERFORM 5-READ-ROUTINE
   PERFORM 10-PROCESS-RECORD UNTIL EOF-HAS-OCCURRED.

PERFORM 20-PROCESS-TOTALS.
   .
   .
   .
5-READ-ROUTINE.
   READ INPUT-FILE AT END MOVE 'Y' TO EOF-FLAG.
```

11.5 EXAMPLE9—A Program to Calculate Monthly Dues

In order to illustrate the topics covered in this chapter we have written a program that can be used to compute payment amounts for members in a homeowners' association. Such associations are formed when many homeowners band together to share neighborhood maintenance costs. The actual maintenance costs are distributed based on different properties of the housing units and which owners choose to use the jointly owned swimming pool. In our example, there will be five basic types of dwellings—duplex units and four different types of units included in single buildings called quadrahomes. The duplexes will be referred to as type 'D' units, while the quadrahome units will be referred to as types 'Q1', 'Q2', 'Q3', and 'Q4'. The rules utilized by our example are as follows:

Rule 1 All units must pay a base amount, which covers exterior maintenance, lawn care, and snow removal.

Rule 2 Owners of units that are duplexes must pay an extra 20% of the base rate to cover garage maintenance.

Rule 3 Owners of Q1 and Q3 quadrahome units must pay an extra 10% of the base rate to pay for the maintenance of sun decks, and an extra

FIGURE 11.8

```
COUPON PAYMENT AMOUNTS FOR A BASE RATE OF 40.00                    PAGE    1


NAME              FIRST ADDRESS LINE    SECOND ADDRESS LINE    TYPE   POOL    AMOUNT

JOHN REYNOLDS     1811 RAINTREE CT.     SYCAMORE, IL 60178     Q1     N       50.00
RAY MARTIN        1702 WILLOW CT.       SYCAMORE, IL 60178     D      Y       54.00
MARY MACKEY       1813 RAINTREE CT.     SYCAMORE, IL 60178     Q4     Y       46.00
JIM MILLER        1815 RAINTREE CT.     SYCAMORE, IL 60178     Q2     N       40.00
HARRY AMES        1817 RAINTREE CT.     SYCAMORE, IL 60178     Q3     Y       56.00
```

15% of the base rate for garage maintenance (their garages are smaller than those that go with the duplexes).

Rule 4 All owners of the pool must pay an extra 15% of the base rate.

The first input record contains the base amount that all homeowners must pay. The remaining records each represent a single dwelling. The record includes the owner's name, address, type of the dwelling, and whether or not the owner wishes to use the pool. The program produces a report similar to the one shown in Fig. 11.8.

The flowcharts for the program are given in Figs. 11.9–11.11. You should study the program that follows in Fig. 11.12 to see examples of class conditions, nested IF statements, and complex conditions.

FIGURE 11.9   Logic of EXAMPLE9.

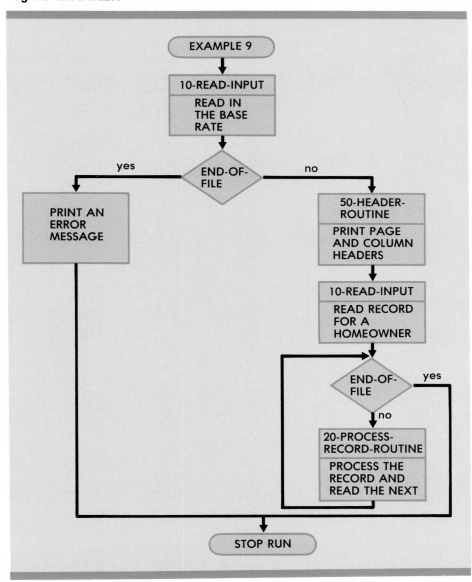

FIGURE 11.10   Logic of EXAMPLE9.

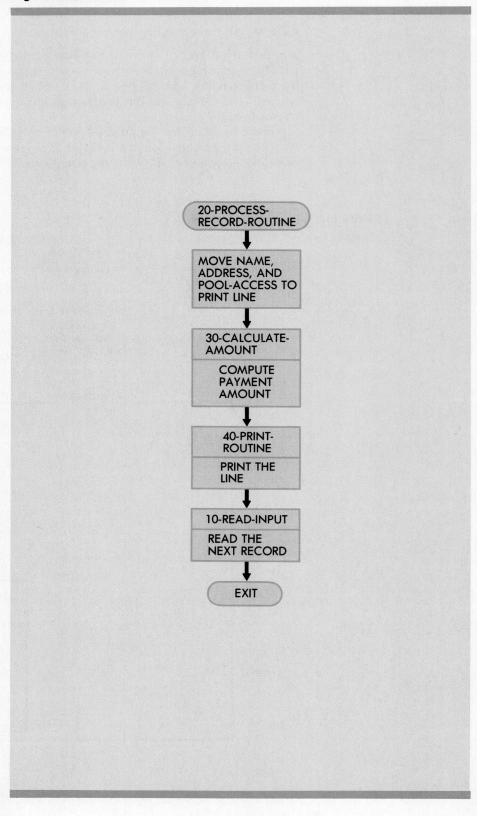

FIGURE 11.11   Logic of EXAMPLE9.

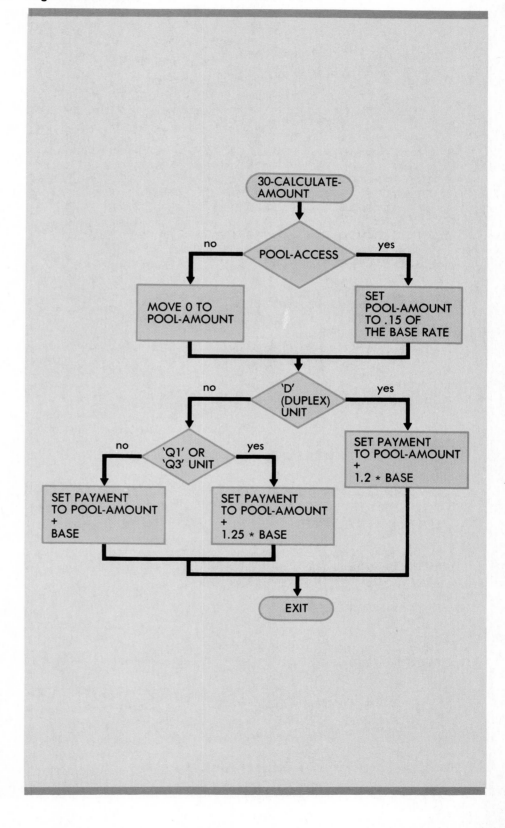

FIGURE 11.12   EXAMPLE9—a program to calculate monthly dues.

```
      IDENTIFICATION DIVISION.
      PROGRAM-ID. EXAMPLE9.
      AUTHOR. W E SINGLETARY.

     ****************************************************************
     *
     * THIS PROGRAM IS DESIGNED TO CALCULATE MONTHLY DUES FOR A
     * HOMEOWNERS' ASSOCIATION.  THERE ARE TWO TYPES OF BUILDINGS
     * OWNED BY MEMBERS OF THE ASSOCIATION - DUPLEXES AND
     * QUADRAHOMES.  A DUPLEX CONTAINS 2 DWELLINGS, WHICH ARE
     * IDENTICAL.  A QUADRAHOME CONTAINS FOUR UNITS, WHICH ALL
     * HAVE SLIGHTLY DIFFERENT DESIGNS.  WE SHALL CALL THESE
     * DIFFERENT TYPES OF UNITS Q1, Q2, Q3, AND Q4.   THE RULES
     * FOR CALCULATING MONTHLY PAYMENTS ARE AS FOLLOWS:
     *
     *    1. ALL UNITS MUST PAY A "BASE" AMOUNT, WHICH COVERS
     *       EXTERIOR MAINTENANCE, LAWN CARE, AND SNOW REMOVAL.
     *
     *    2. OWNERS OF A DUPLEX MUST PAY AN EXTRA 20% OF THE BASE
     *       RATE TO COVER GARAGE MAINTENANCE.
     *
     *    3. OWNERS OF Q1 AND Q3 QUADRAHOME UNITS MUST PAY AN EXTRA
     *       15% OF BASE RATE FOR THEIR (SOMEWHAT SMALLER)
     *       GARAGES.
     *
     *    4. OWNERS OF Q1 AND Q3 UNITS MUST PAY AN EXTRA 10%
     *       OF THE BASE RATE TO PAY FOR MAINTAINING SUN DECKS.
     *
     *    5. ALL USERS OF THE POOL (USE OF THE POOL IS OPTIONAL)
     *       MUST PAY AN EXTRA 15% OF THE BASE RATE.
     *
     *
     ****************************************************************

      ENVIRONMENT DIVISION.

      CONFIGURATION SECTION.
      SOURCE-COMPUTER. IBM-370.
      OBJECT-COMPUTER. IBM-370.

      SPECIAL-NAMES.
          C01 IS TOP-OF-PAGE.

      INPUT-OUTPUT SECTION.
      FILE-CONTROL.

          SELECT INPUT-FILE ASSIGN TO UR-S-SYSIN.
          SELECT OUTPUT-FILE ASSIGN TO UR-S-SYSPRINT.
```

```
     DATA DIVISION.
     FILE SECTION.

 ************************************************************************
 *
 *  THIS FILE IS USED TO READ THE INPUT RECORDS.
 *  THE FIRST RECORD IN THE FILE CONTAINS JUST THE BASE RATE.
 *  ALL OF THE REMAINING RECORDS REPRESENT HOMEOWNERS.
 *  EACH HOMEOWNER RECORD WILL CONTAIN THE FOLLOWING FIELDS:
 *
 *
 *     1. THE OWNER'S NAME
 *     2. THE ADDRESS
 *     3. THE TYPE OF UNIT (D, Q1, Q2, Q3, OR Q4)
 *     4. WHETHER OR NOT POOL ACCESS IS DESIRED
 *
 *
 ************************************************************************

     FD   INPUT-FILE
          LABEL RECORDS ARE OMITTED
          DATA RECORDS ARE BASE-AMOUNT-RECORD HOMEOWNER-RECORD.

     01   BASE-AMOUNT-RECORD.
          05   BASE-AMOUNT-IN   PIC 999V99.
          05   FILLER           PIC X(75).

     01   HOMEOWNER-RECORD.
          05   NAME-IN          PIC X(20).
          05   ADDRESS-1-IN     PIC X(20).
          05   ADDRESS-2-IN     PIC X(20).
          05   TYPE-UNIT-IN     PIC X(2).
               88   UNIT-IS-DUPLEX              VALUE IS 'D '.
               88   UNIT-HAS-GARAGE-AND-SUNDECK
                                               VALUE IS 'Q1'
                                                        'Q3'.
          05   POOL-ACCESS-IN   PIC X.
               88   UNIT-HAS-POOL              VALUE IS 'P'.
          05   FILLER           PIC X(17).
```

continued

FIGURE 11.12 Continued

```
***********************************************************
*
* THIS FILE IS USED TO PRINT THE REPORT.   ONE LINE WILL BE
* PRINTED FOR EACH HOMEOWNER.
*
***********************************************************

   FD   OUTPUT-FILE
        LABEL RECORDS ARE OMITTED
        DATA RECORD IS PRINT-BUFF.

   01   PRINT-BUFF           PIC X(133).

   WORKING-STORAGE SECTION.

***********************************************************
*
* EOF-FLAG IS SET TO 'Y' WHEN END-OF-FILE OCCURS.
*
* BASE-AMOUNT SAVES THE VALUE FROM THE FIRST INPUT RECORD
*
* POOL-AMOUNT GETS SET TO 0 OR .15 * BASE-AMOUNT
*
* N-LINES IS SET TO THE NUMBER OF LINES TO ADVANCE BEFORE
*          PRINTING A LINE
*
* LINE-COUNT CONTAINS THE NUMBER OF THE NEXT LINE ON A PAGE.
*
* PAGE-NO CONTAINS THE PAGE NUMBER OF THE NEXT PAGE OF THE
*          REPORT.
*
* PRINT-LINE IS USED TO BUILD THE LINES TO BE PRINTED.
*
* PAGE-HEADER AND COLUMN-HEADER ARE USED TO PRINT HEADERS AT
*          THE TOP OF THE FIRST PAGE OF OUTPUT.
*
***********************************************************

   01   MISC.
        05   EOF-FLAG          PIC X          VALUE IS 'N'.
             88   EOF-HAS-OCCURRED            VALUE IS 'Y'.
        05   BASE-AMOUNT       PIC 999V99.
        05   POOL-AMOUNT       PIC 999V99.
```

```
01   PRINT-VARIABLES.
     05   N-LINES         PIC 9.
     05   LINE-COUNT      PIC 99.
     05   PAGE-NO         PIC 999        VALUE IS 1.


01   PRINT-LINE.
     05   FILLER          PIC X(6).
     05   NAME-OUT        PIC X(20).
     05   FILLER          PIC X(2).
     05   ADDRESS-1-OUT   PIC X(20).
     05   FILLER          PIC X(2).
     05   ADDRESS-2-OUT   PIC X(20).
     05   FILLER          PIC X(3).
     05   TYPE-UNIT-OUT   PIC X(2).
     05   FILLER          PIC X(4).
     05   POOL-ACCESS-OUT PIC X(1).
     05   FILLER          PIC X(4).
     05   AMOUNT-OUT      PIC ZZZ.99.

01   PAGE-HEADER.
     05   FILLER          PIC X(1).
     05   FILLER          PIC X(8)       VALUE IS SPACES.
     05   FILLER          PIC X(42)      VALUE IS
          'COUPON PAYMENT AMOUNTS FOR A BASE RATE OF '.
     05   BASE-AMOUNT-OUT PIC ZZZ.99.
     05   FILLER          PIC X(20)      VALUE IS SPACES.
     05   FILLER          PIC X(5)       VALUE IS 'PAGE '.
     05   PG-NUM          PIC ZZ9.

01   COLUMN-HEADER.
     05   FILLER          PIC X(1).
     05   FILLER          PIC X(5)       VALUE IS SPACES.
     05   FILLER          PIC X(20)      VALUE IS 'NAME'.
     05   FILLER          PIC X(2)       VALUE IS SPACES.
     05   FILLER          PIC X(20)      VALUE IS
          'FIRST ADDRESS LINE'.
     05   FILLER          PIC X(2)       VALUE IS SPACES.
     05   FILLER          PIC X(20)      VALUE IS
          'SECOND ADDRESS LINE'.
     05   FILLER          PIC X(2)       VALUE IS SPACES.
     05   FILLER          PIC X(4)       VALUE IS 'TYPE'.
     05   FILLER          PIC X(2)       VALUE IS SPACES.
     05   FILLER          PIC X(4)       VALUE IS 'POOL'.
     05   FILLER          PIC X(2)       VALUE IS SPACES.
     05   FILLER          PIC X(6)       VALUE IS 'AMOUNT'.
```

continued

FIGURE 11.12   Continued

```
     PROCEDURE DIVISION.
         OPEN INPUT INPUT-FILE
             OUTPUT OUTPUT-FILE.

         PERFORM 10-READ-INPUT.
         IF EOF-HAS-OCCURRED
             MOVE ' *** EMPTY INPUT FILE ***' TO PRINT-BUFF
             WRITE PRINT-BUFF AFTER ADVANCING TOP-OF-PAGE
         ELSE
             MOVE BASE-AMOUNT-IN TO BASE-AMOUNT-OUT
             MOVE BASE-AMOUNT-IN TO BASE-AMOUNT
             PERFORM 50-HEADER-ROUTINE
             PERFORM 10-READ-INPUT
             PERFORM 20-PROCESS-RECORD-ROUTINE
                 UNTIL EOF-HAS-OCCURRED.

         CLOSE INPUT-FILE
             OUTPUT-FILE.

         STOP RUN.


    ***********************************************************************
    *
    * THIS ROUTINE JUST READS A HOMEOWNER RECORD.
    *
    ***********************************************************************

     10-READ-INPUT.
         READ INPUT-FILE AT END MOVE 'Y' TO EOF-FLAG.


    ***********************************************************************
    *
    * THIS ROUTINE PROCESSES THE INPUT RECORD THAT HAS ALREADY BEEN
    * READ AND THEN ATTEMPTS TO READ THE NEXT RECORD.
    *
    ***********************************************************************

     20-PROCESS-RECORD-ROUTINE.
         MOVE SPACES TO PRINT-LINE.
         MOVE NAME-IN TO NAME-OUT.
         MOVE ADDRESS-1-IN TO ADDRESS-1-OUT.
         MOVE ADDRESS-2-IN TO ADDRESS-2-OUT.
         MOVE TYPE-UNIT-IN TO TYPE-UNIT-OUT.
         MOVE POOL-ACCESS-IN TO POOL-ACCESS-OUT.
         PERFORM 30-CALCULATE-AMOUNT.
         PERFORM 40-PRINT-ROUTINE.
         PERFORM 10-READ-INPUT.
```

```
****************************************************************
*
* THIS ROUTINE CALCULATES THE PAYMENT AMOUNT FOR THE CURRENT
* HOMEOWNER.
*
****************************************************************

 30-CALCULATE-AMOUNT.
     IF UNIT-HAS-POOL
         COMPUTE POOL-AMOUNT ROUNDED = .15 * BASE-AMOUNT
     ELSE
         COMPUTE POOL-AMOUNT = 0.

     IF UNIT-IS-DUPLEX
         COMPUTE AMOUNT-OUT ROUNDED = (1.2 * BASE-AMOUNT) +
                                       POOL-AMOUNT
     ELSE
         IF UNIT-HAS-GARAGE-AND-SUNDECK
             COMPUTE AMOUNT-OUT ROUNDED = (1.25 * BASE-AMOUNT) +
                                           POOL-AMOUNT
         ELSE
             COMPUTE AMOUNT-OUT ROUNDED = BASE-AMOUNT +
                                           POOL-AMOUNT.

****************************************************************
*
* THIS ROUTINE PRINTS A LINE (STARTING ON A NEW PAGE IF
* NECESSARY).
*
****************************************************************

 40-PRINT-ROUTINE.
     IF LINE-COUNT > 50
         PERFORM 50-HEADER-ROUTINE.
     WRITE PRINT-BUFF FROM PRINT-LINE
         AFTER ADVANCING N-LINES.
     ADD N-LINES TO LINE-COUNT.
     MOVE 1 TO N-LINES.
```

continued

FIGURE 11.12 Continued

```
**************************************************************
*
* THIS ROUTINE IS INVOKED TO PRINT PAGE AND COLUMN HEADERS..
* IT RESETS THE LINE-COUNT TO 6 (THE NUMBER OF THE NEXT LINE
* ON THE PAGE).
*
**************************************************************

    50-HEADER-ROUTINE.
        MOVE PAGE-NO TO PG-NUM.
        ADD 1 TO PAGE-NO.
        WRITE PRINT-BUFF FROM PAGE-HEADER
            AFTER ADVANCING TOP-OF-PAGE.
        WRITE PRINT-BUFF FROM COLUMN-HEADER
            AFTER ADVANCING 3 LINES.
        MOVE 2 TO N-LINES.
        MOVE 6 TO LINE-COUNT.
```

SUMMARY

Class conditions are used to verify that a data item contains only numeric or alphabetic digits. Class conditions, relation conditions, and condition names are all simple conditions. Complex conditions can be formed from simple conditions using the three logical operators: AND, OR, and NOT.

Nested IF statements can be used with complex conditions in order to formulate arbitrarily intricate decisions. Nested IF statements should always be carefully indented to reflect the hierarchical structure of the alternatives.

When forming complex conditions (that can be used in either IF statements or PERFORM statements), be sure that all of the simple conditions can be evaluated.

Be very careful with the AT END condition on READ statements. Remember that the statement (or block of statements) executed when end-of-file occurs should be terminated by a period. It is frequently convenient to use a small routine that can be PERFORMed to READ input records and set the end-of-file flag.

REVIEW QUESTIONS

11.1 Does the NUMERIC class condition allow leading blanks and a sign?

11.2 Why is the ALPHABETIC class condition seldom used to verify fields that contain names?

11.3 What are the three types of simple conditions that have been discussed so far?

[handwritten notes in left margin:] Allows a sign but not leading blanks / names can have hypens periods apostrophy's / program will abend to illegal characters

[handwritten answer to 11.3:] Relational condition / Class conditions / condition names

[handwritten margin notes:]

IF NOT EOF-FLAG='N' AND ERROR-FLAG='N'

Not ERROR HAS OCCURED AND WHOLE IS-NUMERIC

order of evaluation will not matter, Parentheses will make it harder to read each condition will probably be evaluated

11.4 If a complex condition is formed from three simple conditions using two AND operators, does the order that the simple conditions occur matter? Should parentheses be used to make the groupings clear?

11.5 Give a complex condition that contains no OR operators in which the use of parentheses can make a difference.

11.6 Can a structure of the form

```
IF C1
    IF C2
        S1.
```

always be replaced with the following structure?

```
IF (C1 AND C2)
    S1.
```

[handwritten:] Can have a situation where C2 can only be evaluated when C1 is true.

P R O G R A M M I N G   E X E R C I S E S

11.1 Suppose that you work for a mail order company that sells computer programs. The company has just run a sale that went as follows:

a) All preferred customers (these are old customers who buy regularly from you) can purchase one program at 10% off the standard price, two programs at 15% off, and three or more programs at 20% off.

b) New customers get either 10% or $10 off their purchase, whichever is more. New customers will have special coupons that were mailed to them with this offer.

c) All other customers get 5% off on one program and 8% off on two or more programs.

d) Illinois residents should pay a 5% sales tax (none of the other customers must pay a sales tax).

The clerks trying to figure the bills have decided that these rules will lead to numerous errors unless you write a program that will help them calculate the correct amounts. The input to your program will be records that conform to the following format:

[handwritten margin note:] B>C AND D>1 AND G>H

Columns	Contents
1–20	Name
21	Customer code ('P' for preferred, 'N' for new, and spaces otherwise)
22	Illinois resident code ('I' for an Illinois resident)
23–77	Up to 11 five-digit amounts representing purchases (Each field has a 999V99 format.)

For each input record, your program should display the values from the record, as well as the correct amount to charge the customers. The numeric fields in columns 23–77 represent the "list price" of the purchased items, and spaces will occur in unused fields. Your program should print page and column headers, and print 55 lines per page.

11.2   Suppose that you work for a company in which employees fill in time cards to record the number of hours that they worked. You are to write a program that accumulates the total time worked by each employee. The program should accept as input a series of records in the following format:

Columns	Contents
1–9	Employee's social security number
11–15	Starting time (HH:MM)
17–21	Ending time

You are to assume that each of the HH and MM values contains numeric digits, but you must make sure that they are in the correct ranges (01 to 12 for hours, and 00 to 59 for minutes). There may be numerous records for a single employee, but there will be at most 50 employees. You may assume that no employee ever works for more than 23 consecutive hours. Your program will have to keep a table in working storage that accumulates the total times for all of the employees. Whenever an invalid input record is detected, it should be displayed with an appropriate error message. After all of the input records have been read and the totals have been accumulated in working storage, your program should print the totals for each of the employees in the table.

    Before leaving this problem, you should consider the complexities involved in taking the difference between two points in time when you cannot limit the period to less than 24 hours. Consider the problem of taking differences between different years (with, perhaps, leap years included in the interval). This problem has been complicated by the fact that most data processing systems store the year as just two digits (assuming that the year 2000 is still some time off). Furthermore, it is frequently necessary to take differences between points in time recorded in different time zones (this can even happen in one location when clocks are reset by an hour forward or backward).

11.3   Write a program that produces final grades for students. Each input record will conform to the following format:

Columns	Contents
1–20	Name
21–38	Up to 6 three-digit test scores

The student's grade is computed by calculating the average of the highest five scores. If there are missing scores, treat them as if they were 000. For each input record, the program should display the name, the highest five scores, the total, the average, and the assigned grade. Grades are assigned according to the following cutoffs:

90–100	A
80–89	B
70–79	C
60–69	D
Less than 60	F

Your program should print page and column headers, and should print up to 55 lines per page.

DEBUGGING A PROGRAM

INTRODUCTION   Before discussing the principles of "debugging" a program, let us spend a few sentences describing the origin of the term. The term originated in an incident that occurred in 1945. It involved the operation of the Mark II, a computer being developed for performing military computations. Unlike today's machines, the Mark II had numerous mechanical and electromechanical components. One day the machine stopped operating and a search was required to determine the exact cause. An unfortunate moth had gotten caught in a relay and was beaten to death. The problem was cured by carefully removing the moth with a tweezers. From that point on the process of fixing a computer or a computer program has been referred to as **debugging.**

Once a program has been coded, it must still be tested. Any errors will have to be detected and corrected. The object is to eventually produce a program that consistently performs as desired. There are a few simple principles that can be used to minimize the effort required to debug a program. The first principle is as follows:

Principle 1   Before a program is submitted for its first test, it should be listed and carefully deskchecked.

It is normally a very good practice to have someone else "deskcheck" (or "walk through") your code before continuing. In a classroom environment this will depend on the rules established by your instructor. However, most good, experienced programmers regularly deskcheck each others' code.

It seems to be extremely difficult for beginners to accept this principle. Novices have a strong tendency to believe that it is faster to "let the machine find the errors." Grasping that this is categorically wrong is a major step toward good debugging skills.

The reasons for checking a program carefully by reading it before ever submitting it for execution are twofold.

1. If the program is very long, several errors are normally detected. The time spent checking the program is usually much less than the time that would have been spent tracking down the errors individually.
2. The time spent reviewing the program can be used to determine what verifications must be made in order to ensure the accuracy of the results. This topic will be covered in the next section.

Note that "saving machine time" is not a major reason for deskchecking. The main reason is to save *your* time.

12.1 Verification Techniques

As you check over a program, examine it in light of the following principle:

Principle 2 A program should be broken up into sections of code that perform separate functions (frequently these are subroutines, but sometimes a single routine can be broken into sections, as well). Determine how to verify that each section is performing its function correctly, and add the required statements.

For example, suppose that SORTTAB is a program to read in a table of words, sort the table, and print the sorted words. The program can immediately be broken into three major sections.

1. The section that reads in a table of words
2. The section that sorts the table
3. The section that prints the table

The last two sections might be further subdivided into smaller sections.

To verify that the section to read in the table has worked correctly, it is necessary to display the contents of the table. Assuming that the section to read the table has executed properly, the results of the sort can be verified by again displaying the contents of the table. Finally, the output of the print routine can be checked by examining the values that actually get printed.

Most of the debugging time spent on assignments from this text should be spent deskchecking, inserting DISPLAYs to verify results, and carefully checking the produced output. There is one more principle relating to verification.

Principle 3 If a program is large enough to contain several routines, test the routines separately.

As an illustration of this principle, consider the SORTTAB program. A reasonable way to write such a program would be as follows:

Step 1 Write the sections that read and print the table. Run this short program; DISPLAY the words as they are read to verify that everything is working properly.

Step 2 While you are debugging the read and print routines, code the sort routine.

Step 3 Now add the sort routine and debug it. Assuming that the read and print routines are thoroughly debugged, you can be sure that the errors that do occur are due to problems in the sort logic itself.

There are several benefits to this approach.

1. Most errors are easy to locate, since only a small amount of untested code is used in each run.
2. Debugging can begin earlier. This makes the process less vulnerable to unforeseen disasters (such as the machine breaking down for a day).
3. It is easier to make an accurate estimate concerning progress. If all of the program is coded, but none of it has been debugged, it is hard to say when the program will be finished. On the other hand, if three-fourths of the

routines are coded and one-half are debugged, there is some basis for projecting the time required to complete the project.

Because the sort example is used throughout the remainder of this chapter, let's consider the code used to verify that the read and print routines work properly. The code and printout from a sample run is included in Fig. 12.1.

FIGURE 12.1   SORTTAB—a program with a stub.

```
        IDENTIFICATION DIVISION.
        PROGRAM-ID. SORTTAB.
        AUTHOR. W E SINGLETARY.

        ************************************************************
        *
        * THIS PROGRAM READS INPUT RECORD, EACH OF WHICH CONTAINS
        * A SINGLE WORD IN COLUMNS 1-20.  THE WORDS ARE FIRST STORED
        * INTO WORD-TABLE (BY THE ROUTINE READ-WORDS).  THEN THE
        * ENTIRE SET OF WORDS IN THE TABLE IS PRINTED BY
        * PRINT-WORDS.  THE WORDS ARE THEN SORTED INTO ASCENDING
        * ORDER BY SORT-WORDS.  FINALLY, THE SORTED TABLE IS
        * PRINTED OUT AGAIN USING PRINT-WORDS.
        *
        ************************************************************

        ENVIRONMENT DIVISION.
        CONFIGURATION SECTION.

        SOURCE-COMPUTER. IBM-370.
        OBJECT-COMPUTER. IBM-370.

        INPUT-OUTPUT SECTION.
        FILE-CONTROL.

            SELECT INPUT-FILE ASSIGN TO UR-S-SYSIN.
            SELECT PRINT-FILE ASSIGN TO UR-S-SYSPRINT.

        DATA DIVISION.
        FILE SECTION.

        FD   INPUT-FILE
             LABEL RECORDS ARE OMITTED
             DATA RECORD IS INPUT-RECORD.

        01   INPUT-RECORD.
             02   WORD-IN         PIC X(20).
             02   FILLER          PIC X(60).

        FD   PRINT-FILE
             LABEL RECORDS ARE OMITTED
             DATA RECORD IS PRINT-BUFF.

        01   PRINT-BUFF           PIC X(133).
```

continued

FIGURE 12.1 Continued

```
     WORKING-STORAGE SECTION.

     ***********************************************************
     *
     * EOF-FLAG                  SET TO 'Y' WHEN END-OF-FILE IS REACHED.
     *
     * TEMP-VAL                  THIS FIELD IS USED WHEN SWITCHING
     *                           TWO ENTRIES IN THE TABLE
     *
     * NUM-ENT                   SET TO HOLD THE NUMBER OF ENTRIES
     *                           IN THE TABLE
     *
     * I, J, AND K               SUBSCRIPTS USED TO REFERENCE ENTRIES
     *                           IN THE TABLE.
     *
     * WORD-TABLE                THE TABLE CONTAINING WORDS
     *
     * PRINT-LINE                USED TO PRINT OUT THE WORDS IN THE
     *                           TABLE
     *
     ***********************************************************

1    01  MISC-FIELDS.
         05  EOF-FLAG            PIC X       VALUE IS 'N'.
             88  EOF-OCCURRED                VALUE IS 'Y'.

         05  TEMP-VAL            PIC X(20).
         05  NUM-ENT             PIC 99.

     01  SUBSCRIPTS.
         02  I                   PIC 99.
         02  J                   PIC 99.
         02  K                   PIC 99.

     01  WORD-TABLE.
         02  WORD-ENTRY          PIC X(20) OCCURS 50 TIMES.

     01  PRINT-LINE.
         02  FILLER              PIC X.
2        02  FILLER              PIC X(12) VALUE IS 'TABLE ENTRY '.
         02  ENT-NUM             PIC Z9.
3        02  FILLER              PIC X(10) VALUE IS ' CONTAINS '.
         02  WORD-OUT            PIC X(20).
```

```
4      PROCEDURE DIVISION.

       ******************************************************************
       *
       * THIS IS THE MAIN LOGIC.  IT JUST READS THE WORDS INTO
       * WORD-TABLE, PRINTS THEM OUT, SORTS THEM, AND THEN
       * PRINTS THEM OUT AGAIN.
       *
       ******************************************************************

5          OPEN INPUT INPUT-FILE
                OUTPUT PRINT-FILE.

6          PERFORM READ-WORDS.
7          PERFORM PRINT-WORDS.

8          PERFORM SORT-WORDS.

9          PERFORM PRINT-WORDS.

10         CLOSE INPUT-FILE
                 PRINT-FILE.

11         STOP RUN.

       ******************************************************************
       *
       * THIS ROUTINE READS THE INPUT RECORDS, EACH OF WHICH
       * CONTAINS A SINGLE WORD.  THE WORDS ARE STORED INTO
       * WORD-TABLE AND NUM-ENT IS SET TO THE NUMBER OF WORDS
       * THAT WERE READ.
       *
       ******************************************************************

       READ-WORDS.
12         MOVE 0 TO NUM-ENT.
13         READ INPUT-FILE AT END MOVE 'Y' TO EOF-FLAG.
15         DISPLAY 'EOF-FLAG=' EOF-FLAG.

16         PERFORM LOAD-1-ENTRY UNTIL EOF-OCCURRED.

       ******************************************************************
       *
       * THIS LITTLE ROUTINE JUST MOVES ONE ENTRY INTO THE TABLE AND
       * TRYS TO READ THE NEXT INPUT RECORD.
       *
       ******************************************************************

       LOAD-1-ENTRY.
17         ADD 1 TO NUM-ENT.
18         MOVE WORD-IN TO WORD-ENTRY (NUM-ENT).
19         DISPLAY 'ADDED WORD ' WORD-IN ' AT POSITION ' NUM-ENT.
20         READ INPUT-FILE AT END MOVE 'Y' TO EOF-FLAG.
22         DISPLAY 'EOF-FLAG=' EOF-FLAG.
```

continued

FIGURE 12.1   Continued

```
     ****************************************************************
     *
     * THIS ROUTINE PRINTS OUT THE WORDS IN WORD-TABLE.
     *
     ****************************************************************

     PRINT-WORDS.
23       MOVE ' *** THE WORDS IN THE TABLE ARE AS FOLLOWS:' TO
             PRINT-BUFF.
24       WRITE PRINT-BUFF AFTER ADVANCING 2 LINES.

25       PERFORM PRINT-1-ENTRY
             VARYING I FROM 1 BY 1 UNTIL I > NUM-ENT.

     ****************************************************************
     *
     * THIS ROUTINE PRINTS OUT A SINGLE WORD IN THE TABLE.
     *
     ****************************************************************

     PRINT-1-ENTRY.
26       MOVE WORD-ENTRY (I) TO WORD-OUT.
27       MOVE I TO ENT-NUM.
28       WRITE PRINT-BUFF FROM PRINT-LINE
             AFTER ADVANCING 1.
```

```
****************************************************************
*
* THIS ROUTINE SORTS THE WORDS IN WORD-TABLE.  IT USES
* THE FOLLOWING BASIC ALGORITHM:
*
*       A.  FIRST, THINK OF THE TABLE AS SEPARATED INTO
*           TWO SECTIONS.  THE LEFT SECTION IS THE "SORTED"
*           SECTION.  THE ENTRIES IN THE SECTION ALL OCCUR
*           IN ASCENDING ORDER.  WHEN WE FIRST ENTER THIS
*           ROUTINE, THE LEFT (SORTED) SECTION ONLY CONTAINS
*           ONE ENTRY.  THE REST OF THE ENTRIES TO THE
*           RIGHT OF THE SORTED SECTION WE SHALL CALL THE
*           THE "UNSORTED" SECTION.  INITIALLY, THIS INCLUDES
*           ALL BUT THE ENTRY IN WORD-ENTRY (1).
*
*       B.  NOW TAKE THE FIRST ENTRY IN THE UNSORTED SECTION.
*           WE WISH TO ADD IT TO THE SORTED SECTION.  TO
*           DO THIS, WE COMPARE IT TO THE WORD THAT OCCURS
*           JUST TO ITS LEFT.  IF THE WORDS ARE OUT OF ORDER,
*           WE SWITCH THEM.  NOW WE HAVE 2 ENTRIES IN THE
*           SORTED SECTION.
*
*       C.  TAKE THE FIRST ENTRY THAT REMAINS IN THE UNSORTED
*           SECTION.  ADD IT TO THE SORTED SECTION.  THIS
*           REQUIRES CHECKING IT AGAINST THE ENTRY TO ITS
*           LEFT (AND SWITCHING THEM, IF THEY ARE OUT OF
*           ORDER) UNTIL EITHER THERE ARE NO MORE ENTRIES
*           TO THE LEFT, OR THE ENTRIES ARE IN THE CORRECT
*           ORDER.  REPEAT THIS STEP UNTIL NO MORE ENTRIES
*           REMAIN IN THE UNSORTED SECTION.
*
* ACTUALLY, STEPS B AND C CAN BE COMBINED (SINCE B IS
* A SPECIAL CASE OF C).  THE ACTUAL CODE USES TWO
* SUBROUTINES.  SORT-1-ENTRY TAKES THE FIRST ENTRY IN
* THE UNSORTED PART OF THE TABLE AND ADDS IT TO THE
* SORTED SECTION.  TO DO THIS IT WILL CALL ONE-SWITCH
* EVERY TIME TWO ENTRIES MUST BE SWITCHED.
*
****************************************************************


  SORT-WORDS.


THERE ARE NO STATEMENTS FLAGGED IN THIS COMPILE
```

continued

FIGURE 12.1 Continued

```
EOF-FLAG=N
ADDED WORD CATS                         AT POSITION 01
EOF-FLAG=N
ADDED WORD ANTELOPES                    AT POSITION 02
EOF-FLAG=N
ADDED WORD ZEBRAS                       AT POSITION 03
EOF-FLAG=N
ADDED WORD DOGS                         AT POSITION 04
EOF-FLAG=N
ADDED WORD BEARS                        AT POSITION 05
EOF-FLAG=N
ADDED WORD TIGERS                       AT POSITION 06
EOF-FLAG=N
ADDED WORD ANTEATERS                    AT POSITION 07
EOF-FLAG=N
ADDED WORD CAMELS                       AT POSITION 08
EOF-FLAG=Y
*** THE WORDS IN THE TABLE ARE AS FOLLOWS:
TABLE ENTRY   1 CONTAINS CATS
TABLE ENTRY   2 CONTAINS ANTELOPES
TABLE ENTRY   3 CONTAINS ZEBRAS
TABLE ENTRY   4 CONTAINS DOGS
TABLE ENTRY   5 CONTAINS BEARS
TABLE ENTRY   6 CONTAINS TIGERS
TABLE ENTRY   7 CONTAINS ANTEATERS
TABLE ENTRY   8 CONTAINS CAMELS
*** THE WORDS IN THE TABLE ARE AS FOLLOWS:
TABLE ENTRY   1 CONTAINS CATS
TABLE ENTRY   2 CONTAINS ANTELOPES
TABLE ENTRY   3 CONTAINS ZEBRAS
TABLE ENTRY   4 CONTAINS DOGS
TABLE ENTRY   5 CONTAINS BEARS
TABLE ENTRY   6 CONTAINS TIGERS
TABLE ENTRY   7 CONTAINS ANTEATERS
TABLE ENTRY   8 CONTAINS CAMELS
```

This listing differs from the listings presented thus far. All of the previous program listings have been copies of the source program as it would be presented to the compiler. In contrast, Fig. 12.1 presents the source listing produced by the compiler. That is the reason for certain differences, such as the numbering of program statements for purposes of identification. This listing has been altered in three minor respects.

1. Certain information, extraneous to this discussion, produced by the compiler at the beginning of the listing has been deleted. This would normally include the date and the time that the program was run, an identification of the facility, and the program identification.

2. The page numbers produced by the compiler have been deleted.

3. Certain information produced by the compiler at the end of the listing has been deleted. This would normally include the time required to compile the program, the time required to execute the program, the number of lines printed, and other statistics.

In this case, since the program is not extremely large, the whole program was coded before debugging began. However, the sort routine was not included in this first debugging run. This run was successful and confirmed that the read and print routines perform properly. In the next section we will continue by studying the debugging of the sort routine.

Note that the routine SORT-WORDS is included in this run, although it does not actually do anything. Such a routine is called a **stub.** A stub is used to allow the main logic to be debugged, even though the real SORT-WORDS routine has not been even coded yet.

12.2 Working from an Abnormally Terminated Program

When a program ends abnormally due to an error, information is normally printed that can be used to locate the error. Exactly what information is displayed depends on the COBOL compiler and run-time environment that you are using. In most cases, however, it is possible to determine exactly what COBOL statement was being executed when the error occurred. In some cases the contents of all of the data fields will be printed, as well. In this discussion we will assume that the last statement that was being executed can be determined. If you find yourself in a situation where this is not true (as on many of the microcomputer versions of COBOL), you must debug using only verification techniques.

To illustrate how to proceed when a program "abends" (abnormally terminates), we shall need an example. Figure 12.2 shows the output of SORTTAB after adding a version of the SORT-WORDS routine. We have included only the new PROCEDURE DIVISION, since the rest of the program was not altered. Because of some as yet undiscovered error, the program abended. In this section the basic techniques for locating such an error will be covered.

Please read through the source listing before continuing. You may very well have spotted the bug. If so, do not let that distract you from the goal of learning how to approach such a situation.

A great deal could be said about the art of locating the exact cause of an abend. However, following just a few basic principles will make the task of locating most bugs quite straightforward.

Principle 4 Find out exactly what caused the abnormal termination.

To do this, examine the output created by the program. Notice that it is exactly as expected until the following two lines appear:

```
***** ERROR 67 SUBSCRIPT OR INDEX NAME OUT OF RANGE.
PROGRAM WAS EXECUTING LINE 32 IN ROUTINE SORTTAB  WHEN TERMINATION OCCURRED.
```

These lines give you information that is crucial for determining exactly what went wrong. The second line indicates exactly what statement in the

FIGURE 12.2 A program with a bug.

```
       PROCEDURE DIVISION.

       *****************************************************************
       *
       * THIS IS THE MAIN LOGIC.  IT JUST READS THE WORDS INTO
       * WORD-TABLE, PRINTS THEM OUT, SORTS THEM, AND THEN
       * PRINTS THEM OUT AGAIN.
       *
       *****************************************************************

5          OPEN INPUT INPUT-FILE
               OUTPUT PRINT-FILE.

6          PERFORM READ-WORDS.
7          PERFORM PRINT-WORDS.

8          PERFORM SORT-WORDS.

9          PERFORM PRINT-WORDS.

10         CLOSE INPUT-FILE
               PRINT-FILE.

11         STOP RUN.

       *****************************************************************
       *
       * THIS ROUTINE READS THE INPUT RECORDS, EACH OF WHICH
       * CONTAINS A SINGLE WORD.  THE WORDS ARE STORED INTO
       * WORD-TABLE AND NUM-ENT IS SET TO THE NUMBER OF WORDS
       * THAT WERE READ.
       *
       *****************************************************************

       READ-WORDS.
12         MOVE 0 TO NUM-ENT.
13         READ INPUT-FILE AT END MOVE 'Y' TO EOF-FLAG.
15         DISPLAY 'EOF-FLAG=' EOF-FLAG.

16         PERFORM LOAD-1-ENTRY UNTIL EOF-OCCURRED.

       *****************************************************************
       *
       * THIS LITTLE ROUTINE JUST MOVES ONE ENTRY INTO THE TABLE AND
       * TRYS TO READ THE NEXT INPUT RECORD.
       *
       *****************************************************************

       LOAD-1-ENTRY.
17         ADD 1 TO NUM-ENT.
18         MOVE WORD-IN TO WORD-ENTRY (NUM-ENT).
19         DISPLAY 'ADDED WORD ' WORD-IN ' AT POSITION ' NUM-ENT.
20         READ INPUT-FILE AT END MOVE 'Y' TO EOF-FLAG.
22         DISPLAY 'EOF-FLAG=' EOF-FLAG.
```

```
     **************************************************************
     *
     * THIS ROUTINE PRINTS OUT THE WORDS IN WORD-TABLE.
     *
     **************************************************************

        PRINT-WORDS.
23          MOVE ' *** THE WORDS IN THE TABLE ARE AS FOLLOWS:' TO
                PRINT-BUFF.
24          WRITE PRINT-BUFF AFTER ADVANCING 2 LINES.

25          PERFORM PRINT-1-ENTRY
                VARYING I FROM 1 BY 1 UNTIL I > NUM-ENT.

     **************************************************************
     *
     * THIS ROUTINE PRINTS OUT A SINGLE WORD IN THE TABLE.
     *
     **************************************************************

        PRINT-1-ENTRY.
26          MOVE WORD-ENTRY (I) TO WORD-OUT.
27          MOVE I TO ENT-NUM.
28          WRITE PRINT-BUFF FROM PRINT-LINE
                AFTER ADVANCING 1.

     **************************************************************
     *
     * THIS ROUTINE SORTS THE WORDS IN WORD-TABLE.  IT USES
     * THE FOLLOWING BASIC ALGORITHM:
     *
     *     A.  FIRST, THINK OF THE TABLE AS SEPARATED INTO
     *         TWO SECTIONS.  THE LEFT SECTION IS THE "SORTED"
     *         SECTION.  THE ENTRIES IN THE SECTION ALL OCCUR
     *         IN ASCENDING ORDER.  WHEN WE FIRST ENTER THIS
     *         ROUTINE, THE LEFT (SORTED) SECTION ONLY CONTAINS
     *         ONE ENTRY.  THE REST OF THE ENTRIES TO THE
     *         RIGHT OF THE SORTED SECTION WE SHALL CALL THE
     *         THE "UNSORTED" SECTION.  INITIALLY, THIS INCLUDES
     *         ALL BUT THE ENTRY IN WORD-ENTRY (1).
     *
     *     B.  NOW TAKE THE FIRST ENTRY IN THE UNSORTED SECTION.
     *         WE WISH TO ADD IT TO THE SORTED SECTION.  TO
     *         DO THIS, WE COMPARE IT TO THE WORD THAT OCCURS
     *         JUST TO ITS LEFT.  IF THE WORDS ARE OUT OF ORDER,
     *         WE SWITCH THEM.  NOW WE HAVE 2 ENTRIES IN THE
     *         SORTED SECTION.
```

continued

FIGURE 12.2   Continued

```
*        C.   TAKE THE FIRST ENTRY THAT REMAINS IN THE UNSORTED
*             SECTION.  ADD IT TO THE SORTED SECTION.  THIS
*             REQUIRES CHECKING IT AGAINST THE ENTRY TO ITS
*             LEFT (AND SWITCHING THEM, IF THEY ARE OUT OF
*             ORDER) UNTIL EITHER THERE ARE NO MORE ENTRIES
*             TO THE LEFT, OR THE ENTRIES ARE IN THE CORRECT
*             ORDER.  REPEAT THIS STEP UNTIL NO MORE ENTRIES
*             REMAIN IN THE UNSORTED SECTION.
*
* ACTUALLY, STEPS B AND C CAN BE COMBINED (SINCE B IS
* A SPECIAL CASE OF C).  THE ACTUAL CODE USES TWO
* SUBROUTINES.  SORT-1-ENTRY TAKES THE FIRST ENTRY IN
* THE UNSORTED PART OF THE TABLE AND ADDS IT TO THE
* SORTED SECTION.  TO DO THIS IT WILL CALL ONE-SWITCH
* EVERY TIME TWO ENTRIES MUST BE SWITCHED.

*************************************************************

29    SORT-WORDS.
          PERFORM SORT-1-ENTRY
              VARYING I FROM 2 BY 1 UNTIL I > NUM-ENT.

      SORT-1-ENTRY.
*
* NOTE THAT K WILL ALWAYS CONTAIN J + 1.  THUS, WHEN
* TWO WORDS ARE COMPARED, J WILL POINT AT THE ONE ON
* THE LEFT, AND K WILL POINT TO THE ONE ON THE RIGHT.
*
30        COMPUTE J = I - 1.
31        COMPUTE K = J + 1.
32        PERFORM ONE-SWITCH
              UNTIL WORD-ENTRY (J) IS NOT > WORD-ENTRY (K).
      ONE-SWITCH.
33        MOVE WORD-ENTRY (J) TO TEMP-VAL.
34        MOVE WORD-ENTRY (K) TO WORD-ENTRY (J).
35        MOVE TEMP-VAL TO WORD-ENTRY (K).
36        COMPUTE J = J - 1.
37        COMPUTE K = J + 1.
```

```
*****  THERE ARE NO STATEMENTS FLAGGED IN THIS COMPILE

EOF-FLAG=N
ADDED WORD CATS                     AT POSITION 01
EOF-FLAG=N
ADDED WORD ANTELOPES                AT POSITION 02
EOF-FLAG=N
ADDED WORD ZEBRAS                   AT POSITION 03
EOF-FLAG=N
ADDED WORD DOGS                     AT POSITION 04
EOF-FLAG=N
ADDED WORD BEARS                    AT POSITION 05
EOF-FLAG=N
ADDED WORD TIGERS                   AT POSITION 06
EOF-FLAG=N
ADDED WORD ANTEATERS                AT POSITION 07
EOF-FLAG=N
ADDED WORD CAMELS                   AT POSITION 08
EOF-FLAG=Y
***  THE WORDS IN THE TABLE ARE AS FOLLOWS:
TABLE ENTRY  1 CONTAINS CATS
TABLE ENTRY  2 CONTAINS ANTELOPES
TABLE ENTRY  3 CONTAINS ZEBRAS
TABLE ENTRY  4 CONTAINS DOGS
TABLE ENTRY  5 CONTAINS BEARS
TABLE ENTRY  6 CONTAINS TIGERS
TABLE ENTRY  7 CONTAINS ANTEATERS
TABLE ENTRY  8 CONTAINS CAMELS
*****  ERROR 67 SUBSCRIPT OR INDEX NAME OUT OF RANGE.
PROGRAM WAS EXECUTING LINE 32 IN ROUTINE SORTTAB  WHEN TERMINATION
OCCURRED.
```

program was being executed when the error occurred, and the first line gives a clue as to the nature of the error. You should immediately scan the listing and mark statement 32, the location of the error. You should have found the following two lines of code.

```
32     PERFORM ONE-SWITCH
             UNTIL WORD-ENTRY (J) IS NOT > WORD-ENTRY (K).
```

Now the line describing what caused the error should be examined. Beginning programmers frequently find it very difficult to interpret error messages. However, if you keep track of each error message and what caused it, with experience it will become much easier to rapidly determine the immediate causes of bugs. In the case illustrated, the error message is indicating that one of the two subscripts contains an illegal value. Thus, either J or K must somehow have acquired a bad value.

At this point, after analyzing the exact immediate cause of the error, it is time to apply a new principle.

The task of isolating the routine that probably caused the error has been made much easier by our foresight in first debugging the read and print routines. Now we can be reasonably confident that the actual bug is in one of the sort routines. This is quite important. Too often a student will simply peruse page after page of code, hoping that the error will become apparent. If the verification of output is not adequate to isolate the error, carefully add more verification logic and resubmit the program.

Finally, after isolating the section of code that produced the error, use the following principle:

This is the "detective" part of debugging. In the example we are considering, the procedure might go as follows:

a) We know that either J or K somehow contained an illegal value. K must (or at least it appears that way) have a value exactly one greater than J. There are only four statements that alter J or K. They are

```
30      COMPUTE J = I - 1.
31      COMPUTE K = J + 1.
36      COMPUTE J = J - 1.
37      COMPUTE K = J + 1.
```

By examining these statements, you might conclude that either the variable I contained a value that was too high (greater than 50), or J was decremented to a value that was too low.

b) Within the sort routines, I is altered only by the perform statement.

```
29      PERFORM SORT-1-ENTRY
            VARYING I FROM 2 BY 1 UNTIL I > NUM-ENT.
```

It seems reasonable to tentatively conclude that the variable I must have contained a value in the range 2 to the value in NUM-ENT. If this were so, then the error would probably be due to decrementing J to an illegal value.

c) Since J is decremented by 1 each time, and it probably started at a value between 2 and the value in NUM-ENT, it probably has been decremented to 0. How could that happen?

d) By examining the logic of SORT-1-ENTRY, it is clear that ONE-SWITCH should be invoked only when J is the subscript of a valid entry immediately to the left of the entry referenced by K, and the two entries should be switched. Thus, the statement 32 is incorrect. It causes J to be decremented to 0, if the new entry to be inserted must go to the left of all of the entries in the sorted section. One might well be tempted to fix it by using

```
32      PERFORM ONE-SWITCH THRU SWITCH-EXIT
            UNTIL J = 0 OR
                WORD-ENTRY (J) IS NOT > WORD-ENTRY (K).
```

Actually, the proposed "fix" would work for some COBOL compilers and fail for others. The cause for failure is rather subtle, but failure occurs often enough to warrant mentioning it. If both of the conditions are first tested, and then the loop is executed only if both are false, an error will occur. On the other hand, some implementations of COBOL cause only the first condition to be tested if it turns out to be true (i.e., the routine will not be performed if the first condition is true, so the second condition is not even checked if the first condition is true). In these cases the program would execute and compute the correct results. This is referred to as a "latent bug." It might not show up for many years (until a new COBOL compiler is used). The lesson to be learned is that you should make sure that you understand a bug thoroughly before attempting to fix it. Then make the correction carefully.

One way to correct the problem would be to use the version of the SORT routines which is shown in Fig. 12.3. Here the new variable should be declared in the WORKING-STORAGE section with the following line:

```
05  FOUND-CORRECT-LOCATION    PIC X.
```

FIGURE 12.3.

```
SORT-WORDS.
    PERFORM SORT-1-ENTRY
        VARYING I FROM 2 BY 1 UNTIL I > NUM-ENT.



SORT-1-ENTRY.
    COMPUTE J = I - 1.
    COMPUTE K = J + 1.
    MOVE 'N' TO FOUND-CORRECT-LOCATION.

    PERFORM TRY-SWITCH
        UNTIL J = 0 OR
            FOUND-CORRECT-LOCATION = 'Y'.



TRY-SWITCH.
    IF WORD-ENTRY (J) > WORD-ENTRY (K)
        MOVE WORD-ENTRY (J) TO TEMP-VAL
        MOVE WORD-ENTRY (K) TO WORD-ENTRY (J)
        MOVE TEMP-VAL TO WORD-ENTRY (K)
        COMPUTE J = J - 1
        COMPUTE K = J + 1
    ELSE
        MOVE 'Y' TO FOUND-CORRECT-LOCATION.
```

SUMMARY

Being able to debug a program is a skill required of any programmer. A good way to develop the ability to rapidly debug a program is to study the following six principles and consistently apply them:

Principle 1   Before a program is submitted for its first test, it should be listed and carefully read through to check it.

Principle 2   A program should be broken up into sections of code that perform separate functions (frequently these are subroutines, but sometimes a single routine can be broken into sections, as well). Determine how to verify that each section is performing its function correctly, and add the required statements.

Principle 3   If a program is large enough to contain several routines, test the routines separately.

Principle 4   Find out exactly what caused the abnormal termination.

Principle 5   Isolate the error. Determine which section of code produced unexpected, erroneous results.

Principle 6   Ask "What could have caused the error?" Work backward from the error.

Finally, after each troublesome bug, reevaluate your attack on the error. Determine whether you approached it methodically, or whether you wasted time and effort. Try to synthesize your experience into general rules. Learn from your errors, so that you can avoid repeating them.

REVIEW QUESTIONS

12.1   How would you react to the following statement:

It used to make sense to deskcheck programs because computers were so incredibly expensive. Now that machines are becoming inexpensive and the cost of a human programmer's time is going up, it makes more sense to just submit your program to the computer immediately after coding it. Let the machine find the compile errors, and debugging occurs so rapidly in an interactive environment that there is no point in wasting a human's time looking for minor errors.

12.2   How would you distinguish between verification and working from the output of an abnormally terminated program?

12.3   What is meant by the term *stub*? Why are stubs used?

12.4   What is meant by the term *abend*?

12.5   What does it mean to *isolate the error*? How can this be achieved?

12.6   What types of errors could occur during execution of the following COBOL statement:

```
COMPUTE AMOUNT = (TIME / BILL (LAST)) * 2.6
```

12.7   What types of errors could occur during the execution of the following COBOL statement:

```
MOVE AMOUNT-IN TO AMOUNT-OUT
```

CHAPTER THIRTEEN

STRUCTURED PROGRAMMING REVISITED

INTRODUCTION The first part of this book is designed to introduce you to the use of structured COBOL. We have introduced the three basic constructs that are allowed in a structured program: a **sequence** of statements, an **if-then-else** structure, and a **do-while** structure. By now you have learned the elements of COBOL required to implement these structures, and you have written a number of programs that required you to compose patterns of logic using these structures. Now we are going to examine some techniques and notations that can be extremely useful in formulating complex patterns of logic.

Some people seem to have a natural ability to create algorithms to solve problems. Others find it quite difficult. The same is true of learning to speak, yet the vast majority of people learn to communicate quite effectively. And just as everyone eventually learns to speak, most students can learn to formulate algorithms and write the corresponding programs, if they learn to approach such problems properly. In this chapter we are going to introduce an extremely useful method for formulating the logic of programs. It is called the technique of **stepwise refinement**. By mastering this approach, you can improve your ability to create patterns of logic quite dramatically.

This chapter also introduces two new notations for representing the logic of a program, **pseudo-code** and **Warnier diagrams**. Throughout this book we have used flowcharts to represent the logic of programs. However, the use of flowcharts has several disadvantages, which led to the creation of such alternatives. Each of these choices has significant advantages and numerous advocates. We will illustrate the relative merits of these notations by using them to describe the logic of an example program. Which notation you elect to use will often depend on factors beyond your control (e.g., many programming shops prefer that all employees use the same notation). However, all of these notations are excellent and convey essentially the same information. What is important is that you become proficient in the use of at least one of them.

13.1 Stepwise Refinement

Stepwise refinement is a method of attacking complex problems. It is based on a very simple idea: Try to break a problem up into simpler subproblems. Thus, to create the logic for a complex program, you should try to determine what major steps are required. Then formulate the solution to the complex problem in terms of these major steps. This allows you to concentrate on the overall logic, without worrying about the detailed solutions of the subproblems. Basically, you create the logic, deferring the details of the major steps. Once the overall logic seems correct, you attack the subproblems using the same approach.

To clarify these concepts, let us consider a specific example. Suppose that you work for a small computer store. Every time a customer purchases anything, a record giving the customer's name and address is added to a file. This file has been growing for the last three months, and your manager has now decided that he wishes to make a list of all of the customers who have made purchases. The list should contain one entry per customer, even though the customer may have made many purchases. You have a program that will read in a file and write out the records sorted in order. So the first thing that you do is to run your sort program. Now you have a file in which the records occur in order. However, the file may contain several consecutive records for the same customer. You must write a program that prints only one name and address for each customer in the file. That program should print four lines for each customer (the name and three lines of address). There should be one blank line between sets of four lines, and your program should print the records for 11 customers on each page (except, perhaps, the last page).

How should you approach the problem of creating the logic for the program? First, you should carefully study the description of the problem until it all makes sense to you. Then you must specify the highest level logic. The highest level logic for this program is shown in Fig. 13.1.

Within the logic illustrated in Fig. 13.1, it is assumed that you can "print one entry," which includes starting on a new page, if necessary. Further, it is assumed that you can "read the next name and address." This does not mean "read the next record," since that could cause several records to be printed for the same customer. To "read the next name and address," the program must read records until the record for the next customer is encountered. Thus, Fig. 13.1 does not specify the entire logic; it specifies a plan for attacking the problem. If you can specify the logic for each of the steps in the flowchart, then the plan will have been successfully completed.

Let us work through the subproblems in order. First, you will need to determine what is meant by the block "Initialize." It seems clear that this will have to include opening the files. In addition, you may have to initialize a few fields in working storage. You may already know which fields will be required, but you can defer specifying them until you have worked out solutions to the other subproblems.

The next subproblem is to "print one entry." The only real problem you will encounter here is exactly how to determine when to proceed to a new page. Discussion of a previous program introduced the idea of a "line counter" that kept track of the next line to be printed on a page. Use that same idea here, or you can count the number of customer records that have been printed on the current page. Either approach involves using a field in working storage to keep track of the position on the page. Normally, the line counter would be used, since that approach is quite general. In this case, however, using the

FIGURE 13.1 The logic required to LIST the customers in a file.

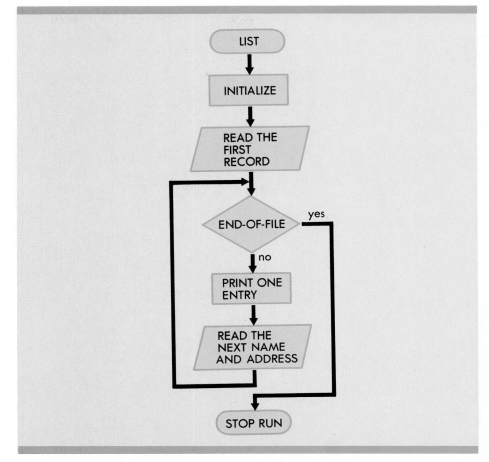

customer counter seems slightly easier. To use the customer counter, add "Initialize the customer counter to 0" to the Initialize logic. The print logic then becomes that shown in the flowchart in Fig. 13.2.

Now only one subproblem remains: to create the logic to read until a new customer is found (or end-of-file occurs). To do this, use a field in working storage to save the last name and address. Then when a record is read, it can be compared against that of the previous customer. If they are the same, the program must continue reading; else the new customer has been successfully read. Again, it is important to add "Initialize the previous customer to spaces" to the logic for Initialize. Now the logic for the routine becomes that shown in Fig. 13.3. The logic for the "terminate" subproblem is quite simple: Just close the two files.

At this point we have a complete, well-structured algorithm. You could use this logic to write a COBOL program that would perform correctly. However, because you normally must implement a loop in COBOL by PERFORMing a separate paragraph, you will have to break READ-NEXT into two separate paragraphs. The resulting form, which is more suitable for many versions of COBOL, would be as shown in Fig. 13.4.

Notice how we have progressed from a very general statement of the problem down to logic that is well-structured and suitable for implementation in COBOL. This was done by first working out the overall logic, deferring the

FIGURE 13.2 The PRINT logic.

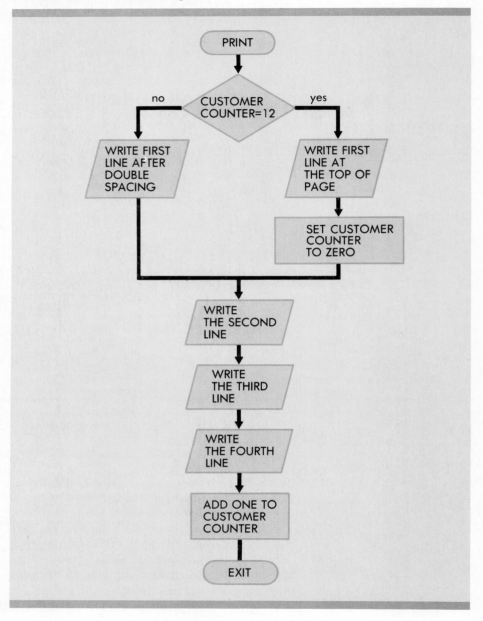

details of the major subproblems. Then the subproblems were attacked one at a time, until the entire logic was finished. Finally, some minor modifications were made that were required in order to implement the logic in COBOL.

Now you are ready to try the approach on a more difficult problem. Suppose that you must write a program that takes as input two of the sorted name and address files. Your program must again print exactly one entry per customer, where a customer can appear in either or both of the input files. How would you approach the problem of creating the logic for such a program? Please take a few minutes to try to work out the logic before continuing.

The overall logic for this problem is identical to the logic you used for

FIGURE 13.3 The logic to read the next customer's record.

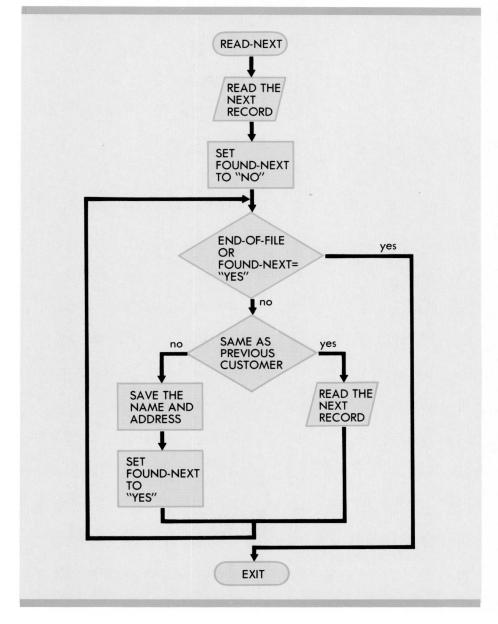

the previous problem! In fact only the subproblem "Read the next name and address" will change dramatically. Thus, you can approach the logic of this fairly complex program in exactly the same way that you approached the logic of the last program. What logic should be used for READ-NEXT? Suppose that you have a routine READ-FROM-TWO that would read the next record in order from the two input files. This routine could be invoked to move the "next" record into a specified field in working storage. It would determine which file the next record should be taken from, and move the record to an area in working storage. Then the logic of READ-NEXT would be that shown in Fig. 13.5.

FIGURE 13.4 The converted READ logic.

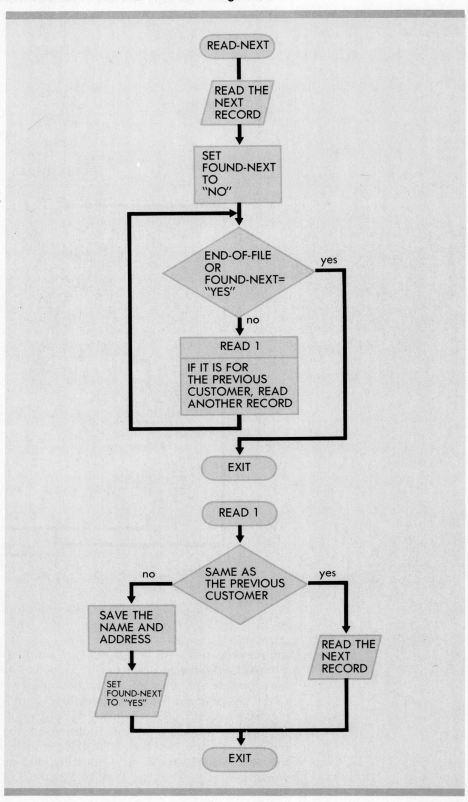

FIGURE 13.5 Logic to read from two files.

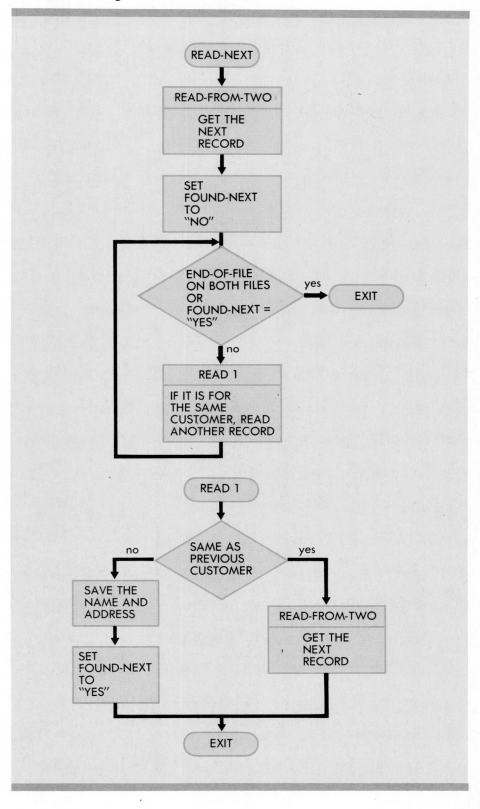

FIGURE 13.6 Logic of the READ-FROM-TWO routine.

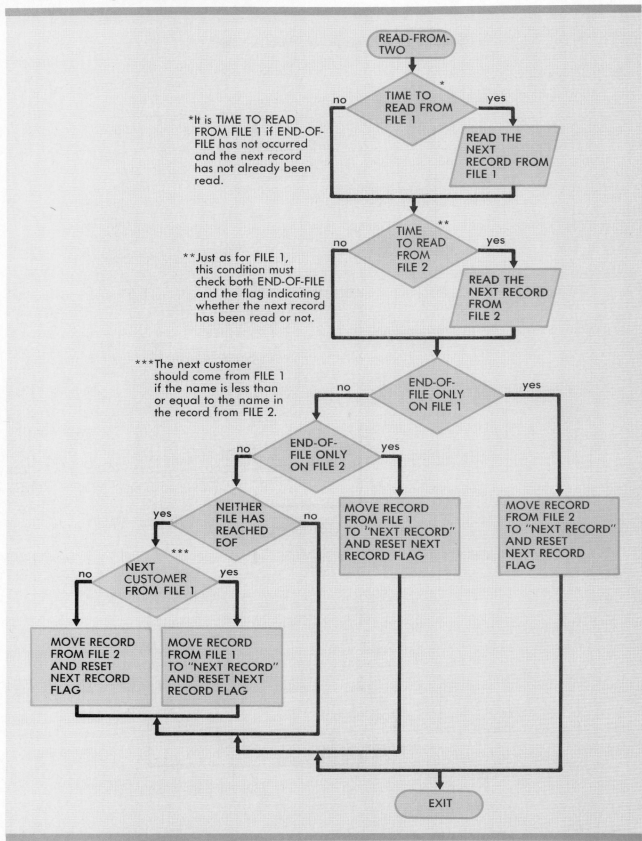

READ-FROM-TWO

TIME TO READ FROM FILE 1 *

*It is TIME TO READ FROM FILE 1 if END-OF-FILE has not occurred and the next record has not already been read.

READ THE NEXT RECORD FROM FILE 1

TIME TO READ FROM FILE 2 **

**Just as for FILE 1, this condition must check both END-OF-FILE and the flag indicating whether the next record has been read or not.

READ THE NEXT RECORD FROM FILE 2

***The next customer should come from FILE 1 if the name is less than or equal to the name in the record from FILE 2.

END-OF-FILE ONLY ON FILE 1

END-OF-FILE ONLY ON FILE 2

NEITHER FILE HAS REACHED EOF

NEXT CUSTOMER FROM FILE 1 ***

MOVE RECORD FROM FILE 2 AND RESET NEXT RECORD FLAG

MOVE RECORD FROM FILE 1 TO "NEXT RECORD" AND RESET NEXT RECORD FLAG

MOVE RECORD FROM FILE 1 TO "NEXT RECORD" AND RESET NEXT RECORD FLAG

MOVE RECORD FROM FILE 2 TO "NEXT RECORD" AND RESET NEXT RECORD FLAG

EXIT

Now the problem of creating the logic of READ-NEXT has been reduced to the subproblem of creating the logic of READ-FROM-TWO. This logic requires a little thought, since now you must keep track of end-of-file for each of the input files. Furthermore, in order to find out which record to return (the next record from the first file, or the next record from the second file), you will have to read each file. The solution involves the use of two end-of-file flags and two flags that indicate whether or not the next record has already been read from each file. All four flags must be initialized to 'N' in the Initialize logic. Again, we have logic that is detailed enough to be used to code a COBOL program.

13.2 Implementing Structured Logic in COBOL

In the last section we discussed the use of stepwise refinement to create a structured algorithm. In the first example, we found it necessary to modify the completed logic to conform to the restrictions of COBOL. The fact that some structured logic must be modified to allow a natural translation into COBOL

FIGURE 13.7 Correctly structured, but must be modified.

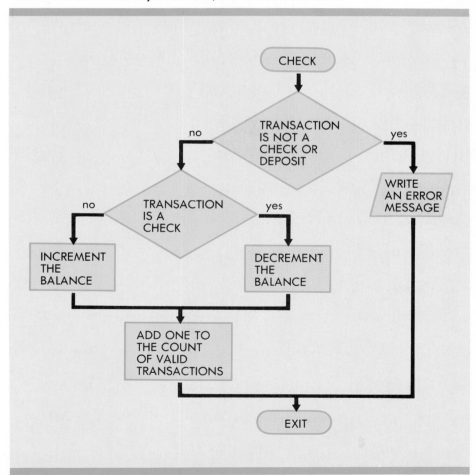

has led to proposed changes in COBOL. These changes will be implemented over the next few years, and then it will be possible to implement easily any structured logic in COBOL. Until then, however, programmers should be aware of certain restrictions imposed by the existing dialects of COBOL. In Chapter 11 we discussed a number of restrictions imposed by the current definition of the COBOL language. In this section we mention these restrictions again, because you will find it useful to be able to recognize these potential problem areas quickly.

FIGURE 13.8 The logic required for COBOL.

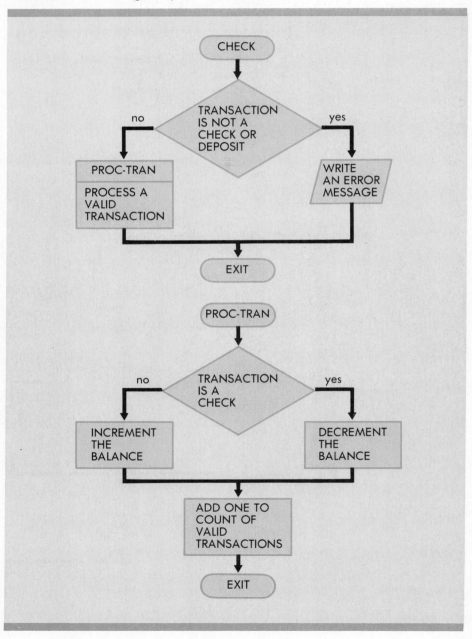

One major restriction of COBOL is that loops implemented with the PER-FORM verb must involve another paragraph. That is, the logic that forms the body of the loop (the instructions that are PERFORMed) must reside in a separate paragraph. In the first example in the last section, this required creating a small routine called READ1, which contained the statements in the body of the loop.

Another restriction involves nested IF statements. Consider the logic shown in the flowchart in Fig. 13.7, which is properly structured. This simple logic cannot be implemented in COBOL. Instead, you must use two routines as shown in the flowcharts in Fig. 13.8.

Finally, as you have been warned in previous chapters, clauses like the AT END clause on READ statements are terminated at the end of a sentence. This means that logic such as that shown in the flowchart in Fig. 13.9 will not work. Again, two routines will be required; they are flowcharted in Fig. 13.10. These deficiencies in COBOL will be corrected as the language is updated.

FIGURE 13.9 A common error with the use of READ.

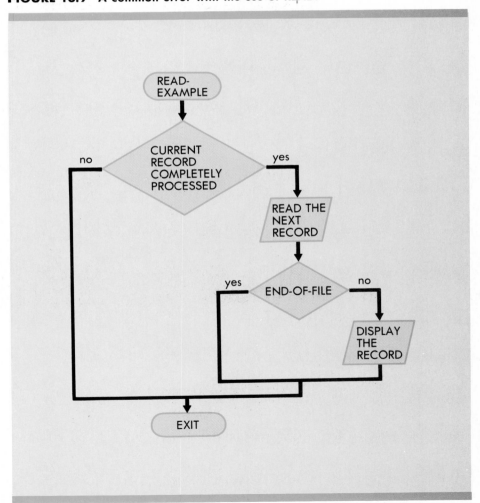

FIGURE 13.10 The correct use of READ.

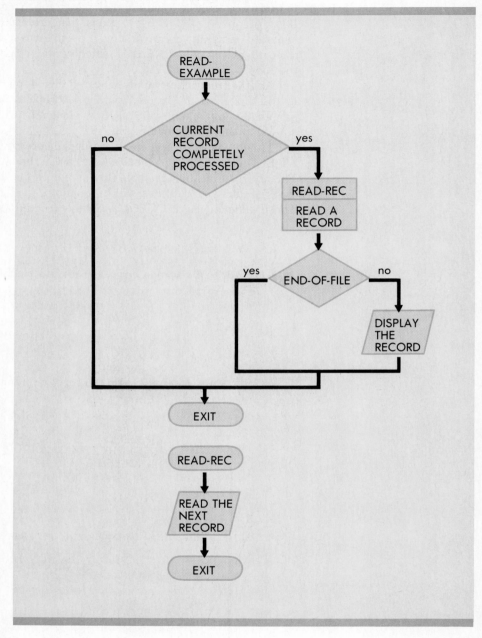

13.3 **Pseudo-code**

Throughout this text we have emphasized the significance of the basic control structures that can be used in forming well-structured programs. We have represented all of our logic with flowcharts. Flowcharts are the most widely used tool for representing patterns of logic, because of their visual impact. A well-drawn flowchart is one of the clearest representations of a program's logic.

However, there are several drawbacks to the use of flowcharts. The major drawback is simply that they cannot easily be kept in machine-readable form with the program itself. That is, the flowchart and the program are normally stored separately. This almost inevitably leads to the unfortunate situation where the program gets updated, but the flowchart does not. The second major difficulty in the use of flowcharts is related to the first: it is hard to update a flowchart. A small alteration can require a significant amount of time redrawing the logic. These two drawbacks have caused people to investigate alternatives for representing the logic of programs.

By far the most popular alternative to flowcharting is the use of **pseudo-code**. A variety of different dialects for pseudo-code have been created and are in wide use. Some dialects, such as the Systems Design Language, popularized by Kenneth Orr, have fairly precise rules of syntax. Others are somewhat less formal. However, all versions are quite similar. In all cases the idea is to describe the logic of the program in English sentences, with indenting and a few keywords used to make the control structure apparent. To illustrate the notion, let us reconsider the logic for a routine discussed earlier in this chapter. Figure 13.11 includes both a flowchart and pseudo-code for the same routine.

Here, the logic of the routine is enclosed by

```
READ-NEXT:  procedure
              .
              .
              .
            endproc
```

The lines describing the actual steps of READ-NEXT are indented. Names of routines or variables are given in uppercase. Note the correspondence between the boxes in the flowchart and the lines in the pseudo-code. By examining the pseudo-code, it should be apparent that loops are represented by

```
do while  (condition)
  .
  .
  .
enddo
```

where the body of the loop is indented. The if-then-else construct is represented by

```
if (condition)
  .
  .
else
  .
endif
```

Within these simple constructs, steps of logic are described in English. You can make your descriptions as detailed as you like. In the case of pseudo-code, you are not restricted by the number of words that can be included in a box.

Throughout the remainder of this book, we will use both flowcharts and pseudo-code wherever they seem appropriate. We urge you to become familiar with both techniques, as well as the alternative described in the next section. Each has its strengths and weaknesses.

FIGURE 13.11

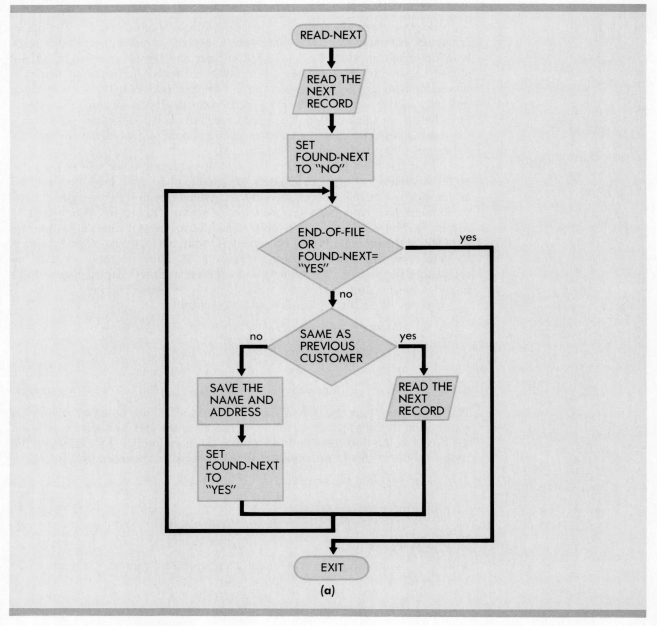

(a)

```
READ-NEXT: procedure
              read the next record
              FOUND-NEXT = no
              do while (not end-of-file) and (FOUND-NEXT = no)
                  if same as previous customer
                      read the next record
                  else
                      save the name and address
                      FOUND-NEXT = yes
                  endif
              enddo
          endproc
```
(b)

13.4 Warnier Diagrams

Yet another notation for describing structured logic is the **Warnier diagram**. The Warnier diagram was invented by Jean-Dominique Warnier as a tool for describing not only program logic, but systems flow and file structures, as well. Its use in the United States is due largely to the writings of Kenneth Orr. In this section we will discuss only the use of Warnier diagrams to represent structured logic and compare the advantages of such diagrams with those of flowcharts and pseudo-code.

Figure 13.12 gives the logic of the LIST program from Section 13.1 as it would be represented using Warnier diagrams. The rules for representing logic using these diagrams are as follows:

Rule 1 The logic for a single routine is expanded within a single curly bracket. Thus, the logic of LIST appears within the leftmost bracket.

Rule 2 To expand the details of the logic for a step, enclose the detailed logic within another curly bracket just to the right of the step being expanded.

Rule 3 To represent a sequence of steps, simply list them in order. The small number in parentheses under each step is the number of times that it is executed. If you study the first two steps of LIST, which represent a sequence construct (refer back to the flowchart of LIST in Fig. 13.1), you should see that they each are executed once.

Rule 4 To represent an iteration, such as the loop to "Process Records" in the LIST logic, a value other than 1 is specified as the number of times that the step is executed.

Rule 5 To represent the logic of an if-then-else construct, use the technique illustrated in the expansion of "Print Current Record". Here

$$\text{NUM-ON-PAGE} = 12 \atop (0,1) \quad \Big\{$$

indicates that the expansion to the right is executed either 0 or 1 times, depending on whether or not the condition is true. A horizontal line over a condition means the negation of the condition. Thus,

$$\overline{\text{NUM-ON-PAGE}=12} \atop (0,1) \quad \Big\{$$

indicates that the expansion of this step is executed exactly when NUM-ON-PAGE is not 12. The two conditions are separated by

which means that only one of these expansions will be executed.

First, note that there is a very close correspondence between the logic displayed by a flowchart, by pseudo-code, and by a Warnier diagram. There are, however, some differences between the use of Warnier diagrams and the other two approaches. The Warnier diagram much more successfully conveys the spirit of stepwise refinement. You can readily visualize the methodic expansion of steps into more detailed expositions. On the other hand, loops are not represented in as much detail. In particular, the exact termination condition is not specified in a Warnier diagram, although it is frequently specified as a note at the edge of the diagram. In addition, such diagrams can become quite sizable and, frequently, must be split at appropriate points.

FIGURE 13.12 The logic to list the customers in a file.

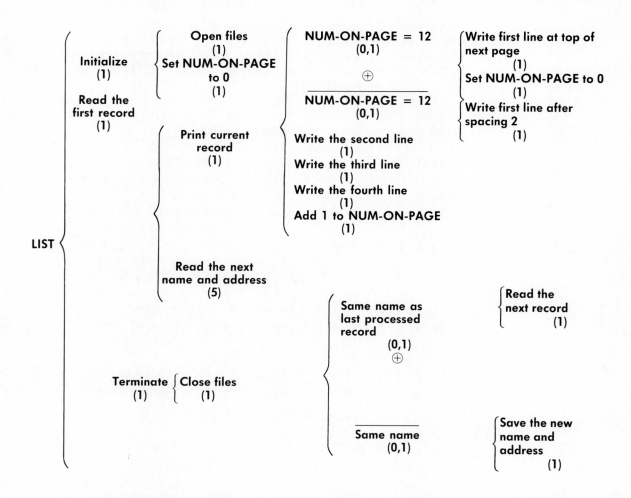

SUMMARY

In this chapter we have presented the basic tool of stepwise refinement. It is one of the most critical concepts for a programmer to grasp. Then we presented two new techniques for representing structured logic, pseudo-code, and Warnier diagrams. Flowcharts offer a visual representation of the detailed structured logic in a better way than either of these new techniques. However, they do not convey the basic stepwise refinement as well as the Warnier diagrams, and they cannot be put into machine-readable form as conveniently as pseudo-code. All three techniques have substantial strengths, which has resulted in sharp controversy concerning their relative merits. We urge you to become comfortable with all three techniques, since you will quite probably encounter them all if you make a career of programming.

There are a number of other tools that have been proposed for representing structured logic. None of these other tools, however, is very widely used. If you master these three techniques, you will have little difficulty picking up any new notation.

REVIEW QUESTIONS

13.1 What are the three basic constructs that can be used in a structured program?

13.2 Describe what is meant by "stepwise refinement."

13.3 Describe at least three patterns of structured logic that cannot be implemented in current versions of COBOL.

13.4 How is a loop represented in pseudo-code? How is an if-then-else construct represented in pseudo-code?

13.5 What advantages does pseudo-code have over flowcharting?

13.6 What advantages does a Warnier diagram have over pseudo-code or a flowchart?

13.7 What advantages does a flowchart have over a Warnier diagram?

EXERCISES

13.1 Suppose that you have a table of integers. To be specific, suppose that the table contains NUM-ENT values. Create the logic to remove duplicate entries from the table, resetting NUM-ENT to the number of entries in the compressed table. Represent the logic using a flowchart, pseudo-code, and a Warnier diagram.

13.2 This exercise is just like 13.1, but here you may assume that the integers in the table occur in ascending order (i.e., the table is sorted).

13.3 Suppose that you have a file of name-and-address records. That is, each record in the file contains four lines of a customer's name and address. Flowchart the logic required to print name and address labels from the input records. This will require double-spacing for the first line, and single-spacing the remaining lines in an input record.

13.4 This problem is just like Exercise 13.3, except that the labels are to be printed "two-up." That is, the printed labels should look like

```
        JOHN DOE               MARY STEVENS
        1823 LARAMIE DRIVE     2 MARSHALL AVENUE
        INDUSTRIAL PARK        LAKE GEORGE, MA 06738
        JENSON, IN 49824


        MARK EDWARDS           ROBERT JACKSON
              .                      .

              .                      .
```

Represent your logic with a Warnier diagram. Can your solution be generalized? That is, could a small change allow the program to be used for "four-up" labels?

13.5   Present (using pseudo-code) logic that can be used to merge two sorted input files. That is, the program will take as input two files of records that are ordered. To be specific, suppose that the files contain name-and-address records. It will produce as output a new sorted file, which will contain all of the records that occur in the two input files. After completing the logic, estimate how many changes would be required to handle four input files. How might you go about organizing the logic?

13.6   Using Warnier diagrams, create the logic to delete records from a file. That is, the logic should describe a program that would take as input two files:

a) Each record in the first file contains a customer's social security number, name, and address. The records occur in ascending order based on the social security numbers.

b) Each record in the second file contains just a social security number. These records also occur in order based on the social security numbers.

The program would produce a single file composed of records from the first file that have social security numbers that do not occur in the second file.

CHAPTER FOURTEEN

PROGRAMMING METHODOLOGIES

INTRODUCTION So far we have concentrated on the specific details of the COBOL language and the problems involved in writing correct programs using the language. We will now consider the entire **life-cycle** of a program. By viewing the act of programming as a component in a larger process, a number of significant insights can be gained, the most important being that the creation of a data processing system normally requires the coordinated work of several people—a group effort. The implications of this rather harmless sounding observation may well surprise you. The most critical problems encountered in most programming projects are not technical. They revolve around the central problem of creating an environment in which a number of people can effectively contribute in a joint effort.

We will break the problem of creating a useful data processing system into four distinct phases—**systems analysis**, **coding**, **testing**, and **maintenance**. The tools and methodologies appropriate to each of the four phases are quite distinct, although they are related.

Program documentation can serve several quite distinct purposes. Tools such as flowcharts, pseudo-code, and Warnier diagrams can be used to help the programmer develop a correct solution. They can also be used to communicate a solution to co-workers. Additional tools for recording and communicating a correct solution, **hierarchy charts** and **input-process-output diagrams**, can also be useful. These tools are particularly important in the maintenance phase of the life-cycle. Since maintenance activity consumes as much as 75–80% of the labor in many programming departments, such productivity aids tend to be taken very seriously.

In addition to aids for documenting programs, methodologies have arisen for the actual process of creating the solution. We will briefly discuss some of the more popular methodologies, in particular, **chief programmer teams** and **code reviews**. These approaches have evolved (and are evolving) as tools to control projects. That is, they create an environment in which the development of a large system composed of many programs proceeds in a more predictable manner. In addition, they tend to establish some level of quality control, which normally leads to a more reliable end product.

* Frederick P. Brooks, Jr., *Mythical Man Month* (Reading, Mass.: Addison-Wesley, 1974), p. 4.

When such reviews can take place without evoking a defensive reaction on the part of those whose code is being reviewed, they serve a truly useful

14.1 The Life-cycle of a System

to conjecture that all programs and systems should be done by individuals working singly.

purpose. A great deal of work has been done exploring the problem of creating an environment where reviews are treated as a positive, productive experience, rather than an attack on the author of the work. Minor variations on the theme of code review are the procedures characterized as "structured walk-throughs," "inspections," and "technical reviews." In all cases, the emphasis should be to enhance the quality of the final product by locating errors as soon as possible in a cooperative, nondefensive environment. Code reviews should not be used as a vehicle for criticizing or evaluating the author of the code.

14.5 Documenting a Program with HIPO Diagrams

In Chapter 13 we discussed several design and documentation aids—flowcharts, pseudo-code, and Warnier diagrams. These can all be used successfully to aid in developing and representing the logic of a program. However, they have not proven completely adequate as means for documenting a completed program or system. It is not that they fail to convey information well; they just do not convey all of the necessary information in the most useful form. It is very hard to convey exactly why this is true based on the experiences that you have had programming the assignments in this text. Those programs are simply too small to result in the types of problems associated with larger programs and systems. In fact, it may very well appear to be the case that you can easily write programs without even developing the logic using the tools presented in Chapter 13. In any event, a well-annotated structured program might seem to be quite adequate as a final product.

As we pointed out earlier, much of the programming effort expended on a program is frequently spent in the maintenance stage of its life-cycle. In large, complex programs it becomes increasingly important that useful, concise documentation be developed by the original programmer. This will be apparent to you once you have attempted to locate an error in a program that someone else has written. Hence, we are going to present in this section some basic techniques for documenting large programs which have proven useful. We urge you to study these techniques and to use them on your future programs, so that you will be prepared to use them in those situations in which they are truly necessary.

One of the most widely utilized documentation techniques is the HIPO package developed by IBM. HIPO documentation includes both **hierarchy charts** and **input-process-output diagrams**. The hierarchy charts offer a visual overview of the different routines in a program, while the input-process-output diagrams present the detailed functionality of each routine. HIPO diagrams were not designed just to document completed programs. Rather, they were created to allow documentation to evolve in an orderly manner throughout the life-cycle of the system. They can be used to document the entire system, as well as the individual programs in the system.

Three separate types of HIPO documentation packages would normally be created during the life-cycle of a system:

1. An **initial design package** is developed during the analysis and design stage of a system, which specifies the functions that the system must perform. It is used to enhance communication between the end-users, the designers, and management.

2. The **detailed design package** is developed by programmers from the initial design package (with help from the analysts) as a basis for specifying

the detailed design before coding the programs in the system. Then as the system is actually coded, this package is updated to reflect the final system accurately.

3. The **maintenance package** is the documentation that is used as a reference for corrections and enhancements to the system. Normally, the detailed design evolves during development into the final maintenance package.

The creation of the initial design package is beyond the scope of our discussion, although much of what we will say would apply to the creation of the original HIPO package.

A HIPO package contains a hierarchy chart, which is frequently referred to as a **visual table of contents**. A hierarchy chart can be used to display the hierarchical relation of the routines in a program. For example, Fig. 14.1 presents a hierarchy chart for the simple payroll program, EXAMPLE5, discussed in Chapter 7.

Notice that the hierarchy chart offers a mechanism for quickly locating the routines that perform each function. In programs that have over 10 to 20 separate routines, this quick reference can be very useful.

Besides the hierarchy chart, a HIPO package contains input-process-output diagrams, which express the function of each module. In large systems, these diagrams are broken into two sets: an overview of the system and detailed specifications. For a program as small as EXAMPLE5, it is impossible to talk meaningfully about overview diagrams. However, you can begin to understand what information is conveyed by input-process-output diagrams by studying Figs. 14.2–14.6, which give the detailed diagrams for EXAMPLE5. Notice that the diagram for each module includes the input data items at left, the output items (which may become input to later steps) at right, and the processes that transform the data items in the center. The arrows are used to show access to or storage of data. For diagrams that describe complex functions, the reverse side of the HIPO worksheet offers space for extended descriptions.

IBM offers for sale special forms and templates that make the construction of HIPO packages simpler. They also provide booklets that offer extensive examples and suggested procedures for creating and evaluating HIPO diagrams. Figures 14.7 and 14.8 display the available HIPO worksheets and the template that can be used to draw the diagrams.

FIGURE 14.1   A hierarchy chart for the payroll program.

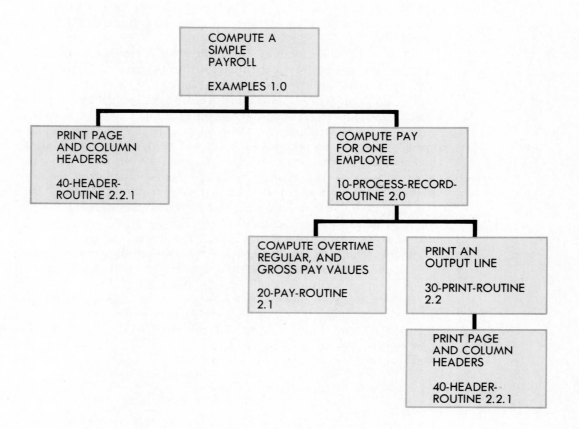

FIGURE 14.2 The logic of EXAMPLE5.

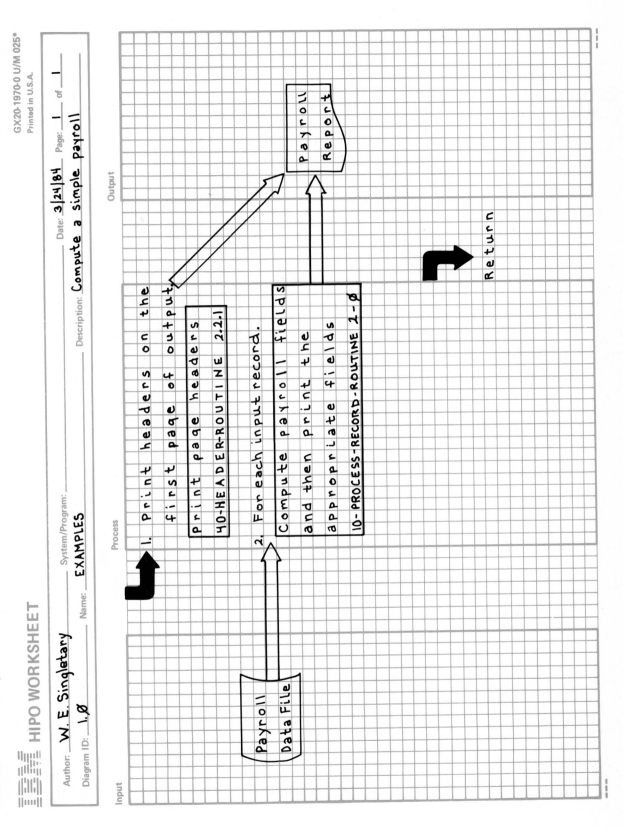

IBM HIPO WORKSHEET

GX20-1970-0 U/M 025*
Printed in U.S.A.

Author: W. E. Singletary   System/Program: ____   Date: 3/24/84   Page: 1 of 1

Diagram ID: 1.0   Name: EXAMPLES   Description: Compute a simple Payroll

Input

Process

1. Print headers on the first page of output.

Print page headers
40-HEADER-ROUTINE 2.2.1

2. For each input record.

Compute payroll fields and then print the appropriate fields
10-PROCESS-RECORD-ROUTINE 1-0

Payroll Data File

Output

Payroll Report

Return

FIGURE 14.3 The logic of EXAMPLE5.

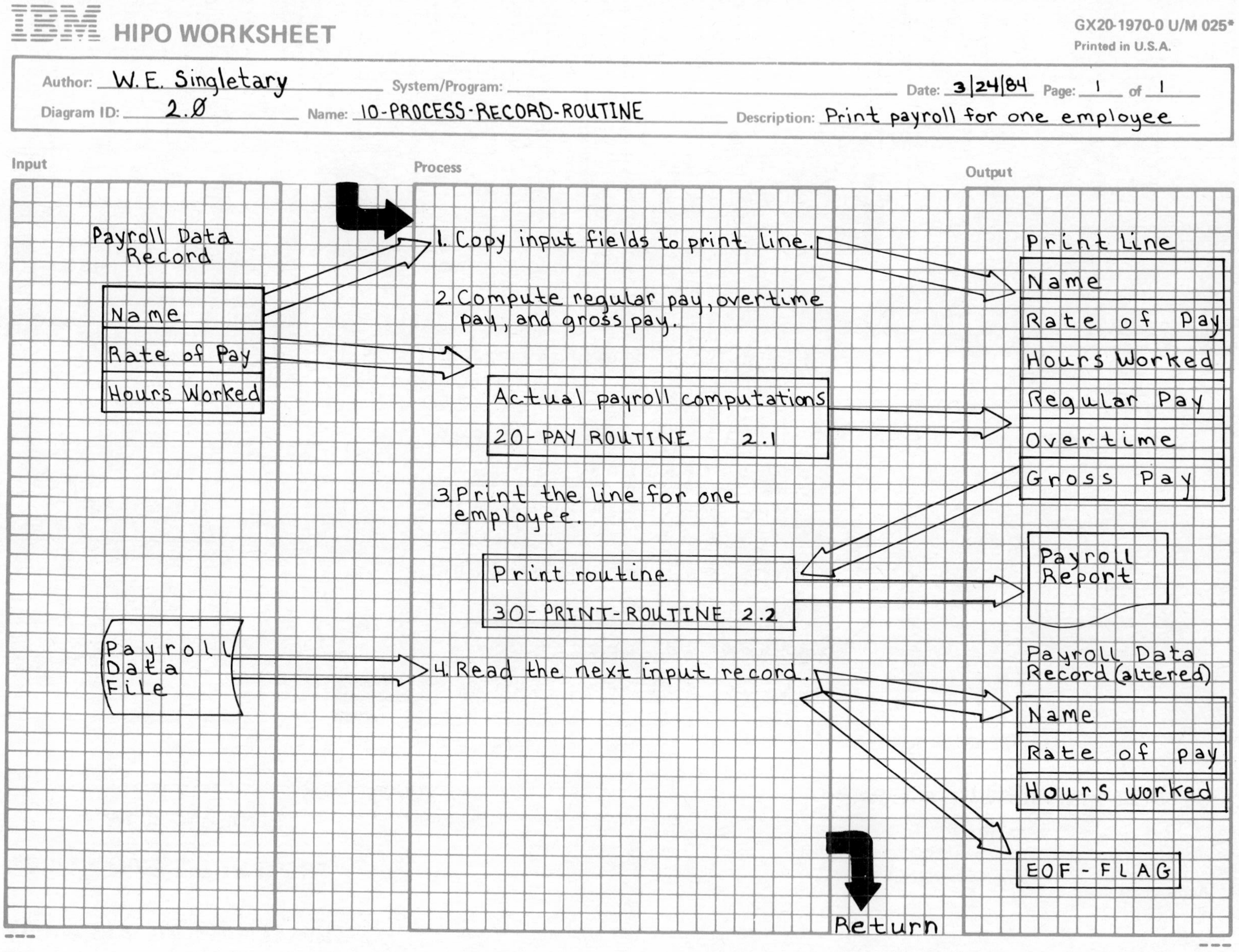

HIPO WORKSHEET

GX20-1970-0 U/M 025*
Printed in U.S.A.

Author: W. E. Singletary   System/Program: Date: 3/24/84   Page: 1 of 1

Diagram ID: 2.0   Name: 10-PROCESS-RECORD-ROUTINE   Description: Print payroll for one employee

Input

Payroll Data Record
- Name
- Rate of Pay
- Hours Worked

Payroll Data File

Process

1. Copy input fields to print line.

2. Compute regular pay, overtime pay, and gross pay.

   Actual payroll computations
   20-PAY ROUTINE 2.1

3. Print the line for one employee.

   Print routine
   30-PRINT-ROUTINE 2.2

4. Read the next input record.

Output

Print Line
- Name
- Rate of Pay
- Hours Worked
- Regular Pay
- Overtime
- Gross Pay

Payroll Report

Payroll Data Record (altered)
- Name
- Rate of pay
- Hours worked

EOF-FLAG

Return

FIGURE 14.4 The logic of EXAMPLE5.

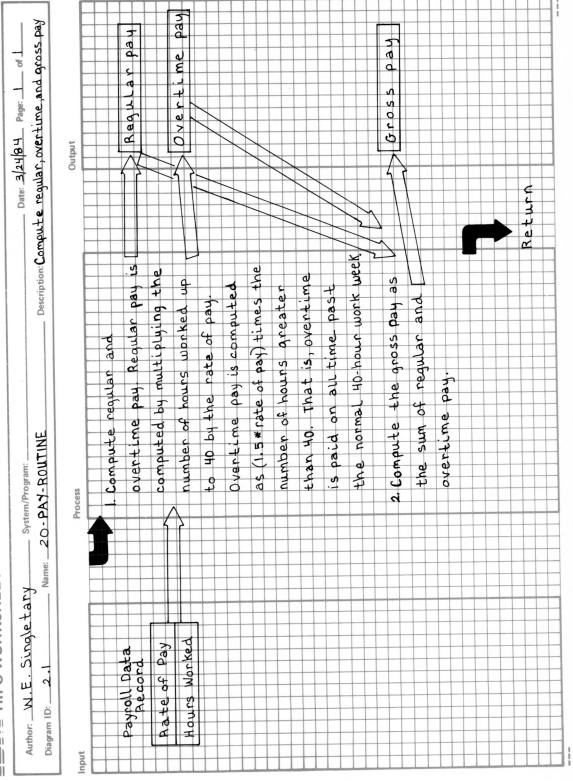

HIPO WORKSHEET

Author: __W.E. Singletary__   System/Program: _____   Date: __3/24/84__   Page: __1__ of __1__

GX20-1970-0 U/M 025*
Printed in U.S.A.

Diagram ID: __2.1__   Name: __20-PAY-ROUTINE__   Description: __Compute regular, overtime, and gross pay__

Input

Payroll Data Record
- Rate of Pay
- Hours Worked

Process

1. Compute regular and overtime pay. Regular pay is computed by multiplying the number of hours worked up to 40 by the rate of pay. Overtime pay is computed as (1.5 * rate of pay) times the number of hours greater than 40. That is, overtime is paid on all time past the normal 40-hour work week.

2. Compute the gross pay as the sum of regular and overtime pay.

Return

Output

Regular pay

Overtime pay

Gross pay

FIGURE 14.5 The logic of EXAMPLE5.

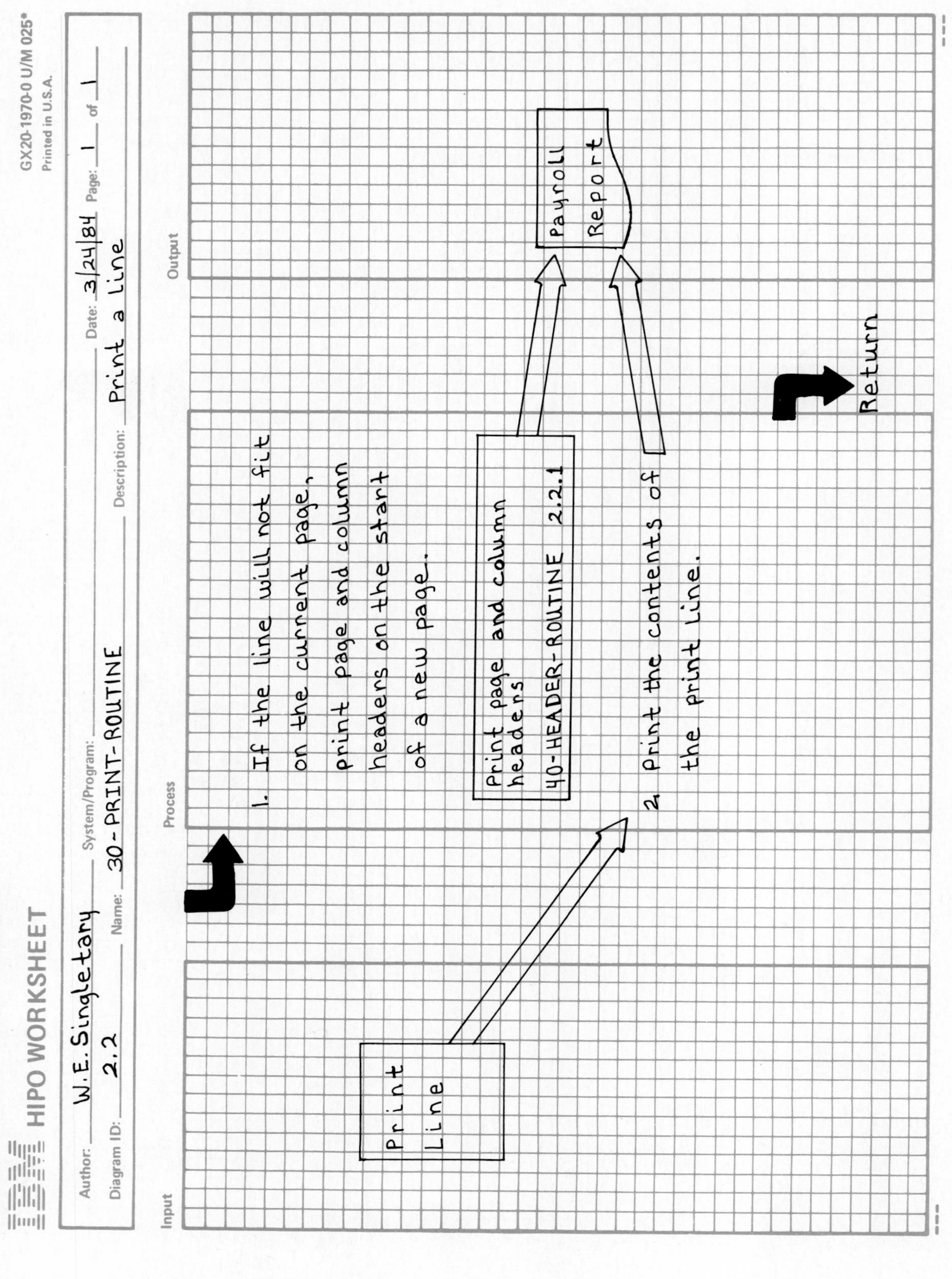

IBM **HIPO WORKSHEET**

GX20-1970-0 U/M 025*
Printed in U.S.A.

Author: _W. E. Singletary_　　System/Program: _____　　Date: _3/24/84_　Page: _1_ of _1_

Diagram ID: _2.2_　Name: _30-PRINT-ROUTINE_　Description: _Print a line_

Input

Print Line

Process

1. If the line will not fit on the current page, print page and column headers on the start of a new page.

   Print page and column headers
   40-HEADER-ROUTINE 2.2.1

2. Print the contents of the print line.

Output

Payroll Report

Return

FIGURE 14.6 The logic of EXAMPLE5.

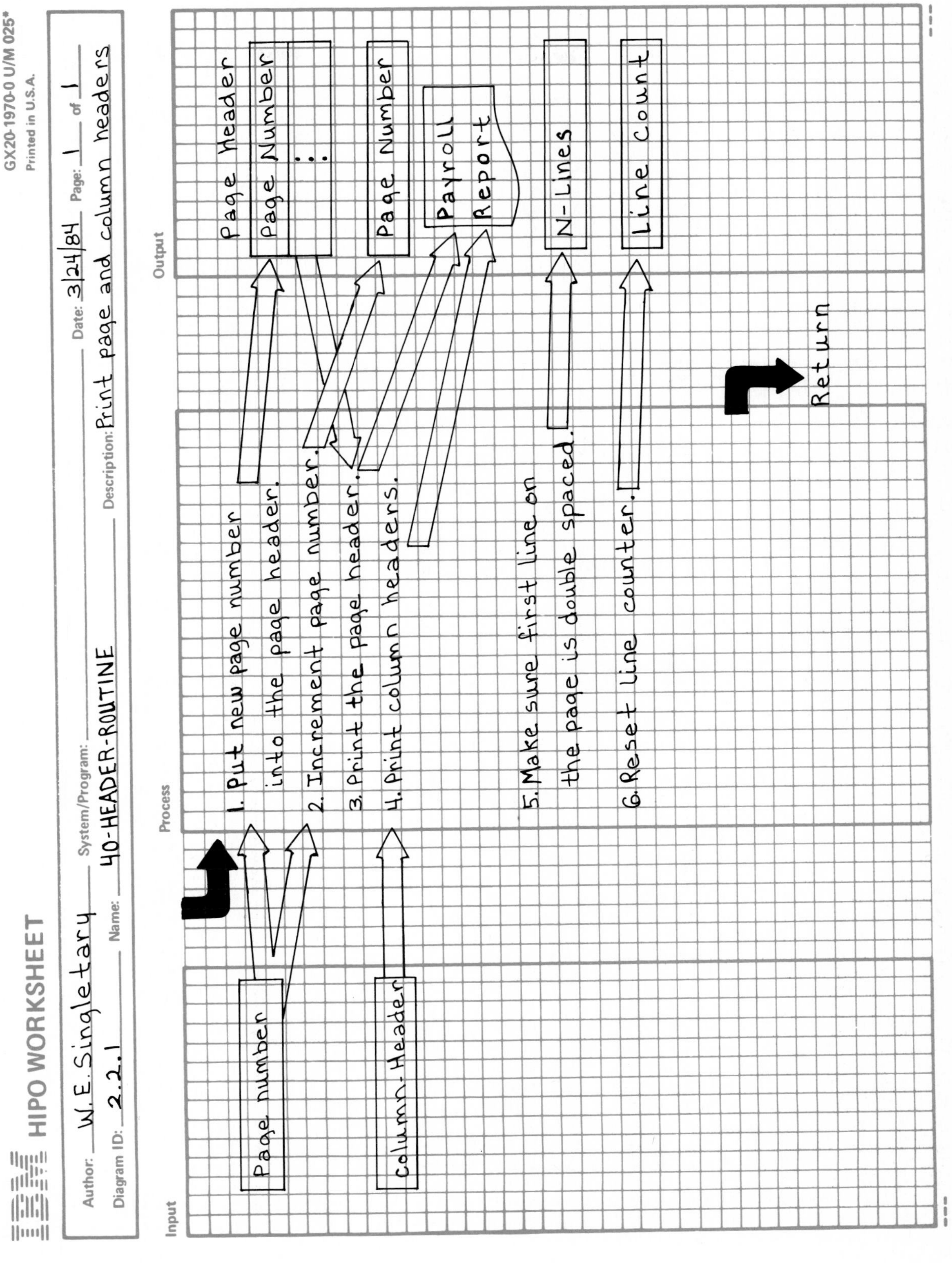

IBM HIPO WORKSHEET

Author: W.E. Singletary   System/Program: Date: 3/24/84   Page: 1 of 1
Diagram ID: 2.2.1   Name: 40-HEADER-ROUTINE   Description: Print page and column headers

GX20-1970-0 U/M 025*
Printed in U.S.A.

Input

Page Number

Column Header

Process

1. Put new page number into the page header.
2. Increment page number.
3. Print the page header.
4. Print column headers.

5. Make sure first line on the page is double spaced.

6. Reset line counter.

Output

Page Header
Page Number
...

Page Number

Payroll Report

N-Lines

Line Count

Return

FIGURE 14.7 The HIPO worksheet.

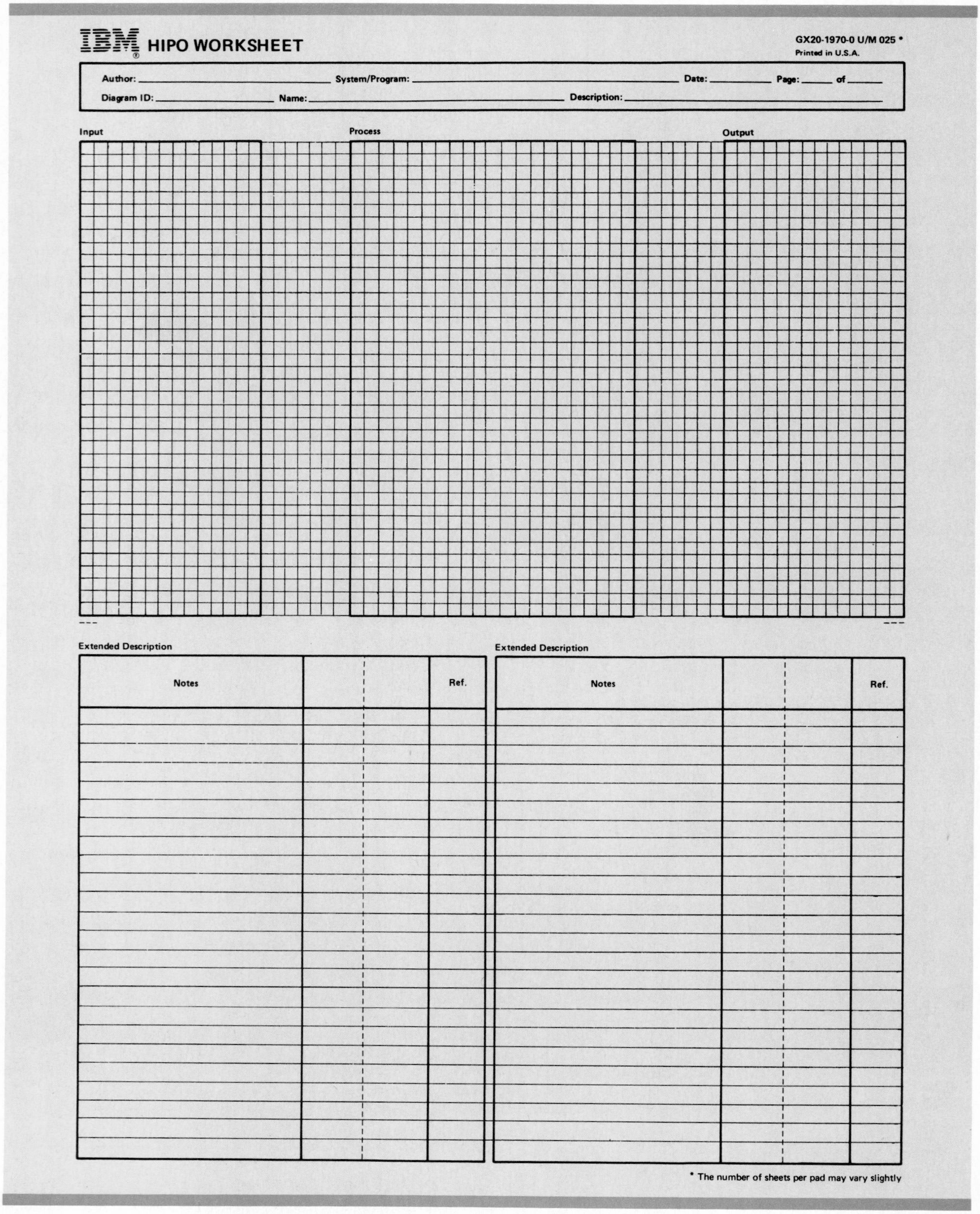
IBM HIPO WORKSHEET

GX20-1970-0 U/M 025 *
Printed in U.S.A.

Author: ____ System/Program: ____ Date: ____ Page: ____ of ____

Diagram ID: ____ Name: ____ Description: ____

Input | Process | Output

Extended Description

Notes		Ref.

Extended Description

Notes		Ref.

* The number of sheets per pad may vary slightly

FIGURE 14.8 The HIPO template.

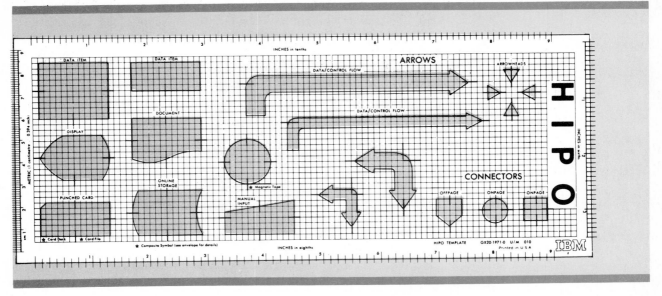

S U M M A R Y

In this chapter we have tried to present the act of programming as one stage in the life-cycle of a system. The creation of most systems is a group activity, requiring the coordinated efforts of several people. Successful group management has proven to be much more difficult than anticipated. Experimentation has resulted in a number of proposed organizational frameworks, including the concept of the chief programmer team.

A chief programmer team includes a chief programmer, a backup programmer, a librarian, and task programmers. The chief programmer is an experienced technician who is responsible for the technical quality of the finished product. The backup programmer aids the chief programmer and must be able to assume the chief programmer's role in an emergency. The librarian offers clerical and organizational support for the team. The task programmers provide programming support.

Code reviews are a major communication vehicle for group projects. They can be used to correct errors at an early stage. However, to be successful, they must occur in a cooperative, nondefensive environment and must be focused on the correction of errors.

Because the programs produced during the coding stage will be used in both the testing and maintenance stages, it is important to include adequate, concise documentation. The tools discussed in Chapter 13, which are excellent aids for program development and the representation of structured logic, should be supplemented with tools that convey an overview of the system and the functions (but not the logic) of the components of the system. This has led to the increased use of documentation techniques such as HIPOs popularized by IBM. A HIPO package includes hierarchy charts to describe the hierarchical relationship of the components of the system, and input-process-output diagrams to describe the functions performed by each component.

A number of different programming methodologies have arisen over the last decade. Many have proved to be quite successful. We certainly have not discussed all of them, and have only presented a cursory overview of those we consider most significant. We have tried to convey the need for formalized communication techniques, which may be difficult to perceive fully until you have worked on a large data processing system. For now it is enough for you to grasp the basic problems and to have an idea of the essential ideas that have been proposed to solve them.

R E V I E W   Q U E S T I O N S

14.1   What are the four stages in the life-cycle of a system?

14.2   Why is the creation of a system normally a group activity?

14.3   How does the chief programmer team differ from the usual management structure? What are the roles of the members of a chief programmer team?

14.4   What types of information do HIPO diagrams convey that the tools discussed in Chapter 13 do not?

14.5   What types of HIPO packages are normally constructed during the life-cycle of a system?

14.6   What types of diagrams are normally included in a HIPO package?

E X E R C I S E S

14.1   Create a HIPO package to document EXAMPLE8.

14.2   Create a HIPO package to document EXAMPLE9.

CHAPTER FIFTEEN

EDITING DATA

INTRODUCTION In all of our examples up to this point, we have not been overly concerned about checking for errors in the input records. Our intent was to expose you as rapidly as possible to features of the COBOL language. It is now time to consider the topic of verifying input data fields, which is normally called **editing** the input data.

If a program accepts input records prepared by humans, it should properly handle the situation in which improper data occurs in one or more records. Abnormal termination of execution is almost always an unacceptable approach. Rather, the program should detect invalid data and display it, so that the user can easily locate and correct the errors. It is almost impossible to overemphasize the importance of editing user-supplied data.

The first topic in this chapter is the common types of editing. Particular techniques are presented for editing numeric fields, fields that can legitimately take on one of a set of designated values, numeric fields in which a check-digit is utilized, and fields that are supposed to contain valid dates. These topics are illustrated by reconsidering a previous example program.

The chapter ends by discussing the special considerations involved in storing data in permanent disk or tape files (called **master files** or **data bases**). The final section explains the appropriate strategy for keeping such data valid and why it is not usually necessary for all programs that access such data to revalidate the contents of each record.

15.1 Editing Numeric Fields

Many of the programs that occur in previous chapters process input records that include numeric data fields. In many cases, if invalid input records were submitted to the program, execution would terminate abnormally (frequently with some rather obscure message). For most situations, this puts too much burden on the user. A properly written program edits each numeric field on an input record to make sure that the contents are acceptable. This must be done before the program attempts any computation that would require such a field to contain valid data.

What does it mean to "make sure that the contents are acceptable"? Normally, this involves two distinct operations.

Step 1 Verify that the field contains a numeric value. This can be done quite easily—unless a sign, leading blanks, or a decimal point are allowed in the field.

Step 2 If there are known limits to the acceptable values for the data, check these bounds. For example, if a field is supposed to contain a valid time in the HH:MM:SS format, then the program should not accept as valid any value of SS (seconds) which is greater than 59.

These two types of editing may seem quite trivial. However, failure to include such simple edit checks has on numerous occasions cost organizations substantial amounts of money. In Section 15.5 we present an enhanced version of the program that printed appointments for the coming week. In the previous version of that program, which occurred in Chapter 10, it was assumed that each input record contained a value in the time slot field that ranged between 1 and 16. Consider how irritating it would be to attempt to use such a program and have it fail (quite mysteriously) due to an invalid value typed in the time slot. The new version prevents such an occurrence by properly editing the contents of the field.

Having discussed the importance of editing numeric fields, let us briefly consider the difficulties that may arise in determining whether or not a field contains a numeric value (and what value). If the field NUM-VAL-1 is supposed to contain only numeric digits, then a simple class test suffices:

```
IF NUM-VAL-1 IS NUMERIC
    MOVE 'Y' TO VALID-DATA
ELSE
    MOVE 'N' TO VALID-DATA.
```

However, input formats should normally be designed for the convenience of the end-user. In these cases, leading blanks might be allowed, the number might not have to be right-justified, a sign might be included, or a decimal point might be included in the field. These situations require more complex editing logic.

Consider the case in which leading blanks are allowed (but the number itself must be right-justified in the field). To make the example concrete, suppose that

```
05  INPUT-FLD-2    PIC X(4).
```

is such a field. COBOL provides the INSPECT statement, which can be used conveniently to handle such editing requirements. The INSPECT statement has some fairly general capabilities for counting and/or replacing characters in a field. Rather than give the most general format for the statement, we will illustrate its more common uses. In this instance, we first move the input field to another field

```
05   NUM-VAL-2     PIC 9(4).
```

which is then altered to remove the leading blanks. The code to edit NUM-VAL-2 would be as follows:

```
MOVE INPUT-FLD-2 TO NUM-VAL-2.
IF NUM-VAL-2 IS = SPACES
    MOVE 'N' TO VALID-DATA
ELSE
    INSPECT NUM-VAL-2
        REPLACING LEADING SPACES WITH ZEROS
    IF NUM-VAL-2 IS NOT NUMERIC
        MOVE 'N' TO VALID-DATA
    ELSE
        MOVE 'Y' TO VALID-DATA.
```

Here the INSPECT is used to replace any leading spaces with zeros.

Now let us consider the case in which an implied decimal point exists, and leading blanks are allowed. In this case, the fields should be declared as

```
05   INPUT-FLD-3               PIC X(6).
         .

         .

         .

05   NUM-VAL-3                 PIC 9(4)V99.
05   NUM-VAL-3-SPLIT REDEFINES NUM-VAL-3.
     10   NUM-VAL-3-HEAD        PIC X(4).
     10   NUM-VAL-3-TAIL        PIC XX.
```

The editing logic would go as follows:

```
MOVE INPUT-FLD-3 TO NUM-VAL-3-SPLIT.
INSPECT NUM-VAL-3-HEAD
    REPLACING LEADING SPACES WITH ZEROS
IF NUM-VAL-3 IS NUMERIC
    MOVE 'Y' TO VALID-DATA
ELSE
    MOVE 'N' TO VALID-DATA.
```

The INSPECT statement can be used to count the number of occurrences of a character, as well as replacing occurrences of characters. To illustrate this capability of the INSPECT statement, let us consider the problem of editing a field that might include a leading sign, where the field might also contain leading spaces. If there are leading spaces, they would precede the sign, which should occur immediately in front of the number. In this case, the fields should be declared as

```
05   INPUT-FLD-4               PIC X(7).
         .

         .

         .

05   NUM-VAL-4                 PIC S9(6)
                                   SIGN IS LEADING
                                   SEPARATE.
```

```
05   NUM-VAL-4-SPLIT REDEFINES NUM-VAL-4.
     10   NUM-VAL-4-HEAD          PIC X.
     10   NUM-VAL-4-TAIL          PIC X(6).
05   NUM-MINUS                    PIC 9.
05   NUM-PLUS                     PIC 9.
```

The code to validate the contents of NUM-VAL-4 would be as follows:

```
MOVE INPUT-FLD-4 TO NUM-VAL-4-SPLIT.
IF NUM-VAL-4 IS = SPACES
    MOVE 'N' TO VALID-DATA
ELSE
    MOVE 0 TO NUM-MINUS
    MOVE 0 TO NUM-PLUS
    INSPECT NUM-VAL-4
        TALLYING NUM-MINUS FOR ALL '-',
                 NUM-PLUS  FOR ALL '+',
        REPLACING FIRST '+' BY ' ',
        REPLACING FIRST '-' BY ' '
    INSPECT NUM-VAL-4
        REPLACING LEADING SPACES BY ZEROS
    IF (NUM-MINUS + NUM-PLUS) > 1
        MOVE 'N' TO VALID-DATA
    ELSE
        IF NUM-VAL-4 IS NOT NUMERIC
            MOVE 'N' TO VALID-DATA
        ELSE
            MOVE 'Y' TO VALID-DATA
            IF NUM-MINUS = 1
                MOVE '-' TO NUM-VAL-4-HEAD.
```

Here the first INSPECT is used to count the number of occurrences of each valid sign and, also, to replace any leading signs with a space. Note that when an INSPECT statement is used to tally the number of occurrences of a character or string, the numeric field that is incremented for each occurrence is not initialized by the INSPECT statement. The second INSPECT then converts leading spaces to zeros. Make sure that you understand why this routine will correctly validate fields of the form '0 +1' and '+ −1234'.

Now consider the case in which the user actually includes a decimal point in the field. In the previous example, there was no decimal point (implied or otherwise). Suppose that the field were to contain two digits to the right of the decimal. This might be the case if a dollar value (either positive or negative) were being entered. The validation logic must remove the decimal point (assuming that the value in the field is "acceptable"), reposition the sign, and replace any leading spaces. In the preceding example, we illustrated all of the required logic except the removal of the decimal point. Here are the required data fields:

```
05   INPUT-FLD-5.
     10   INPUT-FLD-5-LEFT  PIC X(5).
     10   INPUT-FLD-5-DEC   PIC X.
     10   INPUT-FLD-5-RIGHT PIC XX.
          .
          .
          .
```

```
05   NUM-VAL-5                    PIC S9(4)V99
                                  SIGN IS LEADING SEPARATE.
05   NUM-VAL-5-SPLIT-1 REDEFINES NUM-VAL-5.
10   NUM-VAL-5-HEAD     PIC X.
     10  NUM-VAL-5-TAIL     PIC X(6).

05   NUM-VAL-5-SPLIT-2 REDEFINES NUM-VAL-5.
     10   NUM-VAL-5-LEFT    PIC X(5).
     10   NUM-VAL-5-RIGHT   PIC X(2).

05   NUM-MINUS                    PIC 9.
05   NUM-PLUS                     PIC 9.
```

The validation code would be as follows:

```
IF INPUT-FLD-5-DEC IS NOT = '.'
    MOVE 'N' TO VALID-DATA
ELSE
    MOVE INPUT-FLD-5-LEFT TO NUM-VAL-5-LEFT
    MOVE INPUT-FLD-5-RIGHT TO NUM-VAL-5-RIGHT
    IF NUM-VAL-5 IS = SPACES
        MOVE 'N' TO VALID-DATA
    ELSE
        MOVE 0 TO NUM-MINUS
        MOVE 0 to NUM-PLUS
        INSPECT NUM-VAL-5
            TALLYING NUM-MINUS FOR ALL '-',
                     NUM-PLUS  FOR ALL '+',
            REPLACING FIRST '+' BY ' ',
            REPLACING FIRST '-' BY ' '
        INSPECT NUM-VAL-5
            REPLACING LEADING SPACES BY ZEROS
        IF (NUM-MINUS + NUM-PLUS) > 1
            MOVE 'N' TO VALID-DATA
        ELSE
            IF NUM-VAL-5 IS NOT NUMERIC
                MOVE 'N' TO VALID-DATA
            ELSE
                MOVE 'Y' TO VALID-DATA
                IF NUM-MINUS = 1
                    MOVE '-' TO NUM-VAL-5-HEAD.
```

Notice how complex these checks can become. This complexity has caused many programmers to choose shortcuts—approaches that detect many, but not all, input errors. Such an outlook is understandable, but not really correct. As you gain experience in COBOL, you will eventually create general purpose subroutines that perform these editing functions for you (so that you need not recode such logic for every input field). For now it is enough to simply explore the techniques to edit data properly.

Let us now consider another common case: suppose that the field to be edited is left-justified, rather than right-justified. In such cases, you will find it easiest first to right-justify the contents of the field. Then the field can be edited as if it were right-justified originally. Suppose that we wished to right-justify the contents of INPUT-FLD-6 into WORK-FLD-6.

```
05     INPUT-FLD-6.
       10   INPUT-FLD-6-CHAR PIC X OCCURS 7 TIMES.

05     WORK-FLD-6.
       10   WORK-FLD-6-CHAR  PIC X OCCURS 7 TIMES.

05     SUBSCRIPTS.
       10   FROM-SUB          PIC 9.
       10   TO-SUB            PIC 9.
```

The following code would achieve the desired rejustification.

```
MOVE 7 TO TO-SUB.
PERFORM NULL-RTN VARYING FROM-SUB FROM 7 BY -1
    UNTIL (FROM-SUB IS = 1) OR
            (INPUT-FLD-6-CHAR (FROM-SUB) IS NOT =
            SPACE).
PERFORM MOVE-1-CHAR UNTIL FROM-SUB IS = 0.
PERFORM FILL-WITH-BLANK UNTIL TO-SUB IS = 0.
            .
            .
            .

NULL-RTN. EXIT.

MOVE-1-CHAR.
    MOVE INPUT-FLD-6-CHAR (FROM-SUB) TO
        WORK-FLD-6-CHAR (TO-SUB).
    SUBTRACT 1 FROM FROM-SUB.
    SUBTRACT 1 FROM TO-SUB.

FILL-WITH-BLANK.
    MOVE SPACE TO WORK-FLD-6-CHAR (TO-SUB).
    SUBTRACT 1 FROM TO-SUB.
```

Here the use of EXIT in NULL-RTN is done simply to make it clear that the routine contains no other statements. It could be omitted.

You may well be surprised at the complexity introduced by editing numeric input. It is important, however, to understand that erroneous input can lead to very costly mistakes, if it is not detected as soon as possible. The extra effort required to edit input values is almost always justified. There is another point worth mentioning: Because of the complexity of editing logic, and because it is required in almost all COBOL programming environments, some compilers include extensions to the COBOL language designed to make editing easier. These extensions should normally be avoided, because the ability to move the COBOL program from one environment to another usually outweighs the extra coding effort.

15.2 Editing Fields That Take on Designated Values

Some input fields can legitimately take on only values from some designated set. For example, in EXAMPLE8 the program took as input two-character codes that were supposed to represent days. The valid values were

```
M  T  W  TH  F
```

The reworked version of EXAMPLE8 you will find in Section 15.5 includes the logic that should be used whenever it is necessary to verify that the contents of a field is one of a small set of possible values:

```
01  DAY-CODE-TABLE.
    05  FILLER            PIC X(2)      VALUE IS 'M'.
    05  FILLER            PIC X(2)      VALUE IS 'T'.
    05  FILLER            PIC X(2)      VALUE IS 'W'.
    05  FILLER            PIC X(2)      VALUE IS 'TH'.
    05  FILLER            PIC X(2)      VALUE IS 'F'.
01  DAY-ACCESS            REDEFINES DAY-CODE-TABLE.
    05  DAY-CD            PIC X(2) OCCURS 5 TIMES.
            .
            .
            .

    MOVE 'N' TO INVALID-FIELD-FLAG.

    PERFORM 70-GET-DAY VARYING I FROM 1 BY 1
        UNTIL DAY-CODE = DAY-CD (I) OR I = 5.

    IF DAY-CODE IS NOT = DAY-CD (I)
        DISPLAY 'INVALID DAY-CODE'
        MOVE 'Y' TO INVALID-FIELD-FLAG.

70-GET-DAY. EXIT.
```

Here DAY-CODE is the input field that is matched against the values in the table. If it fails to match any table entry, the INVALID-FIELD-FLAG will be set to 'Y'.

15.3 Validation of Check-Digits

Consider a situation in which account numbers are being used as input. It may be extremely important that the numbers are typed correctly, but inevitably occasional mistakes will occur. Is there any way to detect most of these human typing errors? Yes, these errors can be detected, if an extra **check-digit** is included at the end of the account number. For example, if the account numbers would normally be six digits, then a seventh digit might be added as a check-digit. The check-digit can be computed from the first six digits; if the computation is performed and the check-digit contains an unexpected value, then an error must have been made in typing at least one of the seven digits.

Let us illustrate with a specific example. Suppose that we do have seven-digit account numbers, where the last digit is a check-digit. Furthermore, suppose that the check-digit is calculated as follows:

Step 1   Multiply the first of the six digits in the number by 2, the second by 3, the third by 4, the fourth by 5, the fifth by 6, and the sixth by 7.

Step 2   Add the six products together and divide by 10. The remainder can be used as the check-digit.

This is a rather arbitrary choice of how to calculate the check-digit. Let us see how the process works. Suppose that the account number that we assign to a customer should have 836245 as the first six digits. Then the seventh digit, the check-digit, would be calculated as follows:

$$8 \times 2 = 16$$
$$3 \times 3 = 9$$
$$6 \times 4 = 24$$
$$2 \times 5 = 10$$
$$4 \times 6 = 24$$
$$5 \times 7 = 35$$
$$16 + 9 + 24 + 10 + 24 + 35 = 118$$
$$118/10 = 11 \text{ with a remainder of } 8$$

Thus, 8 would be used as the check-digit, giving a seven-digit account number of 8362458. Now consider the most common typing errors. Suppose that a single digit were mistyped. For example, if 8363458 were typed, could the error be detected? If you calculate the check-digit based on the first six digits, it should be 3. Since it is an 8, this error would be detected. Another very common error is the transposition of two digits. Suppose that the second and third digits were transposed, giving 8632458. Then the calculated check-digit would be 5, and again the error would be detected.

    This basic technique of adding a check digit to the end of an account number, a part number, or any other identification number works quite well. It can be used to allow detection of most, but not all, typing errors.

15.4   Validation of Dates

Validation and manipulation of dates and times represent some of the more complex tasks that occur in a data processing environment. Frequently, dates are used for significant computations, such as the number of days of interest due on a loan. In these cases, it is imperative that the originally input dates and times be valid. The editing of times does not introduce significant complexities. Hours, minutes, and seconds are all numeric fields that must be within fixed ranges. Dates do, however, pose some difficulties. This results from the different number of days per month, and the complexities of leap year calculations.

    Before considering the details of editing dates, let us consider some of the more popular ways to represent dates. The most common representation of dates is in the mm/dd/yy format. Thus, 12/15/83 is often used to represent December 15, 1983. A date that is specified by month, day of month, and year is referred to as a Gregorian date. Examples of Gregorian dates in slightly differing formats are as follows:

12/15/83

December 15, 1983

15 December, 1983

831215   (yymmdd)

19831215   (yyyymmdd)

Of these formats, we recommend the last as the preferred format for recording dates in files. The presence of four characters for the year, and ordering dates with the year to the left, makes a variety of computations and comparisons substantially easier. On the other hand, dates should normally be input in formats that are most convenient for the end-user. In this case, the mm/dd/yy format is frequently chosen.

Dates that are used in computations may also be kept in the Julian format. A date in Julian format is specified by the year and the day of the year, where the days in a year are numbered from 1 to 366 (where 366 is used only during leap years). For example, two Julian formats for December 15, 1983 would be

83349   (yyddd—the 349th day of 1983)

1983349   (yyyyddd)

Dates that are used in computations we recommend be stored in files in the second of these Julian formats.

Date and time manipulations should normally be done using service subroutines that can be utilized by everyone in a programming shop. The computations are simply too complex to require everyone to recode them for each program that requires such a computation. A similar comment applies to routines that edit dates in input records. However, you should be somewhat familiar with the required checks, so we are including in our enhanced version of EXAMPLE8 the code needed to verify that the incoming date (in mm/dd/yy Gregorian format) is valid. The code is as shown in Fig. 15.1.

FIGURE 15.1

```
01   LEAP-YEAR-CALCULATION-FIELDS.
     05   YEAR-YYYY              PIC 9(4).
     05   YEAR-4-REM            PIC 9.
     05   YEAR-100-REM          PIC 999.
     05   YEAR-400-REM          PIC 999.
     05   DUMMY-FIELD           PIC 9(4).


01   DAYS-PER-MONTH.
     05   FILLER                PIC 99     VALUE IS 31.
     05   FILLER                PIC 99.
     05   FILLER                PIC 99     VALUE IS 31.
     05   FILLER                PIC 99     VALUE IS 30.
     05   FILLER                PIC 99     VALUE IS 31.
     05   FILLER                PIC 99     VALUE IS 30.
     05   FILLER                PIC 99     VALUE IS 31.
     05   FILLER                PIC 99     VALUE IS 31.
     05   FILLER                PIC 99     VALUE IS 30.
     05   FILLER                PIC 99     VALUE IS 31.
     05   FILLER                PIC 99     VALUE IS 30.
     05   FILLER                PIC 99     VALUE IS 31.
01   MAX-DAYS-IN-MONTH REDEFINES DAYS-PER-MONTH.
     05   MAX-DD                PIC 99 OCCURS 12 TIMES.
                .
                .
                .
                .
```

FIGURE 15.1   Continued

```
********************************************************************
*
* THIS ROUTINE CHECKS A DATE (STORED IN THE FIELDS MM, DD, AND
* YY).  IF THE DATE IS INVALID, THE VALUE 'Y' IS MOVED TO
* DATE-ERROR-FLAG.
*
********************************************************************

40-CHECK-DATE.
    IF (MM IS NOT NUMERIC) OR
       (DD IS NOT NUMERIC) OR
       (YY IS NOT NUMERIC)

        MOVE 'Y' TO DATE-ERROR-FLAG

    ELSE
        IF (MM < 1) OR (MM > 12)
            MOVE 'Y' TO DATE-ERROR-FLAG
        ELSE
            PERFORM 50-CHECK-DD.
```

Note that the routine must determine whether or not the given year is a leap year before it can establish the range for the number of days in the month. The logic of this routine is quite complex, but is not nearly as complex as the problem of determining the difference between points in time. Suppose that workers use time cards to record starting and ending dates and times (a worker may start work on one day and leave during another). If you carefully consider all of the complexities involved in determining how long the worker was on the job (including changing clocks forward or backward an hour, which corresponds to changing a time zone), you will see why general purpose service routines are the only reasonable way to handle date and time processing requirements.

```
*********************************************************************
*
* THIS ROUTINE CHECKS FOR A DAY THAT IS NOT IN A VALID RANGE FOR
* THE MONTH.  THIS IS MADE COMPLEX BY HAVING TO ADJUST FOR
* LEAP YEARS.  A YEAR IS A LEAP YEAR IF
*    A. THE YEAR IS DIVISIBLE BY 4, BUT NOT BY 100
* OR B. THE YEAR IS DIVISIBLE BY 400.
*
* WE GIVE THE PROPER WAY TO DETERMINE A LEAP YEAR, EVEN
* THOUGH THE YEAR WAS ONLY SPECIFIED BY 2 DIGITS.  NORMALLY,
* WE ADVOCATE SPECIFYING ALL YEARS AS FOUR DIGITS.  HOWEVER,
* FOR THIS EXAMPLE, WE HAVE JUST ASSUMED THAT YY VALUES IN
* THE RANGE 0-80 REPRSENT YEARS IN THE RANGE 2000-2080; VALUES
* IN THE RANGE 81-99 REPRESENT YEARS IN THE RANGE 1981-1999.
*
*********************************************************************

 50-CHECK-DD.
    IF YY > 80
        COMPUTE YEAR-YYYY = 1900 + YY
    ELSE
        COMPUTE YEAR-YYYY = 2000 + YY.

    DIVIDE 4 INTO YEAR-YYYY GIVING DUMMY-FIELD
        REMAINDER YEAR-4-REM
    DIVIDE 100 INTO YEAR-YYYY GIVING DUMMY-FIELD
        REMAINDER YEAR-100-REM
    DIVIDE 400 INTO YEAR-YYYY GIVING DUMMY-FIELD
        REMAINDER YEAR-400-REM
    IF ((YEAR-4-REM = 0) AND (YEAR-100-REM IS NOT = 0)) OR
        (YEAR-400-REM = 0)

        MOVE 29 TO MAX-DD (2)
    ELSE
        MOVE 28 TO MAX-DD (2).

    IF DD < 1 OR DD > MAX-DD (MM)
        MOVE 'Y' TO DATE-ERROR-FLAG.
```

15.5 EXAMPLE8 Revisited

We now present a recoded version of EXAMPLE8, the program that printed appointments for the coming week (the original version was presented in Chapter 10). This version properly edits the input data. This program illustrates many of the types of editing that we have discussed in this chapter, and you should note the differences between it and the original version.

FIGURE 15.2 The appointment calendar with editing.

```
     IDENTIFICATION DIVISION.
     PROGRAM-ID. NEWEX8.
     AUTHOR. W E SINGLETARY.

     *************************************************************
     *
     * THIS PROGRAM IS USED TO DISPLAY APPOINTMENTS FOR 1 WEEK.  IT
     * READS IN A "DATE RECORD" AS THE FIRST INPUT RECORD.  THIS
     * RECORD CONTAINS JUST THE DATE OF MONDAY (SO A HEADER OF
     * THE FORM
     *
     *           WEEK OF NOVEMBER  12, 1983
     *
     * CAN BE PRINTED).  AFTER THE DATE RECORD, THERE CAN BE ANY
     * NUMBER OF RECORDS, EACH OF WHICH REPRESENTS A SINGLE
     * APPOINTMENT.  ONCE ALL OF THE APPOINTMENT RECORDS HAVE
     * BEEN READ, THEN ALL OF THE APPOINTMENTS FOR THE WEEK ARE
     * DISPLAYED.
     *
     *************************************************************

     ENVIRONMENT DIVISION.

     CONFIGURATION SECTION.
     SOURCE-COMPUTER. IBM-370.
     OBJECT-COMPUTER. IBM-370.

     SPECIAL-NAMES.
         C01 IS TOP-OF-PAGE.

     INPUT-OUTPUT SECTION.
     FILE-CONTROL.

         SELECT INPUT-FILE ASSIGN TO UR-S-SYSIN.
         SELECT OUTPUT-FILE ASSIGN TO UR-S-SYSPRINT.

     DATA DIVISION.
     FILE SECTION.
```

```
*******************************************************************
*
* THIS FILE IS USED TO READ THE INPUT RECORDS.  THE FIRST
* RECORD IS THE DATE RECORD.  IT SHOULD CONTAIN A DATE OF
* THE FORM MM/DD/YY IN THE FIRST 8 COLUMNS.  ALL OF THE
* REMAINING RECORDS REPRESENT SINGLE APPOINTMENTS.  EACH
* APPOINTMENT SPECIFIES
*
*    A) A NAME
*    B) A DAY OF THE WEEK (M, T, W, TH, F).  HERE SINGLE
*       LETTER CODES SHOULD BE FOLLOWED BY A BLANK.
*    C) AN APPOINTMENT SLOT.  THE DAY FROM 8:30AM TO 4:30PM
*       IS DIVIDED INTO 16 HALF-HOUR SLOTS.
*    D) A NOTE INDICATING THE REASON FOR THE APPOINTMENT
*
*******************************************************************


    FD  INPUT-FILE
        LABEL RECORDS ARE OMITTED
        DATA RECORDS ARE DATE-RECORD, APPT-RECORD.

    01  DATE-RECORD.
        05  DATE-OF-MONDAY.
            10  MM              PIC 99.
            10  FILLER          PIC X.
            10  DD              PIC 99.
            10  FILLER          PIC X.
            10  YY              PIC 99.
        05  FILLER              PIC X(72).

    01  APPT-RECORD.
        05  NAME-IN             PIC X(20).
        05  DAY-CODE            PIC XX.
        05  SLOT                PIC 99.
        05  REASON-IN           PIC X(20).
        05  FILLER              PIC X(36).



*******************************************************************
*
* THIS FILE IS USED TO PRINT THE APPOINTMENTS.  ONLY A SINGLE
* PAGE IS PRINTED, WITH A SEPARATE COLUMN FOR EACH OF THE
* DAYS (MONDAY - FRIDAY).
*
*******************************************************************


    FD  OUTPUT-FILE
        LABEL RECORDS ARE OMITTED
        DATA RECORD IS PRINT-BUFF.

    01  PRINT-BUFF              PIC X(133).
```

continued

FIGURE 15.2 Continued

```
   WORKING-STORAGE SECTION.

   ************************************************************
   *
   * EOF-FLAG IS SET TO 'Y' WHEN END-OF-FILE OCCURS.
   *
   * DATE-ERROR-FLAG GETS SET TO 'Y' IF THE DATE RECORD IS INVALID
   *
   * INVALID-FIELD-FLAG GETS SET TO 'Y' WHEN AN INPUT FIELD
   *     IS INVALID
   *
   * YEAR-YYYY IS SET TO THE 4-DIGIT REPRESENTATION OF THE YEAR
   *
   * YEAR-4-REM IS THE REMAINDER AFTER DIVIDING THE YEAR BY 4
   *
   * YEAR-100-REM IS THE REMAINDER AFTER DIVIDING THE YEAR BY 100
   *
   * YEAR-400-REM IS THE REMAINDER AFTER DIVIDING THE YEAR BY 400
   *
   * DUMMY-FIELD IS USED ON DIVISIONS TO HANDLE UNWANTED QUOTIENTS
   *
   * MONTH-TABLE IS USED TO CONVERT THE MONTH NUMBER INTO A
   *     MORE READABLE VERSION IN THE PAGE HEADERS
   *
   * DAYS-PER-MONTH IS A TABLE THAT GIVES THE NUMBER OF DAYS IN
   *     EACH MONTH (DYNAMICALLY ADJUSTED FOR LEAP YEARS)
   *
   * DAY-CODE-TABLE IS USED TO CONVERT THE 2-CHARACTER DAY
   *     CODES INTO NUMBERS FROM 1-5 (SUBSCRIPTS INTO THE
   *     APPOINTMENT TABLE).
   *
   * APPOINTMENT-TABLE CONTAINS THE APPOINTMENTS FOR THE WEEK.
   *
   * I AND J ARE USED AS SUBSCRIPTS.
   *
   * APPT-TIME GIVES THE TIME OF THE NEXT APPOINTMENT
   *
   * PRINT-LINE IS USED TO BUILD THE LINES TO BE PRINTED.
   *
   * PAGE-HEADER-1, PAGE-HEADER-2, AND COLUMN-HEADER ARE USED
   *     TO PRINT HEADERS ON THE PAGE.
   *
   *
   ************************************************************

      01  FLAGS.
          05   EOF-FLAG              PIC X      VALUE IS 'N'.
               88   EOF-HAS-OCCURRED            VALUE IS 'Y'.
          05   DATE-ERROR-FLAG      PIC X      VALUE IS 'N'.
               88  INVALID-DATE-RECORD         VALUE IS 'Y'.
          05   INVALID-FIELD-FLAG  PIC X.
               88  INVALID-FIELD               VALUE IS 'Y'.
```

```
01  LEAP-YEAR-CALCULATION-FIELDS.
    05  YEAR-YYYY           PIC 9(4).
    05  YEAR-4-REM          PIC 9.
    05  YEAR-100-REM        PIC 999.
    05  YEAR-400-REM        PIC 999.
    05  DUMMY-FIELD         PIC 9(4).


01  MONTH-TABLE.
    05  FILLER              PIC X(9)   VALUE IS 'JANUARY'.
    05  FILLER              PIC X(9)   VALUE IS 'FEBRUARY'.
    05  FILLER              PIC X(9)   VALUE IS 'MARCH'.
    05  FILLER              PIC X(9)   VALUE IS 'APRIL'.
    05  FILLER              PIC X(9)   VALUE IS 'MAY'.
    05  FILLER              PIC X(9)   VALUE IS 'JUNE'.
    05  FILLER              PIC X(9)   VALUE IS 'JULY'.
    05  FILLER              PIC X(9)   VALUE IS 'AUGUST'.
    05  FILLER              PIC X(9)   VALUE IS 'SEPTEMBER'.
    05  FILLER              PIC X(9)   VALUE IS 'OCTOBER'.
    05  FILLER              PIC X(9)   VALUE IS 'NOVEMBER'.
    05  FILLER              PIC X(9)   VALUE IS 'DECEMBER'.
01  MONTH-ACCESS            REDEFINES MONTH-TABLE.
    05  MONTH               PIC X(9) OCCURS 12 TIMES.

01  DAYS-PER-MONTH.
    05  FILLER              PIC 99     VALUE IS 31.
    05  FILLER              PIC 99.
    05  FILLER              PIC 99     VALUE IS 31.
    05  FILLER              PIC 99     VALUE IS 30.
    05  FILLER              PIC 99     VALUE IS 31.
    05  FILLER              PIC 99     VALUE IS 30.
    05  FILLER              PIC 99     VALUE IS 31.
    05  FILLER              PIC 99     VALUE IS 31.
    05  FILLER              PIC 99     VALUE IS 30.
    05  FILLER              PIC 99     VALUE IS 31.
    05  FILLER              PIC 99     VALUE IS 30.
    05  FILLER              PIC 99     VALUE IS 31.
01  MAX-DAYS-IN-MONTH REDEFINES DAYS-PER-MONTH.
    05  MAX-DD              PIC 99 OCCURS 12 TIMES.

01  DAY-CODE-TABLE.
    05  FILLER              PIC X(2)   VALUE IS 'M'.
    05  FILLER              PIC X(2)   VALUE IS 'T'.
    05  FILLER              PIC X(2)   VALUE IS 'W'.
    05  FILLER              PIC X(2)   VALUE IS 'TH'.
    05  FILLER              PIC X(2)   VALUE IS 'F'.
01  DAY-ACCESS              REDEFINES DAY-CODE-TABLE.
    05  DAY-CD              PIC X(2) OCCURS 5 TIMES.
```

continued

FIGURE 15.2 Continued

```
01    APPOINTMENT-TABLE.
      05   APPT-FOR-1-DAY        OCCURS 5 TIMES.
           10   ONE-APPT         OCCURS 16 TIMES.
                15   NAME        PIC X(20).
                15   REASON      PIC X(20).

01    SUBSCRIPTS.
      05   I                     PIC 99.
      05   J                     PIC 99.

01    APPT-TIME.
      05   NEXT-HOUR             PIC 99      VALUE IS 8.
      05   NEXT-MINUTES          PIC 99      VALUE IS 30.

01    PRINT-LINE.
      05   FILLER                PIC X(1).
      05   APPT-TIME-OUT.
           10   APPT-HOUR        PIC Z9.
           10   APPT-COLON       PIC X.
           10   APPT-MINUTES     PIC 99.
      05   FILLER                PIC X(3).
      05   ONE-COLUMN            OCCURS 5 TIMES.
           10   NAME-OR-REASON-OUT PIC X(20).
           10   FILLER           PIC X(2).

01    PAGE-HEADER-1.
      05   FILLER                PIC X(1).
      05   FILLER                PIC X(48) VALUE IS SPACES.
      05   FILLER                PIC X(23) VALUE IS
           'A P P O I N T M E N T S'.

01    PAGE-HEADER-2.
      05   FILLER                PIC X(43) VALUE IS SPACES.
      05   FILLER                PIC X(16) VALUE IS
                                 'FOR THE WEEK OF'.
      05   MONTH-OUT             PIC X(9).
      05   FILLER                PIC X      VALUE IS SPACES.
      05   DD-OUT                PIC Z9.
      05   FILLER                PIC X(2)   VALUE IS ', '.
      05   YYYY-OUT.
           10   YY-FIRST-2       PIC X(2)   VALUE IS '19'.
           10   YY-OUT           PIC 99.


01    COLUMN-HEADER.
      05   FILLER                PIC X(12) VALUE IS SPACES.
      05   FILLER                PIC X(22) VALUE IS 'MONDAY'.
      05   FILLER                PIC X(22) VALUE IS 'TUESDAY'.
      05   FILLER                PIC X(22) VALUE IS 'WEDNESDAY'.
      05   FILLER                PIC X(22) VALUE IS 'THURSDAY'.
      05   FILLER                PIC X(22) VALUE IS 'FRIDAY'.
```

```
PROCEDURE DIVISION.
    OPEN INPUT INPUT-FILE
         OUTPUT OUTPUT-FILE.

    PERFORM 10-EMPTY-A-SLOT VARYING I FROM 1 BY 1 UNTIL I > 5
            AFTER J FROM 1 BY 1 UNTIL J > 16.

    PERFORM 20-READ-INPUT.
    IF EOF-HAS-OCCURRED
        MOVE ' *** EMPTY INPUT FILE ***' TO PRINT-BUFF
        WRITE PRINT-BUFF AFTER ADVANCING TOP-OF-PAGE
    ELSE
        PERFORM 30-PROCESS-DATE-RECORD
        IF INVALID-DATE-RECORD
            MOVE ' *** INVALID DATE RECORD ***' TO PRINT-BUFF
            WRITE PRINT-BUFF AFTER ADVANCING TOP-OF-PAGE
        ELSE
            PERFORM 20-READ-INPUT
            PERFORM 60-PROCESS-RECORD-ROUTINE
                UNTIL EOF-HAS-OCCURRED
            PERFORM 80-PRINT-APPOINTMENTS.

    CLOSE INPUT-FILE
          OUTPUT-FILE.

    STOP RUN.

**************************************************************
*
* THIS ROUTINE INITIALIZES AN ENTRY IN THE APPOINTMENT-TABLE
* TO ALL SPACES.
*
**************************************************************

 10-EMPTY-A-SLOT.
    MOVE SPACES TO NAME (I, J).
    MOVE SPACES TO REASON (I, J).

**************************************************************
*
* THIS ROUTINE READS INPUT RECORDS, SETTING EOF-FLAG TO 'Y'
* WHEN END-OF-FILE OCCURS.
*
**************************************************************

 20-READ-INPUT.
     READ INPUT-FILE AT END MOVE 'Y' TO EOF-FLAG.
```

continued

280   Editing Data

FIGURE 15.2 Continued

```
****************************************************************
*
* THIS ROUTINE PROCESSES THE DATE RECORD.  THIS SIMPLY AMOUNTS
* TO CONVERTING THE MONTH AND YEAR INTO THE FORMS REQUIRED
* FOR THE PAGE HEADER AND MOVING THE VALUES INTO THE HEADER.
*
****************************************************************

   30-PROCESS-DATE-RECORD.
       PERFORM 40-CHECK-DATE.
       IF NOT INVALID-DATE-RECORD
           MOVE MONTH (MM) TO MONTH-OUT
           MOVE DD TO DD-OUT
           MOVE YY TO YY-OUT.


****************************************************************
*
* THIS ROUTINE CHECKS A DATE (STORED IN THE FIELDS MM, DD, AND
* YY).  IF THE DATE IS INVALID, THE VALUE 'Y' IS MOVED TO
* DATE-ERROR-FLAG.
*
****************************************************************

   40-CHECK-DATE.
       IF (MM IS NOT NUMERIC) OR
          (DD IS NOT NUMERIC) OR
          (YY IS NOT NUMERIC)

           MOVE 'Y' TO DATE-ERROR-FLAG

       ELSE
           IF (MM < 1) OR (MM > 12)
               MOVE 'Y' TO DATE-ERROR-FLAG
           ELSE
               PERFORM 50-CHECK-DD.
```

```
***************************************************************
*
* THIS ROUTINE CHECKS FOR A DAY THAT IS NOT IN A VALID RANGE FOR
* THE MONTH.  THIS IS MADE COMPLEX BY HAVING TO ADJUST FOR
* LEAP YEARS.  A YEAR IS A LEAP YEAR IF
*    A. THE YEAR IS DIVISIBLE BY 4, BUT NOT BY 100
* OR B. THE YEAR IS DIVISIBLE BY 400.
*
* WE GIVE THE PROPER WAY TO DETERMINE A LEAP YEAR, EVEN
* THOUGH THE YEAR WAS ONLY SPECIFIED BY 2 DIGITS.  NORMALLY,
* WE ADVOCATE SPECIFYING ALL YEARS AS FOUR DIGITS.  HOWEVER,
* FOR THIS EXAMPLE, WE HAVE JUST ASSUMED THAT YY VALUES IN
* THE RANGE 0-80 REPRSENT YEARS IN THE RANGE 2000-2080; VALUES
* IN THE RANGE 81-99 REPRESENT YEARS IN THE RANGE 1981-1999.
*
***************************************************************

   50-CHECK-DD.
       IF YY > 80
           COMPUTE YEAR-YYYY = 1900 + YY
       ELSE
           COMPUTE YEAR-YYYY = 2000 + YY.

       DIVIDE 4 INTO YEAR-YYYY GIVING DUMMY-FIELD
           REMAINDER YEAR-4-REM
       DIVIDE 100 INTO YEAR-YYYY GIVING DUMMY-FIELD
           REMAINDER YEAR-100-REM
       DIVIDE 400 INTO YEAR-YYYY GIVING DUMMY-FIELD
           REMAINDER YEAR-400-REM
       IF ((YEAR-4-REM = 0) AND (YEAR-100-REM IS NOT = 0)) OR
          (YEAR-400-REM = 0)

           MOVE 29 TO MAX-DD (2)
       ELSE
           MOVE 28 TO MAX-DD (2).

       IF DD < 1 OR DD > MAX-DD (MM)
           MOVE 'Y' TO DATE-ERROR-FLAG.
```

continued

FIGURE 15.2 Continued

```
******************************************************************
*
* THIS ROUTINE PROCESSES THE INPUT RECORD THAT HAS ALREADY BEEN
* READ AND THEN ATTEMPTS TO READ THE NEXT RECORD.
*
******************************************************************

 60-PROCESS-RECORD-ROUTINE.
     MOVE 'N' TO INVALID-FIELD-FLAG.

     PERFORM 70-GET-DAY VARYING I FROM 1 BY 1
         UNTIL DAY-CODE = DAY-CD (I) OR I = 5.

     IF DAY-CODE IS NOT = DAY-CD (I)
         DISPLAY 'INVALID DAY-CODE'
         MOVE 'Y' TO INVALID-FIELD-FLAG.

     IF SLOT IS NOT NUMERIC.
         DISPLAY 'INVALID TIME SLOT'
         MOVE 'Y' TO INVALID-FIELD-FLAG
     ELSE
         IF SLOT < 1 OR SLOT > 16
             DISPLAY 'INVALID TIME SLOT'
             MOVE 'Y' TO INVALID-FIELD-FLAG.

     IF INVALID-FIELD
         DISPLAY 'INVALID INPUT RECORD: ' APPT-RECORD
     ELSE
         IF NAME (I, SLOT) = SPACES
             MOVE NAME-IN TO NAME (I, SLOT)
             MOVE REASON-IN TO REASON (I, SLOT)
         ELSE
             DISPLAY 'BOTH ' NAME-IN ' AND ' NAME (I, SLOT)
                     ' ARE SCHEDULED FOR ' DAY-CODE
                     ' SLOT ' SLOT.

     PERFORM 20-READ-INPUT.

******************************************************************
*
* THIS ROUTINE IS A NULL ROUTINE.  ALL OF THE SEARCHING
* LOGIC IS EXPRESSED IN THE PERFORM THAT INVOKES IT.
*
******************************************************************

 70-GET-DAY.
     EXIT.
```

```
****************************************************************
*
* THIS ROUTINE PRINTS THE PAGE OF APPOINTMENTS.
*
****************************************************************

 80-PRINT-APPOINTMENTS.
     WRITE PRINT-BUFF FROM PAGE-HEADER-1
         AFTER ADVANCING TOP-OF-PAGE.
     WRITE PRINT-BUFF FROM PAGE-HEADER-2
         AFTER ADVANCING 2 LINES.
     WRITE PRINT-BUFF FROM COLUMN-HEADER
         AFTER ADVANCING 3 LINES.

     MOVE SPACES TO PRINT-LINE.
     PERFORM 90-PRINT-1-SET VARYING J FROM 1 BY 1
         UNTIL J > 16.

****************************************************************
*
* THIS ROUTINE PRINTS THE APPOINTMENTS FOR A GIVEN TIME OF THE
* DAY.
*
****************************************************************

 90-PRINT-1-SET.
     MOVE NEXT-HOUR TO APPT-HOUR.
     MOVE ':' TO APPT-COLON.
     MOVE NEXT-MINUTES TO APPT-MINUTES.

     IF NEXT-MINUTES = 30
         ADD 1 TO NEXT-HOUR
         MOVE 0 TO NEXT-MINUTES
     ELSE
         MOVE 30 TO NEXT-MINUTES.

     IF NEXT-HOUR > 12
         SUBTRACT 12 FROM NEXT-HOUR.


     PERFORM 100-MOVE-NAMES VARYING I FROM 1 BY 1
         UNTIL I > 5.
     WRITE PRINT-BUFF FROM PRINT-LINE
         AFTER ADVANCING 2.

     MOVE SPACES TO APPT-TIME-OUT.
     PERFORM 110-MOVE-REASONS VARYING I FROM 1 BY 1
         UNTIL I > 5.
     WRITE PRINT-BUFF FROM PRINT-LINE
         AFTER ADVANCING 1.
```

continued

```
**************************************************************
*
* THIS ROUTINE MOVES THE NAMES FOR APPTS AT A GIVEN TIME TO
* THE PRINT LINE.
*
**************************************************************

  100-MOVE-NAMES.
     MOVE NAME (I, J) TO NAME-OR-REASON-OUT (I).


  **************************************************************
  *
  * THIS ROUTINE MOVES THE REASONS FOR APPTS AT A GIVEN TIME TO
  * THE PRINT LINE.
  *
  **************************************************************

  110-MOVE-REASONS.
     MOVE REASON (I, J) TO NAME-OR-REASON-OUT (I).
```

15.6 Editing Data Stored in Files

Up to this point, we have discussed techniques of editing input data. In this final section, we consider the question of exactly when editing takes place in a large data processing system. In such systems data is stored in files that reside on some type of mass storage device, such as magnetic tapes, disks, or diskettes. One of the most common types of programs in such systems simply prints reports based on the stored data. Is it important that such report programs edit their input data, which is taken from the stored files?

The rather surprising answer is "No, report programs usually do not need to edit the fields in the records they use as input." Rather, the fields are edited by the programs that create and update the files stored on the magnetic media. This allows the programs that access the stored data to assume its validity. This is why the report programs that occur in the chapters that follow do not edit their input records.

The topic of updating files maintained on disk or tape will not be covered in this volume. Therefore, we will not be able to explore the details involved in editing such data. However, one comment is worthy of note. Even though data stored in tape and disk files is assumed accurate by the numerous programs that access it, very occasionally invalid data may slip through the edit program. This has led to the simple technique of using a separate program simply to read through the contents of such a file searching for invalid data. Since most of the editing logic to verify the fields exists in the programs that edit the data before storing it in the file, the construction of such a program is normally fairly straightforward. The small amount of effort spent in the coding of such a program is normally a prudent investment.

SUMMARY

It is important that data input by humans be verified before calculations and decisions are based upon it. The cost of having programs fail due to invalid input data greatly exceeds the effort required to edit the data items. In this chapter we have considered some of the more common types of editing:

Editing numeric data

Editing data items that can take on one of a set of values

Editing fields that use check-digits

Editing dates

Each of these types of data poses special editing requirements.

The effort required to edit fields can be reduced by coding general purpose service routines. Such routines normally exist in large programming departments or "shops," and they can substantially reduce the effort required to write programs that edit input data. This is particularly true in the case of editing or processing date and time information.

Data stored in files that reside on mass storage devices is normally edited when the files are created or updated. Those programs that access the data usually assume that the data is valid. It is considered a good idea to code a short program for each such file that simply reads through the file, making as many types of edit checks as possible.

REVIEW QUESTIONS

15.1   Why should input data normally be validated? Give an instance in which validating an input field might not be necessary.

15.2   Consider the following opinion:

> Editing numeric data can be made quite simple by forcing the user to put the sign in the first position, type leading zeros, and to use only implied decimal points. The use of more complex logic is not justified, since it leads to errors in the edit programs and is generally more effort than it's worth.

How would you respond to such a statement?

15.3   Give three instances of data items that can take their values from small sets. How should such items be edited?

15.4   Describe the difference between Julian and Gregorian date formats. What makes the validation of a date in either format complex?

15.5   Why is it generally considered a good idea to store dates in files using four digits to represent the year? Why are dates normally input using an mm/dd/yy format?

15.6   Why is it not necessary for most report programs to edit the data that occurs in their input records?

EXERCISE

Recode the last program that you wrote to include the statements required to edit the input fields.

CHAPTER SIXTEEN

INTRODUCTION TO REPORT LOGIC

INTRODUCTION   In this chapter the basic logic necessary to produce a simple report program is presented. Several concepts must be introduced before the environment for the report can be set.

The notion of a master file and its relation to a data processing system is presented briefly in Section 16.1. In Section 16.2 the particular master file, the RECORD INVENTORY MASTER FILE is discussed in detail and the two reports that are to be produced are displayed.

The two most popular types of sequential files—magnetic tape and magnetic disk—are explored in Section 16.3.

The chapter is rounded out with a discussion of the actual report logic, and the flowcharts and a listing of the program are displayed.

16.1 Master Files

In order to pursue this discussion, it will be necessary to establish some basic terminology. A *file* was defined previously as an organized collection of related data records (such as the files that were used as input to the example programs presented earlier). The fact that the files can be stored on any one of a variety of storage media has also been noted. Of these media, the most commonly used are diskettes, magnetic tape, and magnetic disk packs.

A data processing system is an integrated group of programs that are used to create and manipulate one or more files in order to achieve some specific data processing objectives. Inventory and payroll systems are among the more common data processing systems. The objectives of these systems should be evident.

Among the files to be processed by most data processing systems, there is one particular permanent file that is the central repository of the data to be manipulated. Often an entire system consists simply of a set of programs designed to maintain and utilize the information stored in this one file. Such a file is called a **master file**.

Normally a master file will contain one record for each "item" to be processed. For example, the inventory master file for a company contains one record for each product, and the payroll file contains one record for each employee. Such records are referred to as **item records**. An item record should contain all of the pertinent description, history, and current status information that may be required regarding the related item.

Aside from the information contained in the individual item records, the most critical feature of a master file, just as for any file, is its organization. Generally, the records in a file are organized according to one of two basic schemes: sequentially and by direct access.

The records in a **sequential file** are stored in some particular order. When such a file is read by the machine, the reading must begin with the first record in the file and proceed with the reading of each individual record in the file in the order in which it occurs. For example, all card files are sequential files, since the cards must be read in the order in which they occur in the file.

In the case of **direct access** files it is possible to retrieve data from any particular record in the file directly. That is, any record in the file may be accessed without requiring that any of the previous records in the file be read first. Direct access files may be stored only on devices that have been designed specifically to provide this facility. The most commonly used direct access device is the magnetic disk pack. *Note:* The fact that a file is a direct access file does not necessarily preclude the possibility that the file may be read sequentially. It is the usual case with such files that the way in which they are accessed at a given time depends upon the specific purpose for which they are being used at that particular time.

Only sequential files will be considered in the present discussion. Each record in a sequential master file normally contains a field that is used to identify uniquely the entity described by the record. For example, the records in a payroll master file would, most probably, each contain the social security number of one employee. This unique identifier is called the **key** of the record. Sequential master files are usually ordered according to the contents of the key field. Thus, the records in a payroll master file might occur in ascending order based on the social security number field.

There are occasions when it is desirable to put a file into an order other than the one dictated by the key field. In such cases the file may be reordered by sorting it on one or more fields other than the key field in the item records. The field that determines the order of a file is called the **sort field**. Thus, the key is the normal sort field.

A master file often contains some special records, aside from the item records, which occur at the beginning of the file. These records contain information that pertains to the file itself. The special records that precede the item records are called **header records**. For example, a header record would most likely contain the date that the file was last updated.

Any field that occurs in every item record in a master file may, at some time, be used as a sort field for ordering that file. It is often the case that a master file which is normally ordered on a given key may have to be reordered on a different sort field, depending on the particular use to be made of the file. This process of reordering a file is called **sorting.** For example, a payroll master file that is normally ordered on the social security number field may occasionally have to be reordered using the name field as the sort field for the purpose of producing an alphabetical listing of the employees.

No matter upon which field the master file is sorted, the header records should appear at the beginning of the file after the sort is completed. In order to ensure that this will be the case, all fields in the header records corresponding to fields in the item records that can be used as the key should be assigned values lower than any legitimate values that may be assigned to the corresponding item record fields.

16.2   A Record Inventory Master File

In this section the design of a particular master file will be presented. The example to be considered was chosen because it will be familiar to most, if not all, readers. The first step in the construction of any master file is the formulation of a complete and concise answer to the following question:

> Precisely what are the objectives of the system that will be used to process the master file?

The system that is to be constructed is intended to be used to maintain inventory records for a small business that sells record albums. In this case each item record in the master file will contain information on a single record album (e.g., one item record might be for "Simple Dreams" by Linda Ronstadt, produced by Elektra/Asylum Records). The fields in the master file should contain all of the data elements that might be required to produce reports for the owner of the record shop. To see what fields will actually be required, it is useful to look at some example reports that will be produced by the system. Figures 16.1 and 16.2 show two of the basic types of reports.

The master file will be used to record information relating to record albums. Therefore, it should be given a name indicating the contents of the file. We have chosen the name Record Inventory Master File (RIMF). Since this file will be used to record information and produce reports for several years, it is desirable that we include in the item records all of the data fields that might reasonably be desired in a report for the shop owner (i.e., all of the attributes of albums that might be needed in current or future reports should be included). For our purposes each item record in the RIMF will have to contain at least the following data fields:

1. A code identifying the producer of the album (e.g., COLM for Columbia Records)

FIGURE 16.1 Available stock report.

```
    01/05/83                    JOE'S RECORD SHOP                        PAGE 2

                            PRODUCER CODE - COLM

  VOLUME         ARTIST         TITLE                 IN STOCK      ON ORDER       PRICE
  C 31105        P NERO         SUMMER OF '42             5            0           4.95
  CG 33624       P NERO         THE FIRST TIME EVER       2            0           5.95
  CS 1009        P NERO         I'LL NEVER FALL           3            0           4.95
  CS 2469        SIMON&GAR      SOUNDS OF SILENCE         6            0           4.95
  CS 8192        D BRUBECK      TIME OUT                  0            2           3.95
  CS 9768        BEAUT. DAY     IT'S A BEAUTIFUL DAY      4            0           5.95
  CS 9907        P NERO         MIDNIGHT COWBOY          11            0           6.95
  FC 35625       N DIAMOND      YOU DON'T BRING ME       15            0           6.95
  JC 35305       W NELSON       STARDUST                  0            4           7.95
  KC 30750       P SIMON        PAUL SIMON                7            0           6.95
  KCS 9914       SIMON&GAR      BRIDGE OVER TROUBLED      5            0           5.95
  PC 31350       SIMON&GAR      GREATEST HITS            12            0           6.95
  PC 33540       P SIMON        STILL CRAZY               8            0           7.95

  TOTALS: # VOLUMES =     13                            78            6
```

FIGURE 16.2 Sales history report.

VOLUME	ARTIST	TITLE	PRICE	L WK	2	3	4	5	6	7	8	9	10	11	12
CS 8192	D BRUBECK	TIME OUT	3.95	0	0	1	2	0	0	0	0	0	1	0	0
CS 9768	BEAUT. DAY	IT'S A BEAUTIFUL DAY	5.95	0	1	0	0	2	0	0	0	1	1	0	1
FC 35625	N DIAMOND	YOU DON'T BRING ME	6.95	3	2	0	4	2	3	1	3	0	2	2	3
C 31105	P NERO	SUMMER OF '42	4.95	1	0	1	2	0	1	1	0	2	0	1	1
CG 33624	P NERO	THE FIRST TIME EVER	5.95	2	1	3	0	2	1	0	1	1	2	1	1
CS 1009	P NERO	I'LL NEVER FALL	4.95	1	2	0	1	1	2	1	0	2	1	0	1
CS 9907	P NERO	MIDNIGHT COWBOY	6.95	2	0	0	1	0	1	0	0	0	1	0	0
KC 30750	P SIMON	PAUL SIMON	6.95	4	5	3	1	3	3	2	3	4	3	5	4
PC 33540	P SIMON	STILL CRAZY	7.95	3	3	4	3	0	4	2	5	1	2	1	3
CS 2469	SIMON&GAR	SOUNDS OF SILENCE	4.95	2	1	3	1	0	2	1	0	1	2	0	1
KCS 9914	SIMON&GAR	BRIDGE OVER TROUBLED	5.95	1	0	2	0	2	1	1	0	1	2	1	0
PC 31350	SIMON&GAR	GREATEST HITS	6.95	5	3	4	2	3	1	2	4	3	2	3	1
JC 35305	W NELSON	STARDUST	7.95	11	9	10	8	9	12	10	7	9	10	8	11
				35	27	31	25	24	31	21	23	25	29	22	27

01/05/83   JOE'S RECORD SHOP   PAGE 2

PRODUCER CODE - COLM   SALES HISTORY REPORT

2. A volume identifier (Each album has a character string that identifies that particular album. For example, the Linda Ronstadt album mentioned above has a volume identifier of 6E-104. The producer code and the volume identifier together uniquely determine an album. Hence, the pair of fields— (producer, volume identifier)—together forms the key for each item record.)

3. The artist or group that created the music

4. The title of the album

5. The number of copies in stock (i.e., the number of copies that are in the store)

6. The number of copies on order

7. The price of the album

8. History data giving the number of copies that have sold during each of the last 12 weeks

There are other data fields that could reasonably be included in the item records (such as the date that the album was made). The problem of determining exactly which fields should be included is a significant task that is usually performed by a systems analyst. The basic principles that determine the choice are as follows:

Principle 1 Try to include any field that might be needed on a report or needed to compute a field on some report.

Principle 2 Limit the number of fields. You cannot include all fields that could possibly be used at some point in the future, because there is a cost associated with gathering, inputting, and maintaining the data.

We have chosen to include just the fields given above in the item records of the RIMF.

The next step is to produce an actual record layout for an item record in the RIMF. Such a layout simply designates the position and contents of each field in a record. The layout in Fig. 16.3 is the one that will be used in all the examples which refer to the RIMF.

The 109-character record described in Fig. 16.3 might seem quite large, since all of the input records that we have used before were 80 characters or less in length. However, it is not uncommon for item records to be several thousand characters in length. The incredible storage capacities available on magnetic tapes and disks make it possible to include millions or even billions of characters of data in a single master file.

The RIMF will have a single header record at the front of the file. The format for this record is given in Fig. 16.4. The following points should be noted about this layout:

1. Any field that might at some time be used as a sort field for a sorted version of the RIMF must have a value in the header record that is set to the lowest possible collating value. This is required so that sorting the RIMF will always cause the header record to precede the item records. The COBOL language includes two figurative constants, LOW-VALUE and HIGH-VALUE, which evaluate to the lowest possible collating value and the highest value, respectively.

2. The name of the record shop is included in the header record. This allows more than one record shop to use the same system without having to alter

FIGURE 16.3 RIMF item record format.

Columns	Contents
1–4	Producer code (This code indicates the producer of the album; e.g., RCA or Columbia Records.)
5–19	The volume ID (This is a value assigned by each producer to identify each volume uniquely. There is no fixed format for the codes. They may contain nonnumeric characters.)
20–29	The artist
30–49	The title of the album
50–53	Number of copies in stock
54–57	Number of copies on order
58–61	Price of the album (99V99)
62–109	12 four-digit fields (The first field contains the number of albums sold last week, the second contains the number sold the week before, and so forth. Thus, 12 weeks of sales history are stored.

FIGURE 16.4 RIMF header record format.

Columns	Contents
1–81	All LOW-VALUE (This causes the header to sort to the start of the file.)
82–89	Date that the file was last updated
90–109	The name of the record shop

the programs. Whenever the name of the shop appears in a report, it will be taken from the header record (not from a character constant in the program that produces the report).

3. The date the file was last updated is included in the header record. This will be the date printed at the top of each report, since it reflects the date on which the information in the report was "current."

The design of the RIMF is now complete. This file will contain one header record and one item record for each album (but not each copy of an album).

16.3 Tape and Disk Sequential Files

Card files and printer files are usually referred to as unit record files. The processing of files that are not unit record files requires a more general understanding of the ASSIGN clause of the SELECT statement in the environment division and of the file description in the data division. A discussion of these refinements was avoided in the preceding sections but will be treated in detail here. The ASSIGN clause has the following format:

```
ASSIGN TO file-identifier
```

The file-identifier is used to designate which file is to be processed. On many systems it will have the form

```
file-name
```

For example,

```
RIMF.DAT
```

might reference a specific file, RIMF.DAT.

On IBM systems the following format is used:

```
ASSIGN TO class-organization-name
```

The possible classes are UR, UT, and DA.

UR specifies a sequential card file or a printer file.

UT specifies a sequential file.

DA specifies a file with direct organization.

DA can be used if the file is a sequential file residing on a magnetic disk pack, but the authors recommend its use only for direct files. The organization should be specified as either S or D, meaning sequential or direct, respectively.

The name can be any name formed according to the following rules:

Rule 1 The first character of the name must be an alphabetic character.

Rule 2 The name must contain only alphabetic characters or numeric digits.

Rule 3 The length of the name should not exceed eight characters.

This name is used at execution time to designate precisely what physical file is being referenced. The explanation of how this is done is beyond the scope of this book. Be sure to note the general use of the name and make an attempt to choose meaningful names in all cases.

You should be able to decipher the meaning of the following ASSIGN clauses from the preceding discussion.

```
ASSIGN TO UT-S-INPUTFL

ASSIGN TO UR-S-PRINTER

ASSIGN TO DA-D-REQUESTF
```

The first of these clauses designates a sequential (probably noncard) file, the second specifies a file that is to be directed to a printer, and the third specifies a file on a direct access device (such as a magnetic disk pack).

The following file description entry might be used to process the RIMF.

```
FD    RIMF
      LABEL RECORDS ARE STANDARD
      BLOCK CONTAINS 6 RECORDS
      DATA RECORDS ARE RIMF-HDR RIMF-ITEM.
```

In order to understand why the BLOCK CONTAINS clause was introduced and why this form of the LABEL RECORDS clause was specified, an understanding of the rudimentary details of how information is stored on mass storage devices is a necessity. The exact mechanisms for storing files on and retrieving files from magnetic disk packs and magnetic tapes differ drastically. However, for the level of comprehension required here, a discussion of magnetic tapes and an observation that a somewhat similar situation prevails in the case of magnetic disk packs should be sufficient.

A magnetic tape drive is similar in several respects to a common tape recorder. In both cases information is stored on magnetic tapes for future retrieval, and these tapes are normally rewound between uses. Of course, in one case the data is a voice image, while in the other it consists of strings of character images.

As previously mentioned, the storage capacity of the tapes utilized by magnetic tape drives is literally enormous. A single reel of tape may contain several files, each of which contains thousands of records. The way in which this data is organized on the tape is the current topic of concern.

Several special records are found at the front of each file on a given reel of tape. These records, called **label records**, contain information about the particular file that they precede. In general, there are standard formats for the information that occurs in these records. The formats, however, vary with the type of computer used to do the processing. The information in the label records clause is used at execution time to locate the correct file and to determine a variety of miscellaneous facts about that particular file. None of this information actually affects the user's program in any way. The statement

```
LABEL RECORDS ARE STANDARD
```

simply conveys the information that

In the case of an **input** file, the normal means for locating the correct file and preparing it for retrieval are to be followed.

In the case of an **output** file, the normal label records are to be written ahead of the actual data records.

Occasionally a programming shop will utilize nonstandard or user label records. In such a case it is necessary for the programmer to ascertain the techniques established by that particular shop for processing these label records.

When data is stored on a magnetic tape, there is a gap left between the individual records. This gap, or empty space, is referred to as an **interrecord gap**. While the gap is only 0.6 to about 0.75 inches wide, it may exceed the length of tape necessary to store a 100-character record by a factor of as much as 10. This is due to the fact that data is so densely packed on the tape. A typical density factor is 1600 characters per inch. Furthermore, each interrecord gap represents a place where the tape must be physically stopped and restarted. Typically, the time required for starting and stopping a tape is approximately five times as long as the time required to read a 100-character record.

By applying a little arithmetic, you can readily gain an appreciation of the fact that if individual 100-character records were stored on tape, that tape could be 90% blank spaces, and the time occupied in starting and stopping this tape could be 80% of the total time required to read the tape. In order to alleviate this situation it is common practice to store more than one record between interrecord gaps. This technique is called **blocking.** The set of records stored between gaps is called a **block,** and the number of these records is called the **blocking factor.**

You can easily calculate the affect a blocking factor of 10 would have on the length of tape required to store and the length of time required to read a lengthy file of 100-character records. Assume, for example, such a file contained 10,000 records. The number of interrecord gaps would be reduced from 10,000 to 1000. This effectively reduces the length of tape required to store the file by 5400 inches and the amount of time required to read the file to about one-sixth of what it was without blocking.

When records are to be stored on tape or retrieved from tape in blocks, the BLOCK CONTAINS clause is used. The format of this clause is

        BLOCK CONTAINS n RECORDS

where n is the blocking factor. If the BLOCK CONTAINS clause is omitted, it is assumed that the blocking factor is 1. The reader is cautioned that a program which reads a blocked file must have the same specified blocking factor as that specified in the program that created the file.

In the case of IBM systems, the BLOCK CONTAINS clause may be specified as

        BLOCK CONTAINS 0 RECORDS

for an input file. In this case the system will examine the standard label records to determine the correct blocking factor.

16.4 The Logic of a Simple Report

In this section we wish to consider a general pattern of logic—the logic of reports. It has become widely recognized that most reports can be coded using minor variations of one basic pattern of logic. Since report programs are the most common type of program in many systems, it will be very useful to you to master this general pattern.

We shall build up to the general pattern in stages. Let us first consider the extremely simple report shown in Fig. 16.5.

FIGURE 16.5 Available inventory report.

```
        JOE'S RECORD SHOP                        PAGE 1

     VOLUMES IN THE RECORD INVENTORY MASTER FILE

   PRODUCER   VOL-ID     TITLE          ARTIST      IN-STOCK

    APPL      613-214    GREATEST HITS  BEATLES        8
    APPL      613-379    POSTCARD       HOPKINS        2
    APPL      618-012    TRY AGAIN      LOSERS        13
    APPL      620-967    BREAKOUT       JONES          4
     .          .          .             .            .
     .          .          .             .            .
     .          .          .             .            .

   TOTAL # ALBUMS IN STOCK = 2,314
```

This report simply lists all of the albums in the file. One line is printed for each item record. Page and column headers are printed on each page, and a final totals line is printed at the end of the report.

The logic to produce this report is displayed in Figs. 16.6–16.12. This logic is well worth considering in detail. The flowchart for the MAIN-LOGIC routine is presented in Fig. 16.6. This routine contains the overall logic of the report. It invokes PROC-HDR to process the header record. If no errors occur (such as an empty file or missing header record), READ-ITEM-RECORD is used to read the first item record. PRINT-REPORT processes the item records, printing the report.

The flowchart for PROC-HDR is given in Fig. 16.7. This routine processes the header record on the master file. There are two basic types of errors that could be detected—the file might be empty or the header record might be missing. If neither of these errors is detected, the fields in the header record are saved. If a program were to be written that accessed a file which was created without a header record, this entire routine would be omitted (altering MAIN-LOGIC slightly).

The flowchart for READ-ITEM-RECORD is given in Fig. 16.8. This routine is used to read the next record from the RIMF. It places the next key (or HIGH-VALUES at end-of-file) into a field in working storage.

FIGURE 16.6 Prototypical report logic.

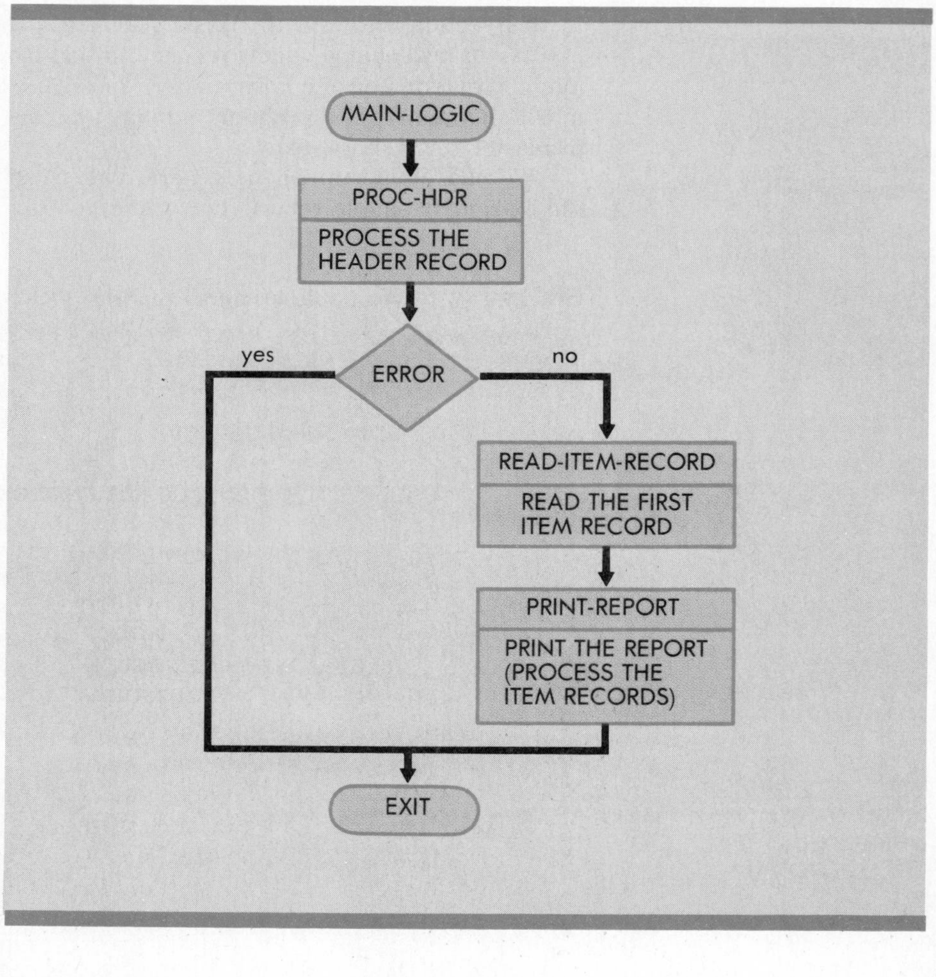

FIGURE 16.7 Prototypical report logic.

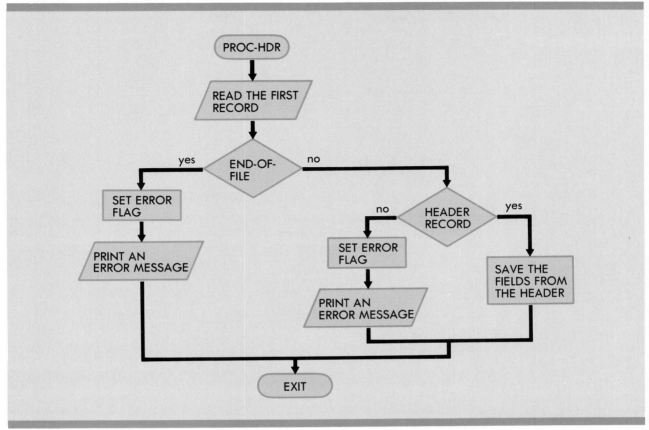

The flowchart for PRINT-REPORT is given in Fig. 16.9. This routine contains the logic to process the item records and produce the desired report. It first zeroes the totals accumulator and prints the first page and column headers. Actually, the totals accumulator need not be zeroed if it was initialized to zero when it was defined.

The flowchart for PROC-1-RECORD is given in Fig. 16.10. This routine prints a line for a single item record, accumulates totals, and reads the next record.

The flowchart for PRINT-ROUTINE is given in Fig. 16.11. This routine prints the next line of the report, after printing page and column headers if necessary. Note the use of LINE-COUNT to determine when headers must be printed and N-LINES to control single- and double-spacing.

The flowchart for HEADER-ROUTINE is given in Fig. 16.12. This routine just prints the page and column headers. It resets LINE-COUNT to indicate which line is next on the page and sets N-LINES to 2 to force double-spacing for the first line after the headers.

Now let us consider how this logic must be modified to produce the report depicted in Fig. 16.1. That report is broken into sections—one for each record producer. That is, the file is sorted into ascending order on the sort field made up of the producer code and the volume ID fields. All of the records with the same producer are used to produce one section of the report.

FIGURE 16.8 Prototypical report logic.

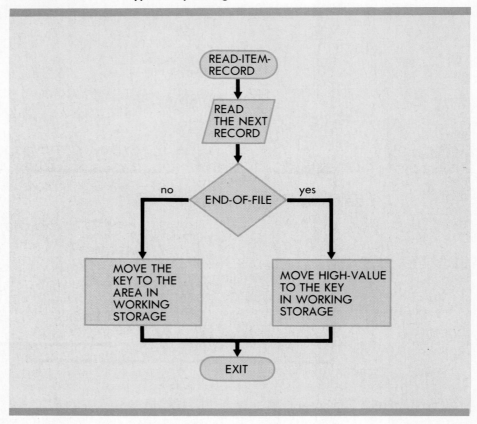

In a case such as the one we are considering, it is useful to view the file as follows:

Header record

All of the records used to create the first section of the report

All of the records used to create the second section of the report

.

.

.

The file should be visualized as a sequence of "groups," each group being a sequence of records with the same producer code. The end of a group is detected when the value in the producer code is not the same in two adjacent records. The end of a group is called a **control break**.

Control breaks separate the sequence of item records into groups that are used to produce the sections of the report. Each group has an associated set of subtotals. Sometimes main groups are broken into smaller groups, each with associated subtotals. In this case the smaller groups are separated by low-level control breaks. The larger groups are separated by higher level control breaks. Thus, there is a significant resemblance between the hierarchical organization of groups in the file and the hierarchical structure of the subtotals in the report. The groupings are characterized by the control breaks.

FIGURE 16.9 Prototypical report logic.

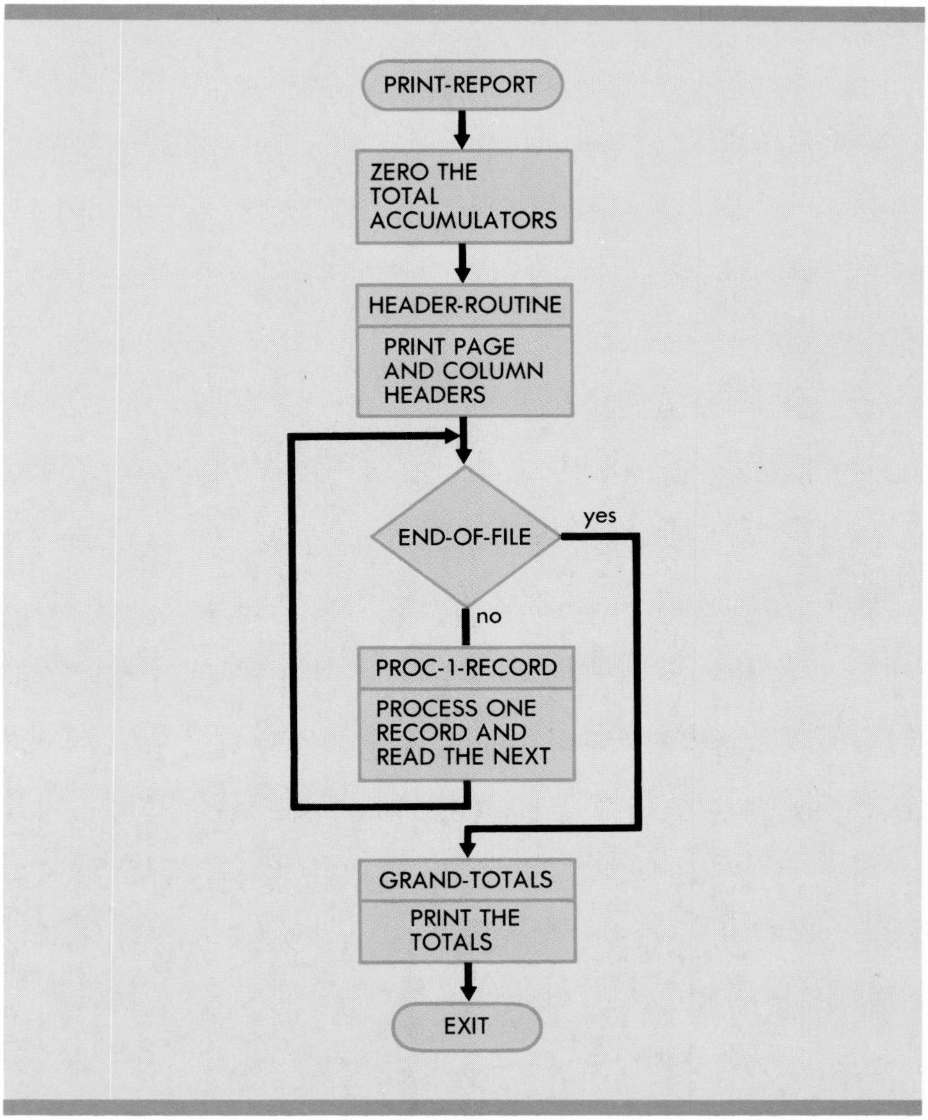

Now let us see how the logic to produce this slightly more complex report differs from the logic that we just covered: MAIN-LOGIC, PROC-HDR, READ-ITEM-RECORD, PRINT-ROUTINE and HEADER-ROUTINE are not altered at all. The new flowchart for PRINT-REPORT is given in Fig. 16.13. There are three major changes in the logic:

1. There are now two sets of totals accumulators, one for final totals and one for subtotals (which are printed when a control break is detected). The PRINT-REPORT routine processes only the final totals.

2. HEADER-ROUTINE is not invoked, since headers are printed at the start of each section of the report.

3. PROC-1-GROUP is invoked to process all of the records for one producer, rather than using PROC-1-RECORD to process a single record.

FIGURE 16.10 Prototypical report logic.

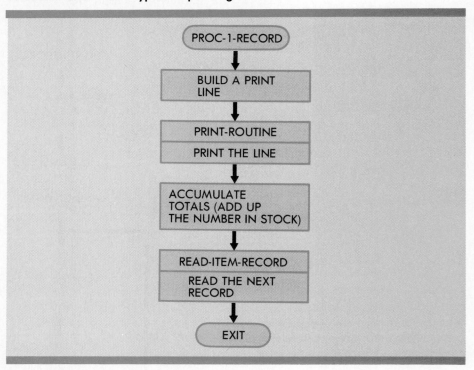

FIGURE 16.11 Prototypical report logic.

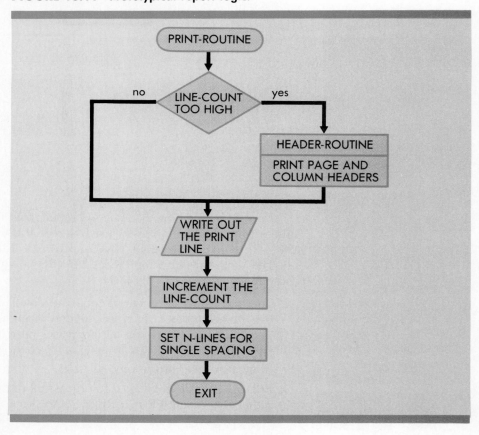

FIGURE 16.12 Prototypical report logic.

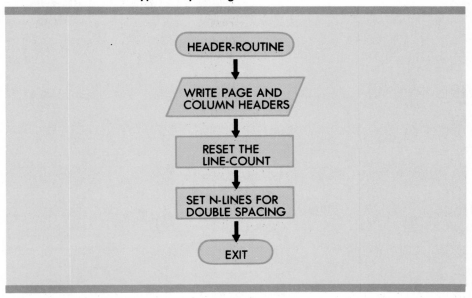

FIGURE 16.13 Modifications for a control break.

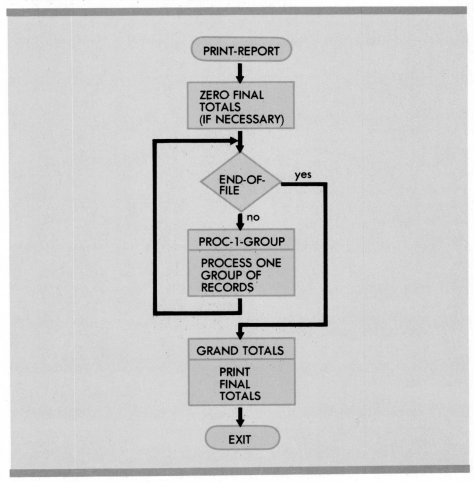

The flowchart for PROC-1-GROUP is given in Fig. 16.14. This should begin to look familiar. It is very similar to PRINT-REPORT. This is because each processes a sequence of "data units" and produces totals at the end. PRINT-REPORT processes a sequence of groups of records. PROC-1-GROUP processes a sequence of individual records.

FIGURE 16.14 Modifications for a control break.

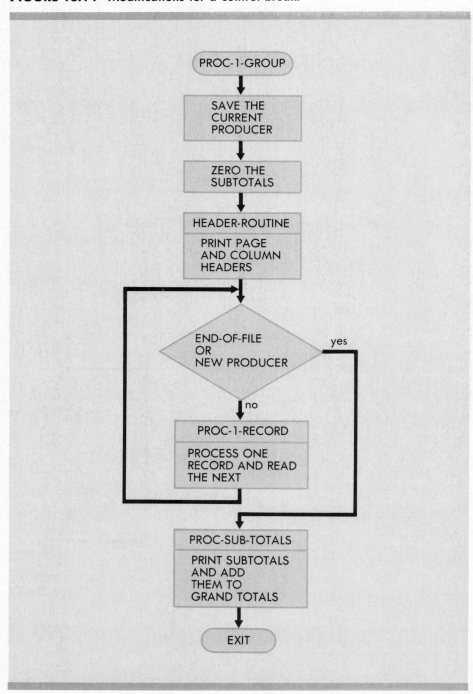

FIGURE 16.15 Modifications for a control break.

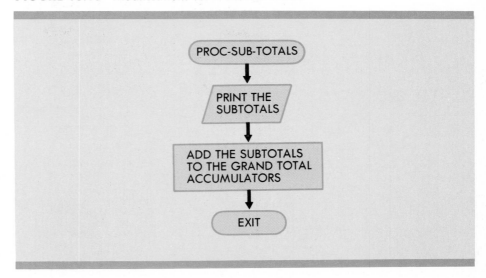

PROC-1-RECORD is just as it was before, but it should be noted that it accumulates only the subtotals. It need not worry about the final totals. When the subtotals are printed in PROC-SUB-TOTALS, the subtotals are added into the final totals as shown in Fig. 16.15. This is called "rolling the totals forward." The routine to print the grand totals, GRAND-TOTALS, is not flowcharted, since it is a single step.

The listing of the program to produce the report is in Fig. 16.16. Notice that it implements the logic of the flowcharts exactly.

FIGURE 16.16 Report with control breaks and summary totals.

```
      IDENTIFICATION DIVISION.
      PROGRAM-ID. REPORT1.
      AUTHOR. R OVERBEEK.

      **********************************************************************
      *
      * THIS PROGRAM PRODUCES A REPORT, USING THE RIMF AS INPUT.
      * THE PROGRAM ASSUMES THAT THE FILE IS SORTED INTO
      * ASCENDING ORDER ON THE FIRST 19 COLUMNS.  CONTROL BREAKS
      * WILL OCCUR BASED ON THE PRODUCER (COLUMNS 1-4).  THE
      * REPORT LISTS THE ALBUMS FOR EACH PRODUCER - WITH SUBTOTALS
      * SHOWING THE NUMBER OF TITLES, NUMBER OF ALBUMS IN STOCK,
      * AND THE NUMBER ON ORDER.  GRAND TOTALS GIVE THE SAME VALUES
      * FOR ALL PRODUCERS ADDED TOGETHER.
      *
      **********************************************************************
```

FIGURE 16.16 Continued

```
        ENVIRONMENT DIVISION.
        CONFIGURATION SECTION.
        SOURCE-COMPUTER. IBM-370.
        OBJECT-COMPUTER. IBM-370.

        SPECIAL-NAMES.
            C01 IS TOP-OF-PAGE.

        INPUT-OUTPUT SECTION.
        FILE-CONTROL.
            SELECT RIMF ASSIGN TO UT-S-RIMF.
            SELECT PRINT-FILE ASSIGN TO UR-S-SYSPRINT.

        DATA DIVISION.
        FILE SECTION.


****************************************************************
*
* THIS FD DESCRIBES THE RECORD INVENTORY MASTER FILE (RIMF).
* THE FILE HAS A SINGLE HEADER RECORD AND ONE ITEM RECORD PER
* ALBUM TITLE IN THE FILE (THE PRODUCER AND VOLUME ID TOGETHER
* FORM A UNIQUE KEY FOR EACH ITEM RECORD).
*
****************************************************************

    FD  RIMF
        LABEL RECORDS ARE STANDARD
        BLOCK CONTAINS 0 RECORDS
        DATA RECORDS ARE RIMF-HDR RIMF-ITEM.

    01  RIMF-HDR.
        05   FILLER                PIC X(81).
        05   DATE-LAST-UPDATED     PIC X(8).
        05   SHOP-NAME             PIC X(20).

    01  RIMF-ITEM.
        05   RIMF-KEY.
             10   PRODUCER         PIC X(4).
                  88   HEADER-REC              VALUE IS LOW-VALUE.
             10   VOLUME-ID        PIC X(15).
        05   ARTIST                PIC X(10).
        05   ALBUM-TITLE           PIC X(20).
        05   COPIES-IN-STOCK       PIC 9999.
        05   COPIES-ON-ORDER       PIC 9999.
        05   PRICE-OF-ALBUM        PIC 99V99.
        05   SALES-HISTORY         PIC S9999 OCCURS 12 TIMES.
```

```
****************************************************************
*
* THIS FILE IS USED TO PRINT THE REPORT.
*
****************************************************************

  FD   PRINT-FILE
       LABEL RECORDS ARE OMITTED
       DATA RECORD IS PRINT-BUFF.

  01   PRINT-BUFF                PIC X(133).

  WORKING-STORAGE SECTION.

****************************************************************
*
* EOF-FLAG              SET TO 'Y' WHEN END-OF-FILE OCCURS
*
* ERROR-FLAG            SET TO 'Y' IF A SERIOUS ERROR IS
*                       DETECTED (A MISSING HEADER RECORD)
*
* PAGE-NO               PAGE NUMBER OF THE NEXT REPORT PAGE
*
* N-LINES               NUMBER OF LINES TO SPACE BEFORE
*                       PRINTING
*
* LINE-COUNT            NUMBER OF THE NEXT LINE ON A PAGE
*
* SUB-ON-ORDER          ACCUMULATES THE SUBTOTAL OF VOLUMES
*                       ON ORDER
*
* SUB-IN-STOCK          ACCUMULATES THE SUBTOTAL OF VOLUMES
*                       IN STOCK
*
* SUB-NUMBER-TITLES     ACCUMULATES THE SUBTOTAL OF THE NUMBER
*                       OF TITLES
*
* TOT-ON-ORDER          ACCUMULATES THE GRAND TOTAL OF VOLUMES
*                       ON ORDER
*
* TOT-IN-STOCK          ACCUMULATES THE GRAND TOTAL OF VOLUMES
*                       IN STOCK
*
* TOT-NUMBER-TITLES     ACCUMULATES THE GRAND TOTAL OF THE
*                       NUMBER OF TITLES
*
* CURRENT-PRODUCER      USED TO DETECT CONTROL BREAKS
*
* LAST-PROD-READ        HOLDS THE PRODUCER OF LAST RECORD
*
****************************************************************

  01   FLAGS.
       05   EOF-FLAG            PIC X      VALUE IS 'N'.
            88   EOF-HAS-OCCURRED          VALUE IS 'Y'
       05   ERROR-FLAG          PIC X      VALUE IS 'N'.
```

continued

FIGURE 16.16 Continued

```
01   PRINT-CONTROL-FIELDS.
     05   LINE-COUNT          PIC 99.
     05   PAGE-NO             PIC 999      VALUE IS 1.
     05   N-LINES             PIC 9.

01   SUB-TOTAL-ACCUMULATORS.
     05   SUB-ON-ORDER        PIC 9(7).
     05   SUB-IN-STOCK        PIC 9(7).
     05   SUB-NUMBER-TITLES   PIC 9(7).

01   GRAND-TOTAL-ACCUMULATORS.
     05   TOT-ON-ORDER        PIC 9(7)     VALUE IS 0.
     05   TOT-IN-STOCK        PIC 9(7)     VALUE IS 0.
     05   TOT-NUMBER-TITLES   PIC 9(7)     VALUE IS 0.

01   SAVED-PRODUCER-CODES.
     05   CURRENT-PRODUCER    PIC X(4).
     05   LAST-PROD-READ      PIC X(4).

01   PAGE-HEADER.
     05   FILLER              PIC X(6)     VALUE IS SPACES.
     05   PAGE-HDR-DATE       PIC X(8).
     05   FILLER              PIC X(25)    VALUE IS SPACES.
     05   PAGE-HDR-SHOP       PIC X(20).
     05   FILLER              PIC X(20)    VALUE IS SPACES.
     05   FILLER              PIC X(5)     VALUE IS 'PAGE'.
     05   PG-NUM              PIC ZZ9.

01   COLUMN-HDR-1.
     05   FILLER              PIC X(39)    VALUE IS SPACES.
     05   FILLER              PIC X(16)    VALUE IS
                                          'PRODUCER CODE - '.
     05   COL-HDR-PRODUCER    PIC X(4).

01   COLUMN-HDR-2.
     05   FILLER              PIC X(1).
     05   FILLER              PIC X(6)     VALUE IS 'VOLUME'.
     05   FILLER              PIC X(10)    VALUE IS SPACES.
     05   FILLER              PIC X(6)     VALUE IS 'ARTIST'.
     05   FILLER              PIC X(10)    VALUE IS SPACES.
     05   FILLER              PIC X(5)     VALUE IS 'TITLE'.
     05   FILLER              PIC X(15)    VALUE IS SPACES.
     05   FILLER              PIC X(8)     VALUE IS 'IN STOCK'.
     05   FILLER              PIC X(5)     VALUE IS SPACES.
     05   FILLER              PIC X(8)     VALUE IS 'ON ORDER'.
     05   FILLER              PIC X(3)     VALUE IS SPACES.
     05   FILLER              PIC X(5)     VALUE IS 'PRICE'.
```

```
01   PRINT-LINE.
     05   FILLER                  PIC X.
     05   VOLUME-ID-OUT           PIC X(15).
     05   FILLER                  PIC X.
     05   ARTIST-OUT              PIC X(10).
     05   FILLER                  PIC X(6).
     05   TITLE-OUT               PIC X(20).
     05   FILLER                  PIC X.
     05   IN-STOCK-OUT            PIC ZZZ9.
     05   FILLER                  PIC X(10).
     05   ON-ORDER-OUT            PIC ZZZ9.
     05   FILLER                  PIC X(4).
     05   PRICE-OUT               PIC ZZ.99.

01   SUB-TOTAL-LINE.
     05   FILLER                  PIC X.
     05   FILLER                  PIC X(20)  VALUE IS
                                  'TOTALS: # VOLUMES = '.
     05   SUB-TITLES-OUT          PIC ZZZ9.
     05   FILLER                  PIC X(26)  VALUE IS SPACES.
     05   SUB-IN-STOCK-OUT        PIC ZZZ,ZZ9.
     05   FILLER                  PIC X(7)   VALUE IS SPACES.
     05   SUB-ON-ORDER-OUT        PIC ZZZ,ZZ9.

01   TOTS-HDR.
     05   FILLER                  PIC X(41)  VALUE IS SPACES.
     05   FILLER                  PIC X(12)  VALUE IS
                                  'GRAND TOTALS'.

01   TOTS-LINE.
     05   FILLER                  PIC X(41)  VALUE IS SPACES.
     05   TOTS-TYPE               PIC X(15).
     05   TOTS-VAL                PIC ZZZ,ZZ9.


PROCEDURE DIVISION.

******************************************************************
*
* THIS IS THE MAIN LOGIC OF THE REPORT.  YOU SHOULD STUDY IT
* CAREFULLY, SINCE MOST REPORTS WITH A SINGLE CONTROL BREAK
* WILL HAVE VERY SIMILAR LOGIC.
*
******************************************************************

     OPEN INPUT RIMF
          OUTPUT PRINT-FILE.

     PERFORM 10-PROC-HDR.

     IF ERROR-FLAG = 'N'
         PERFORM 30-READ-ITEM-RECORD
         PERFORM 20-PRINT-REPORT.

     CLOSE RIMF PRINT-FILE.
     STOP RUN.
```

continued

FIGURE 16.16 Continued

```
*****************************************************************
*
* THIS ROUTINE PROCESSES THE HEADER RECORD ON THE RIMF.  IT
* SETS THE ERROR-FLAG, IF THE FILE IS EMPTY OR THE HEADER IS
* MISSING.  ELSE, THE SHOP NAME AND DATE THAT THE FILE WAS LAST
* UPDATED ARE PUT INTO THE PAGE HEADER.
*
*****************************************************************

  10-PROC-HDR.
      READ RIMF AT END MOVE 'Y' TO EOF-FLAG.
      IF EOF-HAS-OCCURRED
          MOVE ' *** FILE HAS NO RECORDS ***' TO PRINT-BUFF
          WRITE PRINT-BUFF AFTER ADVANCING TOP-OF-PAGE
          MOVE 'Y' TO ERROR-FLAG
      ELSE
          IF NOT HEADER-REC
              MOVE ' *** HEADER MISSING ON RIMF ***'
                  TO PRINT-BUFF
              WRITE PRINT-BUFF AFTER ADVANCING TOP-OF-PAGE
              MOVE 'Y' TO ERROR-FLAG
          ELSE
              MOVE DATE-LAST-UPDATED TO PAGE-HDR-DATE
              MOVE SHOP-NAME TO PAGE-HDR-SHOP.

*****************************************************************
*
* THIS ROUTINE PRINTS THE REPORT, INCLUDING GRAND TOTALS
*
*****************************************************************

  20-PRINT-REPORT.
      PERFORM 40-PROC-1-GROUP UNTIL EOF-HAS-OCCURRED.
      PERFORM 70-GRAND-TOTALS.

*****************************************************************
*
* THIS ROUTINE READS THE NEXT RECORD FROM THE RIMF FILE,
* SETTING LAST-PROD-READ TO THE KEY (HIGH-VALUE ON EOF).
*
*****************************************************************

  30-READ-ITEM-RECORD.
      READ RIMF AT END MOVE 'Y' TO EOF-FLAG.
      IF EOF-HAS-OCCURRED
          MOVE HIGH-VALUE TO LAST-PROD-READ
      ELSE
          MOVE PRODUCER TO LAST-PROD-READ.
```

```
**************************************************************
*
* THIS ROUTINE PRINTS THE SECTION OF THE REPORT CORRESPONDING
* TO A SINGLE PRODUCER.
*
**************************************************************

 40-PROC-1-GROUP.
     MOVE PRODUCER TO CURRENT-PRODUCER.

     MOVE 0 TO SUB-ON-ORDER.
     MOVE 0 TO SUB-IN-STOCK.
     MOVE 0 TO SUB-NUMBER-TITLES.

     PERFORM 90-HEADER-ROUTINE.
     PERFORM 50-PROC-1-RECORD
         UNTIL LAST-PROD-READ NOT = CURRENT-PRODUCER.

     PERFORM 60-PROC-SUB-TOTALS.

**************************************************************
*
* THIS ROUTINE PRINTS A LINE FOR THE CURRENT ITEM RECORD
* AND ACCUMULATES SUBTOTALS.
*
**************************************************************

 50-PROC-1-RECORD.
     MOVE SPACES TO PRINT-LINE.
     MOVE VOLUME-ID TO VOLUME-ID-OUT.
     MOVE ARTIST TO ARTIST-OUT.
     MOVE ALBUM-TITLE TO TITLE-OUT.
     MOVE COPIES-IN-STOCK TO IN-STOCK-OUT.
     MOVE COPIES-ON-ORDER TO ON-ORDER-OUT.
     MOVE PRICE-OF-ALBUM TO PRICE-OUT.
     PERFORM 80-PRINT-ROUTINE.

     ADD 1 TO SUB-NUMBER-TITLES.
     ADD COPIES-IN-STOCK TO SUB-IN-STOCK.
     ADD COPIES-ON-ORDER TO SUB-ON-ORDER.

     PERFORM 30-READ-ITEM-RECORD.
```

continued

FIGURE 16.16 Continued

```
*****************************************************************
*
* THIS ROUTINE PRINTS SUBTOTALS AND ADDS THE SUBTOTALS TO
* THE GRAND TOTALS.
*
*****************************************************************

  60-PROC-SUB-TOTALS.
      MOVE SUB-NUMBER-TITLES TO SUB-TITLES-OUT.
      MOVE SUB-IN-STOCK TO SUB-IN-STOCK-OUT.
      MOVE SUB-ON-ORDER TO SUB-ON-ORDER-OUT.
      WRITE PRINT-BUFF FROM SUB-TOTAL-LINE
          AFTER ADVANCING 3 LINES.

      ADD SUB-NUMBER-TITLES TO TOT-NUMBER-TITLES.
      ADD SUB-IN-STOCK TO TOT-IN-STOCK.
      ADD SUB-ON-ORDER TO TOT-ON-ORDER.

*****************************************************************
*
* THIS ROUTINE PRINTS GRAND TOTALS.
*
*****************************************************************

  70-GRAND-TOTALS.
      WRITE PRINT-BUFF FROM TOTS-HDR AFTER ADVANCING TOP-OF-PAGE.

      MOVE '# TITLES' TO TOTS-TYPE.
      MOVE TOT-NUMBER-TITLES TO TOTS-VAL.
      WRITE PRINT-BUFF FROM TOTS-LINE AFTER ADVANCING 2 LINES.

      MOVE 'IN STOCK =' TO TOTS-TYPE.
      MOVE TOT-IN-STOCK TO TOTS-VAL.
      WRITE PRINT-BUFF FROM TOTS-LINE AFTER ADVANCING 1.

      MOVE 'ON ORDER' TO TOTS-TYPE.
      MOVE TOT-ON-ORDER TO TOTS-VAL.
      WRITE PRINT-BUFF FROM TOTS-LINE AFTER ADVANCING 1.

*****************************************************************
*
* THIS ROUTINE PRINTS A LINE (STARTING ON A NEW PAGE IF
* NECESSARY).
*
*****************************************************************

  80-PRINT-ROUTINE.
      IF LINE-COUNT > 50
          PERFORM 90-HEADER-ROUTINE.
      WRITE PRINT-BUFF FROM PRINT-LINE
          AFTER ADVANCING N-LINES.
      ADD N-LINES TO LINE-COUNT.
      MOVE 1 TO N-LINES.
```

```
**************************************************************
*
* THIS ROUTINE IS INVOKED TO PRINT PAGE AND COLUMN HEADERS..
* IT RESETS THE LINE-COUNT TO 6 (THE NUMBER OF THE NEXT LINE
* ON THE PAGE).
*
**************************************************************

90-HEADER-ROUTINE.
     MOVE PAGE-NO TO PG-NUM.
     ADD 1 TO PAGE-NO.
     WRITE PRINT-BUFF FROM PAGE-HEADER
          AFTER ADVANCING TOP-OF-PAGE.

     MOVE CURRENT-PRODUCER TO COL-HDR-PRODUCER.
     WRITE PRINT-BUFF FROM COLUMN-HDR-1
          AFTER ADVANCING 2 LINES.
     WRITE PRINT-BUFF FROM COLUMN-HDR-2
          AFTER ADVANCING 2 LINES.

     MOVE 2 TO N-LINES.
     MOVE 6 TO LINE-COUNT.
```

SUMMARY

The central file in any data processing system is called a master file. This is a file containing all of the information that is to be utilized by the reports the system is to produce.

The two most popular mass storage devices are magnetic tape and magnetic disk drives. A magnetic tape may only be used to store a sequential file, but the files on a magnetic disk may be accessed either sequentially or directly.

Virtually all report programs that contain only a single control break can be designed using basically the same underlying logic as outlined in this chapter.

REVIEW QUESTIONS

16.1   What is a master file?

16.2   What types of records does a master file normally contain?

16.3   What characterizes a sequential file? A direct access file?

16.4   Name three popular input/output devices associated with sequential files only.

16.5   What is an interrecord gap?

16.6   What is a blocking factor?

16.7   What advantage can be gained through the use of blocking factors greater than 1?

16.8   What is a label record?

16.9   What types of files require the use of a blocking factor?

16.10 What is a control break?

PROGRAMMING EXERCISES

16.1   Suppose that a group of doctors have decided to automate their billing procedures. They have decided to keep a single master file containing information about what is owed to them by their patients. The master file contains a single header record and any number of item records. The formats of these records in the file are

HEADER RECORD

Columns	Contents
1–20	LOW-VALUE
21–28	Date that the file was last updated
29–211	LOW-VALUE

ITEM RECORDS

1–20	Name
21–40	First line of address
41–60	Second line of address
61–80	Third line of address
81–89	Social security number
90–99	Phone number (including area code)
100–107	Date opened
108–127	Name of doctor
128–211	Seven entries in the following format:

1–7	Amount owed (S9(5)V99)
8–12	Service charge (S9(3)V99)

These last seven entries reflect amounts that have been owed

Less than 1 month

More than 1 but less than 2 months

More than 2 but less than 3 months

More than 3 but less than 4 months

More than 4 but less than 5 months

More than 5 but less than 6 months

More than 6 months, respectively.

Normally, the records in the master file occur in ascending order based on positions 81 to 89 (social security number). You may assume, however, that the file that will be used as input for this exercise has been sorted into the following order:

1. It will be in ascending order based on positions 108 to 127.
2. It will be in ascending order (within the groups created by 108 to 127) on positions 1–20.

You are to produce a report conforming to the format that is shown in the following example. There should be a separate section of the report for each doctor (i.e., for each unique value of the field in positions 108–127). Each section should conclude with a line reporting the number of accounts for that doctor and total amount owed to him. At the end of the report a single line, printed on a new page, should give the total number of accounts (item records).

```
 11/04/81                            DR. ADAMS                           PAGE 1

    NAME            ADDRESS         SOC-SEC-#      PHONE #     OPENED   M  OWED   SER.CH.

JOHN DOE        315 ROMAN COURT  998-54-3401  815-758-6632  10/11/79  0  27.40     .00
                DE KALB, IL                                           1  36.18     .98
                                                                      2  80.14    1.86
                                                                      3  42.00    1.00
                                                                      4  18.00    1.05
MARY SMITH . . . .
         .
         .
         .
 #ACCOUNTS = 10                                             TOTAL AMOUNT = $9482.13
```

16.2   When communities require money to fund a project, they frequently issue municipal bonds. A bond may be purchased, and it represents the following agreement:

The community agrees to pay a fixed amount (the par value) to the purchaser of the bond on some date in the future (the maturity date). The community also agrees to make two interest payments a year to the holder of the bond.

These bonds are often purchased in quite large numbers by institutions such as banks. The collection of bonds held by a given bank is referred to as the municipal bond portfolio maintained by the bank. Suppose that a given bank keeps a master file reflecting its municipal bond holdings. The master file contains a single header record and one item record per bond in the portfolio. The formats of the records in the master file are

HEADER RECORD

Columns	Contents
1–90	LOW-VALUE
91–98	Date the file was last updated
99–114	LOW-VALUE

ITEM RECORD

1–30	First line of description
31–60	Second line of description
61–90	Third line of description
91–100	Par value of the bond (9(8)V99)
101–105	Rate of interest paid on the bond (99V999)
106	Twice a year interest will be paid on the bond. This field contains a single-digit code indicating the two months during which the interest check is expected: 1 = January and July 2 = February and August . . . 6 = June and December
107–114	Maturity date (mm/dd/yy)

Create a report patterned after the section displayed below. There should be a separate section of the report (with subtotals) for each distinct value in positions 113 to 114 of the item records; that is, a separate section of the report should be printed for each year-of-maturity value. Do not reset the page counter to 1 after each section. At the end of the report print final totals (total number of bonds and total par value) on a new page.

```
   10/11/81            MUNICIPAL BOND LIST BY YEAR OF MATURITY          PAGE 1

                       YEAR OF MATURITY = 1987

  DESCRIPTION                  PAR VALUE   RATE OF INTEREST   INT. CODE   MATURITY

PUBLIC WORKS BOND ISSUE - 68   20,000.00        5.500            2        01/01/87
HARRINGTON HEIGHTS
ILLINOIS

ROYAL VALLEY SCHOOL BOND - 69  150,000.00       6.125            4        03/01/87
ROYAL COUNTY
MICHIGAN

        .                          .               .              .
        .                          .               .              .
        .                          .               .              .

        TOTAL PAR VALUE = 12,020,000.00   TOTAL # BONDS = 439
```

16.3 Suppose that you work in the data processing division of a small company that distributes heating and plumbing supplies. The company will have up to 10 salesmen selling products at any given time. Each distinct product has a six-digit product number assigned to it. The first two digits of the product number are used to denote a general class of product. Thus

026516

might describe a particular type of faucet fixture where the 02 is the general class of faucet fixture. A master file exists with one header record and one item record for every type of item sold by the company. The formats of these records are

HEADER RECORD

Columns	Contents
1–26	LOW-VALUE
27–34	Date the file was last updated
35–153	LOW-VALUE

ITEM RECORDS

1–6	Product number
7–26	Description of product
27–33	Price of product
34–153	One entry for each of the ten salesmen. The format of each entry is
	6 Units sold last year
	6 Units sold this year

Write a program to produce the report depicted below. A separate section with subtotals should be printed for each group of records with the same values in positions 1 and 2. Totals should appear on a separate page at the end of the report.

05/23/81	SALES REPORT FOR ITEM 02				PAGE 10
PRODUCT NUMBER	DESCRIPTION	PRICE	SALESMAN	LAST YR	THIS YR
024680	FAUCET FIXTURE – A	10.89	1	20	18
			2	17	13
			3	31	14
			8	5	15
			10	10	17
025289	FAUCET FIXTURE – B	11.42	2	13	33
			3	4	21
			5	20	22
			8	12	24
			10	13	16
.	.	.	.	.	.
.	.	.	.	.	.

TOTAL AMOUNTS – LAST YEAR = $5,539.20   THIS YEAR $6,453.48

REPORT
LOGIC
REVISITED

INTRODUCTION   In practice, few report programs are as basic as the one presented in the preceding chapter. Most reports require the use of two, three, or more control breaks for the purpose of accumulating subtotals. The logic required to implement the additional control breaks is discussed in this chapter.

One new language feature, the MOVE statement with the CORRESPONDING option is also introduced. We include a discussion and a demonstration of this statement here for completeness. Beware, though, for unless you exercise extreme caution in the use of the CORRESPONDING option, unexpected results can occur. Many experts discourage use of this option altogether.

see example on page 319.

17.1 The MOVE Statement with the Corresponding Option

By now, you are probably acutely aware of the large number of MOVE statements often required to transfer data fields from one storage area to another. There is a technique that facilitates a significant reduction in the required number of MOVE statements. Before this technique is discussed, however, an understanding of the mechanism that allows data items in two or more records to have the same name is necessary.

In the examples introduced thus far, all of the data names in a given program have been unique. The assignment of unique data names ensured that any reference made to a particular data item was totally unambiguous. While it is true that all references to data items must be unambiguous, it is not the case that all data names need be unique. The reason for this is that the COBOL language allows data names to be qualified. The following example shows the qualification of data names.

```
01        MASTER-RECORD.
          05   NAME              PIC X(20).
          05   SOC-SEC           PIC X(9).
          05   ADDR1             PIC X(20).
          05   ADDR2             PIC X(25).
          05   CURRENT-BAL       PIC 999V99.

01        PRINT-LINE.
          05   FILLER            PIC X(20).
          05   NAME              PIX X(20).
          05   FILLER            PIC X(10).
          05   SOC-SEC           PIC X(9).
          05   FILLER            PIC X(10).
          05   CURRENT-BAL       PIC ZZZZ.99.
```

The descriptions of MASTER-RECORD and PRINT-LINE in the example may be legitimately included in the same program. In order to reference unambiguously a field such as NAME, either of the following references could be used.

```
NAME IN MASTER-RECORD
```

or

```
NAME IN PRINT-LINE
```

In general, a name can be qualified by use of the format

$$\text{name-1} \left\{ \begin{matrix} \underline{\text{IN}} \\ \underline{\text{OF}} \end{matrix} \right\} \text{name-2}$$

where name-1 is used in the detailed description of name-2. Thus,

```
MOVE NAME IN MASTER-RECORD TO NAME OF PRINT-LINE
```

is a valid COBOL statement. A name may be qualified as many times as necessary in order to ensure that a reference is unambiguous. For example,

```
SOC-SEC-1 IN SOC-SEC IN PRINT-RECORD
```

is a twice-qualified reference to SOC-SEC-1. If you must qualify a reference to an entry in a table, the qualification comes before the subscript. Hence,

```
OVERDUE IN MASTER-RECORD (WEEK-SUBSCRIPT)
```

is correct, but

```
OVERDUE (WEEK-SUBSCRIPT) IN MASTER-RECORD
```

is not.

The CORRESPONDING option in a MOVE statement makes it possible to capitalize on the fact that different data items may have the same name. The format of this form of the MOVE statement is

$$\underline{MOVE} \left\{ \begin{array}{l} \underline{CORR} \\ \underline{CORRESPONDING} \end{array} \right\} \text{data-name-1} \ \underline{TO} \ \text{data-name-2}$$

where data-name-1 and data-name-2 are both names of group data items. A statement in this format has the effect of causing all data items in data-name-1 which correspond to data items in data-name-2 to be moved to the corresponding data items in data-name-2. Basically, two data items correspond when they have the same name. As an example, the following statement:

```
MOVE CORRESPONDING MASTER-RECORD TO PRINT-LINE
```

has the same effect as the three MOVE statements

```
MOVE NAME IN MASTER-RECORD TO NAME IN PRINT-LINE
MOVE SOC-SEC IN MASTER-RECORD TO SOC-SEC IN PRINT-LINE
MOVE CURRENT-BAL IN MASTER-RECORD TO
    CURRENT-BAL IN PRINT-LINE.
```

Those items in the sending field which fail to correspond to items in the receiving field are ignored. For example, ADDR-1 and ADDR-2 are not affected by the MOVE statement.

Three refinements must be added to complete the definition of corresponding data items.

1. At least one of the two corresponding data items must be an elementary item (an item that is not further subdivided).

2. Any data item in data-name-1 or data-name-2 that contains an OCCURS clause is ignored.

3. The corresponding data items in data-name-1 and data-name-2 must have identical qualifiers (i.e., all intervening names must be identical).

To illustrate these points, assume that PERSON-1, PERSON-2, and MAIN-RECORD are defined as follows:

```
01      PERSON-1.
        05   STATUS1.
             10   MARITAL-CODE      PIC X(1).
             10   CHILDREN          PIC 99.
        05   NAME                   PIC X(20).
        05   BALANCE                PIC 9999V99.
        05   MAIN-ADDRESS.
             10   LINE-1            PIC X(20).
             10   LINE-2            PIC X(20).


01      PERSON-2.
        05   NAME                   PIC X(20).
        05   BALANCE OCCURS 5 TIMES PIC 9999V99.
        05   STATUS1.
             10   VETERAN-CODE      PIC X(1).
```

```
                    10    AGE              PIC 999.
                    10    CHILDREN         PIC 99.
              05    OFFICE-ADDRESS.
                    10    LINE-1           PIC X(20).
                    10    LINE-2           PIC X(20).

      01          MAIN-RECORD.
            05    EMPLOYEE.
                  10    STATUS1.
                        15    MARITAL-CODE   PIC X.
                        15    SEX            PIC X.
                        15    CHILDREN       PIC 99.
```

In this case, the statement

```
      MOVE CORRESPONDING PERSON-1 TO PERSON-2
```

has the same effect as the two statements

```
      MOVE CHILDREN IN STATUS1 IN PERSON-1 TO
            CHILDREN IN STATUS1 IN PERSON-2.
      MOVE NAME IN PERSON-1 TO NAME IN PERSON-2
```

The two STATUS-1 items fail to correspond because neither is an elementary item, and the BALANCE item in PERSON-2 is ignored because it contains an OCCURS clause. The address lines do not correspond because the qualifiers, MAIN-ADDRESS and OFFICE-ADDRESS, are not identical. Similarly,

```
      MOVE CORR PERSON-1 TO EMPLOYEE
```

is equivalent to

```
      MOVE MARITAL-CODE IN PERSON-1 TO MARITAL-CODE IN
            EMPLOYEE
      MOVE CHILDREN IN PERSON-1 TO CHILDREN IN EMPLOYEE
```

The fact that PERSON-1 and EMPLOYEE do not have identical level numbers does not matter. All that matters is that the intervening qualifier, STATUS1, is the same.

It should be clear that conciseness in a program can be achieved through the judicious use of duplicate names and the CORRESPONDING option. It should be noted, however, that since the CORRESPONDING option has the same effect as several MOVE statements, it should not be used where a simple MOVE statement would suffice. For example, if one record is to be moved into another area having an identical format, a single MOVE statement (without the CORRESPONDING option) should be used. Further illustrations of the MOVE CORRESPONDING statement occur in the program discussed in the following section.

17.2 Reports Revisited

In the first report program that we presented, the notion of control break was introduced. In that report two routines, PRINT-REPORT and PROC-1-GROUP, had very similar patterns of logic. Each processed a contiguous set of records from the file. PRINT-REPORT processed the entire set of item records, while PROC-1-GROUP processed a group of item records that all had the same value in the producer field.

It is sometimes necessary to introduce still smaller subgroups. Each type of subgroup is characterized by the field that is used to determine when a control break occurs. If you think carefully about it, you can see how this affects the logic of a report. At the highest level, PRINT-REPORT processes a sequence of the largest subgroups (by repeatedly invoking a routine like PROC-1-GROUP). The routine to process a major subgroup will process a sequence of smaller subgroups (again by invoking a routine similar to PROC-1-GROUP to process each of the smaller subgroups). The routine that processes the lowest level subgroups processes a sequence of records (by invoking PROC-1-RECORD for each record).

The logic for processing a group is very basic to a report. It is essentially the pattern shown in Fig. 17.1.

FIGURE 17.1 The logic to process a group of records.

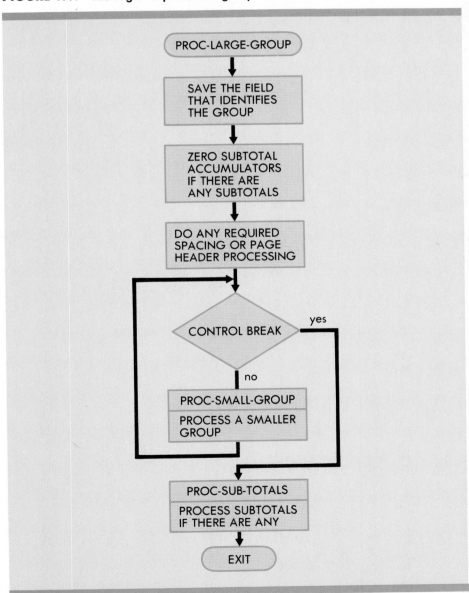

A report is basically characterized by the types of subgroups that must be processed. For each type, a pattern similar to PROC-LARGE-GROUP will be required. The peculiarities of each such routine will normally involve the spacing or page header processing, and the subtotal processing (some groups may not require subtotals).

To illustrate these concepts, consider the program in Fig. 17.2. It prints a sales history report. This report can be run using either a sorted version of the RIMF or a sorted extract file as input. The input file must be sorted into large groups, based on the contents of the PRODUCER field. Each large group should be broken into smaller groups, based on the ARTIST field. Finally, each group of records having the same values in the PRODUCER and ARTIST fields should be arranged in descending order based on the SALES-HISTORY (1) field.

FIGURE 17.2   **Report with multiple control breaks.**

```
      IDENTIFICATION DIVISION.
      PROGRAM-ID. REPORT2.
      AUTHOR. R OVERBEEK.

     ******************************************************************
     *
     * THIS PROGRAM PRODUCES A REPORT, USING THE RIMF AS INPUT.
     * THE PROGRAM ASSUMES THAT THE FILE IS SORTED INTO
     * ASCENDING ORDER ON A KEY FORMED BY (COL. 1-4, 20-29).  THE
     * REPORT HAS TWO CONTROL BREAKS.  THE LOWEST LEVEL CONTROL
     * BREAK OCCURS WHEN THE ARTIST CHANGES; ALL THAT HAPPENS WHEN
     * THE ARTIST CHANGES IS THAT THE FIRST RECORD OF THE NEW ARTIST
     * IS DOUBLE-SPACED (AND THE REST OF THE ALBUMS FOR THE SAME
     * ARTIST ARE SINGLE-SPACED).  WHEN A CONTROL BREAK IS CAUSED
     * BY A CHANGE IN THE PRODUCER (THE HIGHER LEVEL CONTROL BREAK),
     * SUBTOTALS ARE PRINTED.  THE SECTION OF THE REPORT FOR THE
     * NEXT PRODUCER STARTS ON A NEW PAGE.
     *
     * THE REPORT GIVES A SUMMARY OF THE HISTORICAL DATA IN THE
     * RIMF (OR IN AN EXTRACTED SUBSET OF THE RIMF).
     *
     ******************************************************************

      ENVIRONMENT DIVISION.
      CONFIGURATION SECTION.
      SOURCE-COMPUTER. IBM-370.
      OBJECT-COMPUTER. IBM-370.

      SPECIAL-NAMES.
          C01 IS TOP-OF-PAGE.

      INPUT-OUTPUT SECTION.
      FILE-CONTROL.
          SELECT INPUT-FILE ASSIGN TO UT-S-EXTRFILE.
          SELECT PRINT-FILE ASSIGN TO UR-S-SYSPRINT.
```

```
       DATA DIVISION.
       FILE SECTION.

  *****************************************************************
  *
  * THIS FD DESCRIBES THE RECORD INVENTORY MASTER FILE (RIMF).
  * THE FILE HAS A SINGLE HEADER RECORD AND ONE ITEM RECORD PER
  * ALBUM TITLE IN THE FILE (THE PRODUCER AND VOLUME ID TOGETHER
  * FORM A UNIQUE KEY FOR EACH ITEM RECORD).
  *
  *****************************************************************

   FD  INPUT-FILE
       LABEL RECORDS ARE STANDARD
       BLOCK CONTAINS 0 RECORDS
       DATA RECORDS ARE RIMF-HDR RIMF-ITEM.

   01  RIMF-HDR.
       05  FILLER                PIC X(81).
       05  DATE-LAST-UPDATED     PIC X(8).
       05  SHOP-NAME             PIC X(20).

   01  RIMF-ITEM.
       05  RIMF-KEY.
           10  PRODUCER          PIC X(4).
               88  HEADER-REC              VALUE IS LOW-VALUE.
           10  VOLUME-ID         PIC X(15).
       05  ARTIST                PIC X(10).
       05  ALBUM-TITLE           PIC X(20).
       05  COPIES-IN-STOCK       PIC 9999.
       05  COPIES-ON-ORDER       PIC 9999.
       05  PRICE-OF-ALBUM        PIC 99V99.
       05  SALES-HISTORY         PIC S9999    OCCURS 12 TIMES.

  *****************************************************************
  *
  * THIS FILE IS USED TO PRINT THE REPORT.
  *
  *****************************************************************

   FD  PRINT-FILE
       LABEL RECORDS ARE OMITTED
       DATA RECORD IS PRINT-BUFF.

   01  PRINT-BUFF               PIC X(133).
```

continued

FIGURE 17.2 Continued

```
    WORKING-STORAGE SECTION.

    ************************************************************
    *
    * I                        USED AS A SUBSCRIPT
    *
    * N-LINES                  SET TO THE NUMBER OF LINES TO
    *                          ADVANCE BEFORE PRINTING
    *
    * EOF-FLAG                 SET TO 'Y' WHEN END-OF-FILE OCCURS
    *
    * ERROR-FLAG               SET TO 'Y' IF A SERIOUS ERROR IS
    *                          DETECTED (A MISSING HEADER RECORD)
    *
    * PAGE-NO                  PAGE NUMBER OF THE NEXT REPORT PAGE
    *
    * LINE-COUNT               NUMBER OF THE NEXT LINE ON A PAGE
    *
    * CURRENT-PRODUCER         USED TO DETECT CONTROL BREAKS
    *
    * CURRENT-ARTIST           USED TO DETECT CONTROL BREAKS
    *
    * LAST-PROD-READ           HOLDS THE PRODUCER ON LAST RECORD
    *
    * LAST-ARTIST              HOLDS THE ARTIST ON LAST RECORD
    *
    * SUB-TOTALS               ACCUMULATES THE SUBTOTALS OF THE
    *                          SALES HISTORY FIELDS
    *
    * TOTALS                   ACCUMULATES THE TOTALS FOR THE SALES
    *                          HISTORY FIELDS
    *
    ************************************************************

    01  I                        PIC 99.

    01  FLAGS.
        05   EOF-FLAG             PIC X        VALUE IS 'N'.
             88  EOF-HAS-OCCURRED              VALUE IS 'Y'.
        05   ERROR-FLAG           PIC X        VALUE IS 'N'.

    01  PRINT-CONTROL-FIELDS.
        05   LINE-COUNT           PIC 99.
        05   N-LINES              PIC 9.
        05   PAGE-NO              PIC 999      VALUE IS 1.

    01  SAVED-CONTROL-BREAK-FIELDS.
        05   CURRENT-PRODUCER     PIC X(4).
        05   CURRENT-ARTIST       PIC X(10).
        05   LAST-PROD-READ       PIC X(4).
        05   LAST-ARTIST          PIC X(10).
```

```
01  ACCUMULATORS.
    05   SUB-TOTALS              PIC 999999  OCCURS 12 TIMES.
    05   TOTALS                  PIC 999999  OCCURS 12 TIMES.

01  PAGE-HEADER.
    05   FILLER                  PIC X(6)    VALUE IS SPACES.
    05   PAGE-HDR-DATE           PIC X(8).
    05   FILLER                  PIC X(25)   VALUE IS SPACES.
    05   PAGE-HDR-SHOP           PIC X(20).
    05   FILLER                  PIC X(20)   VALUE IS SPACES.
    05   FILLER                  PIC X(5)    VALUE IS 'PAGE'.
    05   PG-NUM                  PIC ZZ9.

01  COLUMN-HDR-1.
    05   FILLER                  PIC X(21)   VALUE IS SPACES.
    05   FILLER                  PIC X(16)   VALUE IS
                                      'PRODUCER CODE - '.
    05   COL-HDR-PRODUCER        PIC X(4).
    05   FILLER                  PIC X(10)   VALUE IS SPACES.
    05   FILLER                  PIC X(37)   VALUE IS
                        'S A L E S   H I S T O R Y   R E P O R T'.

01  COLUMN-HDR-2.
    05   FILLER                  PIC X(1).
    05   FILLER                  PIC X(6)    VALUE IS 'VOLUME'.
    05   FILLER                  PIC X(10)   VALUE IS SPACES.
    05   FILLER                  PIC X(6)    VALUE IS 'ARTIST'.
    05   FILLER                  PIC X(10)   VALUE IS SPACES.
    05   FILLER                  PIC X(5)    VALUE IS 'TITLE'.
    05   FILLER                  PIC X(16)   VALUE IS SPACES.
    05   FILLER                  PIC X(5)    VALUE IS 'PRICE'.
    05   FILLER                  PIC X(2)    VALUE IS SPACES.
    05   FILLER                  PIC X(5)    VALUE IS ' L WK'.
    05   FILLER                  PIC X(5)    VALUE IS '    2'.
    05   FILLER                  PIC X(5)    VALUE IS '    3'.
    05   FILLER                  PIC X(5)    VALUE IS '    4'.
    05   FILLER                  PIC X(5)    VALUE IS '    5'.
    05   FILLER                  PIC X(5)    VALUE IS '    6'.
    05   FILLER                  PIC X(5)    VALUE IS '    7'.
    05   FILLER                  PIC X(5)    VALUE IS '    8'.
    05   FILLER                  PIC X(5)    VALUE IS '    9'.
    05   FILLER                  PIC X(5)    VALUE IS '   10'.
    05   FILLER                  PIC X(5)    VALUE IS '   11'.
    05   FILLER                  PIC X(5)    VALUE IS '   12'.
```

continued

FIGURE 17.2 Continued

```
      01  PRINT-LINE.
          05  FILLER              PIC X.
          05  VOLUME-ID           PIC X(15).
          05  FILLER              PIC X.
          05  ARTIST              PIC X(10).
          05  FILLER              PIC X(6).
          05  ALBUM-TITLE         PIC X(20).
          05  FILLER              PIC X.
          05  PRICE-OF-ALBUM      PIC ZZ.99.
          05  FILLER              PIC X(2).
          05  HISTORY-OUT OCCURS 12 TIMES.
              10  FILLER          PIC X.
              10  ONE-HISTORY-VAL PIC ZZZ9.

      01  TOTS-LINE.
          05  FILLER              PIC X(61).
          05  SALES-HIST OCCURS 12 TIMES.
              10  FILLER          PIC X.
              10  ONE-TOT-VAL     ·PIC ZZZ9.

      01  TOTS-HDR.
          05  FILLER              PIC X(41)   VALUE IS SPACES.
          05  FILLER              PIC X(12)   VALUE IS
                                  'GRAND TOTALS'.

      PROCEDURE DIVISION.

      ****************************************************************
      *
      * THIS IS THE MAIN LOGIC OF THE REPORT.  THIS REPORT HAS TWO
      * LEVELS OF CONTROL BREAKS (BESIDES THE FINAL CONTROL BREAK).
      *
      ****************************************************************

          OPEN INPUT INPUT-FILE
              OUTPUT PRINT-FILE.

          PERFORM 10-PROC-HDR.

          IF ERROR-FLAG = 'N'
              PERFORM 40-READ-ITEM-RECORD
              PERFORM 20-PRINT-REPORT.

          CLOSE INPUT-FILE PRINT-FILE.
          STOP RUN.
```

```
    ***********************************************************
    *
    * THIS ROUTINE PROCESSES THE HEADER RECORD.  IT
    * SETS THE ERROR-FLAG, IF THE FILE IS EMPTY OR THE HEADER IS
    * MISSING.  ELSE, THE SHOP NAME AND DATE THAT THE FILE WAS LAST
    * UPDATED ARE PUT INTO THE PAGE HEADER.
    *
    ***********************************************************

     10-PROC-HDR.
         READ INPUT-FILE AT END MOVE 'Y' TO EOF-FLAG.
         IF EOF-HAS-OCCURRED
             MOVE ' *** FILE HAS NO RECORDS ***' TO PRINT-BUFF
             WRITE PRINT-BUFF AFTER ADVANCING TOP-OF-PAGE
             MOVE 'Y' TO ERROR-FLAG
         ELSE
             IF NOT HEADER-REC
                 MOVE ' *** HEADER MISSING ON INPUT FILE ***'
                     TO PRINT-BUFF
                 WRITE PRINT-BUFF AFTER ADVANCING TOP-OF-PAGE
                 MOVE 'Y' TO ERROR-FLAG
             ELSE
                 MOVE DATE-LAST-UPDATED TO PAGE-HDR-DATE
                 MOVE SHOP-NAME TO PAGE-HDR-SHOP.

    ***********************************************************
    *
    * THIS ROUTINE PRINTS THE REPORT, INCLUDING GRAND TOTALS
    *
    ***********************************************************

     20-PRINT-REPORT.
         PERFORM 30-ZERO-TOTS
             VARYING I FROM 1 BY 1 UNTIL I > 12.

         PERFORM 50-PROC-1-PRODUCER
             UNTIL EOF-HAS-OCCURRED.

         PERFORM 120-GRAND-TOTALS.

    ***********************************************************
    *
    * THIS ROUTINE JUST ZEROS OUT THE ACCUMULATORS FOR THE FINAL
    * TOTALS.
    *
    ***********************************************************

     30-ZERO-TOTS.
         MOVE 0 TO TOTALS (I).
```

continued

FIGURE 17.2 Continued

```
*********************************************************************
*
* THIS ROUTINE READS THE NEXT RECORD FROM THE INPUT-FILE,
* SETTING EOF-FLAG TO 'Y' WHEN END-OF-FILE OCCURS
*
*********************************************************************

  40-READ-ITEM-RECORD.
      READ INPUT-FILE AT END MOVE 'Y' TO EOF-FLAG.
      IF EOF-HAS-OCCURRED
          MOVE HIGH-VALUE TO LAST-PROD-READ
      ELSE
          MOVE PRODUCER TO LAST-PROD-READ
          MOVE ARTIST IN RIMF-ITEM TO LAST-ARTIST.

*********************************************************************
*
* THIS ROUTINE PRINTS THE SECTION OF THE REPORT CORRESPONDING
* TO A SINGLE PRODUCER.
*
*********************************************************************

  50-PROC-1-PRODUCER.
      MOVE PRODUCER TO CURRENT-PRODUCER.

      PERFORM 60-ZERO-SUB-TOTS
          VARYING I FROM 1 BY 1 UNTIL I > 12.

      PERFORM 150-HEADER-ROUTINE.

      PERFORM 70-PROC-1-ARTIST
          UNTIL LAST-PROD-READ NOT = CURRENT-PRODUCER.

      PERFORM 100-PROC-SUB-TOTALS.

*********************************************************************
*
* THIS ROUTINE JUST ZEROS OUT THE ACCUMULATORS FOR THE
* SUB-TOTALS.
*
*********************************************************************

  60-ZERO-SUB-TOTS.
      MOVE 0 TO SUB-TOTALS (I).
```

```
*******************************************************************
*
* THIS ROUTINE PROCESSES ALL OF THE RECORDS FOR A SINGLE ARTIST.
*
*******************************************************************

  70-PROC-1-ARTIST.
      MOVE ARTIST IN RIMF-ITEM TO CURRENT-ARTIST.
      MOVE 2 TO N-LINES.

      PERFORM 80-PROC-1-RECORD
          UNTIL LAST-PROD-READ NOT = CURRENT-PRODUCER OR
                LAST-ARTIST NOT = CURRENT-ARTIST.

*******************************************************************
*
* THIS ROUTINE PRINTS A LINE FOR THE CURRENT ITEM RECORD
* AND ACCUMULATES SUBTOTALS.
*
*******************************************************************

  80-PROC-1-RECORD.
      MOVE SPACES TO PRINT-LINE.
      MOVE CORR RIMF-ITEM TO PRINT-LINE.
      MOVE VOLUME-ID IN RIMF-ITEM TO VOLUME-ID IN PRINT-LINE.
      PERFORM 90-MOVE-SALES-HIST
          VARYING I FROM 1 BY 1 UNTIL I > 12.
      PERFORM 140-PRINT-ROUTINE.
      MOVE 1 TO N-LINES.

      PERFORM 40-READ-ITEM-RECORD.

*******************************************************************
*
* THIS ROUTINE JUST MOVES ONE SALES HISTORY VALUE TO THE
* PRINT LINE.
*
*******************************************************************

  90-MOVE-SALES-HIST.
      MOVE SALES-HISTORY (I) TO ONE-HISTORY-VAL (I).
      ADD SALES-HISTORY (I) TO SUB-TOTALS (I).
```

continued

FIGURE 17.2 Continued

```
**********************************************************************
*
* THIS ROUTINE PRINTS SUBTOTALS AND ADDS THE SUBTOTALS TO
* THE GRAND TOTALS.
*
**********************************************************************

 100-PROC-SUB-TOTALS.
     MOVE SPACES TO TOTS-LINE.
     PERFORM 110-MOVE-AND-ADD-A-SUB
         VARYING I FROM 1 BY 1 UNTIL I > 12.

     WRITE PRINT-BUFF FROM TOTS-LINE AFTER ADVANCING 3 LINES.

**********************************************************************
*
* THIS ROUTINE MOVES ONE SUB-TOTAL TO THE TOTS-LINE AND
* ADDS THE SUB-TOTAL TO THE CORRESPONDING FINAL TOTAL.
*
**********************************************************************

 110-MOVE-AND-ADD-A-SUB.
     MOVE SUB-TOTALS (I) TO ONE-TOT-VAL (I).
     ADD SUB-TOTALS (I) TO TOTALS (I).

**********************************************************************
*
* THIS ROUTINE PRINTS GRAND TOTALS.
*
**********************************************************************

 120-GRAND-TOTALS.
     WRITE PRINT-BUFF FROM TOTS-HDR AFTER ADVANCING TOP-OF-PAGE.

     MOVE SPACES TO TOTS-LINE.
     PERFORM 130-MOVE-ONE-TOTAL
         VARYING I FROM 1 BY 1 UNTIL I > 12.

     WRITE PRINT-BUFF FROM TOTS-LINE
         AFTER ADVANCING 2 LINES.

**********************************************************************
*
* THIS ROUTINE JUST MOVES ONE FINAL TOTAL TO THE TOTALS LINE
*
**********************************************************************

 130-MOVE-ONE-TOTAL.
     MOVE TOTALS (I) TO ONE-TOT-VAL (I).
```

```
*********************************************************************
*
* THIS ROUTINE PRINTS A LINE (STARTING ON A NEW PAGE IF
* NECESSARY).
*
*********************************************************************

 140-PRINT-ROUTINE.
     IF LINE-COUNT > 50
         PERFORM 150-HEADER-ROUTINE.
     WRITE PRINT-BUFF FROM PRINT-LINE
         AFTER ADVANCING N-LINES.

     ADD N-LINES TO LINE-COUNT.

*********************************************************************
*
* THIS ROUTINE IS INVOKED TO PRINT PAGE AND COLUMN HEADERS..
* IT RESETS THE LINE-COUNT TO 6 (THE NUMBER OF THE NEXT LINE
* ON THE PAGE).
*
*********************************************************************

 150-HEADER-ROUTINE.
     MOVE PAGE-NO TO PG-NUM.
     ADD 1 TO PAGE-NO.
     WRITE PRINT-BUFF FROM PAGE-HEADER
         AFTER ADVANCING TOP-OF-PAGE.

     MOVE CURRENT-PRODUCER TO COL-HDR-PRODUCER.
     WRITE PRINT-BUFF FROM COLUMN-HDR-1
         AFTER ADVANCING 2 LINES.

     WRITE PRINT-BUFF FROM COLUMN-HDR-2
         AFTER ADVANCING 2 LINES.

     MOVE 2 TO N-LINES.
     MOVE 6 TO LINE-COUNT.
```

Figure 16.2 illustrates some output from the report. Notice that each group of records with the same ARTIST value begins with a double-spaced line. The remaining lines for the group are single-spaced. There are no subtotals for the smallest groups. The logic for the program includes three routines similar to PROC-LARGE-GROUP. These routines are PRINT-REPORT, PROC-1-PRODUCER, and PROC-1-ARTIST. A thorough understanding of this report should give the reader a good introduction to the logic of reports.

SUMMARY

The MOVE statement with the CORRESPONDING option should be used with caution, if at all. Most report programs require more than a single control break. Once the logic to add an additional control break is understood, multiple control breaks, to whatever depth, should pose no particular problems.

REVIEW QUESTIONS

17.1 What restriction applies to whether items are group or elementary items in order to correspond in the use of a MOVE statement with a CORRESPONDING option?

17.2 Do restrictions also pertain to items that contain an OCCURS clause?

17.3 Why should you avoid use of MOVE statements with the CORRESPONDING option?

17.4 Why are multiple control breaks required in many report programs?

PROGRAMMING EXERCISES

17.1 Create a report for the doctor billing system that lists for each doctor his patients, ordered on the date in which they first started visiting the doctor. To create the report, use the master file as input, but assume that it has been sorted as follows:

The records all occur in ascending order on columns 108–127 (the doctor's name).

The records for a single doctor occur in ascending order on columns 100–107 (the date that the patient first came to the doctor).

The report should have control breaks on the doctor's name and the year that the account was opened (columns 126–127), as well as at the end of the report. The final grand total should contain just the number of accounts in the file and should be printed on a separate page. Each page of the report should look like

```
PATIENT REPORT BY DATE OF FIRST VISIT          PAGE 8
                        DOCTOR BAKER

       PATIENT          DATE OF FIRST VISIT

JAMES MORRIS               08/13/81
MARY ADAMS                 11/02/81
JERRY BLACK                12/15/81

       TOTAL NUMBER OF NEW PATIENTS IN 1981 = 3

LINDA CARTER               01/08/82
TAMMY MORRIS               02/18/82
TOM SMITH                  04/27/82
JIM BAKER                  07/30/82
MARY JONES                 10/11/82

          TOTAL NUMBER OF NEW PATIENTS IN 1982 = 5

TOTAL NUMBER OF PATIENTS FOR DOCTOR   BAKER = 27
```

The last line of this page shows the line printed when a control break occurs due to a change in the doctor's name. The patients for the next doctor should begin on a new page.

17.2   Create a summary report for the municipal bond reporting system. The report gives the total par value of bonds that mature during each year. Within each year the report shows for each month the number of bonds for which interest checks are expected. Thus, a page of the report would look like

```
03/10/83   M U N I C I P A L   B O N D   S U M M A R Y        PAGE 2

                 YEAR          COUPON CODE    NUMBER OF BONDS

                  84                1               4
                                    2               3
                                    3               5
                                    4               3
                                    5               3
                                    6               4

          TOTAL PAR VALUE = $220,000

                  85                1               2
                                    2               4
                                    3               3
                                    4               3
                                    5               3
                                    6               4

          TOTAL PAR VALUE = $270,000
```

At the end of the report, a grand total giving the total par value and the total number of bonds should be printed (on a separate page).

CHAPTER EIGHTEEN

THE REPORT WRITER

INTRODUCTION Most data processing programs are report programs similar to those presented in Chapters 16 and 17. The Report Writer feature of COBOL represents an attempt to reduce the time required to code such a program by using the fact that most report programs follow one basic pattern of logic. Instead of specifying the detailed logic of a report in the PROCEDURE DIVISION, one can describe the format in the DATA DIVISION and use just a few statements in the PROCEDURE DIVISION to invoke the Report Writer; the Report Writer then uses the general logic of a report program to produce the report.

Heading lines are the normal headers printed at the top of each page.
Detail lines make up the body of the report and are produced from the item records in the report file.
Footing lines are the subtotal and total lines.

Closely associated lines (e.g., the lines in the header or in a group of subtotals), are commonly referred to as **heading groups**, **detail groups**, and **footing groups**. A rough description of a report can be produced by specifying the format, spacing, and content of

1. the heading group to be printed at the top of each page,
2. the detail group to be printed for each item in the report,
3. the footing group to be printed whenever subtotals are displayed, and
4. the footing group to be printed at the completion of the report.

To complete the description of a particular report, one must specify when subtotals should occur. Chapter 16 reveals that subtotals occur when two successive detail groups contain different values for some critical field (the field referred to as the **subtotal key**). Such an occurrence is called a **control break**.

Now, when a detailed description of the groups of lines in a report (called the report groups) and of the control breaks is given in the DATA DIVISION, very few actual statements have to be used in the PROCEDURE DIVISION. It is necessary to process only the input file and designate the points at which a detail group should be printed. The Report Writer automatically maintains a LINE-COUNTER and a PAGE-COUNTER, prints headers, and produces subtotals when appropriate. The following sections present the details of the process described previously.

18.1 **Changes to the Data Division**

In this section, the statements required to specify the precise format of a report will be presented. A specific example will be used to illustrate points as they are discussed. We have selected a report quite similar to the one produced by the program in Section 16.4. The report produced by the example program in this section prints album totals for each producer and prints grand totals on a separate page.

The first change to be noted occurs in the FD entry for the output file to which the report is directed, PRINT-FILE. If the Report Writer is invoked to produce the report, no description of the records is presented in the FD entry. Thus, the DATA RECORD IS clause and the description of the corresponding print line are omitted. In their place a REPORT clause of the following format is used

    RE<u>PORT</u> IS report-name

where report-name is just an arbitrary label that is used to connect the particular FD entry with the description of the report, which occurs later in the DATA DIVISION.

The complete description of the report referenced in the FD entry occurs in a new section following the WORKING-STORAGE SECTION, the REPORT SECTION. This section has a **report description** (RD) entry followed by descriptions of the groups of lines which make up the report (report description entries). The RD entry is used to specify

1. when control breaks should occur,
2. the number of lines produced per page,
3. the line number of the line where the header group should begin,
4. the number of the line where the first detail group should begin.

The format of the RD entry is

    R<u>D</u> report name   [CONTROL clause]
                          [PAGE LIMIT clause]

The CONTROL clause is used to specify when control breaks should occur. Its format is

$$\begin{Bmatrix} \underline{CONTROL} \text{ IS} \\ \underline{CONTROLS} \text{ ARE} \end{Bmatrix} \begin{Bmatrix} \text{identifier-1} \\ \underline{FINAL} \\ \underline{FINAL} \text{ identifier-1} \end{Bmatrix}$$

The meaning of each of the possible forms is as follows:

    CONTROL IS identifier-1

This indicates that the field identifier-1 should be checked whenever a detail group is printed. If the value in identifier-1 changes, a control break occurs. When a control break occurs, the appropriate footing group is printed before the next detail group.

    CONTROL IS FINAL

When FINAL is coded, it indicates that a control break should occur after the last detail group is printed. This would be used to print totals at the end of a report.

    CONTROLS ARE FINAL identifier-1

In this case, two levels of control breaks are specified. A control break associated with FINAL is said to be of higher order than a control break associated with identifier-1. This means that, while the control breaks associated with identifier-1 are the same as those described in case 1, the control break associated with FINAL causes the same footing group described in case 1 to be printed, and, in addition, causes the footing group described in case 2 to be printed. If a FINAL control break occurs, a control for identifier-1 will automatically occur; the footing group associated with the lower order control break is then printed before the footing group associated with the FINAL control break.

Hence, in the example program,

```
CONTROLS ARE FINAL PRODUCER
```

means

1. Whenever the value of PRODUCER changes between the points where two successive detail groups are printed, a footing group associated with the PRODUCER control breaks should be printed before the second data group.

2. When the FINAL control break occurs, it will be just as if a PRODUCER control break had immediately preceded it.

The format for the PAGE LIMIT clause is

$$\underline{PAGE} \begin{bmatrix} \underline{LIMIT} \ IS \\ \underline{LIMITS} \ ARE \end{bmatrix} integer\text{-}1 \ \underline{LINES}$$
$$[\underline{HEADING} \ integer\text{-}2] \ [\underline{FIRST} \ \underline{DETAIL} \ integer\text{-}3]$$

Integer-1 gives the maximum number of lines to be printed per page.

Integer-2 gives the line number where the first line of the heading group is printed.

Integer-3 gives the line number where the first line of the first detail group for a given page is printed.

Thus, in the example:

```
RD   PRODUCER-LISTS CONTROLS ARE FINAL COURSE
                    PAGE LIMIT IS 52 LINES
                    HEADING 1 FIRST DETAIL 7.
```

the report description entry establishes where the control breaks are to occur, the maximum number of lines per page, the location of the start of the header group, and the location where the detail groups begin on a page.

The remainder of the REPORT SECTION contains report group descriptions, which are used to describe each of the heading, detail, and footing groups in the report. In the example there are four such group descriptions—one for the page header groups, one for the detail groups, one for the footing groups caused by control breaks indicated by a change in PRODUCER, and one for the FINAL footing group. There are actually three distinct formats illustrated by these group description entries:

```
FORMAT 1

01  [data-name-1]
    TYPE clause
    [LINE clause]
    [NEXT GROUP clause]
```

This first format is used to begin a report group description. The data-name-1 entry, which is optional, should be specified for detail groups for reasons that will be clarified in the next section. The TYPE clause is used to specify the type of group being described and has the following format:

$$\underline{TYPE} \text{ IS} \begin{Bmatrix} \underline{PAGE\ HEADING} \\ \underline{DETAIL} \\ \underline{CONTROL\ FOOTING} \begin{Bmatrix} identifier\text{-}1 \\ \underline{FINAL} \end{Bmatrix} \end{Bmatrix}$$

The options allow one to specify a heading, detail, or footing group. In the case of a footing group, one must add an extra entry to indicate specifically what type of control break would cause the footing to be printed.

The LINE clause is used to describe exactly what line the group should begin on. Its format is

$$\underline{LINE} \text{ NUMBER IS} \begin{Bmatrix} integer\text{-}1 \\ \underline{PLUS}\ integer\text{-}2 \\ \underline{NEXT\ PAGE} \end{Bmatrix}$$

If integer-1 is specified, the first line of the report group begins at that exact line of the page (lines are numbered 1, 2, 3, ... starting at 1 from the top). If PLUS integer-2 is used, the first line of the group will be integer-2 lines past the last line printed (unless the end of a page occurs). NEXT PAGE is used to force the group to begin on the next page. If NEXT PAGE is coded or if the end of a page occurs with the PLUS integer-2 option, a header is automatically printed at the top of the next page before printing the report group.

The NEXT GROUP clause specifies how the printer is to be advanced after the last line of the report group is printed. It has the following format:

$$\underline{NEXT\ GROUP} \text{ IS} \begin{Bmatrix} integer\text{-}1 \\ \underline{PLUS}\ integer\text{-}2 \\ \underline{NEXT\ PAGE} \end{Bmatrix}$$

where the options are similar to those offered by the LINE clause. Thus,

```
01  TYPE IS CONTROL FOOTING PRODUCER
    LINE NUMBER IS PLUS 2 NEXT GROUP NEXT PAGE.
```

begins a footing group to be printed when the field PRODUCER changes value between detail groups. A double space should occur before printing the first subtotal line of the group (in this case the only line), and the next report group should be printed on the next page.

The second format is

```
FORMAT 2

Level-number LINE clause
```

where level-number can be anything from 02 to 49. This format is used when there is more than one line in the report group. In the example, the heading group contains more than one line, so this format is utilized.

The third format is used to describe a specific field in a line of the group and has the following format:

```
FORMAT 3

Level-number  [data-name-1]
              COLUMN NUMBER IS integer-1
              PICTURE clause
```

$$\begin{Bmatrix} \underline{\text{SO}}\underline{\text{URCE}} \text{ IS identifier-1} \\ \underline{\text{VA}}\underline{\text{LUE}} \text{ IS literal-1} \\ \underline{\text{SUM}} \text{ identifier-2} \end{Bmatrix}$$

In this case, integer-1 specifies what column in the report the field should begin in. The PICTURE clause is simply the usual clause used to specify the format of a field. If

```
SOURCE IS identifier-1
```

is specified, the field in the report line takes its value from identifier-1. If PAGE-COUNTER is specified, the current page number is inserted into the field in the report line. If

```
VALUE IS literal-1
```

is used, literal-1 is put into the report line. If

```
SUM identifier-2
```

is used, the field attains its value from a series of summations. In this case, a special SUM counter is established to accumulate the desired value. If data-name-1 was used in Format 3, the SUM counter may be referred to by that name; otherwise, it is unnamed. The SUM counter is incremented as follows:

1. If identifier-1 is not the name of some other SUM counter, then the SUM counter is incremented every time that a detail group containing

```
SOURCE IS identifier-1
```

is printed.

2. If identifier-1 is the name of another SUM counter, then SUM is incremented whenever identifier-1 is displayed in a footing group.

Each time that a SUM counter is displayed in a footing group, the counter is reset to zero. Thus,

```
05  SUB-TOT
        COLUMN IS 84 PIC ZZ9 SUM NO-OF-TITLES.
```

defines a SUM counter, SUB-TOT, which is incremented whenever NO-OF-TITLES is displayed in one of the detail lines. In the FINAL footing group

```
05  COLUMN IS 82 PIC ZZZZ9 SUM SUB-TOT.
```

defines an unnamed SUM counter that is incremented just before SUB-TOT is reset to zero each time that subtotals are displayed.

The reader should, at this point, see quite clearly how the REPORT SECTION in the example was used to specify the format of the report PRODUCER-LISTS. In the next section, the instructions in the PROCEDURE DIVISION that are required to produce the report are discussed.

18.2 Changes to the **PROCEDURE DIVISION**

Once a report has been completely described in the DATA DIVISION, only a few statements are required in the PROCEDURE DIVISION to generate the report. These statements are as follows:

1. The report file must be opened, just as any output file must be opened.

2. The statement

```
INITIATE report-name
```

must be issued. This initializes the PAGE-COUNTER, the LINE-COUNTER, and all SUM counters.

3. Whenever a detail line should be printed, the following statement should be executed:

```
GENERATE data-name-1
```

where data-name-1 is the name given to some detail group. This causes the detail group to be printed. If page headers or subtotals should be generated, they will all be printed automatically by the Report Writer.

4. After all the detailed lines have been printed, the program should execute

```
TERMINATE report-name
```

which causes the FINAL control break.

5. The file should be closed before ending execution of the program.

The example program in Fig. 18.1 illustrates the features introduced in this chapter. The brevity of this program should emphasize to the reader that a large number of commands can be saved by utilizing a powerful facility such as the Report Writer.

FIGURE 18.1 A report using the Report Writer.

```
       IDENTIFICATION DIVISION.
       PROGRAM-ID. REPORT1.
       AUTHOR. R OVERBEEK.


       *************************************************************
       *
       * THIS PROGRAM PRODUCES A REPORT, USING THE RIMF AS INPUT.
       * THE PROGRAM ASSUMES THAT THE FILE IS SORTED INTO
       * ASCENDING ORDER ON THE FIRST 19 COLUMNS.  CONTROL BREAKS
       * WILL OCCUR BASED ON THE PRODUCER (COLUMNS 1-4).  THE
       * REPORT LISTS THE ALBUMS FOR EACH PRODUCER -- WITH SUBTOTALS
       * SHOWING THE NUMBER OF TITLES, NUMBER OF ALBUMS IN STOCK,
       * AND THE NUMBER ON ORDER.  GRAND TOTALS GIVE THE SAME VALUES
       * FOR ALL PRODUCERS ADDED TOGETHER.
       *
       *************************************************************

       ENVIRONMENT DIVISION.
       CONFIGURATION SECTION.
       SOURCE-COMPUTER. IBM-370.
       OBJECT-COMPUTER. IBM-370.
       INPUT-OUTPUT SECTION.
       FILE-CONTROL.
           SELECT RIMF ASSIGN TO UT-S-RIMF.
           SELECT PRINT-FILE ASSIGN TO UR-S-SYSPRINT.
```

```
        DATA DIVISION.
        FILE SECTION.

   *******************************************************************
   *
   * THIS FD DESCRIBES THE RECORD INVENTORY MASTER FILE (RIMF).
   * THE FILE HAS A SINGLE HEADER RECORD AND ONE ITEM RECORD PER
   * ALBUM TITLE IN THE FILE (THE PRODUCER AND VOLUME ID TOGETHER
   * FORM A UNIQUE KEY FOR EACH ITEM RECORD).
   *
   *******************************************************************

    FD  RIMF
        LABEL RECORDS ARE STANDARD
        BLOCK CONTAINS 0 RECORDS
        DATA RECORDS ARE RIMF-HDR RIMF-ITEM.

    01  RIMF-HDR.
        05  FILLER               PIC X(81).
        05  DATE-LAST-UPDATED    PIC X(8).
        05  SHOP-NAME            PIC X(20).

    01  RIMF-ITEM.
        05  RIMF-KEY.
            10  PRODUCER         PIC X(4).
                88  HEADER-REC   VALUE IS LOW-VALUE.
            10  VOLUME-ID        PIC X(15).
        05  ARTIST               PIC X(10).
        05  ALBUM-TITLE          PIC X(20).
        05  COPIES-IN-STOCK      PIC 9999.
        05  COPIES-ON-ORDER      PIC 9999.
        05  PRICE-OF-ALBUM       PIC 99V99.
        05  SALES-HISTORY        PIC S9999 OCCURS 12 TIMES.

   *******************************************************************
   *
   * THIS FILE IS USED TO PRINT THE REPORT.
   *
   *******************************************************************

    FD  PRINT-FILE
        LABEL RECORDS ARE OMITTED
        REPORT IS PRODUCER-REPORT.
```

continued

FIGURE 18.1   Continued

```
   WORKING-STORAGE SECTION.

   **********************************************************************
   *
   * EOF-FLAG                    SET TO 'Y' WHEN END-OF-FILE OCCURS
   *
   * ERROR-FLAG                  SET TO 'Y' IF A SERIOUS ERROR IS
   *                             DETECTED (A MISSING HEADER RECORD)
   *
   * CONSTANT-1                  A CONSTANT VALUE OF 1
   *
   * PAGE-HDR-DATE               DATE FROM THE RIMF HEADER
   *
   * PAGE-HDR-SHOP               USE TO SAVE SHOP NAME FROM
   *                             RIMF HEADER
   *
   * LAST-PROD-READ              HOLDS THE PRODUCER OF LAST RECORD
   *
   **********************************************************************

      01  FLAGS.
          05  EOF-FLAG             PIC X VALUE IS 'N'.
              88  EOF-HAS-OCCURRED    VALUE IS 'Y'.
          05  ERROR-FLAG          PIC X VALUE IS 'N'.

      01  MISC.
          05  CONSTANT-1          PIC 9 VALUE IS 1.
          05  PAGE-HDR-DATE       PIC X(8).
          05  PAGE-HDR-SHOP       PIC X(20).
          05  LAST-PROD-READ      PIC X(4).

   REPORT SECTION.
   RD  PRODUCER-REPORT
       CONTROLS ARE FINAL LAST-PROD-READ
       PAGE LIMIT IS 50 LINES
       HEADING 1
       FIRST DETAIL 7.
```

```
01    TYPE IS PAGE HEADING.
      05    LINE NUMBER IS 1.
            10    COLUMN IS 7     PIC X(8)   SOURCE IS PAGE-HDR-DATE.
            10    COLUMN IS 40    PIC X(20)  SOURCE IS PAGE-HDR-SHOP.
            10    COLUMN IS 80    PIC X(5)   VALUE IS 'PAGE'.
            10    COLUMN IS 85    PIC ZZ9    SOURCE IS PAGE-COUNTER.

      05    LINE NUMBER IS 3.
            10    COLUMN IS 40    PIC X(16)
                        VALUE IS 'PRODUCER CODE -'.
            10    COLUMN IS 56    PIC X(4)   SOURCE IS LAST-PROD-READ.
      05    LINE NUMBER IS 5.
            10    COLUMN IS 2     PIC X(6)   VALUE IS 'VOLUME'.
            10    COLUMN IS 18    PIC X(6)   VALUE IS 'ARTIST'.
            10    COLUMN IS 34    PIC X(5)   VALUE IS 'TITLE'.
            10    COLUMN IS 54    PIC X(8)   VALUE IS 'IN STOCK'.
            10    COLUMN IS 67    PIC X(8)   VALUE IS 'ON ORDER'.
            10    COLUMN IS 78    PIC X(5)   VALUE IS 'PRICE'.

01    A-DETAIL-LINE TYPE IS DETAIL
            LINE NUMBER IS PLUS 1.
      05    COLUMN IS 2           PIC X(15)  SOURCE IS VOLUME-ID.
      05    COLUMN IS 18          PIC X(10)  SOURCE IS ARTIST.
      05    COLUMN IS 34          PIC X(20)  SOURCE IS ALBUM-TITLE.
      05    COLUMN IS 55          PIC ZZZ9   SOURCE IS COPIES-IN-STOCK.
      05    COLUMN IS 69          PIC ZZZ9   SOURCE IS COPIES-ON-ORDER.
      05    COLUMN IS 77          PIC ZZ.99  SOURCE IS PRICE-OF-ALBUM.
      05                          PIC 9      SOURCE IS CONSTANT-1.

01    TYPE IS CONTROL FOOTING LAST-PROD-READ
            LINE NUMBER IS PLUS 3
            NEXT GROUP NEXT PAGE.
      05    COLUMN IS 2           PIC X(20)
                                  VALUE IS 'TOTALS: # VOLUMES = '.
      05    SUB-TITLES
            COLUMN IS 22    PIC ZZZ9   SUM CONSTANT-1.
      05    SUB-IN-STOCK
            COLUMN IS 52    PIC ZZZ,ZZ9 SUM COPIES-IN-STOCK.
      05    SUB-ON-ORDER
            COLUMN IS 66    PIC ZZZ,ZZ9 SUM COPIES-ON-ORDER.

01    TYPE IS CONTROL FOOTING FINAL.
      05    LINE NUMBER IS NEXT PAGE.
            10    COLUMN IS 42    PIC X(12) VALUE IS 'GRAND TOTALS'.
      05    LINE NUMBER IS PLUS 2.
            10    COLUMN IS 42    PIC X(8)  VALUE IS 'TITLES'.
            10.   COLUMN IS 57    PIC ZZZ,ZZ9 SUM SUB-TITLES.
      05    LINE NUMBER IS PLUS 1.
            10    COLUMN IS 42    PIC X(10) VALUE IS 'IN STOCK ='.
            10    COLUMN IS 57    PIC ZZZ,ZZ9 SUM SUB-IN-STOCK.
      05    LINE NUMBER IS PLUS 1.
            10    COLUMN IS 42    PIC X(10) VALUE IS 'ON ORDER ='.
            10    COLUMN IS 57    PIC ZZZ,ZZ9 SUM SUB-ON-ORDER.
```

continued

FIGURE 18.1 Continued

```
    PROCEDURE DIVISION.

    ****************************************************************
    *
    * THIS IS THE MAIN LOGIC OF THE REPORT.  YOU SHOULD STUDY IT
    * CAREFULLY, SINCE MOST REPORTS WITH A SINGLE CONTROL BREAK
    * WILL HAVE VERY SIMILAR LOGIC.
    *
    ****************************************************************

        OPEN INPUT RIMF
            OUTPUT PRINT-FILE.

        PERFORM 10-PROC-HDR.

        IF ERROR-FLAG = 'N'
            INITIATE PRODUCER-REPORT
            PERFORM 30-READ-ITEM-RECORD
            PERFORM 20-PROC-A-RECORD
                UNTIL EOF-HAS-OCCURRED
            TERMINATE PRODUCER-REPORT.

        CLOSE RIMF PRINT-FILE.
        STOP RUN.

    ****************************************************************
    *
    * THIS ROUTINE PROCESSES THE HEADER RECORD.  IT
    * SETS THE ERROR-FLAG IF THE FILE IS EMPTY OR THE HEADER IS
    * MISSING.  ELSE, THE SHOP NAME AND DATE THAT THE FILE WAS LAST
    * UPDATED ARE PUT INTO THE PAGE HEADER.
    *
    ****************************************************************

    10-PROC-HDR.
        READ RIMF AT END MOVE 'Y' TO EOF-FLAG.
        IF EOF-HAS-OCCURRED
            DISPLAY '*** FILE HAS NO RECORDS ***'
            MOVE 'Y' TO ERROR-FLAG
        ELSE
            IF NOT HEADER-REC
                DISPLAY '*** HEADER MISSING ON RIMF ***'
                MOVE 'Y' TO ERROR-FLAG
            ELSE
                MOVE DATE-LAST-UPDATED TO PAGE-HDR-DATE
                MOVE SHOP-NAME TO PAGE-HDR-SHOP.
```

```
******************************************************************
*
* THIS ROUTINE PRINTS THE REPORT, INCLUDING GRAND TOTALS
*
******************************************************************

 20-PROC-A-RECORD.
     GENERATE A-DETAIL-LINE.
     PERFORM 30-READ-ITEM-RECORD.

******************************************************************
*
* THIS ROUTINE READS THE NEXT RECORD FROM THE RIMF,
* MOVING THE KEY TO WORKING STORAGE (HIGH-VALUE ON EOF).
*
******************************************************************

 30-READ-ITEM-RECORD.
     READ RIMF AT END MOVE 'Y' TO EOF-FLAG.
     IF EOF-HAS-OCCURRED
         MOVE HIGH-VALUE TO LAST-PROD-READ
     ELSE
         MOVE PRODUCER TO LAST-PROD-READ.
 READ-ITEM-EXIT. EXIT.
```

There are two peculiarities of the program worth noting. First, consider the sum counter SUB-TITLES. This is defined as acquiring its value by summing the values in CONSTANT-1 (i.e., whenever CONSTANT-1 is used as a source when a detail group is printed, it is added into SUB-TITLES). CONSTANT-1 is used as a source in A-DETAIL-LINE. But note that no column is specified on the entry using CONSTANT-1 as a source. This will cause CONSTANT-1 to be summed into SUB-TITLES, but it will not be displayed when A-DETAIL-LINE is printed (because there is no column specified). This is a standard "trick" used to count detail groups when using the Report Writer.

The second point worth noting is that, unlike the version of the report that appears in Chapter 14, header lines are printed on the last page. It is possible, but difficult, to suppress these lines.

The Report Writer is a useful tool for writing simple, standard reports. Although it is possible to handle most unusual features, it frequently leads to a program that is hard to understand and debug. So it is probably best to use the Report Writer only when creating relatively standard reports. For reports with extra embellishments, it is normally easier just to code the logic as a variation of the patterns presented in Chapters 16 and 17.

Only the basic ideas of the Report Writer have been presented in this book. A multitude of options have been omitted. Since it is necessary to utilize many of these options in order to generate a complex report, you may want to continue your study of the Report Writer by examining a standard ANS COBOL reference manual.

SUMMARY

The Report Writer facility of ANS COBOL offers a convenient way to code straightforward reports. By describing the characteristics of the desired report in the REPORT SECTION, most of the logic normally required to produce a report, such as identifying control breaks and processing subtotals, can be completely avoided.

In order to describe the report, the programmer specifies the features of the heading groups, detail groups, and footing groups that make up the report. In addition, the programmer must specify the fields that can be used to determine control breaks. This information is specified in the Report Description (RD), which occurs in the REPORT SECTION.

Assuming that the RD is properly coded, the programmer can use an INITIATE statement to cause initialization processing, GENERATE statements to create the desired report body, and a TERMINATE statement to end the report. These three statements replace most of the logic normally required to produce reports.

REVIEW QUESTIONS

18.1   What three categories are used to characterize lines in a report?

18.2   How does the programmer indicate that the Report Writer will be used to create the report?

18.3   What information is specified in the CONTROL clause?

18.4   When is a SUM counter used?

18.5   What statement is used to cause a detail group to be printed? Can the use of such a statement cause more than one group of lines to be printed?

18.6   How can you control the number of lines printed per page when you use the Report Writer?

PROGRAMMING EXERCISES

18.1   In Exercise 1 at the end of Chapter 17, you were asked to generate a simple report. Recode that report using the Report Writer feature of COBOL.

18.2   In Exercise 2 at the end of Chapter 16, you were asked to produce a report from the municipal bond master file. Recode that assignment using the Report Writer.

18.3   Rewrite the report described in Exercise 3 at the end of Chapter 17, using the Report Writer.

COBOL
RESERVED
WORDS

The following is a list of reserved words:

ACCEPT	CODE	DELETE
ACCESS	CODE-SET	DELIMITED
ADD	COLLATING	DELIMITER
ADVANCING	COLUMN	DEPENDING
AFTER	COMMA	DESCENDING
ALL	COMMUNICATION	DESTINATION
ALPHABETIC	COMP	DETAIL
ALSO	COMPUTATIONAL	DISABLE
ALTER	COMPUTE	DISPLAY
ALTERNATE	CONFIGURATION	DIVIDE
AND	CONTAINS	DIVISION
ARE	CONTROL	DOWN
AREA	CONTROLS	DUPLICATES
AREAS	COPY	DYNAMIC
ASCENDING	CORR	
ASSIGN	CORRESPONDING	EGI
AT	COUNT	ELSE
AUTHOR	CURRENCY	EMI
		ENABLE
BEFORE	DATA	END
BLANK	DATE	END-OF-PAGE
BLOCK	DATE-COMPILED	ENTER
BOTTOM	DATE-WRITTEN	ENVIRONMENT
BY	DAY	EOP
	DE	EQUAL
CALL	DEBUG-CONTENTS	ERROR
CANCEL	DEBUG-ITEM	ESI
CD	DEBUG-LINE	EVERY
CF	DEBUG-NAME	EXCEPTION
CH	DEBUG-SUB-1	EXIT
CHARACTER	DEBUG-SUB-2	EXTEND
CHARACTERS	DEBUG-SUB-3	
CLOCK-UNITS	DEBUGGING	FD
CLOSE	DECIMAL-POINT	FILE
COBOL	DECLARATIVES	FILE-CONTROL

FILLER	LINKAGE	QUEUE
FINAL	LOCK	QUOTE
FIRST	LOW-VALUE	QUOTES
FOOTING	LOW-VALUES	
FOR		RANDOM
FROM	MEMORY	RD
	MERGE	READ
GENERATE	MESSAGE	RECEIVE
GIVING	MODE	RECORD
GO	MODULES	RECORDS
GREATER	MOVE	REDEFINES
GROUP	MULTIPLE	REEL
	MULTIPLY	REFERENCES
HEADING		RELATIVE
HIGH-VALUE		RELEASE
HIGH-VALUES	NATIVE	REMAINDER
	NEGATIVE	REMOVAL
I-O	NEXT	RENAMES
I-O-CONTROL	NO	REPLACING
IDENTIFICATION	NOT	REPORT
IF	NUMBER	REPORTING
IN	NUMERIC	REPORTS
INDEX		RERUN
INDEXED	OBJECT-COMPUTER	RESERVE
INDICATE	OCCURS	RESET
INITIAL	OF	RETURN
INITIATE	OFF	REVERSED
INPUT	OMITTED	REWIND
INPUT-OUTPUT	ON	REWRITE
INSPECT	OPEN	RF
INSTALLATION	OPTIONAL	RH
INTO	OR	RIGHT
INVALID	ORGANIZATION	ROUNDED
IS	OUTPUT	RUN
	OVERFLOW	
JUST		SAME
JUSTIFIED	PAGE	SD
	PAGE-COUNTER	SEARCH
KEY	PERFORM	SECTION
	PF	SECURITY
LABEL	PH	SEGMENT
LAST	PIC	SEGMENT-LIMIT
LEADING	PICTURE	SELECT
LEFT	PLUS	SEND
LENGTH	POINTER	SENTENCE
LESS	POSITION	SEPARATE
LIMIT	POSITIVE	SEQUENCE
LIMITS	PRINTING	SEQUENTIAL
LINAGE	PROCEDURE	SET
LINAGE-COUNTER	PROCEDURES	SIGN
LINE	PROCEED	SIZE
LINE-COUNTER	PROGRAM	SORT
LINES	PROGRAM-ID	SORT-MERGE

SOURCE	TAPE	VALUE
SOURCE-COMPUTER	TERMINAL	VALUES
SPACE	TERMINATE	VARYING
SPACES	TEXT	
SPECIAL-NAMES	THAN	
STANDARD	THROUGH	WHEN
STANDARD-1	THRU	WITH
START	TIME	WORDS
STATUS	TIMES	WORKING-STORAGE
STOP	TO	WRITE
STRING	TOP	
SUB-QUEUE-1	TRAILING	ZERO
SUB-QUEUE-2	TYPE	ZEROES
SUB-QUEUE-3		ZEROS
SUBTRACT		
SUM	UNIT	+
SUPPRESS	UNSTRING	−
SYMBOLIC	UNTIL	*
SYNC	UP	/
SYNCHRONIZED	UPON	**
	USAGE	>
TABLE	USE	<
TALLYING	USING	=

APPENDIX B

GENERAL COBOL FORMATS

General Format for **IDENTIFICATION DIVISION**

```
IDENTIFICATION DIVISION.
PROGRAM-ID. program-name.
[AUTHOR. [comment-entry] ...]
[INSTALLATION. [comment-entry] ...]
[DATE-WRITTEN. [comment-entry] ...]
[DATE-COMPILED. [comment-entry] ...]
[SECURITY. [comment-entry] ...]
```

General Format for **ENVIRONMENT DIVISION**

```
ENVIRONMENT DIVISION.
CONFIGURATION SECTION.
SOURCE-COMPUTER. computer-name [WITH DEBUGGING MODE] .
OBJECT-COMPUTER. computer-name
     ⎡              ⎧WORDS     ⎫⎤
     ⎢, MEMORY SIZE integer ⎨CHARACTERS⎬⎥
     ⎣              ⎩MODULES   ⎭⎦
     [, PROGRAM COLLATING SEQUENCE IS alphabet-name]
     [, SEGMENT-LIMIT IS segment-number] .
[SPECIAL-NAMES. [, implementor-name
     ⎡IS mnemonic-name [, ON STATUS IS condition-name-1 [, OFF STATUS IS condition-name-2]]⎤
     ⎢IS mnemonic-name [, OFF STATUS IS condition-name-2 [, ON STATUS IS condition-name-1]]⎥ ...
     ⎨ON STATUS IS condition-name-1 [, OFF STATUS IS condition-name-2]                      ⎬
     ⎣OFF STATUS IS condition-name-2 [, ON STATUS IS condition-name-1]                      ⎦

        ⎡            ⎧STANDARD-1                                    ⎫⎤
        ⎢            ⎪NATIVE                                        ⎪⎥
  ,     ⎢            ⎪implementor-name                              ⎪⎥ ...
        ⎢alphabet-name IS⎨       ⎡⎧THROUGH⎫ literal-2              ⎤⎬
        ⎢            ⎪literal-1⎢⎨THRU   ⎬                         ⎥⎪
        ⎢            ⎪       ⎣ALSO literal-3[, ALSO literal-4]...⎦⎪
        ⎢            ⎪    ⎡       ⎡⎧THROUGH⎫ literal-6          ⎤⎤⎪
        ⎢            ⎩    ⎣literal-5⎢⎨THRU  ⎬                   ⎥⎦⎭ ...
        ⎣                 ⎣ALSO literal-7[, ALSO literal-8]...⎦
     [, CURRENCY SIGN IS literal-9]
     [, DECIMAL-POINT IS COMMA] .]

[INPUT-OUTPUT SECTION.
FILE-CONTROL.
    {file-control-entry} ...
[I-O-CONTROL.

     ⎡           ⎡  ⎧file-name-1     ⎫⎤
     ⎢; RERUN ⎢ON ⎨implementor-name⎬⎥
                  ⎩                ⎭
```

GENERAL FORMAT FOR ENVIRONMENT DIVISION (continued)

```
        ⎧⎡               ⎧REEL⎫     ⎤⎫
        ⎪⎢[END OF]       ⎨UNIT⎬     ⎥⎪
 EVERY  ⎨⎢               ⎩    ⎭ OF file-name-2⎥⎬ ...
        ⎪⎢integer-1 RECORDS         ⎥⎪
        ⎪⎢integer-2 CLOCK-UNITS     ⎥⎪
        ⎩⎣condition-name            ⎦⎭


    ⎡        ⎡RECORD    ⎤                                      ⎤
    ⎢; SAME  ⎢SORT      ⎥ AREA FOR file-name-3 {, file-name-4} ...⎥ ...
    ⎣        ⎣SORT-MERGE⎦                                      ⎦
   [; MULTIPLE FILE TAPE CONTAINS file-name-5 [POSITION integer-3]
       [, file-name-6 [POSITION integer-4]] ... ] ... .]]
```

General Format For File Control Entry

FORMAT 1:
SELECT [OPTIONAL] file-name
   ASSIGN TO implementor-name-1 [, implementor-name-2] ...
   ⎡; RESERVE integer-1 ⎡AREA ⎤⎤
   ⎣   ⎣AREAS⎦⎦
   [; ORGANIZATION IS SEQUENTIAL]
   [; ACCESS MODE IS SEQUENTIAL]
   [;FILE STATUS IS data-name-1] .

FORMAT 2:
SELECT file-name
   ASSIGN TO implementor-name-1 [, implementor-name-2] ...
   ⎡; RESERVE integer-1 ⎡AREA ⎤⎤
   ⎣   ⎣AREAS⎦⎦
   ; ORGANIZATION IS RELATIVE
   ⎡   ⎧SEQUENTIAL [, RELATIVE KEY IS data-name-1]⎫⎤
   ⎢; ACCESS MODE is ⎨⎧RANDOM ⎫   ⎬⎥
   ⎣   ⎩⎩DYNAMIC⎭, RELATIVE KEY IS data-name-1   ⎭⎦
   [; FILE STATUS IS data-name-2] .

FORMAT 3:
SELECT file-name
   ASSIGN TO implementor-name-1 [, implementor-name-2] ...
   ⎡; RESERVE integer-1 ⎡AREA ⎤⎤
   ⎣   ⎣AREAS⎦⎦
   ; ORGANIZATION IS INDEXED
   ⎡   ⎧SEQUENTIAL⎫⎤
   ⎢; ACCESS MODE IS   ⎨RANDOM   ⎬⎥
   ⎣   ⎩DYNAMIC   ⎭⎦
   ; RECORD KEY IS data-name-1
   [; ALTERNATE RECORD KEY IS data-name-2 [WITH DUPLICATES]] ...
   [; FILE STATUS IS data-name-3] .
FORMAT 4:
SELECT file-name ASSIGN TO implementor-name-1 [, implementor-name-2] ...

General Format for Data Division

DATA DIVISION.
[FILE SECTION.
[FD file-name
   ⎡; BLOCK CONTAINS [integer-1 TO] integer-2 ⎧RECORDS   ⎫⎤
   ⎣   ⎩CHARACTERS⎭⎦
```
```

```
    [; RECORD CONTAINS [integer-3 TO] integer-4 CHARACTERS]
      ;LABEL {RECORD IS    }{STANDARD}
             {RECORDS ARE   }{OMITTED }
      [;VALUE OF implementor-name-1 IS {data-name-1}
                                       {literal-1  }
             [, implementor-name-2 IS {data-name-2}] ...]
                                      {literal-2  }
      [; DATA {RECORD is   } data-name-3 [, data-name-4] ...]
              {RECORDS ARE }
      [; LINAGE IS {data-name-5} LINES [, WITH FOOTING AT {data-name-6}]
                   {integer-5  }                          {integer-6  }
             [, LINES AT TOP {data-name-7}][, LINES AT BOTTOM {data-name-8}]]
                             {integer-7  }                    {integer-8  }
    [; CODE-SET IS alphabet-name]
    [; {REPORT IS   } report-name-1 [, report-name-2] ...].
       {REPORTS ARE }
[record-description-entry] ... ] ...

[SD  file-name
    [; RECORD CONTAINS [integer-1 TO] integer-2 CHARACTERS]
    [; DATA {RECORD IS   } data-name-1 [, data-name-2] ...].
            {RECORDS ARE }
{record-description-entry} ...] ...]
[WORKING-STORAGE SECTION.
[77-level-description-entry] ...]
[record-description-entry ]

[LINKAGE SECTION.
[77-level-description-entry] ...]
[record-description-entry ]

[COMMUNICATION SECTION.
[communication-description-entry
[record-description-entry] ...] ...]

[REPORT SECTION.
[RD   report-name
    [; CODE literal-1]
    [; {CONTROL IS  } {data-name-1 [, data-name-2] ...              }]
       {CONTROLS ARE} {FINAL [, data-name-1 [, data-name-2] ...]    }
    [; PAGE [LIMIT IS  ] integer-1 [LINE ] [, HEADING integer-2]
            [LIMITS ARE]           [LINES]
          [, FIRST DETAIL integer-3] [, LAST DETAIL integer-4]
          [, FOOTING integer-5]].
   {report-group-description-entry} ...] ...]
```

General Format for Data Description Entry

```
FORMAT 1:
level-number {data-name-1}
             {FILLER     }
    [; REDEFINES data-name-2]
    [; {PICTURE} IS character-string]
       {PIC    }
    [; [USAGE IS] {COMPUTATIONAL}]
                  {COMP         }
                  {DISPLAY      }
                  {INDEX        }
    [; [SIGN IS] {LEADING } [SEPARATE CHARACTER]]
                 {TRAILING}
    [; OCCURS {integer-1 TO integer-2 TIMES DEPENDING ON data-name-3}
              {integer-2 TIMES                                      }
```

$$\left[\begin{Bmatrix} \underline{\text{ASCENDING}} \\ \underline{\text{DESCENDING}} \end{Bmatrix} \text{KEY IS data-name-4 [, data-name-5]} \dots\right] \dots$$

$$\qquad \text{[INDEXED BY index-name-1 [, index-name-2]} \dots \text{]]}$$

$$\left[; \begin{Bmatrix} \underline{\text{SYNCHRONIZED}} \\ \underline{\text{SYNC}} \end{Bmatrix} \begin{bmatrix} \underline{\text{LEFT}} \\ \underline{\text{RIGHT}} \end{bmatrix}\right]$$

$$\left[; \begin{Bmatrix} \underline{\text{JUSTIFIED}} \\ \underline{\text{JUST}} \end{Bmatrix} \text{RIGHT}\right]$$

[; <u>BLANK</u> WHEN <u>ZERO</u>]

[; <u>VALUE</u> IS literal] .

<u>FORMAT 2</u>:

66 data-name-1; <u>RENAMES</u> data-name-2 $\left[\begin{Bmatrix} \underline{\text{THROUGH}} \\ \underline{\text{THRU}} \end{Bmatrix} \text{data-name-3}\right]$.

<u>FORMAT 3</u>:

88 condition-name; $\begin{Bmatrix} \underline{\text{VALUE}} \text{ IS} \\ \underline{\text{VALUES}} \text{ ARE} \end{Bmatrix}$ literal-1 $\left[\begin{Bmatrix} \underline{\text{THROUGH}} \\ \underline{\text{THRU}} \end{Bmatrix} \text{literal-2}\right]$

$$\left[, \text{literal-3} \left[\begin{Bmatrix} \underline{\text{THROUGH}} \\ \underline{\text{THRU}} \end{Bmatrix} \text{literal-4}\right]\right] \dots \quad .$$

General Format for Communication Description Entry

<u>FORMAT 1</u>:

<u>CD</u> cd-name;

$$\text{FOR [}\underline{\text{INITIAL}}\text{] INPUT} \begin{bmatrix} \text{[[; SYMBOLIC } \underline{\text{QUEUE}} \text{ IS data-name-1]} \\ \text{[; SYMBOLIC } \underline{\text{SUB-QUEUE-1}} \text{ IS data-name-2]} \\ \text{[; SYMBOLIC } \underline{\text{SUB-QUEUE-2}} \text{ IS data-name-3]} \\ \text{[; SYMBOLIC } \underline{\text{SUB-QUEUE-3}} \text{ IS data-name-4]} \\ \text{[; } \underline{\text{MESSAGE}} \underline{\text{DATE}} \text{ IS data-name-5]} \\ \text{[; } \underline{\text{MESSAGE}} \underline{\text{TIME}} \text{ IS data-name-6]} \\ \text{[; SYMBOLIC } \underline{\text{SOURCE}} \text{ IS data-name-7]} \\ \text{[; } \underline{\text{TEXT}} \underline{\text{LENGTH}} \text{ IS data-name-8]} \\ \text{[; } \underline{\text{END}} \underline{\text{KEY}} \text{ IS data-name-9]} \\ \text{[; } \underline{\text{STATUS}} \underline{\text{KEY}} \text{ IS data-name-10]} \\ \text{[; } \underline{\text{MESSAGE}} \underline{\text{COUNT}} \text{ IS data-name-11]]} \\ \text{[data-name-1, data-name-2, } \dots \text{, data-name-11]} \end{bmatrix}$$

<u>FORMAT 2</u>:

<u>CD</u> cd-name; FOR <u>OUTPUT</u>

    [; <u>DESTINATION</u> <u>COUNT</u> IS data-name-1]

    [; <u>TEXT</u> <u>LENGTH</u> IS data-name-2]

    [; <u>STATUS</u> <u>KEY</u> IS data-name-3]

    [; <u>DESTINATION</u> <u>TABLE</u> <u>OCCURS</u> integer-2 TIMES

        [; <u>INDEXED</u> BY index-name-1 [, index-name-2] ...]]

    [; <u>ERROR</u> <u>KEY</u> IS data-name-4]

    [; SYMBOLIC <u>DESTINATION</u> IS data-name-5] .

General Format for Report Group Description Entry

<u>FORMAT 1</u>:

01 [data-name-1]

$$\left[; \underline{\text{LINE}} \text{ NUMBER IS} \begin{Bmatrix} \text{integer-1 [ON } \underline{\text{NEXT}} \underline{\text{PAGE}}\text{]} \\ \underline{\text{PLUS}} \text{ integer-2} \end{Bmatrix}\right]$$

$$\left[; \underline{\text{NEXT}} \underline{\text{GROUP}} \text{ IS} \begin{Bmatrix} \text{integer-3} \\ \underline{\text{PLUS}} \text{ integer-4} \\ \underline{\text{NEXT}} \underline{\text{PAGE}} \end{Bmatrix}\right]$$

```
                    ┌ ┌REPORT HEADING┐           ┐
                    │ │RH            │           │
                    │ └──────────────┘           │
                    │ ┌PAGE HEADING┐             │
                    │ │PH          │             │
                    │ └────────────┘             │
                    │ ┌CONTROL HEADING┐┌data-name-2┐│
                    │ │CH             ││FINAL      ││
        ; TYPE is   │ └───────────────┘└───────────┘│
                    │ ┌DETAIL┐                    │
                    │ │DE    │                    │
                    │ └──────┘                    │
                    │ ┌CONTROL FOOTING┐┌data-name-3┐│
                    │ │CF             ││FINAL      ││
                    │ └───────────────┘└───────────┘│
                    │ ┌PAGE FOOTING┐             │
                    │ │PF          │             │
                    │ └────────────┘             │
                    │ ┌REPORT FOOTING┐           │
                    │ │RF            │           │
                    └ └──────────────┘           ┘

      [; [USAGE IS] DISPLAY] .


FORMAT 2:
level-number [data-name-1]
      [; LINE NUMBER IS {integer-1 [ON NEXT PAGE]}]
                        {PLUS integer-2         }
      [; [USAGE IS] DISPLAY] .


FORMAT 3:
level-number [data-name-1]
      [; BLANK WHEN ZERO]
      [; GROUP INDICATE]
      [;  {JUSTIFIED} RIGHT]
          {JUST     }
      [; LINE NUMBER IS {integer-1 [ON NEXT PAGE]}]
                        {PLUS integer-2         }
      [; COLUMN NUMBER IS integer-3]
       ;  {PICTURE} IS character-string
          {PIC    }
      ┌ ; SOURCE IS identifier-1                        ┐
      │ ; VALUE IS literal                              │
      │{; SUM identifier-2 [, identifier-3] ...         │
      │    [UPON data-name-2 [, data-name-3] ...]} ...  │
      │    [RESET on {data-name-4}]                     │
      │              {FINAL      }                      │
      └ [; [USAGE IS] DISPLAY].                         ┘
```

General Format for PROCEDURE DIVISION

```
FORMAT 1:
PROCEDURE DIVISION [USING data-name-1 [, data-name-2] ...] .
[DECLARATIVES.
{section-name SECTION [segment-number] .  declarative-sentence
[paragraph-name. [sentence] ...] ...} ...
END DECLARATIVES.]
{section-name SECTION [segment-number] .
[paragraph-name. [sentence] ...] ...} ...


FORMAT 2:
PROCEDURE DIVISION [USING data-name-1 [, data-name-2] ...] .
{paragraph-name. [sentence] ...} ...
```

General Format for Verbs

<u>ACCEPT</u> identifier [<u>FROM</u> mnemonic-name]

<u>ACCEPT</u> identifier <u>FROM</u> $\begin{Bmatrix} \underline{DATE} \\ \underline{DAY} \\ \underline{TIME} \end{Bmatrix}$

<u>ACCEPT</u> cd-name MESSAGE <u>COUNT</u>

<u>ADD</u> $\begin{Bmatrix} identifier-1 \\ literal-1 \end{Bmatrix} \begin{bmatrix} , identifier-2 \\ , literal-2 \end{bmatrix}$ ... <u>TO</u> identifier-m [<u>ROUNDED</u>]

    [, identifier-n [<u>ROUNDED</u>]] ... [; ON <u>SIZE</u> <u>ERROR</u> imperative-statement]

<u>ADD</u> $\begin{Bmatrix} identifier-1 \\ literal-1 \end{Bmatrix} ' \begin{Bmatrix} identifier-2 \\ literal-2 \end{Bmatrix} \begin{bmatrix} , identifier-3 \\ , literal-3 \end{bmatrix}$ ...

    <u>GIVING</u> identifier-m [<u>ROUNDED</u>] [, identifier-n [<u>ROUNDED</u>]] ...

    [; ON <u>SIZE</u> <u>ERROR</u> imperative-statement]

<u>ADD</u> $\begin{Bmatrix} \underline{CORRESPONDING} \\ \underline{CORR} \end{Bmatrix}$ identifier-1 <u>TO</u> identifier-2 [<u>ROUNDED</u>]

    [; ON <u>SIZE</u> <u>ERROR</u> imperative-statement]

<u>ALTER</u> procedure-name-1 <u>TO</u> [<u>PROCEED</u> <u>TO</u>] procedure-name-2

    [, procedure-name-3 <u>TO</u> [<u>PROCEED</u> <u>TO</u>] procedure-name-4] ...

<u>CALL</u> $\begin{Bmatrix} identifier-1 \\ literal-1 \end{Bmatrix}$ [<u>USING</u> data-name-1 [, data-name-2] ...]

    [; ON <u>OVERFLOW</u> imperative-statement]

<u>CANCEL</u> $\begin{Bmatrix} identifier-1 \\ literal-1 \end{Bmatrix} \begin{bmatrix} , identifier-2 \\ , literal-2 \end{bmatrix}$ ...

<u>CLOSE</u> file-name-1 $\begin{bmatrix} \begin{Bmatrix} \underline{REEL} \\ \underline{UNIT} \end{Bmatrix} \begin{bmatrix} \textbf{WITH NO REWIND} \\ \textbf{FOR } \underline{\textbf{REMOVAL}} \end{bmatrix} \\ \textbf{WITH} \begin{Bmatrix} \underline{\textbf{NO REWIND}} \\ \underline{\textbf{LOCK}} \end{Bmatrix} \end{bmatrix}$

$\begin{bmatrix} , \text{file-name-2} \begin{bmatrix} \begin{Bmatrix} \underline{REEL} \\ \underline{UNIT} \end{Bmatrix} \begin{bmatrix} \textbf{WITH NO REWIND} \\ \textbf{FOR } \underline{\textbf{REMOVAL}} \end{bmatrix} \\ \textbf{WITH} \begin{Bmatrix} \underline{\textbf{NO REWIND}} \\ \underline{\textbf{LOCK}} \end{Bmatrix} \end{bmatrix} \end{bmatrix}$ ...

<u>CLOSE</u> file-name-1 [WITH <u>LOCK</u>] [, file-name-2 [WITH <u>LOCK</u>]] ...

<u>COMPUTE</u> identifier-1 [<u>ROUNDED</u>] [, identifier-2 [<u>ROUNDED</u>]] ...

    = arithmetic-expression [; ON <u>SIZE</u> <u>ERROR</u> imperative-statement]

<u>DELETE</u> file-name RECORD [; <u>INVALID</u> KEY imperative-statement]

<u>DISABLE</u> $\begin{Bmatrix} \underline{INPUT} \text{ [}\underline{TERMINAL}\text{]} \\ \underline{OUTPUT} \end{Bmatrix}$ cd-name WITH <u>KEY</u> $\begin{Bmatrix} identifier-1 \\ literal-1 \end{Bmatrix}$

<u>DISPLAY</u> $\begin{Bmatrix} identifier-1 \\ literal-1 \end{Bmatrix} \begin{bmatrix} , identifier-2 \\ , literal-2 \end{bmatrix}$ ... [<u>UPON</u> mnemonic-name]

<u>DIVIDE</u> $\begin{Bmatrix} identifier-1 \\ literal-1 \end{Bmatrix}$ <u>INTO</u> identifier-2 [<u>ROUNDED</u>]

    [, identifier-3 [<u>ROUNDED</u>]] ... [; ON <u>SIZE</u> <u>ERROR</u> imperative-statement]

<u>DIVIDE</u> $\begin{Bmatrix} identifier-1 \\ literal-1 \end{Bmatrix}$ <u>INTO</u> $\begin{Bmatrix} identifier-2 \\ literal-2 \end{Bmatrix}$ <u>GIVING</u> identifier-3 [<u>ROUNDED</u>]

    [, identifier-4 [<u>ROUNDED</u>]] ... [; ON <u>SIZE</u> <u>ERROR</u> imperative-statement]

<u>DIVIDE</u> $\begin{Bmatrix} identifier-1 \\ literal-1 \end{Bmatrix}$ <u>BY</u> $\begin{Bmatrix} identifier-2 \\ literal-2 \end{Bmatrix}$ <u>GIVING</u> identifier-3 [<u>ROUNDED</u>]

    [, identifier-4 [<u>ROUNDED</u>]] ... [; ON <u>SIZE</u> <u>ERROR</u> imperative-statement]

<u>DIVIDE</u> $\begin{Bmatrix} identifier-1 \\ literal-1 \end{Bmatrix}$ <u>INTO</u> $\begin{Bmatrix} identifier-2 \\ literal-2 \end{Bmatrix}$ <u>GIVING</u> identifier-3 [<u>ROUNDED</u>]

    <u>REMAINDER</u> identifier-4 [; ON <u>SIZE</u> <u>ERROR</u> imperative-statement]

<u>DIVIDE</u> $\begin{Bmatrix} identifier-1 \\ literal-1 \end{Bmatrix}$ <u>BY</u> $\begin{Bmatrix} identifier-2 \\ literal-2 \end{Bmatrix}$ <u>GIVING</u> identifier-3 [<u>ROUNDED</u>]

    <u>REMAINDER</u> identifier-4 [; ON <u>SIZE</u> <u>ERROR</u> imperative-statement]

<u>ENABLE</u> $\begin{Bmatrix} \underline{INPUT} \text{ [}\underline{TERMINAL}\text{]} \\ \underline{OUTPUT} \end{Bmatrix}$ cd-name WITH <u>KEY</u> $\begin{Bmatrix} identifier-1 \\ literal-1 \end{Bmatrix}$

<u>ENTER</u> language-name [routine-name] .

<u>EXIT</u> [<u>PROGRAM</u>] .

<u>GENERATE</u> $\begin{Bmatrix} \text{data-name} \\ \text{report-name} \end{Bmatrix}$

<u>GO</u> TO [procedure-name-1]

<u>GO</u> TO procedure-name-1 [, procedure-name-2] ... , procedure-name-n

    <u>DEPENDING</u> ON identifier

<u>IF</u> condition; $\begin{Bmatrix} \text{statement-1} \\ \underline{NEXT} \ \underline{SENTENCE} \end{Bmatrix} \begin{Bmatrix} ; \ \underline{ELSE} \ \text{statement-2} \\ ; \ \underline{ELSE} \ \underline{NEXT} \ \underline{SENTENCE} \end{Bmatrix}$

<u>INITIATE</u> report-name-1 [, report-name-2] ...

General COBOL Formats

INSPECT identifier-1 TALLYING
$$\left\{ \text{, identifier-2 } \underline{\text{FOR}} \left\{ , \left\{ \left\{ \begin{array}{l} \underline{\text{ALL}} \\ \underline{\text{LEADING}} \\ \underline{\text{CHARACTERS}} \end{array} \right\} \left\{ \begin{array}{l} \text{identifier-3} \\ \text{literal-1} \end{array} \right\} \right\} \left[\left\{ \begin{array}{l} \underline{\text{BEFORE}} \\ \underline{\text{AFTER}} \end{array} \right\} \text{INITIAL} \left\{ \begin{array}{l} \text{identifier-4} \\ \text{literal-2} \end{array} \right\} \right] \right\} \dots \right\} \dots$$

INSPECT identifier-1 REPLACING
$$\left\{ \begin{array}{l} \underline{\text{CHARACTERS}} \ \underline{\text{BY}} \left\{ \begin{array}{l} \text{identifier-6} \\ \text{literal-4} \end{array} \right\} \left[\left\{ \begin{array}{l} \underline{\text{BEFORE}} \\ \underline{\text{AFTER}} \end{array} \right\} \text{INITIAL} \left\{ \begin{array}{l} \text{identifier-7} \\ \text{literal-5} \end{array} \right\} \right] \\ \left\{ , \left\{ \begin{array}{l} \underline{\text{ALL}} \\ \underline{\text{LEADING}} \\ \underline{\text{FIRST}} \end{array} \right\} \right\} \left\{ , \left\{ \begin{array}{l} \text{identifier-5} \\ \text{literal-3} \end{array} \right\} \ \underline{\text{BY}} \left\{ \begin{array}{l} \text{identifier-6} \\ \text{literal-4} \end{array} \right\} \left[\left\{ \begin{array}{l} \underline{\text{BEFORE}} \\ \underline{\text{AFTER}} \end{array} \right\} \text{INITIAL} \left\{ \begin{array}{l} \text{identifier-7} \\ \text{literal-5} \end{array} \right\} \right] \right\} \dots \right\} \dots$$

INSPECT identifier-1 TALLYING
$$\left\{ \text{, identifier-2 } \underline{\text{FOR}} \left\{ , \left\{ \left\{ \begin{array}{l} \underline{\text{ALL}} \\ \underline{\text{LEADING}} \\ \underline{\text{CHARACTERS}} \end{array} \right\} \left\{ \begin{array}{l} \text{identifier-3} \\ \text{literal-1} \end{array} \right\} \right\} \left[\left\{ \begin{array}{l} \underline{\text{BEFORE}} \\ \underline{\text{AFTER}} \end{array} \right\} \text{INITIAL} \left\{ \begin{array}{l} \text{identifier-4} \\ \text{literal-2} \end{array} \right\} \right] \right\} \dots \right\} \dots$$

REPLACING
$$\left\{ \begin{array}{l} \underline{\text{CHARACTERS}} \ \underline{\text{BY}} \left\{ \begin{array}{l} \text{identifier-6} \\ \text{literal-4} \end{array} \right\} \left[\left\{ \begin{array}{l} \underline{\text{BEFORE}} \\ \underline{\text{AFTER}} \end{array} \right\} \text{INITIAL} \left\{ \begin{array}{l} \text{identifier-7} \\ \text{literal-5} \end{array} \right\} \right] \\ \left\{ , \left\{ \begin{array}{l} \underline{\text{ALL}} \\ \underline{\text{LEADING}} \\ \underline{\text{FIRST}} \end{array} \right\} \right\} \left\{ , \left\{ \begin{array}{l} \text{identifier-5} \\ \text{literal-3} \end{array} \right\} \ \underline{\text{BY}} \left\{ \begin{array}{l} \text{identifier-6} \\ \text{literal-4} \end{array} \right\} \left[\left\{ \begin{array}{l} \underline{\text{BEFORE}} \\ \underline{\text{AFTER}} \end{array} \right\} \text{INITIAL} \left\{ \begin{array}{l} \text{identifier-7} \\ \text{literal-5} \end{array} \right\} \right] \right\} \dots \right\} \dots$$

MERGE file-name-1 ON $\left\{ \begin{array}{l} \underline{\text{ASCENDING}} \\ \underline{\text{DESCENDING}} \end{array} \right\}$ KEY data-name-1 [, data-name-2] ...

$\left[\text{ON} \left\{ \begin{array}{l} \underline{\text{ASCENDING}} \\ \underline{\text{DESCENDING}} \end{array} \right\} \text{KEY data-name-3 [, data-name-4] ...} \right]$ ...

[COLLATING $\underline{\text{SEQUENCE}}$ IS alphabet-name]

$\underline{\text{USING}}$ file-name-2, file-name-3 [, file-name-4] ...

$\left\{ \begin{array}{l} \underline{\text{OUTPUT}} \ \underline{\text{PROCEDURE}} \text{ IS section-name-1 } \left[\left\{ \begin{array}{l} \underline{\text{THROUGH}} \\ \underline{\text{THRU}} \end{array} \right\} \text{section-name-2} \right] \\ \underline{\text{GIVING}} \text{ file-name-5} \end{array} \right\}$

$\underline{\text{MOVE}} \left\{ \begin{array}{l} \text{identifier-1} \\ \text{literal} \end{array} \right\} \underline{\text{TO}}$ identifier-2 [, identifier-3] ...

$\underline{\text{MOVE}} \left\{ \begin{array}{l} \underline{\text{CORRESPONDING}} \\ \underline{\text{CORR}} \end{array} \right\}$ identifier-1 $\underline{\text{TO}}$ identifier-2

$\underline{\text{MULTIPLY}} \left\{ \begin{array}{l} \text{identifier-1} \\ \text{literal-1} \end{array} \right\} \underline{\text{BY}}$ identifier-2 [$\underline{\text{ROUNDED}}$]

[, identifier-3 [$\underline{\text{ROUNDED}}$]] ... [; ON $\underline{\text{SIZE}}$ $\underline{\text{ERROR}}$ imperative-statement]

$\underline{\text{MULTIPLY}} \left\{ \begin{array}{l} \text{identifier-1} \\ \text{literal-1} \end{array} \right\} \underline{\text{BY}} \left\{ \begin{array}{l} \text{identifier-2} \\ \text{literal-2} \end{array} \right\} \underline{\text{GIVING}}$ identifier-3 [$\underline{\text{ROUNDED}}$]

[, identifier-4 [$\underline{\text{ROUNDED}}$]] ... [; ON $\underline{\text{SIZE}}$ $\underline{\text{ERROR}}$ imperative-statement]

$\underline{\text{OPEN}} \left\{ \begin{array}{l} \underline{\text{INPUT}} \text{ file-name-1 } \left[\begin{array}{l} \underline{\text{REVERSED}} \\ \underline{\text{WITH}} \ \underline{\text{NO}} \ \underline{\text{REWIND}} \end{array} \right] \left[\text{, file-name-2 } \left[\begin{array}{l} \underline{\text{REVERSED}} \\ \underline{\text{WITH}} \ \underline{\text{NO}} \ \underline{\text{REWIND}} \end{array} \right] \right] \dots \\ \underline{\text{OUTPUT}} \text{ file-name-3 } [\text{WITH } \underline{\text{NO}} \ \underline{\text{REWIND}}] [, \text{file-name-4 } [\text{WITH } \underline{\text{NO}} \ \underline{\text{REWIND}}]] \dots \\ \underline{\text{I-O}} \text{ file-name-5 } [, \text{file-name-6}] \dots \\ \underline{\text{EXTEND}} \text{ file-name-7 } [, \text{file-name-8}] \dots \end{array} \right\} \dots$

$\underline{\text{OPEN}} \left\{ \begin{array}{l} \underline{\text{INPUT}} \text{ file-name-1 } [, \text{file-name-2}] \dots \\ \underline{\text{OUTPUT}} \text{ file-name-3 } [, \text{file-name-4}] \dots \\ \underline{\text{I-O}} \text{ file-name-5 } [, \text{file-name-6}] \dots \end{array} \right\} \dots$

$\underline{\text{PERFORM}}$ procedure-name-1 $\left[\left\{ \begin{array}{l} \underline{\text{THROUGH}} \\ \underline{\text{THRU}} \end{array} \right\} \text{procedure-name-2} \right]$

$\underline{\text{PERFORM}}$ procedure-name-1 $\left[\left\{ \begin{array}{l} \underline{\text{THROUGH}} \\ \underline{\text{THRU}} \end{array} \right\} \text{procedure-name-2} \right] \left\{ \begin{array}{l} \text{identifier-1} \\ \text{integer-1} \end{array} \right\} \underline{\text{TIMES}}$

$\underline{\text{PERFORM}}$ procedure-name-1 $\left[\left\{ \begin{array}{l} \underline{\text{THROUGH}} \\ \underline{\text{THRU}} \end{array} \right\} \text{procedure-name-2} \right] \underline{\text{UNTIL}}$ condition-1

$\underline{\text{PERFORM}}$ procedure-name-1 $\left[\left\{ \begin{array}{l} \underline{\text{THROUGH}} \\ \underline{\text{THRU}} \end{array} \right\} \text{procedure-name-2} \right]$

$\underline{\text{VARYING}} \left\{ \begin{array}{l} \text{identifier-2} \\ \text{index-name-1} \end{array} \right\} \underline{\text{FROM}} \left\{ \begin{array}{l} \text{identifier-3} \\ \text{index-name-2} \\ \text{literal-1} \end{array} \right\}$

$\underline{\text{BY}} \left\{ \begin{array}{l} \text{identifier-4} \\ \text{literal-2} \end{array} \right\} \underline{\text{UNTIL}}$ condition-1

$\left[\underline{\text{AFTER}} \left\{ \begin{array}{l} \text{identifier-5} \\ \text{index-name-3} \end{array} \right\} \underline{\text{FROM}} \left\{ \begin{array}{l} \text{identifier-6} \\ \text{index-name-4} \\ \text{literal-3} \end{array} \right\} \right.$

GENERAL FORMAT FOR VERBS (continued)

```
        BY {identifier-7} UNTIL condition-2
           {literal-4   }

       [AFTER {identifier-8 } FROM {identifier-9 }
              {index-name-5}      {index-name-6 }
                                  {literal-5    }


          BY {identifier-10} UNTIL condition-3]]
             {literal-6    }
```

READ file-name RECORD [INTO identifier] [; AT END imperative-statement]

READ file-name [NEXT] RECORD [INTO identifier]

  [; AT END imperative-statement]

READ file-name RECORD [INTO identifier] [; INVALID KEY imperative-statement]

READ file-name RECORD [INTO identifier]

  [; KEY IS data-name]

  [; INVALID KEY imperative-statement]

RECEIVE cd-name {MESSAGE} INTO identifier-1 [; NO DATA imperative-statement]
                {SEGMENT}

RELEASE record-name [FROM identifier]

RETURN file-name RECORD [INTO identifier] ; AT END imperative-statement

REWRITE record-name [FROM identifier]

REWRITE record-name [FROM identifier] [; INVALID KEY imperative-statement]

```
SEARCH identifier-1 [VARYING {identifier-2 }] [; AT END imperative-statemet-1]
                             {index-name-1 }

   ; WHEN condition-1 {imperative-statement-2}
                      {NEXT SENTENCE         }

   [; WHEN condition-2 {imperative-statement-3}] ...
                       {NEXT SENTENCE         }

SEARCH ALL identifier-1 [; AT END imperative-statement-1]

   ; WHEN {                  {IS EQUAL TO}{identifier-3           }
          {data-name-1       {IS=        }{literal-1              }
          {condition-name-1               {arithmetic-expression-1}

          [AND {               {IS EQUAL TO}{identifier-4           }] ...
               {data-name-2    {IS =       }{literal-2              }
               {condition-name-2            {arithmetic-expression-2}


          {imperative-statement-2}
          {NEXT SENTENCE         }

SEND cd-name FROM identifier-1

                                  {WITH identifier-2}
SEND cd-name [FROM identifier-1] {WITH ESI         }
                                  {WITH EMI         }
                                  {WITH EGI         }

 [{BEFORE} ADVANCING {{{identifier-3}[LINE ]}}]
  {AFTER }            {{{integer     }[LINES]}}
                      {                       }
                      {{mnemonic-name}        }
                      {PAGE         }

SET {identifier-1 [, identifier-2] ...} TO {identifier-3}
    {index-name-1 [, index-name-2] ...}    {index-name-3}
                                           {integer-1   }

SET index-name-4 [, index-name-5 ... {UP BY  }{identifier-4}
                                     {DOWN BY}{integer-2   }

SORT file-name-1 ON {ASCENDING }KEY data-name-1 [, data-name-2]...
                    {DESCENDING}
                    [ON {ASCENDING }KEY data-name-3 [, data-name-4]...]...
                        {DESCENDING}


 [COLLATING SEQUENCE IS alphabet-name]
 {INPUT PROCEDURE IS section-name-1 [{THROUGH} section-name-2]}
 {                                   {THRU   }                }
 {USING file-name-2 [, file-name-3] ...                       }

 {OUTPUT PROCEDURE IS section-name-3 [{THROUGH} section-name-4]}
 {                                    {THRU   }                }
 {GIVING file-name-4                                           }
```

```
START file-name [ KEY { IS EQUAL TO                    }  data-name ]
                      { IS =                            }
                      { IS GREATER THAN                 }
                      { IS >                            }
                      { IS NOT LESS THAN                }
                      { IS NOT <                         }

    [; INVALID KEY imperative-statement]

STOP { RUN     }
     { literal }

STRING { identifier-1 } [ , identifier-2 ] ... DELIMITED BY { identifier-3 }
       { literal-1    } [ , literal-2    ]                  { literal-3    }
                                                            { SIZE         }

      [ , { identifier-4 } [ , identifier-5 ] ... DELIMITED BY { identifier-6 } ] ...
          { literal-4    } [ , literal-5    ]                  { literal-6    }
                                                               { SIZE         }

    INTO identifier-7 [WITH POINTER identifier-8]

    [; ON OVERFLOW imperative-statement]

SUBTRACT { identifier-1 } [ , identifier-2 ] ... FROM identifier-m [ROUNDED]
         { literal-1    } [ , literal-2    ]

    [, identifier-n [ROUNDED]] ... [; ON SIZE ERROR imperative-statement]

SUBTRACT { identifier-1 } [ , identifier-2 ] ... FROM { identifier-m }
         { literal-1    } [ , literal-2    ]          { literal-m    }

    GIVING identifier-n [ROUNDED] [, identifier-o [ROUNDED]] ...

    [; ON SIZE ERROR imperative-statement]

SUBTRACT { CORRESPONDING } identifier-1 FROM identifier-2 [ROUNDED]
         { CORR          }

    [; ON SIZE ERROR imperative-statement]

SUPPRESS PRINTING

TERMINATE report-name-1 [, report-name-2] ...

UNSTRING identifier-1

    [ DELIMITED BY [ALL] { identifier-2 } [ , OR [ALL] { identifier-3 } ] ... ]
                         { literal-1    }              { literal-2    }

    INTO identifier-4 [, DELIMITER IN identifier-5] [, COUNT IN identifier-6]
        [, identifier-7 [, DELIMITER IN identifier-8] [, COUNT IN identifier-9]] ...

    [WITH POINTER identifier-10] [TALLYING IN identifier-11]

    [; ON OVERFLOW imperative-statement]

USE AFTER STANDARD { EXCEPTION } PROCEDURE ON { file-name-1 [, file-name-2] ... } .
                   { ERROR     }              { INPUT                           }
                                              { OUTPUT                          }
                                              { I-O                             }
                                              { EXTEND                          }

USE AFTER STANDARD { EXCEPTION } PROCEDURE ON { file-name-1 [, file-name-2] ... } .
                   { ERROR     }              { INPUT                           }
                                              { OUTPUT                          }
                                              { I-O                             }

USE BEFORE REPORTING identifier.

USE FOR DEBUGGING ON { cd-name-1                       }
                     { [ALL REFERENCES OF] identifier-1 }
                     { file-name-1                      }
                     { procedure-name-1                 }
                     { ALL PROCEDURES                   }

    [ cd-name-2                        ]
    [ [ALL REFERENCES OF] identifier-2 ] ....
    [ , file-name-2                    ]
    [ procedure-name-2                 ]
    [ ALL PROCEDURES                   ]

WRITE record-name [FROM identifier-1]

    [ { BEFORE } ADVANCING { { { identifier-2 } [ LINE  ] } } ]
    [ { AFTER  }           { { { integer      } [ LINES ] } } ]
    [                      { { mnemonic-name }             } ]
    [                      { { PAGE          }             } ]

    [ ; AT { END-OF-PAGE } imperative-statement ]
    [      { EOP         }                      ]

WRITE record-name [FROM identifier] [; INVALID KEY imperative-statement]
```

General Format for Conditions

RELATION CONDITION:

```
                          ┌ IS [NOT] GREATER THAN ┐
┌ identifier-1          ┐ │ IS [NOT] LESS THAN    │ ┌ identifier-2           ┐
│ literal-1             │ │ IS [NOT] EQUAL TO     │ │ literal-2              │
│ arithmetic-expression-1│ │ IS [NOT] >            │ │ arithmetic-expression-2│
└ index-name-1         ┘ │ IS [NOT] <            │ └ index-name-2           ┘
                          └ IS [NOT] =            ┘
```

CLASS CONDITION:

```
identifier IS [NOT] ┌ NUMERIC    ┐
                    └ ALPHABETIC ┘
```

SIGN CONDITION:

```
                              ┌ POSITIVE ┐
arithmetic-expression IS [NOT]│ NEGATIVE │
                              └ ZERO     ┘
```

CONDITION-NAME CONDITION:

condition-name

SWITCH-STATUS CONDITION:

condition-name

NEGATED SIMPLE CONDITION:

NOT simple-condition

COMBINED CONDITION:

```
          ┌ ┌ AND ┐           ┐
condition │ │ OR  │ condition │ ...
          └ └    ┘           ┘
```

ABBREVIATED COMBINED RELATION CONDITION:

```
                   ┌ ┌ AND ┐                                  ┐
relation-condition │ │ OR  │ [NOT] [relational-operator] object│ ...
                   └ └    ┘                                   ┘
```

Miscellaneous Formats

QUALIFICATION:

```
┌ data-name-1     ┐ ┌ ┌ OF ┐           ┐
│ condition-name  │ │ │ IN │ data-name-2│ ...
└               ┘ └ └   ┘           ┘

                ┌ ┌ OF ┐             ┐
paragraph-name  │ │ IN │ section-name │
                └ └   ┘             ┘

          ┌ ┌ OF ┐            ┐
text-name │ │ IN │ library-name│
          └ └   ┘            ┘
```

SUBSCRIPTING:

```
┌ data-name      ┐
│ condition-name │ (subscript-1 [, subscript-2 [, subscript-3]])
└              ┘
```

INDEXING:

```
┌ data-name      ┐ ┌ ┌ index-name-1 [{±} literal-2] ┐
│ condition-name │ │ │ literal-1                    │
└              ┘ └ └                              ┘

  ┌   ┌ index-name-2 [{±} literal-4] ┐┌   ┌ index-name-3 [{±} literal-6] ┐┐┐
  │ , │ literal-3                    ││ , │ literal-5                    │││
  └   └                            ┘└   └                            ┘┘┘
```

IDENTIFIER: FORMAT 1

```
            ┌ ┌ OF ┐           ┐
data-name-1 │ │ IN │ data-name-2│ ... [(subscript-1 [, subscript-2
            └ └   ┘           ┘
  [, subscript-3]])]
```

IDENTIFIER: FORMAT 2

```
            ┌ ┌ OF ┐           ┐     ┌ ┌ index-name-1 [{±} literal-2] ┐
data-name-1 │ │ IN │ data-name-2│ ...│ │ literal-1                    │
            └ └   ┘           ┘     └ └                              ┘

  ┌   ┌ index-name-2 [{±} literal-4] ┐┌   ┌ index-name-3 [{±} literal-6] ┐┐┐
  │ , │ literal-3                    ││ , │ literal-5                    │││
  └   └                            ┘└   └                            ┘┘┘
```

General Format for COPY Statement

```
          ┌ ┌ OF ┐            ┐
COPY text-name │ │ IN │ library-name│
          └ └   ┘            ┘

  ┌            ┌   ┌ ==pseudo-text-1== ┐    ┌ ==pseudo-text-2== ┐┐    ┐
  │ REPLACING  │ , │ identifier-1      │ BY │ identifier-2      ││ ...│
  │            │   │ literal-1         │    │ literal-2         ││    │
  │            └   └ word-1            ┘    └ word-2            ┘┘    │
  └                                                                 ┘
```

GLOSSARY

Introduction

The terms in this chapter are defined in accordance with their meaning as used in this document describing COBOL and may not have the same meaning for other languages.

These definitions are also intended to be either reference material or introductory material to be reviewed prior to reading the detailed language specifications. For this reason, these definitions are, in most instances, brief and do not include detailed syntactical rules.

Definitions

Abbreviated Combined Relation Condition. The combined condition that results from the explicit omission of a common subject or a common subject and common relational operator in a consecutive sequence of relation conditions.

Access Mode. The manner in which records are to be operated upon within a file.

Actual Decimal Point. The physical representation, using either of the decimal point characters period (.) or comma (,), of the decimal point position in a data item.

Alphabet-Name. A user-defined word, in the SPECIAL-NAMES paragraph of the ENVIRONMENT DIVISION, that assigns a name to a specific character set and/or collating sequence.

Alphabetic Character. A character that belongs to the following set of letters: A, B, C, D, E, F, G, H, I, J, K, L, M, N, O, P, Q, R, S, T, U, V, W, X, Y, Z, and the space.

Alphanumeric Character. Any character in the computer's character set.

Alternate Record Key. A key, other than the prime record key, whose contents identify a record within an indexed file.

Arithmetic Expression. An arithmetic expression can be an identifier or a numeric elementary item, a numeric literal, such identifiers and literals separated by arithmetic operators, two arithmetic expressions separated by an arithmetic operator, or an arithmetic expression enclosed in parentheses.

Arithmetic Operator. A single character, or a fixed two-character combination, that belongs to the following set:

Character	Meaning
+	Addition
−	Subtraction
*	Multiplication
/	Division
**	Exponentiation

Ascending Key. A key upon the values of which data is ordered starting with the lowest value of key up to the highest value of key in accordance with the rules for comparing data items.

Assumed Decimal Point. A decimal point position that does not involve the existence of an actual character in a data item. The assumed decimal point has logical meaning but no physical representation.

At End Condition. A condition caused:

1. During the execution of a READ statement for a sequentially accessed file.
2. During the execution of a RETURN statement, when no next logical record exists for the associated SORT or MERGE file.
3. During the execution of a SEARCH statement, when the search operation terminates without satisfying the condition specified in any of the associated WHEN phrases.

Block. A physical unit of data that is normally composed of one or more logical records. For mass storage files, a block may contain a portion of a logical record. The size of a block has no direct relation to the size of the file within which the block is contained or to the size of the logical record(s) that are either continued within the block or that overlap the block. The term is synonymous with physical record.

Body Group. Generic name for a report group of TYPE DETAIL, CONTROL HEADING, or CONTROL FOOTING.

Called Program. A program that is the object of a CALL statement combined at object time with the calling program to produce a run unit.

Calling Program. A program that executes a CALL to another program.

Cd-Name. A user-defined word that names an MCS interface area described in a communication description entry within the COMMUNICATION SECTION of the DATA DIVISION.

Character. The basic indivisible unit of the language.

Character Position. A character position is the amount of physical storage required to store a single standard data format character described as usage is DISPLAY. Further characteristics of the physical storage are defined by the implementor.

Character-String. A sequence of contiguous characters that form a COBOL word, a literal, a PICTURE character-string, or a comment-entry.

Class Condition. The proposition, for which a truth value can be determined, that the content of an item is wholly alphabetic or is wholly numeric.

Clause. An ordered set of consecutive COBOL character-strings whose purpose is to specify an attribute of an entry.

COBOL Character Set. The complete COBOL character set consists of the 51 characters listed below:

Character	Meaning
0,1,...,9	Digit
A,B,...,Z	Letter
	Space (blank)
+	Plus sign
−	Minus sign (hyphen)
*	Asterisk
/	Stroke (virgule, slash)
=	Equal sign
$	Currency sign
,	Comma (decimal point)
;	Semicolon
.	Period (decimal point)
"	Quotation mark
(	Left parenthesis
)	Right parenthesis
>	Greater than symbol
<	Less than symbol

COBOL Word. (See *Word*.)

Collating Sequence. The sequence in which the characters that are acceptable in a computer are ordered for purposes of sorting, merging, and comparing.

Column. A character position within a print line. The columns are numbered from 1, by 1, starting at the leftmost character position of the print line and extending to the rightmost position of the print line.

Combined Condition. A condition that is the result of connecting two or more conditions with the 'AND' or the 'OR' logical operator.

Comment-Entry. An entry in the IDENTIFICATION DIVISION that may be any combination of characters from the computer character set.

Comment Line. A source program line represented by an asterisk in the indicator area of the line and any characters from the computer's character set in area A and area B of that line. The comment line serves only for documentation in a program. A special form of comment line represented by a stroke (/) in the indicator area of the line and any characters from the computer's character set in area A and area B of that line causes page ejection prior to printing the comment.

Communication Description Entry. An entry in the COMMUNICATION SECTION of the DATA DIVISION that is composed of the level-indicator CD, followed by a cd-name, and then followed by a set of clauses as required. It describes the interface between the Message Control System (MCS) and the COBOL program.

Communication Device. A mechanism (hardware or hardware/software) capable of sending data to a queue and/or receiving data from a queue. This mechanism may be a computer or a peripheral device. One or more programs containing communication description entries and residing within the same computer define one or more of these mechanisms.

Communication Section. The section of the DATA DIVISION that describes the interface areas between the MCS and the program, composed of one or more CD description entries.

Compile Time. The time at which a COBOL source program is translated, by a COBOL compiler, to a COBOL object program.

Compiler Directing Statement. A statement, beginning with a compiler directing verb, that causes the compiler to take a specific action during compilation.

Complex Condition. A condition in which one or more logical operators act upon one or more conditions. (See Negated Simple Condition, Combined Condition, Negated Combined Condition.)

Computer-Name. A system-name that identifies the computer upon which the program is to be compiled or run.

Condition. A status of a program at execution time for which a truth value can be determined. Where the term 'condition' (condition-1, condition-2, ...) appears in these language specifications in or in reference to 'condition' (condition-1, condition-2, ...) of a general format, it is a conditional expression consisting of either a simple condition optionally parenthesized, or a combined condition consisting of the syntactically correct combination of simple conditions, logical operators, and parentheses, for which a truth value can be determined.

Condition-Name. A user-defined word assigned to a specific value, set of values, or range of values, within the complete set of values that a conditional variable may possess; or the user-defined word assigned to a status of an implementor-defined switch or device.

Condition-Name Condition. The proposition, for which a truth value can be determined, that the value of a conditional variable is a member of the set of values attributed to a condition-name associated with the conditional variable.

Conditional Expression. A simple condition or a complex condition specified in an IF, PERFORM, or SEARCH statement. (See Simple Condition and Complex Condition.)

Conditional Statement. A conditional statement specifies that the truth value of a condition is to be determined and that the subsequent action of the object program is dependent on this truth value.

Conditional Variable. A data item one or more values of which has a condition-name assigned to it.

Configuration Section. A section of the ENVIRONMENT DIVISION that describes overall specifications of source and object computers.

Connective. A reserved word that is used to:

1. Associate a data-name, paragraph-name, condition-name, or text-name with its qualifier.
2. Link two or more operands written in a series.
3. Form conditions (logical connectives). (See *Logical Operator.*)

Contiguous Items. Items that are described by consecutive entries in the

DATA DIVISION, and that bear a definite hierarchical relationship to each other.

Control Break. A change in the value of a data item that is referenced in the CONTROL clause. More generally, a change in the value of a data item that is used to control the hierarchical structure of a report.

Control Break Level. The relative position within a control hierarchy at which the most major control break occurred.

Control Data Item. A data item, a change in whose contents may produce a control break.

Control Data-Name. A data-name that appears in a CONTROL clause and refers to a control data item.

Control Footing. A report group that is presented at the end of the control group of which it is a member.

Control Group. A set of body groups that is presented for a given value of a control data item or of FINAL. Each control group may begin with a CONTROL HEADING, end with a CONTROL FOOTING, and contain DETAIL report groups.

Control Heading. A report group that is presented at the beginning of the control group of which it is a member.

Control Hierarchy. A designated sequence of report subdivisions defined by the positional order of FINAL and the data-names within a CONTROL clause.

Counter. A data item used for storing numbers or number representations in a manner that permits these numbers to be increased or decreased by the value of another number, or to be changed or reset to zero or to an arbitrary positive or negative value.

Currency Sign. The character '$' of the COBOL character set.

Currency Symbol. The character defined by the CURRENCY SIGN clause in the SPECIAL-NAMES paragraph. If no CURRENCY SIGN clause is present in a COBOL source program, the currency symbol is identical to the currency sign.

Current Record. The record that is available in the record area associated with the file.

Current Record Pointer. A conceptual entity that is used in the selection of the next record.

Data Clause. A clause that appears in a data description entry in the DATA DIVISION and provides information describing a particular attribute of a data item.

Data Description Entry. An entry in the DATA DIVISION that is composed of a level-number followed by a data-name, if required, and then followed by a set of data clauses, as required.

Data Item. A character or a set of contiguous characters (excluding in either case literals) defined as a unit of data by the COBOL program.

Data-Name. A user-defined word that names a data item described in a data description entry in the DATA DIVISION. When used in the general formats, 'data-name' represents a word that can neither be subscripted, indexed, nor qualified unless specifically permitted by the rules for that format.

Debugging Line. A debugging line is any line with 'D' in the indicator area of the line.

Debugging Section. A debugging section is a section that contains a USE FOR DEBUGGING statement.

Declaratives. A set of one or more special purpose sections, written at the beginning of the PROCEDURE DIVISION, the first of which is preceded by the key word DECLARATIVES and the last of which is followed by the key words END DECLARATIVES. A declarative is composed of a section header, followed by a USE compiler directing sentence, followed by a set of zero, one or more associated paragraphs.

Declarative-Sentence. A compiler-directing sentence consisting of a single USE statement terminated by the separator period.

Delimiter. A character or a sequence of contiguous characters that identify the end of a string of characters and separates that string of characters from the following string of characters. A delimiter is not part of the string of characters that it delimits.

Descending Key. A key upon the values of which data is ordered starting with the highest value of key down to the lowest value of key, in accordance with the rules for comparing data items.

Destination. The symbolic identification of the receiver of a transmission from a queue.

Digit Position. A digit position is the amount of physical storage required to store a single digit. This amount may vary depending on the usage of the data item describing the digit position. Further characteristics of the physical storage are defined by the implementor.

Division. A set of zero, one or more sections of paragraphs, called the division body, that are formed and combined in accordance with a specific set of rules. There are four (4) divisions in a COBOL program: IDENTIFICATION, ENVIRONMENT, DATA, and PROCEDURE.

Division Header. A combination of words followed by a period and a space that indicates that beginning of a division. The division headers are

```
IDENTIFICATION DIVISION.
ENVIRONMENT DIVISION.
DATA DIVISION.
PROCEDURE DIVISION [USING data-name-1 [data-name-2]
. . .].
```

Dynamic Access. An access mode in which specific logical records can be obtained from or placed into a mass storage file in a nonsequential manner (see *Random Access*) and obtained from a file in a sequential manner (see *Sequential Access*), during the scope of the same OPEN statement.

Editing Character. A single character or a fixed two-character combination belonging to the following set.

Character	Meaning
B	Space
0	Zero
+	Plus
−	Minus
CR	Credit
DB	Debit

Z	Zero suppress
*	Check protect
$	Currency sign
,	Comma (decimal point)
.	Period (decimal point)
/	Stroke (virgule, slash)

Elementary Item. A data item that is described as not being further logically subdivided.

End of Procedure Division. The physical position in a COBOL source program after which no further procedures appear.

Entry. Any descriptive set of consecutive clauses terminated by a period and written in the IDENTIFICATION DIVISION, ENVIRONMENT DIVISION, or DATA DIVISION of a COBOL source program.

Environment Clause. A clause that appears as part of an ENVIRONMENT DIVISION entry.

Execution Time. (See *Object Time.*)

Extend Mode. The state of a file after execution of an OPEN statement, with the EXTEND phrase specified, for that file and before the execution of a CLOSE statement for that file.

Figurative Constant. A compiler generated value referenced through the use of certain reserved words.

File. A collection of records.

File Clause. A clause that appears as part of any of the following DATA DIVISION entries:

File description (FD)

Sort-merge file description (SD)

Communication description (CD)

FILE-CONTROL. The name of an ENVIRONMENT DIVISION paragraph in which the data files for a given source program are declared.

File Description Entry. An entry in the File Section of the DATA DIVISION that is composed of the level-indicator FD, followed by a file-name, and then followed by a set of file clauses as required.

File-Name. A user-defined word that names a file described in a file description entry or a sort-merge file description entry within the File Section of the DATA DIVISION.

File Organization. The permanent logical file structure established at the time that a file is created.

File Section. The section of the DATA DIVISION that contains file description entries and sort-merge file description entries together with their associated record descriptions.

Format. A specific arrangement of a set of data.

Group Item. A named contiguous set of elementary or group items.

High Order End. The leftmost character of a string of characters.

I-O-CONTROL. The name of an ENVIRONMENT DIVISION paragraph in which object program requirements for specific input-output techniques, re-run points, sharing of same areas by several data files, and multiple file storage on a single input-output device are specified.

Relational Operator. A reserved word, a relation character, a group of consecutive reserved words, or a group of consecutive reserved words and relation characters used in the construction of a relation condition. The permissible operators and their meaning are

Relational Operator	Meaning
IS [NOT] GREATER THAN IS [NOT] >	Greater than or not greater than
IS [NOT] LESS THAN IS [NOT] <	Less than or not less than
IS [NOT] EQUAL TO IS [NOT] =	Equal to or not equal to

Relative File. A file with relative organization.

Relative Key. A key whose contents identify a logical record in a relative file.

Relative Organization. The permanent logical file structure in which each record is uniquely identified by an integer value greater than zero, which specifies the record's logical ordinal position in the file.

Report Clause. A clause, in the Report Section of the DATA DIVISION, that appears in a report description entry or a report group description entry.

Report Description Entry. An entry in the Report Section of the DATA DIVISION that is composed of the level-indicator RD, followed by a report name, followed by a set of report clauses as required.

Report File. An output file whose file description entry contains a REPORT clause. The contents of a report file consist of records that are written under control of the Report Writer Control System.

Report Footing. A report group that is presented only at the end of a report.

Report Group. In the Report Section of the DATA DIVISION, an 01 level-number entry and its subordinate entries.

Report Group Description Entry. An entry in the Report Section of the DATA DIVISION that is composed of the level-number 01, the optional data-name, a TYPE clause, and an optional set of report clauses.

Report Heading. A report group that is presented only at the beginning of a report.

Report Line. A division of a page representing one row of horizontal character positions. Each character position of a report line is aligned vertically beneath the corresponding character position of the report line above it. Report lines are numbered from 1, by 1, starting at the top of the page.

Report-Name. A user-defined word that names a report described in a report description entry within the Report Section of the DATA DIVISION.

Report Section. The section of the DATA DIVISION that contains one or more report description entries and their associated report group description entries.

Report Writer Control System (RWCS). An object time control system, provided by the implementor, that accomplishes the construction of reports.

Report Writer Logical Record. A record that consists of the Report Writer print line and associated control information necessary for its selection and vertical positioning.

Reserved Word. A COBOL word specified in the list of words which may be used in COBOL source programs, but which must not appear in the programs as user-defined words or system-names.

Routine-Name. A user-defined word that identifies a procedure written in a language other than COBOL.

Run Unit. A set of one or more object programs which function, at object time, as a unit to provide problem solutions.

RWCS. (See *Report Writer Control System.*)

Section. A set of zero, one, or more paragraphs or entries, called a section body, the first of which is preceded by a section header. Each section consists of the section header and the related section body.

Section Header. A combination of words followed by a period and a space that indicates the beginning of a section in the ENVIRONMENT, DATA, and PROCEDURE DIVISION.

In the ENVIRONMENT and DATA DIVISIONs, a section header is composed of reserved words followed by a period and a space. The permissible section headers are

In the ENVIRONMENT DIVISION,

```
CONFIGURATION SECTION.
INPUT-OUTPUT SECTION.
```

In the DATA DIVISION,

```
FILE SECTION.
WORKING-STORAGE SECTION.
LINKAGE SECTION.
COMMUNICATION SECTION.
REPORT SECTION.
```

In the PROCEDURE DIVISION, a section header is composed of a section-name, followed by the reserved word SECTION, followed by a segment-number (optional), followed by a period and a space.

Section-Name. A user-defined word which names a section in the PROCEDURE DIVISION.

Segment-Number. A user-defined word that classifies sections in the PROCEDURE DIVISION for purposes of segmentation. Segment-numbers may contain only the characters 0, 1, ..., 9. A segment-number may be expressed either as a one or two digit number.

Sentence. A sequence of one or more statements, the last of which is terminated by a period followed by a space.

Separator. A punctuation character used to delimit character-strings.

Sequential Access. An access mode in which logical records are obtained from or placed into a file in a consecutive predecessor-to-successor logical record sequence determined by the order of records in the file.

Sequential File. A file with sequential organization.

Sequential Organization. The permanent logical file structure in which a record is identified by a predecessor-successor relationship established when the record is placed into the file.

Sign Condition. The proposition, for which a truth value can be determined, that the algebraic value of a data item or an arithmetic expression is either less than, greater than, or equal to zero.

Simple Condition. Any single condition chosen from the set

Relation condition

Class condition

Condition-name condition

Switch-status condition

Sign condition

(Simple-condition)

Sort File. A collection of records to be sorted by a SORT statement. The sort file is created and can be used by the sort function only.

Sort-Merge File Description Entry. An entry in the File Section of the DATA DIVISION that is composed of the level-indicator SD, followed by a file-name, and then followed by a set of file clauses as required.

The symbolic identification of the originator of a transmission to a queue.

SOURCE-COMPUTER. The name of an ENVIRONMENT DIVISION paragraph in which the computer environment, within which the source program is compiled, is described.

Source Item. An identifier designated by a SOURCE clause that provides the value of a printable item.

Source Program. Although it is recognized that a source program may be represented by other forms and symbols, in this document it always refers to a syntactically correct set of COBOL statements beginning with an IDENTIFICATION DIVISION and ending with the end of the PROCEDURE DIVISION. In contexts where there is no danger of ambiguity, the word "program" alone may be used in place of the phrase "source program."

Special Character. A character that belongs to the following set.

Character	Meaning
+	Plus sign
−	Minus sign
*	Asterisk
/	Stroke (virgule, slash)
=	Equal sign
$	Currency sign
,	Comma (decimal point)
;	Semicolon
.	Period (decimal point)
"	Quotation mark
(	Left parenthesis
)	Right parenthesis
>	Greater than symbol
<	Less than symbol

Special-Character Word. A reserved word that is an arithmetic operator or a relation character.

SPECIAL-NAMES. The name of an ENVIRONMENT DIVISION paragraph in which implementor-names are related to user specified mnemonic-names.

Special Registers. Compiler generated storage areas whose primary use is to store information produced in conjunction with the use of specific COBOL features.

Standard Data Format. The concept used in describing the characteristics of data in a COBOL DATA DIVISION under which the characteristics or properties of the data are expressed in a form oriented to the appearance of the data on a printed page of infinite length and breadth, rather than a form oriented to the manner in which the data is stored internally in the computer, or on a particular external medium.

Statement. A syntactically valid combination of words and symbols written in the PROCEDURE DIVISION beginning with a verb.

Sub-Queue. A logical hierarchical division of a queue.

Subject of Entry. An operand or reserved word that appears immediately following the level indicator or the level-number in a DATA DIVISION entry.

Subprogram. (See *Called Program.*)

Subscript. An integer whose value identifies a particular element in a table.

Subscripted Data-Name. An identifier that is composed of a data-name followed by one or more subscripts enclosed in parentheses.

Sum Counter. A signed numeric data item established by a SUM clause in the Report Section of the DATA DIVISION. The sum counter is used by the Report Writer Control System to contain the result of designated summing operations that take place during production of a report.

Switch-Status Condition. The proposition, for which a truth value can be determined, that an implementor-defined switch, capable of being set to an "on" or "off" status, has been set to a specific status.

System-Name. A COBOL word which is used to communicate with the operating environment.

Table. A set of logically consecutive items of data that are defined in the DATA DIVISION by means of the OCCURS clause.

Table Element. A data item that belongs to the set of repeated items comprising a table.

Terminal. The originator of a transmission to a queue, or the receiver of a transmission from a queue.

Text-Name. A user-defined word which identifies library text.

Text-Word. Any character-string or separator, except space, in a COBOL library or in pseudo-text.

Truth Value. The representation of the result of the evaluation of a condition in terms of one of two values:

True

False

Unary Operator. A plus ($+$) or a minus ($-$) sign, which precedes a variable or a left parenthesis in an arithmetic expression and which has the effect of multiplying the expression of $+1$ or -1, respectively.

Unit. A module of mass storage the dimensions of which are determined by each implementor.

User-Defined Word. A COBOL word that must be supplied by the user to satisfy the format of a clause or statement.

Variable. A data item whose value may be changed by execution of the object program. A variable used in an arithmetic expression must be a numeric elementary item.

Verb. A word that expresses an action to be taken by a COBOL compiler or object program.

Word. A character-string of not more than 30 characters which forms a user-defined word, a system-name, or a reserved word.

Working-Storage Section. The section of the DATA DIVISION which describes working-storage data items, composed either of noncontiguous items or of working-storage records or of both.

77-Level-Description-Entry. A data description entry that describes a noncontiguous data item with the level-number 77.

ANSWERS TO REVIEW QUESTIONS

Chapter 1

1.1 The abacus is the oldest computing device discussed in the chapter.

1.2 Pascal and Leibniz.

1.3 Charles Babbage was the inventor of the analytical engine.

1.4 Howard Aiken is normally given credit as the person responsible for creating the first general purpose computer, the IBM/Harvard Mark I.

1.5 Mauchly and Eckert designed the ENIAC, BINAC, and UNIVAC computers.

1.6 Vacuum tubes characterized the first-generation computers. Transistors were used in the second generation, and integrated circuits characterized the third generation.

1.7 Normally, a hardware configuration is made up of the computer itself, output devices, input devices, and auxiliary storage devices.

1.8 The major components of a computer are the input ports, output ports, memory, and a central processing unit (CPU).

1.9 There are a wide variety of input devices in common use. In particular, card readers, terminals, tape drives, disk drives, and magnetic ink character readers (micr) have all been used as input devices.

1.10 Four common output devices are line printers, on-line terminals, magnetic tape drives, and magnetic disk drives.

1.11 The three most commonly used auxiliary storage devices are the hard disk, floppy disk, and tape drives.

1.12 The control unit and the arithmetic-logic unit together make up the CPU. The control generates the signals that coordinate all of the major components of the computer, while the arithmetic-logic unit evaluates all arithmetic and logical expressions.

1.13 Video display terminals and typewriter terminals are both in common use.

1.14 Floppy disk drives are the most common type of auxiliary storage device used on microcomputers.

1.15 The most common floppy disk drives available on microcomputers have storage capacities that range from about 140k to 1.2 megabytes.

Chapter 2

2.1   Machine instructions are encoded in a computer's memory as a sequence of binary bits (i.e., as a sequence of 0's and 1's). This is the form that a computer can process, but it is extremely difficult for most humans to comprehend such an encoded version of the instructions.

2.2   An assembler language is a language for writing programs that allows the use of mnemonics for the operation codes. Thus, an assembler instruction might look like

```
ST      R1,ANSWER
```

in contrast to the encoded machine instruction, which might look like

```
01011000001100000101100
```

2.3   The major disadvantage of writing programs in machine or assembler language (rather than a language like COBOL) is that the programs can be run on only one type of machine. One main reason for creating a language like COBOL is to allow versions of the same program to be run on computers by manufacturers such as IBM, Honeywell, and Digital Equipment Corporation and on a wide variety of other types of computers.

2.4   The original specifications for COBOL were outlined in the report of the Conference on Data Systems Languages (CODASYL), which appeared in 1960.

2.5   COBOL is an acronym for COmmon Business Oriented Language.

2.6   A computer program is a detailed set of instructions written in strict accordance with the rules of some programming language.

2.7   The rules that specify how statements in a language must be formed are called the **syntax** of the language.

2.8   Both syntactic and logical errors can be made in the construction of a program.

2.9   Compilers can detect syntax errors, but usually do not detect logical errors.

2.10 The four major steps in developing a program are understanding the problem to be solved, formulating an algorithm to solve the problem, translating the algorithm into a programming language, and executing the program on some computer (normally, one would use trial data on the first attempts to execute the program to ensure that the program works properly).

2.11 Flowcharts are graphs that are used to graphically or schematically describe the logic of a program.

2.12 The five flowchart symbols used in this text are

INPUT/OUTPUT:

PROCESS:

DECISION:

TERMINAL:

SUBROUTINE:

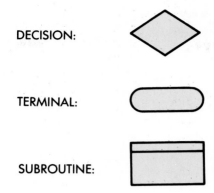

2.13 The first large-scale application of structured programming in a commercial setting took place in 1969–1972 in the New York Times Project carried out by IBM.

2.14 The three basic constructs allowed in a structured program are

Sequence structure:

Decision structure:

Loop structure:

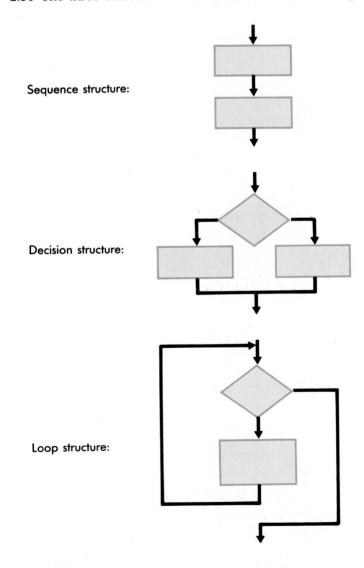

2.15 The four major advantages listed in the text are

a) Ease of comprehension (clarity) due to the fact that each segment of code has a single entry and exit

b) Functional independence of modules

c) Ease of modification

d) Verifiability. The correctness of the program can be confirmed by first confirming the correctness of the independent submodules.

Chapter 3

3.1 Columns 1–6 are used to contain page and line numbers. These fields are optional and are seldom actually filled in.

3.2 The COBOL segments are the DIVISION, SECTION, PARAGRAPH, and FILE DESCRIPTION. These all require segment headers.

3.3 Segment headers must begin in the A margin (columns 8–11).

3.4 An asterisk in column 7 indicates a comment card.

3.5 A user-supplied name can contain the characters A–Z, the numeric digits 0–9, and the hyphen (-).

3.6 The maximum length of a user-supplied name is 30 characters.

3.7 The divisions in a COBOL program are as follows:

IDENTIFICATION	identifies the program name and the programmer
ENVIRONMENT	describes the computing environment and names the files processed by the program
DATA	specifies the data items processed by the program
PROCEDURE	the actual statements that describe the logic of the program

3.8 Hardware devices are assigned to files in accordance with the SELECT statements, which occur in the FILE-CONTROL SECTION in the ENVIRONMENT DIVISION.

3.9 The OPEN statement in the PROCEDURE DIVISION determines whether a file is input or output.

3.10 The COBOL verbs that occur in the statements in EXAMPLE1 are OPEN, READ, MOVE, WRITE, CLOSE, and STOP.

Chapter 4

4.1 The WORKING-STORAGE SECTION is used to describe the data items that do not occur in the records of external data files.

4.2 The VALUE clause may be used to assign initial values to data items.

4.3 The AT END phrase in a READ statement is used to indicate what processing should occur when end-of-file is detected. Normally, an end-of-file "flag" is set when the condition occurs.

4.4 The scope of the AT END normally extends to the next period. That is, all of the statements between the words AT END and the next period will be executed only when the end-of-file condition occurs.

4.5   The allowable relational operators are

```
<
IS LESS THAN
>
IS GREATER THAN
=
IS EQUAL TO

IS NOT <
IS NOT LESS THAN
IS NOT >
IS NOT GREATER THAN
IS NOT =
IS NOT EQUAL TO
```

Here the words IS, THAN, and TO are all optional.

4.6   A subroutine is a paragraph that performs a well-defined function and follows the main routine in the PROCEDURE DIVISION. Note that the term "subroutine" is not part of the ANS COBOL standard. However, we are using the term in a manner consistent with what some programmers call "internal subroutines."

4.7   They must follow the main routine (i.e., after the STOP RUN statement in the main routine).

4.8   The two formats are

```
PERFORM paragraph-header
```

and

```
PERFORM paragraph-header-1 UNTIL condition-1.
```

4.9   The loop is implemented with the second form of the PERFORM statement.

4.10 A paragraph is terminated by the next paragraph, the next section, or the end of the program.

Chapter 5

5.1   The three types of constants are as follows:

Numeric constant	10
Nonnumeric constant (literal)	'Y'
Figurative constant	SPACES

5.2   The value is assigned during compilation (it is in the data item at the point when execution actually begins).

5.3   VALUE clauses used to assign initial values to data items can be used only in the WORKING-STORAGE SECTION.

5.4   The SPECIAL-NAMES paragraph was used to establish a correspondence between C01 and the user-supplied name TOP-OF-PAGE. This caused the use of AFTER ADVANCING TOP-OF-PAGE to mean "after advancing the printer to C01." On most systems C01 means "the top of the next page."

5.5 The SPECIAL-NAMES paragraph occurs in the CONFIGURATION SECTION of the ENVIRONMENT DIVISION.

5.6 The vertical positioning of print lines is controlled by using the AFTER ADVANCING phrase in the WRITE statement.

5.7 AFTER ADVANCING 10 LINES.

5.8 The record descriptions of page and column headers should be put in the WORKING-STORAGE SECTION.

5.9 By putting page and column headers in the WORKING-STORAGE section, rather than describing them as records in the output file, you allow yourself to assign initial values to fields in the record.

5.10 The FROM phrase is a convenient way to avoid having to specify a MOVE to the output buffer. Thus,

```
WRITE OUTPUT-LINE FROM PAGE-HEADER
      AFTER ADVANCING TOP-OF-PAGE
```

could have been used in EXAMPLE3 to replace

```
MOVE PAGE-HEADER TO OUTPUT-LINE.
WRITE OUTPUT-LINE AFTER ADVANCING TOP-OF-PAGE.
```

Chapter 6

6.1 Only X's can be used in the PICTURE for an alphanumeric data item. You can, of course, use a repeat factor. Thus, both XXXX and X(4) would be legitimate.

6.2 The PICTURE for a numeric data item can contain all 9's or a single V with a set of 9's. Optionally, it may contain a leading S to indicate a signed value.

6.3 A numeric edited item can contain 9's, Z's, and a single decimal point (.).

6.4 The character V is used to represent an implied decimal point.

6.5 The V is not counted in the length of the field.

6.6 The Z is used to cause leading 0's to be replaced with blanks. All digits other than leading zeros are inserted just as if the Z were a 9.

6.7 Yes.

6.8 Yes.

6.9 In all cases, if the first of the two formats is used, field-2 is altered to receive the result of the computation.

6.10 In all cases, if the second of the two formats is used, field-3 is altered.

Chapter 7

7.1 You can express a computation in a compact, more easily readable form.

7.2 The available arithmetic operators are

+	Addition
−	Subtraction
*	Multiplication
/	Division
**	Exponentiation

7.3 You use parentheses to indicate how the evaluation should occur, which is the convention used in high school algebra. There are rules for the order of evaluation in cases in which the parentheses are omitted. However, we advise you to always include the parentheses in those cases where the order of evaluation would make a difference.

7.4 They can be one or more COBOL statements.

7.5 We suggest the following format.

```
IF condition
     COBOL statement
     COBOL statement
        .
        .
        .

ELSE
     COBOL statement
     COBOL statement
        .
        .
        .

     COBOL statement.
```

If the ELSE is not used, then the format would be

```
IF condition
     COBOL statement
     COBOL statement
        .
        .
        .

     COBOL statement.
```

7.6 The next period.

7.7 Whenever it is unnecessary. That is, whenever there are no statements to be executed exactly when the condition does not hold.

7.8 According to the algebraic values of the operands. Zero is considered unique (i.e., $-0 = +0$), and unsigned values are considered positive.

7.9 The numeric field (which must be an integer) is converted to an alphanumeric item of the same size, and then the comparison proceeds.

7.10 The length of an operand is the total number of characters it contains.

Chapter 8

8.1 It must begin with an S.

8.2 It indicates whether the sign is leading or trailing, and whether it occupies a separate character.

8.3 Simple insertion editing is accomplished with the following characters:

```
,
B
/
0
```

8.4   Floating insertion editing is accomplished using two or more occurrences of one of the following symbols as the leftmost symbols in the picture:

$
-
+

8.5   The floating insertion character should appear immediately to the left of the leftmost position that might be occupied by a digit from the sending field, it should occur in all digits to the left of the decimal (all digits, in the case of an integer), and two occurrences of the insertion character must precede any comma or decimal point.

8.6   When an asterisk is used in the digit positions, leading zeros are replaced by the *.

8.7   CR and DB.

8.8   A numeric data item can be moved to an alphanumeric, numeric, or numeric edited receiving field.

8.9   A numeric edited field can be moved only to an alphanumeric field.

8.10   No.

8.11   It allows you to round off arithmetic values, which is frequently quite important.

8.12   They can be used to make a program more readable. In addition, they can make it easier to modify programs in those cases where a specific code value might change.

Chapter 9

9.1   A table is a data item composed of entries that have the same format. The items in the table are accessed using subscripts. An OCCURS clause is used to declare the entries that occur in the table.

9.2   A subscript is an integer or integer-valued data item that is used to specify an entry in a table.

9.3   No.

9.4   In the phrase

```
VARYING field-1 FROM field-2 BY field-3
```

field-1 gives the field whose value is altered, starting from field-2, in increments specified by field-3.

9.5   Without the OCCURS clause, separate data items would have to be used to specify all of the entries in a table. In addition, all of the logic required to process the table entries would have to specify precisely which entry was being operated upon. The added complexity and code could be quite large.

9.6   It allows the programmer to avoid using separate statements to initialize and increment the subscript used to reference the entries in a table.

Chapter 10

10.1   To allow the programmer the convenience of introducing a new grouping of data items without having to renumber all of the level numbers of the items being grouped. With modern text editors, it is fairly quick and easy to alter sets of level numbers, so much of the original motivation for incrementing by 5 no longer applies. However, it is a very widely used convention.

10.2 The programmer normally defines a field that occurs in the same position in all of the records which is used to determine exactly what type of record is being processed.

10.3 It must follow the definition with the actual values.

10.4 Some programmers view it as an esoteric language construct. That is, it is used so rarely that many programmers do not understand its use. We believe that, when used properly, it is clearer than the alternatives. However, you would do well to follow the conventions established by the company that employs you.

Chapter 11

11.1 The NUMERIC class allows a sign but does not allow leading blanks.

11.2 Because names can validly contain hyphens, periods, and apostrophes. In addition, programs will not abend if illegal characters are included.

11.3 Relation conditions, condition names, and class conditions.

11.4 No, the order of evaluation will not matter. Parentheses should not be used in such a case—they just make the condition harder to read. It should be noted that all of the conditions must be capable of evaluation.

11.5 The condition

```
NOT ERROR-HAS-OCCURRED AND WAGE IS NUMERIC
```

could be parenthesized as

```
NOT (ERROR-HAS-OCCURRED AND WAGE IS NUMERIC)
```

or

```
(NOT ERROR-HAS-OCCURRED) AND (WAGE IS NUMERIC)
```

Now consider a situation in which the WAGE is not numeric; the logical value of first case is *true*, but the value of second evaluates to *false*.

11.6 No, since you might have a situation in which C2 can only be evaluated if C1 is true.

Chapter 12

12.1 The comment misses the point; subtle bugs can originate from typos and be missed by compilers. Even with interactive debuggers, these bugs can require substantial amounts of time to locate. In the vast majority of cases, the time required to carefully desk check a program will be an excellent investment.

12.2 Working from the output of an abnormally terminated program amounts to working backward to determine "what must have happened."

12.3 A stub is a version of a routine that just displays data items to verify that the routine gets invoked properly. It may also do some minimal computation to allow the routines that invoke it to be tested thoroughly.

It is called a stub because it will be later expanded to the final version of the routine, once the upper level routines are debugged.

12.4 The term **abend** means "abnormal termination," which means that the program quit because a severe error condition was detected.

12.5 To **isolate the error** means to determine the approximate point in the program where the code must be incorrect.

12.6 TIME could contain a nonnumeric value, BILL (LAST) could contain a nonnumeric value, or BILL (LAST) could contain 0.

12.7 AMOUNT-IN might not contain a valid numeric field (which might be required by the PICTURE specified for AMOUNT-OUT). Truncation might occur, but that would not result in an abend.

Chapter 13

13.1 The sequence construct, the if-then-else (or decision) construct, and the do-while (or loop) construct.

13.2 It is a method of approaching complex problems by reducing them to simpler subproblems. Thus, each problem is attacked by formulating an approach that is fairly simple and will work under the assumption that a set of (hopefully simpler) subproblems can be solved.

13.3 The restrictions mentioned in the text were

a) the body of a loop must be a separate routine (which is PERFORMed)

b) structures of the form

```
if (CONDITION-1)
    if (condition-2)
        code-1
    else
        code-2
    endif
    code-3
else
    code-4
endif
```

must be broken up, and

c) logic of the form

```
if (condition)
    read the next record
    if (end-of-file occurred)
        code
    endif
endif
```

must be broken up.

13.4 In pseudo-code, a loop is represented as

```
do while (condition)
    body of the loop
enddo
```

An if-then-else structure is normally represented as

```
if (condition)
     code
else
     code
endif
```

13.5 It is easy to keep pseudo-code in machine-readable form and to modify it, if the logic is altered.

13.6 It makes the process of stepwise refinement more apparent.

13.7 Loops are more completely described by a flowchart, and flowcharts can more easily be kept to manageable sizes.

Chapter 14

14.1 The four stages are analysis and design, coding, testing, and maintenance.

14.2 The creation of a system is normally a group activity because the project would be too large for a single individual to complete within the specified time constraints.

14.3 The main difference is that a highly competent technician (the chief programmer) is responsible for the technical quality of the entire system. That is, the less competent members of the team have their work monitored by a more competent technician, rather than a manager who is not technically competent. The chief programmer is the person responsible for the technical quality of the project. He or she is assisted by a backup programmer, who must be capable of assuming the role of the chief programmer. The librarian performs clerical support functions, and task programmers perform programming tasks.

14.4 The HIPO package includes a hierarchy chart which makes the overall structure of the program visually obvious. In addition, the input-process-output diagrams clearly depict the functions of each module (as opposed to the logic required to perform those functions).

14.5 The initial design package, the detailed design package, and the maintenance package.

14.6 The visual table of contents (or hierarchy chart) and input-process-output diagrams.

Chapter 15

15.1 Because otherwise abends will occur, which is not acceptable in the normal data processing environment. It might not be necessary to validate fields such as names or "comments to be included in a record." These fields are frequently not edited, because failure to edit the fields will not cause abends, and the exact rules for editing the fields are either not known or extremely complex.

15.2 The goal of a data processing system is to make life easier for the people who use it. This rather obvious fact is too often forgotten by those who create such systems. By carefully constructing a set of examples that edit most types of fields, a programmer can learn to easily construct the editing code for new applications.

15.3 Three instances are

   a) the possible grades assigned to students in a class

   b) the possible majors that a student might declare

   c) a set of codes representing days of the week (e.g., M, T, W, TH, F, SA, SU).

   In such cases it is usually easiest to use a table containing the set of valid values.

15.4 The Gregorian date uses the concept of month, while the Julian format does not (it specifies a date as the day within the year). In either case, leap year calculations always introduce an element of complexity.

15.5 You should store four digits, because many software packages that are being constructed now will be in use after the year 2000 (you really should try to produce "timeless" software, although very few systems actually have this quality). On the other hand, input data items should normally be in a form that is most convenient for the user of the system. If they are used to typing dates in a form like 11/13/83, your programs should accept dates in that form.

15.6 Because the data on the input file (which is normally stored on some form of auxiliary storage) is normally edited as the file is constructed. Programs that access this data then assume the editing process worked properly.

Chapter 16

16.1 A master file is the "central repository," or permanent file, used to hold data on the items processed by a data processing system. Occasionally a system will need to process data on several distinct classes of items, requiring the use of multiple master files.

16.2 A master file always contains item records. They frequently contain header records. Very occasionally, they also contain records, called trailer records, that occur at the end of the file (containing totals for the fields that occur in the file); however, this text will not cover the topic of trailer records.

16.3 A sequential file is one in which records must be read in a specified order. A direct access file, on the other hand, has the property that records may be accessed in an arbitrary order.

16.4 Card readers, line printers, and tape drives all require sequential files (i.e., they do not support direct access files).

16.5 An interrecord gap is the space between physical records as they are stored on some magnetic medium.

16.6 The blocking factor is the number of logical records (i.e., records as they are viewed by the program) that are stored per physical record (i.e., per block).

16.7 By blocking records, you avoid wasting storage capacity due to interrecord gaps, and you reduce the number of input-output operations required to read a file.

16.8 A label record is a record that contains information about an entire file and is stored physically just ahead of the file (when the file is stored on magnetic tape).

16.9 Blocking factors are used on files that reside on magnetic media like tapes or magnetic disks.

16.10 The term **control break** refers to the end of a logical group of records within a file.

Chapter 17

17.1 One of the two corresponding items must be elementary.

17.2 Items that contain OCCURS clauses are ignored.

17.3 Actually, you should not avoid their use; just avoid *inappropriate* use. In particular, do not use a MOVE CORRESPONDING when a MOVE without the CORRESPONDING would work equally as well (i.e., when the entire record is moved).

17.4 Multiple control breaks are required when detailed subtotaling is desired. That is, when the file is viewed as a sequence of groups, each of which is further broken down into a sequence of subgroups, your program will have to process multiple control breaks. Note that the term **multiple control breaks** means a hierarchy of control breaks, not just the control breaks that occur between the major groupings within the file.

Chapter 18

18.1 Heading lines, detail lines, and footing lines.

18.2 By using a REPORT clause in the FD for the file. This REPORT clause designates the RD entry that describes the report.

18.3 The CONTROL clause specifies how control breaks are detected.

18.4 A SUM counter is used to sum fields between control breaks. That is, it is used to accumulate subtotals.

18.5 The GENERATE statement is used to print a detail group. A single GENERATE may cause heading and footing groups to be printed, as well as the detail group that is actually specified in the statement.

18.6 With the PAGE LIMIT clause in the RD entry.

I N D E X